**W9-BOM-656**

# LIST OF BOXES

## KEY POINTS BOXES

## LANGUAGE AND CULTURE BOXES

For **ESL Note** and **Net Note** listings see page ix.

# KEYS *for* WRITERS

## A BRIEF HANDBOOK

### THIRD EDITION

---

## ANN RAIMES

*Hunter College, City University of New York*

---

**Houghton Mifflin Company**
Boston   New York

Senior sponsoring editor: Suzanne Phelps Weir
Senior development editor: Martha Bustin
Editorial technology manager: Janet Edmonds
Senior project editor: Rosemary Winfield
Senior production/design coordinator: Jill Haber
Manufacturing manager: Florence Cadran
Marketing manager: Cindy Graff Cohen

Cover: Graphic image by Len Massiglia.

**Credits** (*credits continue on p. 456*)

**Part 1**  Berlin, Irving. "A Pretty Girl Is Like a Melody." *Ziegfeld Follies of 1919*. Copyright © Irving Berlin Music Corp.

Braithwaite, Dawn O. "Viewing Persons with Disabilities as a Culture." *Intercultural Communication*. 6th ed. Ed. Larry A. Samovar and Richard E. Porter. Belmont, CA: Wadsworth, 1991. 36.

Delpit, Lisa. "Language Diversity and Learning." *Other People's Children*. New York: New Press, 1995. 62.

Frost, Robert. "Stopping by Woods on a Snowy Evening." *The Poetry of Robert Frost*. Ed. Edward Connery Lathem. New York: Henry Holt and Co., 1969, 1979. Copyright © 1923 by Henry Holt and Company, Inc., copyright © 1951 by Robert Frost. Reprinted by permission of Henry Holt and Company, LLC.

Gilbert, Matthew. "All Talk, All the Time." *Boston Globe Magazine* 4 June 2000, 9. Reprinted courtesy of the Boston Globe.

Hölldobler, Bert, and Edward O. Wilson. *Journey to the Ants*. Cambridge, Mass.: Harvard University Press, 1994. 29.

King, Martin Luther, Jr. "I Have a Dream." Reprinted by arrangement with the Heirs to the Estate of Martin Luther King, Jr. c/o Writers House, Inc. as agent for the proprietor. Copyright © 1963 by Martin Luther King, Jr., copyright © 1991 Coretta Scott King.

Mallon , Thomas. *A Book of One's Own: People and Their Diaries*. New York: Ticknor and Fields, 1984. 1.

McDowell, Edwin. "With Special E-Fares, Online Bookings Soar." *New York Times* 7 June 2000: H14.

Reed, Ishmael. "America: The Multinational Society." *Writin' Is Fightin'*. New York: Atheneum, 1990. 1. Copyright © 1990 by Atheneum.

Rose, Phyllis. *Parallel Lives: Five Victorian Marriages*. New York: Knopf, 1986. 106.

Soriano, Joanne L. "KCC Service Learning at the Lyon Arboretum" (reflective journal). Kapi'olani Community College. 2 June 1997 <http://leahi.kcc.hawaii.edu/josorian/Service/jo.html>. Reprinted by permission of Joanne L. Soriano.

Tannen, Deborah. *You Just Don't Understand*. New York: Ballantine, 1990. 226.

Toulmin, Stephen. *The Uses of Argument*. 1958. Cambridge: Cambridge University Press, 1964. 101–102.

**Part 2**  "ACLU Urges Boston School to Annul Suspension of Creative Student." American Civil Liberties Union. 27 Apr. 2000 <http://www.aclu.org>. Reprinted by permission of the American Civil Liberties Union, New York, NY.

AltaVista search page: + neuromusicology + intelligence. Reprinted by permission of AltaVista Company, Palo Alto, CA.

City University of New York. Library catalogue (CUNY PLUS) screen for Crawford, James. InfoTrac search results: music and intelligence. Instructional screen images from Expanded Academic ASAP. Reprinted by permission of The Gale Group. Netscape Communicator browser window copyright © 1999 Netscape Communications Corporation. Used with permission.

MetaCrawler search page: neuromusicology intelligence. Copyright © InfoSpace, Inc. All rights reserved. InfoSpace and their designs and related marks are the intellectual property of InfoSpace, Inc.

Newcomb, Amelia. "Suspense and Suspension." *Christian Science Monitor*, 2 May 2000: 13. Reproduced with permission. Copyright © 2000 The Christian Science Monitor. All rights reserved. Online at csmonitor.com.

Stalker, James C. "Official English or English Only." *English Journal* 77 (Mar. 1988): 21.

**Part 5**  Carbone, Nick. *English Online: A Student's Guide to the Internet and World Wide Web*. 3rd ed. Boston: Houghton Mifflin, 2000. Inside front cover. Copyright © 2000 by Houghton Mifflin. Reprinted with permission.

Carlsbad Caverns National Park Chat page <http://www/carlsbad.caverns.national-park.com/wwwboard/carlchat/htm>.

*Printed in the U.S.A.*    Library of Congress Catalog Card Number 2001090677
ISBN 0-618-11523-4    89-QT-06 05 04 03

# Preface

A decade ago I began writing the First Edition of *Keys for Writers* with the view that the best handbook is the one that students will use. As a longtime composition and ESL teacher, I had become frustrated that various assigned handbooks seemed to play little or no significant role in improving students' writing. Despite encouragement, tutorials, and other instruction, many students did not independently open their handbooks to find answers to their particular questions. I wrote *Keys for Writers* to be extremely accessible both in terms of form and content, and I class-tested it every step of the way. From my own ongoing classroom experience, from broad student surveys, and from the thoughtful feedback of many other teachers, I know that *Keys for Writers* has succeeded as a resource that students keep open and at hand, not closed and on a shelf. It is a resource that has helped students to improve their writing.

In the intervening years, technology has touched every aspect of writing and research. It is now true that the best handbook is the one that students will use *and the one that best keeps pace with students' changing needs*. In this third edition, you will find new material that I see my students need as technology advances, requirements evolve, and new theories suggest new classroom approaches. Many of you, both teachers and students, have sent, called, or e-mailed invaluable suggestions to help the book keep pace with current changes and be as accurate and timely as a handbook should be. I am grateful for those shared ideas and delighted to incorporate them. The third edition also retains a wealth of helpful features that are the foundations of *Keys:* an easy two-row system of color-coded tabs; a way to personalize the book with moveable KeyTab® locator cards; a respectful tone; thorough presentations on research and documentation; clear treatment of grammar and style, with abundant examples and concise explanations; and a recognition of the rich diversity of our student population.

With its combination of the familiar and friendly and the new and up-to-date, this edition of *Keys for Writers* becomes, I hope, even more useful—in writing courses, in courses across the curriculum with a writing component, and, with practical coverage of workplace and online issues, in life after graduation as well.

## Designed for Easy Access

**Two rows of color-coded divider tabs**   The simplicity and clarity of two rows of tabs (the first row—red; the second row—gold) make it easy to find information quickly. Students do not have to follow three or more color threads through several layers or banks of tabs. They do not need to stop and puzzle over what category, from an overly large assortment of categories, will hold the information they are looking for. In *Keys for Writers*, students go efficiently to the row of red tabs (Parts 1–5) for "whole paper" issues and to the row of gold tabs (Parts 6–10) for sentence-level issues.

**Color-coded Key to the Book**   This initial menu page aligns the table of contents with the part divider tabs to help students flip directly to the part they need.

**Unique KeyTabs®**   Found in the back of the handbook, the moveable, custom-fit KeyTabs® serve as bookmarks, extended margins, and note cards. Simply insert these locator cards anywhere within *Keys for Writers*, with the top of the Key Tab® extending from the top of the book, and have quick access to whatever information is most helpful and most often consulted. Five KeyTabs® are included with the third edition.

**Key Points boxes**   These concise summary and checklist boxes encourage the development of editing and critical thinking skills. Their format makes vital information stand out for convenient reference.

**Thorough coverage of grammar, in one convenient part**   Part 7, Common Sentence Problems (now including Basic Grammar), gives students one central place to turn when they have grammar questions. Grammar coverage is not split confusingly over several parts, as in other handbooks.

**Superb Index**   The index is extremely thorough and includes many alternate terms to aid students.

## New to the Third Edition

**New Section on Evaluating Sources**   A frequent obstacle for students writing a research paper is how to know what is a scholarly article and what is not. *Keys for Writers,* Third Edition, devotes a whole section to this major subject. It discusses what to look for when evaluating books and articles originating in print and makes a distinction between sources accessed via the Internet and those originated for the Internet. For evaluating Internet sources, a new Key Points box, Developing Your Junk Antennae, provides eight accessible and easy ways of distinguishing the useful from the useless (p. 100).

Updated and expanded technology coverage *Keys for Writers,* Third Edition, contains the latest information on

- **Using the computer in the writing process** Part 1 covers e-mail forums as a means of brainstorming (real student examples illustrate this process); search engines as a means of exploring and focusing ideas; and technology as it supports collaborative writing.

- **Using search engines, keyword searches, online indexes, databases, and subscription services** Thoroughly updated to reflect current developments, Part 2 addresses the merger of libraries and the Web as information resources and presents the latest approaches to doing online searches. It includes the search done for the sample MLA paper in Part 3, with screen shots of a Web page from a full-text article subscription database and from two popular search engines (p. 91).

- **Conducting research in a range of disciplines** A new list, Research Resources in Twenty-four Subject Areas, contains frequently used reference works in print, print and electronic indexes, and Web sites (p. 74). Live and regularly updated links are available at the *Keys for Writers* Web site.

- **Documenting a wide range of electronic sources** Students draw on electronic sources for an increasing amount of their research, and they often have questions about the proper way to document this material in their papers. Parts 3 and 4 (covering MLA, APA, CBE, *Chicago,* and CGOS styles) answer these questions.

- **Using computer tools for editing and proofreading** Screenshots of Microsoft Word show functions for editing and document design. Students are urged to consider both the advantages and limitations of programs that check spelling and grammar, with examples.

- **Communicating online in discussion lists and Web pages; designing documents; and producing scannable resumes and PowerPoint presentations** A new Part 5, Technology: For Communication,

Document Design, and Work, gathers these practical technology-related topics into one place for ease of use.

**Updated and expanded MLA documentation guidelines**   Part 3, MLA Documentation, reflects all changes found in the most recent MLA publications (*MLA Handbook for Writers of Research Papers*, Fifth Edition, 1999, and *MLA Style Manual*, Second Edition, 1998) and on the MLA Web site. Part 3 now covers more types of sources, especially electronic sources, uses fresh and timely new examples throughout, and shows how to document two or more sequential references to the same work, works from online subscription services, online works of art, and other online visual media.

**Updated and expanded APA documentation guidelines**   Part 4 now covers more types of sources, especially electronic sources, and includes more examples and more current examples. It includes all recent changes posted on the APA Web site and included in the *Publication Manual of the American Psychological Association*, 5th ed. Also, new to *Keys* is an APA sample paper on auditory thresholds, including Web sources and graphs, done by a student for a course in experimental psychology (p. 178).

**New coverage of CGOS; updated coverage of CBE and *Chicago* guidelines**   *Columbia Guide to Online Style* (CGOS) is now included as an alternate style for electronic sources. Part 4 also provides up-to-date guidelines on the styles recommended by the Council of Biology Editors (CBE) and the *Chicago Manual of Style*.

**New material on avoiding plagiarism**   Entitled Avoid Even the Suspicion of Plagiarism, this new section includes a list of explicit guidelines for students on this important subject (p. 104).

**Expanded section on Argument**   The Argument section now not only explains the Toulmin approach but covers critical thinking strategies, the need to establish common ground, and ways to structure effective arguments. It is now included in Part 1, The Writing Process, extending the discussion of purpose, audience, thesis, development of ideas, and coherence. A new sample student argument focuses on telemarketing.

**Superior ESL material and integrated ESL notes**   Specific guidance for the ESL writer appears in Part 9, For Multilingual/ESL Writers, and now is also integrated throughout the book in ESL Notes.

**ESL Note**

Grammar Checking Programs, 34
Evidence Used to Support an Argument, 40
Using a Subject and Verb, 286
Position of an Adjective Phrase, 289
Including Subject *it*, 296
No *–s* on Modal Auxiliaries, 313
Using a *be* Auxiliary before the *–ing* Form, 314
Modals before *be, been,* and *being,* 314
Verbs Used Only in Simple Tenses, 316
No Future Tense in Time Clause, 316
Passive Voice with Transitive Verbs Only, 324
Base Form after Modal Auxiliaries, 328
Subject *it* with a Singular Verb, 329
No Plural *–s* Ending on Adjectives, 347
Adverb Placement, 350
Relative vs. Personal Pronouns, 358
Plural and Singular of *hundred, thousand,* and *million,* 393

The Language Guide to Transfer Errors (p. 407) contains references to more languages and many new examples of characteristic errors. Part 9 contains new or revised sections on language learning and errors, unnecessary pronouns, uncountable nouns, basic rules for articles, *the* for specific reference, and article use.

**Helpful tips for using the Internet**   This edition includes

**Net Note**

Web Sites for Generating Ideas and Planning, 6
Search Engines with Subject Categories, 11
Writing and Revising Collaboratively, 19
Finding Electronic Discussion Lists, 50
Online Links to Sources in 24 Subjects, 74
Acknowledging Copied Electronic Material, 107
Problems with Internet Sources, 112
Indentation in an Online Works Cited List, 132
Italics for a Title, Not Underlining, 132
Business Letters Sent by E-mail, 242

**Four-color design**   The new four-color design allows for realistic screen captures from online sources, distinctive charts, graphs, and visuals of all types, and enhanced highlighting of important information.

**Digital Keys 3.0 CD-ROM and Digital Keys 3.0 Online**
Accompanying *Keys for Writers,* Third Edition, is a CD-ROM (shrink-wrapped with the book upon request) and an online handbook. (A pass-

word to the online handbook comes free with every new copy of the student text.) These interactive electronic versions have an all-new design and interface and include the full text of *Keys for Writers,* Third Edition. See below for details.

## A COMPLETE SUPPORT PACKAGE

*Keys for Writers,* Third Edition, is accompanied by a full range of instructional support.

### For Instructors and Students

*Keys for Writers* Web site, including *Digital Keys 3.0 Online*   Go to <college.hmco.com/keys.html>. The expanded Web site now contains an online version of *Digital Keys 3.0.* (A password to the online handbook comes free with every new copy of the student text.) *Digital Keys 3.0 Online* contains the entire *Keys for Writers,* Third Edition, grammar and punctuation exercises, electronic KeyTabs® for making notes and book marking, an index, and a search function that allows students to enter a word and go immediately to that section of the electronic handbook. The Web site features an introduction to *Keys,* information on how to use *Keys* efficiently; links to relevant resources; research templates for keeping track of one's sources; and updated live links to Research Resources in Twenty-four Discipline Areas, a list in the research section of *Keys.*

*Digital Keys 3.0* CD-ROM   *Digital Keys 3.0* contains the entire *Keys for Writers,* Third Edition, grammar and punctuation exercises, electronic KeyTabs®, an index, a search function that allows students to enter a word and go immediately to that section of the electronic handbook, and diagnostic tests. It is available shrink-wrapped with the book upon request.

eLibrary of Exercises   The eLibrary contains a large number of self-quizzes that give students the opportunity to increase grammar and writing skills in thirty areas. Students can use the eLibrary to sharpen their skills and strengthen their knowledge. It contains over seven hundred exercises. Students will be able to work at their own pace wherever is convenient for them—home, computer lab, or classroom.

*Online Internet Research Guide*   The *Online Internet Research Guide,* by Jason Snart of the University of Florida, Gainesville, presents six extended learning modules with practice exercises (tutorials) for using the Internet as a Research Tool: (1) What is the purpose of research?; (2) E-mail, listservs, newsgroups, chat rooms; (3) Surfing and browsing; (4) Evaluating Web information; (5) Building an argument with Web research; and (6) Plagiarism and documentation.

## For Instructors

Instructor's Support Package   In a convenient, three-hole-punched format, this packet is designed to slip into a binder; instructors can then add or take out information as needed. In five parts, this packet provides an overview of the book with sample syllabus and transparency masters on how to use the handbook and CD-ROM; a section on teaching composition to ESL students; a detailed and up-to-date section on using the Internet in the composition classroom, with student tutorials; diagnostic tests on five main areas of grammar, plus answers to numbered items in the *Exercise Booklet*; and approximately sixty-five transparency masters.

*HM ClassPrep*   This CD-ROM contains most of the elements of the Instructor's Support Package in an electronic format so they can be customized to suit the way the instructor teaches his or her class.

Peterson, *The Writing Teacher's Companion*   This acclaimed book gives sound, expert advice on all aspects of teaching composition, from evaluating papers to managing the classroom.

## Available at a Discount When Packaged with *Keys for Writers*, Third Edition

Raimes and Flanagan, *Exercise Booklet*   Contains an abundance of exercises for *Keys for Writers*, Third Edition. Answers for lettered exercises appear at the back so students can check their own work; answers to numbered items are in the Instructor's Support Package.

*Additional KeyTabs®*   Available in packages of five, these movable locator cards allow students to personalize their book.

Raimes, *Identities: Readings from Contemporary Culture*   Designed to work well with *Keys for Writers*, Third Edition, this reader examines issues of identity and culture through units on eight themes, including Name, Family Ties, Education, and Gender.

Carbone, *Writing Online: A Student's Guide to the Internet and World Wide Web,* **Third Edition**   *Writing Online* covers writing collaborative hypertext, using the latest search engines, and much more. *Writing Online's* Web site contains advice on using the Internet and has three activities per chapter.

*American Heritage College Dictionary,* **Third Edition**   This bestselling reference is an indispensable tool and desk reference for students.

**American Heritage English as a Second Language Dictionary** Specially designed to suit the needs of intermediate to advanced ESL students and to prepare them to use standard American dictionaries.

## Acknowledgments

Many people contributed greatly to this edition. For his expert advice on technological matters and for prompt replies to my many e-mails, I am deeply grateful to Manfred Kuechler, a colleague in the Sociology Department at Hunter College; his knowledge of the workings of the Internet and his patience and clear explanations are truly astounding. Thanks go, too, to Hunter College librarians Danise Hoover, Jean Jacques Strayer, and Patricia Woodard and to the students at Hunter College whose writing appears in this book, with special thanks to Jennifer Hopper and Todd Kray for the essays they contributed.

    I am grateful to all of the following reviewers, who gave the manuscript the benefit of their experience, wisdom, and critical eyes:

Pamela J. Balluck, University of Utah
Jennifer Beech, Pacific Lutheran University
Darsie Bowden, Western Washington University
Laurie Bower, University of Nevada, Reno
Jeffrey P. Cain, Sacred Heart University
Bettina Caluori, DeVry Institute—New Brunswick
Linda Clegg, Cerritos College
Robert Cousins, Utah Valley State College
Ned Cummings, Bryant & Stratton College
Ben Davis, Cuyahoga Community College
Virginia B. DeMers, Ringling School of Art and Design

David W. Furniss, University of Wisconsin—River Falls
Lynée Lewis Gaillet, Georgia State University
Thomas Goodman, University of Miami
Beth L. Hewett, Community College of Baltimore County—Essex
John Hyman, American University
Daniel Lowe, Community College of Allegheny County
Mary Sue MacNealy, The University of Memphis
Louis Martin, Elizabethtown College
Marie Nigro, Lincoln University, PA
Lillian Polak, Nassau Community College
Mark Rollins, Ohio University
Jami M. Taylor, ECPI College of Technology
Jane Mueller Ungari, Robert Morris College
Barbara Whitehead, Hampton University
Stephen Wilhoit, University of Dayton
James Wilson, LaGuardia Community College, CUNY
Sallie Wolf, Arapahoe Community College
Randell Wolff, Murray State
Laura W. Zlogar, University of Wisconsin—River Falls

In addition I extend my grateful thanks to the following who helped at earlier stages of composition:

Joseph A. Alvarez, Central Piedmont Community College
Akua Duku Anokye, University of Toledo
Jennie Ariail, University of South Carolina
Lona Bassett, Jones County Junior College
Linda Bergman, Illinois Institute of Technology
Clair Berry, State Technical Institute at Memphis
Curtis W. Bobbit, College of Great Falls
Terry Brown, University of Wisconsin at River Falls
Karen A. Carlton, Humboldt State University
Lisa Davidson, Passaic County Community College
Judith Davis, Old Dominion University
Rob Dornsife, Creighton University
Darlynn R. Fink, Clarion University of Pennsylvania
Dennis Gartner, Frostburg State University
Dorothy Gilbert, California State University, Haywood
Katherine Green, Albuquerque Technical-Vocational Institute
John Gregorian, Contra Costa Community College
Claudia Gresham-Shelton, Stanly Community College
Jane E. Hardy, Cornell University
Christopher Z. Hobson, State University of New York, College at Old Westbury
Franklin E. Horowitz, Columbia University
Michael Hricik, Westmoreland City Community College
Margaret Hughes, Butte College
Mary L. Hurst, Cuyahoga Community College
Mary Kaye Jordan, Ohio University

Ernest H. Johansson, Ohio University
Ann Judd, Seward County Community College
Susan Kincaid, Lakeland Community College
Sally Kurtzman, Arapahoe Community College
Joseph LaBriola, Sinclair Community College
Lindsay Lewan, Arapahoe Community College
Kelly Lowe, Mount Union College
Dianne Luce, Midlands Technical Community College
Mike MacKey, Community College of Denver
Ann Maxham-Kastrinos, Washington State University
Michael G. Moran, University of Georgia
Carolyn O'Hearn, Pittsburgh State University
Liz Parker, Nashville State Technical Institute
Sally Parr, Ithaca College
Kathy Parrish, Southwestern College
Jane Peterson, Richland College
Nelljean M. Rice, Coastal Carolina University
Kenneth Risdon, University of Minnesota at Duluth
Cheryl W. Ruggiero, Virginia Polytechnic Institute
Kristin L. Snoddy, Indiana University at Kokomo
Ellen Sostarich, Hocking College
Amy Ulmer, Pasadena City College
Margaret Urie, University of Nevada
Thomas Villano, Boston University
Colleen Weldele, Palomar College
James D. Williams, University of North Carolina, Chapel Hill
Martin Wood, University of Wisconsin at Eau Claire
Randal Woodland, University of Michigan—Dearborn

Once again, the staff at Houghton Mifflin Company has been a pleasure to work with: warm, supportive, knowledgeable, responsive, and thoroughly professional. Thanks once more to my extended circle of supportive friends for making sure I took time to play tennis and have fun. Above all, thanks for support and encouragement go to my daughters, Emily and Lucy, and especially to my husband, James Raimes, who has been through my book writing before but never complains and, what's more, contributes not only a sharp editorial eye and vast knowledge but also great cooking. I know what it means to say that writing is a collaborative effort.

ANN RAIMES
Hunter College, City University of New York

# The Writing Process

Engaging in the writing process means engaging in a variety of activities: identifying your purpose, audience, and topic; generating ideas; gathering information; establishing a thesis; organizing ideas; drafting; revising; editing; and proofreading. These activities are often artificially distinguished from one another to make them easier to talk about. In reality, however, virtually no one engaged in writing marches neatly through a series of distinct activities.

Writing is not a linear or formulaic procedure but a messy adventure, an exciting process of discovery. Few writers achieve perfection in the first draft. Instead, most of us repeatedly generate ideas, plan, draft, and revise until our ideas, and the expression of them, have evolved into a satisfying final form.

## 1 Getting Started and Finding a Focus

Getting started is hard if you think of a piece of writing as a permanent document. A blank page or an empty screen with its blinking cursor can be daunting, but the act of writing offers an advantage over speaking: you can go back and make changes. If you remind yourself that you are not locked into whatever you first write, starting the process will become much easier than you ever expected it to be.

### 1a Defining your purpose

Before you begin writing, consider the question "What is the main purpose of this piece of writing?" The following questions will help guide you to an answer.

**KEY POINTS**

**Asking about Purpose**

1. Is your main purpose to explain an idea or provide information? Writing with this purpose is called *expository writing*.

2. Is your main purpose to persuade readers to see things your way or to move readers to action? This aim leads to *persuasive writing* or *argumentation*.

*(Continued)*

*(Continued)*

3. Is your main purpose to describe an experiment or a detailed process or to report on laboratory results? Writing with this purpose is frequently referred to as *scientific* or *technical writing*.

4. Is your main purpose to record and express your own experience, observations, ideas, and feelings? In the humanities, such accounts are known as *expressive, autobiographical,* or *personal writing.*

5. Is your main purpose to create an original work of art, such as a poem, story, play, or novel? Writing with this purpose is called *creative writing.*

The first three items listed in the Key Points box (on expository, persuasive, and scientific or technical writing) are generally the main purposes of college writing. Among these categories, however, the overlap can be considerable. Some assignments may require you to explore and test concepts and opinions against what you already know. Other assignments may ask you to blend explanation with persuasion. Whatever you determine to be the main purpose or purposes of a given assignment should guide you as you begin writing.

**1b** Assessing your audience

A good writer connects with his or her audience and keeps readers in mind at all times, as if in a face-to-face communication. Achieving this connection, however, often proves challenging, because not all readers have the same characteristics. Readers come from different regions, communities, ethnic groups, organizations, and academic disciplines. They have different social and economic backgrounds and varied interests. Also, readers' approaches to what they are reading depend on the context or conventions of the material before them. Conventions vary, for instance, in informal letters, scholarly or scientific writing, Internet writing, newspapers and magazines, business interactions, and college papers in various disciplines.

As you get started and as you write and revise, ask yourself the following questions about your readers.

## LANGUAGE AND CULTURE

### Assessing Your Readers' Expectations

- Who will read your piece of writing? What will readers expect in terms of length, format, date of delivery, and content?

- What kinds of texts do your readers usually read and write, and what are the conventions of those texts? For example, if you are writing a business letter to a company in another country, consult a business communications book to find out what readers there expect in a business letter.

- Will your readers expect formal or informal language? The expectations of teenagers online and college professors, for example, differ greatly.

- Will your readers expect you to use technical terms? If so, which terms are in common use?

- What characteristics do you and your readers have in common: nationality, language, culture, race, class, ethnicity, gender? Consider what limitations writing for these readers places on your use of dialect (Australian English is different from Caribbean English, for example), punctuation (British English and American English treat quotations differently— see **49d**), vocabulary, and political and cultural expectations. Cultivate common ground, and try not to alienate readers.

- Is your instructor your main reader? If so, what do you know about the expectations of a reader in his or her academic discipline? Be sure to ask what background information you should include and what you can safely omit. Ask to see a model paper.

For the writing that you do in college, a unique set of conventions prevails. Even if you are certain that your reader (your instructor) knows what article, concept, or story you are writing about, the conventions of academic writing require you to identify the author and title and not simply begin by referring to "This story" or "This article." In most cases, regard your instructor as a stand-in for an audience of general readers, not as an individual expert.

## **1c**    Finding and exploring ideas for writing

Whether you have to generate your own idea for a topic or you already have a clear sense of purpose and topic, you need strategies other than staring at the ceiling or waiting for inspiration to fly in through the window. Professional writers use a variety of techniques to generate ideas at various stages of the process. Diane Ackerman, in her article "Oh Muse! You Do Make Things Difficult!" reports that the poet Dame Edith Sitwell used to lie in an open coffin; French novelist Colette picked fleas from her cat; statesman Benjamin Franklin soaked in the bathtub; and German dramatist Friedrich Schiller sniffed rotten apples stored in his desk.

Perhaps you have developed your own original approach to generating ideas. Perhaps you were taught a more formal way to begin a writing project, such as constructing an outline. If what you do now doesn't seem to produce good results, or if you are ready for a change, try some of the following methods and see how they work. Not every method works equally well for every project or for every writer. Experimenting is a good idea.

**Net Note**    Some Web sites for writers include useful information on generating ideas and planning. Try, for example, the Purdue University Online Writing Lab at <http://owl.english.purdue.edu> and the Writing Center at Colorado State University at <http://www.colostate.edu/Depts/WritingCenter/references/processes.htm>. ∎

*Keeping a journal*    A *journal* can be far more than a personal diary. Many writers carry a notebook and write in it every day. Journal entries can be observations, references, quotations, questions for research, notes on events, and ideas about assigned texts or topics, as well as specific pieces of writing in progress. A journal can also serve as a review for final examinations or essay tests, reminding you of areas of special interest or subjects you didn't understand.

The *double-entry* or *dialectical journal* provides a formalized way for you to think critically about readings and lectures. Two pages or two columns or open windows in your word processor provide the space for interaction. On the left-hand side, write summaries, quotations, and accounts of readings, lectures, and class discussions—that is, record as exactly and concisely as you can what you read or heard. The left-hand side, in short, is reserved for information about the material. On the right-hand side, record your own comments, reactions, and questions about the material. (See **4f** on critical thinking.) The right-hand side is the place to make your own connections between the reading or lecture and your own experience and knowledge.

*Freewriting*   If you do not know what to write about or how to approach a broad subject, try doing five to ten minutes of *freewriting* either on paper or on the computer. When you freewrite, you let one idea lead to another in free association, without concern for correctness. The important thing is to keep writing. If you cannot think of a word or phrase while you are freewriting, simply put in a symbol such as #. On a computer, use the Search command to find your symbol later, when you can spend more time thinking about the word.

Zhe Chen did some freewriting on the topic "name and identity," which led her eventually to an essay topic examining the effects of the Cultural Revolution on family identity.

```
    I have a unusual name, Zhe. My friends in China say
it's a boys name. My friends in America think it has only
one letter. Most of my American friends have difficulty
pronouncing my name.
    Some people ask me why don't I Americanize my name so
it would be easier to pronounce. But I say if I change my
name, it will not be me any more. What else can I write?
When I was seven years old, I asked my mother what my name
meant. "Ask your father," she said as she washed dishes.
It was raining outside, and the room was so quiet that I
could hear the rain puttering(?) on the window-panes. My
father's thoughts returned to another rainy day in 1967
when the Cultural Revolution just begun. Thousands of
people had been banished to countryside and all the
schools were closed. My grandparents fled to Hong Kong
but my father and aunt stayed in China. Life was
difficult. Gangs sent them to the countryside to work.
It was here that my parents met.
    Back to name again. My father named me Zhe. In
Chinese my name means remember and hope. He wanted me
remember the Cultural Revolution and he wanted me to
finish college. He didn't have that chance.
```

*Brainstorming*   Another way to generate ideas is by *brainstorming*—making a freewheeling list of ideas as you think of them. Brainstorming is enhanced if you do it collaboratively in a group, discussing and then listing your ideas. (See also **1h**, Writing collaboratively.) You can then, by yourself or with the group, scrutinize the ideas, arrange them, reorganize them, and add to or eliminate them.

One group of students working collaboratively made the following brainstorming list on the topic "changing a name":

```
voluntary changes--hate name
escape from family and parents
show business
George Eliot (Mary Ann Evans)
Woody Allen (Allen Stewart Konigsberg)
Puff Daddy (Sean Combs)
married women
writers and their pseudonyms--who?
some keep own name, some change, some use both names and
  hyphenate
Hillary Clinton/Hillary Rodham Clinton
immigrants
Ellis Island
forced name changes
political name changes
name changes because of racism or oppression
criminals?
```

Once the students had made the list, they reviewed it, rejected some items, expanded on others, and grouped items. Thus, they developed a range of subcategories that led them to possibilities for further exploration and essay organization:

```
Voluntary Name Changes
authors: George Eliot, Mark Twain, Isak Dinesen
show business: Woody Allen
other "stage names": Bob Dylan, Ringo Starr, Puff Daddy
ethnic and religious identification: Muhammad Ali

Name Changes upon Marriage
reasons for changing or not changing
Hillary Clinton
problem of children's names
alternative: hyphenated name

Forced Name Changes
immigrants on Ellis Island
wartime oppression
slavery
```

***E-mail conversations***    Network with others on a course bulletin board, in a chat room, or in a newsgroup (see **21b**), or set up your own group of students who want to work together to brainstorm over cyberspace. Daniel Kies at College of DuPage in Glen Ellyn, Illinois, set up an "eForum" for his students in English 101 at <http://papyr.com/eforum/messages/12/68html>. Here are some of their communications (used with permission) about an essay assignment on the "techno-future":

---

**By Rick Waters on Thursday, April 27, 2000 - 04:09 pm:**

I don't know how far along all of you are, but I wanted to offer some ideas for Essay 3. We're supposed to describe the techno-future as we see it, and I figured I would give you a reminder on what's been in the works and what's been accomplished lately.

"Smart Homes" are being built. Bill Gates' is probably the extreme (more info at www.usnews.com/usnews/nycut/tech/billgate/gates.htm)
Microchips are being implanted in brains to reverse the effects of blindness and deafness.
The genetics industry is booming.
There's a pill for just about everything nowadays.
There are (3) cars that can actually fly.
"Lawnmower Man Technology" (the effects of virtual teaching - facts being fed into the brain via multiple stimuli at once) has been in testing since 1992.
Materials (not unlike clothing) are being developed to display video images.
Digital phones are being "blended" with Palmtop computers.
And there's a TON more!

---

**By Tabitha Schneider on Thursday, April 27, 2000 - 04:41 pm:**

Rick, I agree with you, the list is infinite in length. By the time we finish our essays, the ideas might be obsolete.
Technology changes rapidly, we will never be right at the cutting edge, unless we are working the techno-future jobs.
What do you all think?

---

**By Jennifer Thomas on Thursday, April 27, 2000 - 10:55 pm:**

Sadly enough, I haven't heard of half the things that Rick mentioned! Am I behind or what! I think that we are far more technologically advanced than the government wants us to know. I am sitting below two skylights in my living-room, and I'm pretty sure if "Big Brother" wanted to, he could probably interrupt this transmission. Scary as it is, technology is far beyond our realm. And we will be left in the dark, until the government decides we are privy to the information. The laptop I write on, although sufficient for my purposes, is an ancient artifact compared to the laptops on the market today. And my laptop can do a lot of stuff. It's far better than my parents' desktop! But yet, still outdated. Technology scares me in certain ways. Did you also know that the purchases you make at stores are tracked by certain barcodes present on coupons? If you don't use the 25 cent ones, they will eventually send you coupons of a higher value. But if you continue to redeem the 25 cent ones, that will be all you get. (For the most part). Every credit card in the country is linked to a profile. I am hesitant to call it a technological age, but more of an information age. The President could probably find out how often you buy peanut butter, what brand, and whether you use a coupon for it. SCARY!
There's food for thought.

***Mapping*** *Mapping*, also called *clustering*, is a visual way of generating and connecting ideas and can be done individually or in a group. Write your topic in a circle at the center of a page, think of ideas related to the topic, and write those ideas on the page around the central topic. Draw lines from the topic to the related ideas. Then add details under each of the ideas you noted. For an assignment on "current issues in education," a student created the following map and saw that it indicated several possibilities for topics, such as school vouchers, home schooling, and the social exclusivity of private schools.

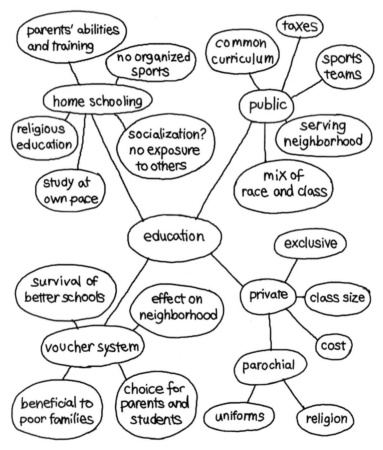

***Using journalists' questions*** Journalists check the coverage of their stories by making sure that they answer six questions—Who? What? When? Where? Why? How?—though not in any set order. A report on a public transit strike, for example, would include details about the union leaders (who they were), the issue of working conditions and benefits (what the situation was), the date and time of the confrontation (when the strike occurred), the place (where it occurred), what caused the confrontation (why it happened), and how the people involved behaved and resolved the strike (how it evolved and ended). If you are telling the story of an event, either as a complete essay or as an example in an essay, asking the journalists' six questions will help you think comprehensively about your topic.

*Using formal sets of prompts*    Sometimes you might find it helpful to use a formal set of directions (known as *prompts*) to suggest new avenues of inquiry. Write down responses to any of the prompts that apply to your topic, and note possibilities for further exploration.

**DEFINE YOUR TERMS**    Look up key words in your topic (like *success, identity, ambition*, and *ethnicity*) in the dictionary, and write down the definition you want to use. Consider synonyms, too.

**INCLUDE DESCRIPTIONS**    Whatever your topic, make your writing more vivid with details about color, light, location, movement, size, shape, sound, taste, and smell. Help your reader "see" your topic, such as a person, place, object, or scientific experiment, as exactly as you see it.

**MAKE COMPARISONS**    Help your reader understand a topic by describing what it might be similar to and different from. For example, how is learning to write like learning to juggle?

**ASSESS CAUSE AND EFFECT**    Convey information on what causes or produces your topic and what effects or results emerge from it. For example, what are the causes and effects of dyslexia? inflation? acid rain? hurricanes? asthma?

**CONSIDER WHAT OTHERS HAVE SAID**    Give your reader information, facts, and statistics on what others say about your topic in interviews, surveys, reading, and research.

*Doing research*    Sometimes, discussing your topic with others, conducting an interview, administering a questionnaire or survey, or doing research can produce good ideas for writing (see **6–8**).

**Net Note**    Internet search engines and directories such as Yahoo! at <http://www.yahoo.com>, AltaVista at <http://www.altavista.com>, WebCrawler at <http://www.webcrawler.com>, and Google at <http://www.google.com> offer subject categories that you can explore and successively narrow down to find a topic suitable for a short essay. For example, a Yahoo! search beginning with "Education" produced more than thirty different categories, such as *bilingual, distance learning, financial aid, organizations, special education,* and *reform.* Clicking on *reform* produced links to eighteen sites (such as *multicultural education reform programs, computers as tutors, guide to math and science reform,* and *about school choice*). Many of the sites included Web pages on topics such as "voucher programs" and "charter schools," as well as links to many other sites, some with bibliographies with further online links. Such directories can suggest a wide range of interesting topics for you to explore.  ■

## **1d**  Finding a topic and focus

In college courses, you might be given any of the following types of assignments for an essay, arranged here from the broadest in scope to the narrowest:

- a free choice of subject;
- a broad subject area, such as "genetic engineering" or "affirmative action";
- a focused and specific topic, such as "the city's plans to build apartments on landfill" or "the treatment of welfare recipients in California";
- an actual question to answer, such as "In what ways is age an issue in cases of driving accidents?"

If you are given a free choice of subject, you will need to narrow your focus to broad subject area, to specific topic, to question. After that, still more narrowing is necessary. You will need a thesis. Your thesis, or claim, is your statement of opinion, main idea, or message that unifies your piece of writing, makes a connection between you and the subject area, lets your reader know where you stand in relation to the topic, and answers the question posed.

Here is one student's movement from subject to thesis over several days of reading, discussion, freewriting, and notetaking:

Subject: College admissions policies
Topic: Affirmative action in college admissions
Question: How do people react to students who are accepted by
colleges under affirmative action policies?
Thesis: The public and the press often unjustly question the
abilities of students accepted into colleges under affirmative
action policies.

**KEY POINTS**

**Subject, Topic, Question, Thesis: A Continuum**

Level 1: Broad *subject area*

↓

Level 2: *Topic* for exploration within that subject area

↓

Level 3: *Key question* that concerns you

↓

Level 4: Your *thesis* (your statement of opinion or your main idea in answer to the question). Often you need to do a great deal of reading and writing before you get to this point.

If you choose a topic and a question that are too broad, you will find it difficult to generate a thesis with focused ideas and examples. Whenever you find yourself thinking, for instance, "There's so much to say about affirmative action—its history, goals, practice, criticisms, successes—that I don't know where to start," narrow your topic. If you begin by choosing a topic and a question that are too narrow, you probably will not find enough material and will end up being repetitive. Whenever you feel you have enough material to fill only a page and can't imagine how you will find more ("What else *can* I say about how my cousin got into college?"), broaden your topic. Above all, stay flexible: you may want to change your topic or your question as you discover more information.

**1e** Formulating a working thesis—and why you need one

Suppose someone were to ask you, "What is the main idea that you want to communicate to your reader in your piece of writing?" The sentence you would give in reply is your thesis, also known as a *claim.* Your thesis tells readers what point you are going to make about your topic, what stand you are going to take. It is not enough to say, "I am writing about bilingual education." Are you going to address bilingual education in elementary, secondary, or higher education? Which readers do you regard as your primary audience? Which geographical areas will you discuss? Will you be concerned with the past or with the present? What do you intend to propose about the area of bilingual education you have selected? In short, what point do you want to make about which aspect of bilingual education—for which readers?

You don't have to know exactly where to put your thesis statement in your essay right now, but having a thesis will focus your thoughts as you read and write. See **4b** for more on the thesis in an argument paper.

### KEY POINTS

**A Good Working Thesis or Claim**

1. narrows your topic to a single main idea that you want to communicate;

2. asserts your position clearly and firmly in a sentence that makes a claim about a topic;

3. states not simply a fact but an opinion;

4. makes a generalization that can be supported by details, facts, and examples within the assigned limitations of time and space;

5. stimulates curiosity and interest in readers and prompts them to think "Why do you say that?" and then read on.

A good thesis statement may be one or more of the following:

1. a strong, thought-provoking, or controversial statement

   ▶ **Bilingual education has not fulfilled its early promise.**

2. a call to action

   ▶ **All inner-city schools should set up bilingual programs.**

3. a question that will be answered in detail in the essay

   ▶ **What can bilingual education accomplish for a child? It can lead to academic and personal development.**

4. a preview or reflection of the structure of the essay

   ▶ **Bilingual education suffers from two main problems: a shortage of trained teachers and a lack of parental involvement.**

After you have formulated your thesis statement, write it on a Post-it® note or an index card and keep it near you as you write. The note or card will remind you to stick to the point. If you still digress as you write, you may need to consider changing your thesis.

*Stating your thesis in your paper*   Even though it is useful to have a working thesis as you read and write drafts, you will eventually need to decide if and where you will include a thesis statement in your essay. Ask your instructor about any special requirements for thesis location. In most academic writing in the humanities and social sciences, a thesis is stated clearly in the essay, usually near the beginning. See your thesis statement as a signpost—both for you as you write your draft and, later, for readers as they read your essay. A clear thesis prepares readers well for the rest of the essay.

Sometimes, though, particularly in descriptive, narrative, and informative writing, you may choose to imply your thesis and not explicitly state it. In such a case, you make your thesis clear by the examples, details, and information you include. You may also choose to state your thesis at the end of your essay instead of the beginning. If so, you present all the evidence to build a case and then make the thesis act as a climax and logical statement about the outcome of the evidence. If you use key words from your thesis as you write, you will keep readers focused on your main idea.

*On not falling in love with your thesis*   A good thesis often takes so long to develop that you might be reluctant to change it. Be willing, however, to refine and change your thesis as you find more information and work with your material. Many writers begin with a tentative working thesis and then find that they come to a new conclusion at the end of the first draft. If that happens to you, start your second draft by focusing on the thesis that emerged during the writing of the first draft. In other words, change your thesis as you go along. Be flexible: it's easier to change a thesis statement to fit new ideas and new evidence that you discover than to find new evidence to fit a thesis. Note that your final thesis statement should take a firm stand on the issue. Flexibility during the writing process is not the same as indecision in the final product.

**1f**   Making an outline

A *scratch outline* is a rough list of numbered points that you intend to cover in your essay. A scratch outline lets you see what ideas you already have, how they connect, what you can do to support and develop them, and what further planning or research you still need to do. One student in the group that made the brainstorming list on page 8 developed the following scratch outline and formulated a tentative thesis:

```
Topic: Changing a name
Question: Why do people change their names?
Tentative thesis: People change their names because they
either have to or want to.
Points:
1. Forced name changes in a new country or a new school
2. Name changes to avoid discrimination or persecution
3. Name changes upon marriage
4. Name changes in show business
5. Voluntary name changes to avoid recognition
   a. Criminals
   b. Writers
```

When this student began to write his draft, however, he changed direction and unified some of his points, developing a more focused thesis (see the formal outline below).

A *formal outline* spells out, in order, what points and supportive details you will use to develop your thesis and arranges them to show the overall form and structure of the essay. You may produce a formal outline before you begin to write, but you are likely to find that making an outline with a high level of detail is more feasible after you have written a draft. Done at this later point, the outline serves as a check on the logic and completeness of what you have written, revealing any gaps, repetition, or illogical steps in the development of your essay.

The student who did the brainstorming (**1c**) and made the scratch outline finally settled on a thesis and made this formal topic outline of an essay draft.

```
Thesis: A voluntary name change is usually motivated by a
desire to avoid or gain recognition.

I.   Name changes to avoid recognition by others

   A. Criminals

   B. Writers

      1. Women writers who adopt men's names
         a. George Eliot (Mary Ann Evans)
         b. George Sand (Amandine Aurore Lucie Dupin)
         c. Isak Dinesen (Karen Blixen)
```

```
      2. Writers who adopt a pseudonym
         a. Mark Twain (Samuel Clemens)
         b. Lewis Carroll (Charles Dodgson)
         c. Amanda Cross (Carolyn Heilbrun)

   C. People wanting to avoid ethnic identification

II.  Name changes to join a group and gain recognition

   A. Married women marking membership in a family

      1. Want to indicate married status
      2. Want to have same name as children

   B. Entertainers choosing eye-catching names

      1. Marilyn Monroe (Norma Jean Baker)
      2. Woody Allen (Allen Stewart Konigsberg)
      3. Ringo Starr (Richard Starkey)
      4. Puff Daddy (Sean Combs)
```

Making this outline allowed the student to see that his draft was basically well structured but that he needed to find out more about criminals and their aliases (I.A.) and about people who change a name to avoid ethnic identification (I.C.).

## 1g Overcoming writer's block

Most students and professional writers, however much they write or even profess to like writing, have at some time or another felt that dreaded block. They sit and stare at the blank screen and keep going to the refrigerator for solace. So it is quite likely that on occasion you will feel overwhelmed with the task of organizing your research findings or frustrated because your writing doesn't seem to "sound right." If so, consider the questions in the Key Points box and try out the strategies.

### KEY POINTS

**Overcoming Writer's Block**

1. Do you have a set of rules that you try to follow in your writing process, such as "Always begin by writing a good introduction" or "Always have a complete outline before starting to write"?

*(Continued)*

*(Continued)*

If you do, consider whether your rules are too rigid or even un-helpful. As you gather ideas and do your preparatory drafting, ignore any self-imposed rules that hinder you.

2. Do you edit as soon as you write, and do you edit often? If you answer yes, your desire to write correctly might be preventing you from thinking about ideas and moving forward. Try journal writing, freewriting, brainstorming, or mapping (see **1c**).

3. Do you feel anxious about writing, even though you have knowl-edge of and interest in your topic? If you do, try using some of the freewriting and brainstorming strategies in **1c**, or begin writing as if you were talking about your topic with a friend.

4. Do you feel that you do not yet know enough about your topic to start writing, even though you may have done a great deal of re-search? If so, try freewriting or try drafting the sections you know most about. Writing will help show you what you know and what you need to know.

If you sit down to a writing task close to the deadline without hav-ing done the necessary preliminary work—reading, interpreting, tak-ing notes, and generating ideas—you probably are suffering not from writer's block but from lack of preparation. To be prepared ade-quately, take time and apply yourself to the task.

## **1h**　 Writing collaboratively

Writing is not necessarily a solitary process. In the academic or busi-ness world, you might be expected to work in formal collaborative structures. Groups, teams, or committees might be formed to draft a proposal or report, or you might be expected to produce documents reflecting the consensus of your section or group.

In such group settings, make sure that you work out a way for every member of the group to contribute. You can do this by assigning each person a set of specific tasks, such as making lists of ideas, draft-ing, analyzing the draft, revising, editing, assembling visuals, and preparing the final document. Schedule regular meetings, and expect everyone to come with a completed written assignment. Build on strengths within the group. For example, for a business report, ask the member skilled in document design and computer graphics to prepare the visual features of the final document (see **24**).

However, make sure that you work collaboratively only when doing so is expected. An instructor who assigns an essay may very well not expect you to work on it with your sister, classmate, or tutor.

**Net Note** In networked computer labs, in distance-learning courses, and in the business world, writing collaboratively is often encouraged—and certainly the technology makes it easy. One person can post an idea or a draft and invite response; or participants can work together on an outline, research, drafting, and editing, with assigned roles. Then all the results and drafts can be posted online, with feedback from peers, the instructor, or the project leader.

Microsoft Word provides useful tools for such collaboration. Click Tools and then Revisions or Track Changes. You can work on a text, highlight changes, and attach the revision to an e-mail message to a colleague, who can click to Accept or Reject each change and compare the original with the revised version (Compare Documents). ■

 Six tips for writing drafts

Writing provides what speech can never provide: the opportunity to revise your ideas and the way you present them. The drafting process lets you make substantive changes as you progress through drafts. You can add, delete, and reorganize sections of your paper. You can rethink your thesis and support. You can change your approach to parts or all of the paper. Writing drafts allows you to work on a piece of writing until you feel you have made it meet your goals.

**KEY POINTS**

**Tips for Drafts**

1. Don't automatically begin at the beginning. Begin by writing the essay parts for which you already have some specific material.

2. Write your first draft as quickly and fluently as you can. Write notes to yourself in capitals or surrounded by asterisks to remind yourself to add or change something or do further research. Some word processing programs have a Comment

*(Continued)*

*(Continued)*

function that allows you to type notes that appear only on the screen, not in a printout. These notes are easily deleted from later drafts. If you use a term frequently (for example, *bilingual education*), abbreviate it (as *b.e.*) and then use tools like Find and Replace to insert the whole phrase throughout your draft.

3. Keep your topic, question, and thesis very much in mind.

4. Avoid the obvious (such as "All people have feelings"). Be specific, and include interesting supporting details.

5. Save all your notes and drafts until your writing is completed and until the course is over. Print out and save a copy of each new draft so that if something happens to the computer or the disk, you have a copy of your work. Some people save every draft under a separate file name. Others prefer to save deleted sections in a separate "dump" file so they can retrieve deleted parts from there.

6. Revise for ideas, interest, and logic; don't merely fix errors. It is often tempting just to correct errors in spelling and grammar and see the result as a new draft. Revising entails more than that. You need to look critically at what you have written, imagine a reader's reaction, and rethink your approach as necessary. See also **3b**.

## 2 Developing and Organizing Ideas

As you plan a paper, you will work on how to organize ideas, how to divide your ideas into paragraphs, how to construct each paragraph, and how to structure the flow of logic in that paper.

### **2a**   Composing unified paragraphs

*Paragraphs* are the building blocks that make up an organized essay or an essay answer on a test. A paragraph is easy to identify on a page; its first line is indented five spaces from the left margin or, in business and online documents, begins with no indentation after a blank line. Each new paragraph signals a progression in your ideas—that is, it moves readers on to a new point.

A paragraph can mark a new point in a narrative, description, explanation, or argument, or it can break up a long discussion or description into manageable chunks that readers can assimilate. Therefore, both logic and aesthetics dictate when it is time to begin a new paragraph. Think of a paragraph as something that gathers together in one place ideas that connect to each other and to the main purpose of the piece of writing. Readers should notice a logical flow of ideas as they read through a paragraph and as they move from one paragraph to another through an essay.

A *unified paragraph,* in academic writing, mirrors the structure of the whole essay: it includes one main idea that the rest of the piece of writing (paragraph or essay) explains, supports, and develops. When you write a paragraph, imagine a reader saying, "Look, I don't have time to read all this. Just tell me in one sentence (or two) what point you are making here." Your reply would express your main point. Each paragraph in an academic essay generally contains a controlling idea expressed in one or two sentences and does not digress or switch topics in midstream. Its content is unified.

The following paragraph is devoted to one topic—tennis—but does not follow through on the promise of the lead sentence to discuss the *trouble* the *backhand* causes *average* players (the key words are italicized).

```
The backhand in tennis causes average weekend players
more trouble than other strokes. Even though the swing is
natural and free-flowing, many players feel intimidated
and try to avoid it. Venus Williams, however, has a great
backhand and she often wins difficult points with it.
Her serve is a powerful weapon, too. When faced by a
backhand coming at them across the net, mid-level play-
ers can't seem to get their feet and body in the best
position. They tend to run around the ball or forget the
swing and give the ball a little poke, praying that it
will not only reach but also go over the net.
```

What is Grand Slam winner Venus Williams doing in a paragraph about average players? What relevance does her powerful serve have to the average player's problems with a backhand? The student revised by cutting out the two sentences about Venus Williams.

*Topic sentence* is the name usually given to the sentence that most directly expresses the main idea of a paragraph. In the paragraph above, it is the first sentence.

When placed first, a topic sentence makes a generalization and serves as a reference point for the rest of the information in the paragraph (see *deductive organization* in **2b**). When placed after one or two other sentences, the topic sentence focuses the details and directs readers' attention to the main idea. When placed at the end of the paragraph, the topic sentence serves to summarize or draw conclusions from the details that precede it (see *inductive organization* in **2c**).

Some paragraphs, such as the short paragraphs typical of newspaper writing or the one-sentence paragraphs that make a quick transition, do not always contain a topic sentence. Sometimes, too, a paragraph contains such clear details that the point is obvious and does not need to be explicitly stated. However, in academic essays, a paragraph in support of your essay's thesis (main point) will usually be unified and focused on one clear topic, whether or not you state it explicitly in one sentence.

## **2b** Including specific details

Details make writing more interesting to read. They lift it from the general and abstract. The paragraph that follows begins with a topic sentence that announces the controlling idea: "Ant queens [. . .] enjoy exceptionally long lives." The authors could have stopped there, expecting us to assume that they are right. We might wonder, however, what "exceptionally long" means in relation to the life of an ant. A month? A year? Seven years? Instead of letting us wonder, the authors develop and support the controlling idea with five examples, organized to build to a convincing climax. Beginning with a generalization and supporting it with specific illustrative details is a common method of organizing a paragraph, known as *deductive organization*. (See p. 23 for an example of *inductive organization*.)

> Ant queens, hidden in the fastness of well-built nests and protected by zealous daughters, enjoy exceptionally long lives. Barring accidents, those of most species last 5 years or longer. A few exceed in natural longevity anything known in the millions of species of other insects, including even the legendary 17-year-old cicadas. One mother queen of an Australian carpenter ant kept in a laboratory nest flourished for 23 years, producing thousands of offspring before she faltered in her reproduction and died, apparently of old age. Several queens of *Lasius flavus*, the little yellow mound-building ant of European meadows, have lived 18 to 22

years in captivity. The world record for ants, and hence for insects generally, is held by a queen of *Lasius niger*, the European black sidewalk ant, which also lives in forests. Lovingly attended in a laboratory nest by a Swiss entomologist, she lasted 29 years.

—Bert Hölldobler and Edward O. Wilson, *Journey to the Ants*

## **2c**    Developing ideas

Whether you are writing a paragraph or an essay, you will do well to keep in mind the image of a skeptical reader always inclined to say something challenging, such as "Why on earth do you think that?" or "What could possibly lead you to that conclusion?" You have to show your reader that your opinion is well founded and supported by experience, knowledge, logical arguments, the work of experts, or reasoned examples. In addition, you want to engage readers and provide vital, unique details. This section shows how you can develop your ideas in logical and interesting ways.

***Tell a story and/or describe a person, object, or scene.***    Choose a pattern of organization that readers will easily grasp. Organize a description by describing from top to bottom, left to right, background to foreground, or even in a circle. Organize the events in a story chronologically so that readers can follow the sequence.

In the following paragraph, a writer tells a story that leads to the point that people with disabilities often face ignorance and insensitivity. Note that she uses *inductive organization,* beginning with background information and the specific details of the story in chronological order and ending with a generalization.

Jonathan is an articulate, intelligent, thirty-five-year-old man who has used a wheelchair since he became a paraplegic when he was twenty years old. He recalls taking an ablebodied woman out to dinner at a nice restaurant. When the waitress came to take their order, she patronizingly asked his date, "And what would he like to eat for dinner?" At the end of the meal, the waitress presented Jonathan's date with the check and thanked her for her patronage. Although it may be hard to believe the insensitivity of the waitress, this incident is not an isolated one. Rather, such an experience is a common one for persons with disabilities.

—Dawn O. Braithwaite, "Viewing Persons with Disabilities as a Culture"

*Develop a point by providing illustrations or examples.*    You saw in the paragraph on pages 22–23 how a statement about the long life of ant queens is supported by a series of examples and facts. The author of the next paragraph uses only one example to develop and illustrate the point made in the opening sentence.

> Print may serve different functions in some communities than it does in others, and some children may be unaccustomed to using print or seeing it used in the ways that schools demand. Shirley Brice Heath, for example, found that the black children in the community she called Trackton engaged with print as a group activity for specific real-life purposes, such as reading food labels when shopping, reading fix-it books to repair or modify toys, reading the names of cars to identify a wished-for model, or reading to participate in church. There was seldom a time anyone in the community would read as a solitary recreational activity; indeed, anyone who did so was thought to be a little strange.
>
> —Lisa Delpit, "Language Diversity and Learning"

*Develop a point by providing facts and statistics.*    The following short newspaper paragraph supports with facts and statistics the assertion made in its first sentence and provides the source of the information.

> Buying tickets online has certainly taken off. Last year, according to Jupiter Communications, the e-commerce research company, online travel spending reached $6.5 billion, or 4.5 percent of all travel spending, and is projected by Jupiter to soar to $28.2 billion in 2005, or 14.2 percent. More to the point, Jupiter said that airline tickets accounted for a whopping 77 percent of online travel purchases last year.
>
> —Edwin McDowell, "With Special E-Fares, Online Bookings Soar"

*Define key terms.*    Sometimes you can effectively clarify and develop a topic by defining terms. Thomas Mallon begins his book on diaries by immediately addressing the terms *diary* and *journal* and deciding to treat them as having the same meaning.

> The first thing we should try to get straight is what to call them. "What's the difference between a diary and a journal?" is one of the questions people interested in these books ask. The two

terms are in fact hopelessly muddled. They're both rooted in the idea of dailiness, but perhaps because of *journal*'s links to the newspaper trade and *diary*'s to *dear*, the latter seems more intimate than the former. (The French blur even this discrepancy by using no word recognizable like *diary;* they just say *journal intime,* which is sexy, but a bit of a mouthful.) One can go back as far as Dr. Johnson's *Dictionary* and find him making the two more or less equal. To him a diary was "an account of the transactions, accidents, and observations of every day; a journal." Well, if synonymity was good enough for Johnson, we'll let it be good enough for us.

—Thomas Mallon, *A Book of One's Own: People and Their Diaries*

***Divide and classify.*** Dividing an object or a concept into parts or separating items into groups gives readers a new way to look at the topic. In the following paragraphs, the writer develops his essay on cell phones by classifying users into three types and devoting one paragraph to each.

Cell phone use has far exceeded practicality. For many, it's even a bit of an addiction, a prop—like a cigarette or a beer bottle—that you can hold up to your mouth. And each person is meeting a different psychological need by clinging to it.

As I see it, the pack breaks down something like this: Some users can't tolerate being alone and have to register on someone, somewhere, all of the time. That walk down [the street] can be pretty lonely without a loved one shouting sweet nothings in your ear.

Others are efficiency freaks and can't bear to lose 10 minutes standing in line at Starbucks. They have to conduct business while their milk is being steamed, or they will implode. The dividing line between work and home has already become permeable with the growth of telecommuting; cell phones contribute significantly to that boundary breakdown.

Then there are those who like to believe they are so very important to the people in their personal and professional lives that they must be in constant touch. "Puffed up" is one way to describe them; "insecure" is another.

—Matthew Gilbert, "All Talk, All the Time"

*Compare and contrast.* When you make a comparison between people, objects, or concepts, examining similarities and differences, different types of development achieve different purposes:

1. You can deal with each subject one at a time in a block style of organization, perhaps summarizing the similarities and differences at the end. This organization works well when each section is short and readers can easily remember the points made.

2. You can select and organize the important points of similarity or difference in a point-by-point style of organization, referring within each point to both subjects.

The following example uses the second approach in comparing John Stuart Mill, a British philosopher and economist, and Harriet Taylor, a woman with whom Mill had a close intellectual relationship. The author, Phyllis Rose, organizes the contrast point by point to emphasize the differences in their facial features, physical behavior, ways of thinking and speaking, and intellectual style. A block organization would have dealt first with all the characteristics of Taylor, followed by all the characteristics of Mill.

> You could see how they complemented each other by the way they looked. What people noticed first about Harriet were her eyes—flashing—and a suggestion in her body of mobility, whereas his features, variously described as chiseled and classical, expressed an inner rigidity. He shook hands from the shoulder. He spoke carefully. Give him facts, and he would sift them, weigh them, articulate possible interpretations, reach a conclusion. Where he was careful, she was daring. Where he was disinterested and balanced, she was intuitive, partial, and sure of herself. She concerned herself with goals and assumptions; he concerned himself with arguments. She was quick to judge and to generalize, and because he was not, he valued her intellectual style as bold and vigorous where another person, more like her, might have found her hasty and simplistic.
>
> —Phyllis Rose, *Parallel Lives: Five Victorian Marriages*

## **2d**   Using transitions and links for coherence

However your individual paragraphs are developed, your readers expect to move with ease from one sentence to the next and from one paragraph to the next, following a clear flow of argument and logic.

When you construct an essay or paragraph, do not cause your readers to grapple with grasshopper prose, which jumps suddenly from one idea to another without obvious links. Instead, a piece of writing needs to be coherent, with all the parts connecting clearly to one another with transitions and links.

*Context links*   A new paragraph introduces a new topic, but that topic should not be entirely separate from what has gone before. Let your reader know the context of the big picture. If you are writing about the expense of exploring Mars and then switch abruptly to the hazards of climbing Everest, a reader will be puzzled. You need to state clearly the connection you see and want your reader to see: "Exploration on our own planet can be as hazardous and as financially risky as space exploration."

*Transitional words and expressions as links*   You can make clear connections between sentences and between paragraphs either by using explicit connecting words like *this, that, these,* and *those* to refer to something mentioned at the end of the previous sentence or paragraph or by using transitional expressions:

TRANSITIONAL EXPRESSIONS

*adding an idea:* also, in addition, further, furthermore, moreover
*contrasting:* however, nevertheless, nonetheless, on the other hand, in contrast, still, on the contrary, rather, conversely
*providing an alternative:* instead, alternatively, otherwise
*showing similarity:* similarly, likewise
*showing order of time or order of ideas:* first, second, third (and so on), then, next, later, subsequently, meanwhile, previously, finally
*showing result:* as a result, consequently, therefore, thus, hence, accordingly, for this reason
*affirming:* of course, in fact, certainly, obviously, to be sure, undoubtedly, indeed
*giving examples:* for example, for instance
*explaining:* in other words, that is
*adding an aside:* incidentally, by the way, besides
*summarizing:* in short, generally, overall, all in all, in conclusion

For punctuation with transitional expressions, see **47e**.

*Word links*   You can also provide coherence by using repeated words; pronouns linked to nouns; words with the same, similar, or opposite meaning; or words linked by context. The writer of the following paragraph maintains coherence not only by using transitional expressions (shown in boldface) but also by repeating words and phrases (italicized) and using pronouns (*she* and *her* to refer to *wife,* and *they* to refer to *Greeks*).

> Entire cultures operate on elaborate systems of *indirectness.* **For example,** I discovered in a small research project that most Greeks assumed that a wife who asked, "Would you like to go to the party?" was hinting that she *wanted to go.* They *felt* that she wouldn't bring it up if she didn't *want to go.* **Furthermore,** they *felt,* she would not state her *preference* outright because that would sound like a demand. *Indirectness* was the appropriate means for communicating her *preference.*
>
> —Deborah Tannen, *You Just Don't Understand*

## 2e Writing introductions and conclusions

Imagine a scene at a party. Someone you have never met before comes up to you and says, "Capital punishment should be abolished immediately." You're surprised. You wonder where this position came from and why you are being challenged with it. You probably think this person rather strange and pushy. Imagine now a reader picking up a piece of your writing. Just like people at a party, your reader needs to know why a topic is being discussed before hearing your opinion on the issue. You need to lead your reader into your thesis and to provide an interesting context for it.

*Introduction*　If you find it difficult to write an introduction because you are not yet clear about your thesis or how you will support it, wait until you have written the body of your essay. You will find something concrete easier to introduce than something you have not yet written.

　When you write an introduction to an essay in the humanities, keep the following points in mind.

**KEY POINTS**

**How to Write a Good Introduction**

**Options**

1. Make sure your first sentence stands alone and does not depend on readers' being aware of the essay title or an assigned question.

*(Continued)*

*(Continued)*

2. Provide context and background information to set up the thesis.

3. Lead readers to expect a statement of your point of view (your thesis).

4. Define key terms that are pertinent to the discussion.

5. Establish the tone of the paper: informative, persuasive, serious, humorous, personal, impersonal, formal, informal.

6. Engage readers' interest, and provide some kind of hook to make readers want to continue reading.

**What to Avoid**

7. Avoid being overly general and telling readers the obvious, such as "Crime is a big problem" or "In this fast-paced world, TV is a popular form of entertainment" or "Since the beginning of time, the sexes have been in conflict."

8. Do not refer to your writing intentions—such as "In this essay, I will . . ." Do not make extravagant claims, such as "This essay will prove that bilingual education works for every student."

9. Do not restate the assigned essay question.

To provide a hook for the reader, an introduction might include any of the following:

surprising statistics          a challenging question
a pithy quotation              interesting background details
an unusual fact                an intriguing opinion statement
a relevant anecdote

Examine the hook in the following example:

On the day before Memorial Day, 1983, a poet called me to describe a city he had just visited. He said that one section included mosques, built by the Islamic people who dwelled there. Attending his reading, he said, were large numbers of Hispanic people, forty thousand of whom lived in the same city. He was not talking about a fabled city located in some mysterious region of the world. The city he'd visited was Detroit.

—Ishmael Reed, "America: The Multinational Society"

Reed introduces the theme of multinationalism in the United States with the hook of an anecdote that leads readers to expect that the city he describes is in an unfamiliar part of the world. He then grabs readers with a surprise in the last sentence—the city is Detroit—and prepares readers for his discussion of a multinational continent.

***Conclusion***  Think of your conclusion as completing a circle. You have taken your readers on a journey from presentation of the topic in your introduction, to your thesis, to supporting evidence and discussion, with specific examples and illustrations. Remind readers of the purpose of the journey. Recall the main idea of the paper, and make a strong statement about it that will stick in their minds.

### KEY POINTS

**How to Write a Good Conclusion**

#### Options

1. Include a summary of the points you have made, but keep it short and use fresh wording.

2. Frame your essay by reminding the reader of something you referred to in your introduction and by reminding the reader of your thesis.

3. End on a strong note: a quotation, a question, a suggestion, a reference to an anecdote in the introduction, a humorous insightful comment, a call to action, or a look to the future.

#### What to Avoid

4. Do not apologize for the inadequacy of your argument ("I do not know much about this problem") or for holding your opinions ("I am sorry if you do not agree with me, but . . .").

5. Do not use the identical wording you used in your introduction.

6. Do not introduce totally new ideas. If you raise a new point at the end, your reader might expect more details.

7. Do not contradict what you said previously.

8. Do not be too sweeping in your conclusions. Do not condemn the whole medical profession, for example, because one person you know had a bad time in one hospital.

## 3 Revising and Editing

Always allow time in your writing schedule for putting a draft away for a while before you look at it with a critical eye.

Revising—making changes to improve a piece of writing—is an essential part of the writing process. It is not a punishment inflicted on inexperienced writers. Good finished products are the result of careful revision. Even Leo Tolstoy, author of the monumental Russian novel *War and Peace,* commented: "I cannot understand how anyone can write without rewriting everything over and over again."

As you revise and edit, address both "big-picture" and "little-picture" concerns. Big-picture revising involves making changes in content and organization. When you revise, you may add or delete details, sections, or paragraphs; alter your thesis statement; vary or strengthen your use of transitions; move material from one position to another; and improve clarity, logic, flow, and style. Little-picture editing involves making adjustments to improve sentence variety and length and correcting errors in grammar, spelling, word choice, mechanics, and punctuation. Both are necessary, but most people like to focus first on the big picture and then turn to fixing up the details.

### 3a Getting feedback and peer review

Ask a friend, colleague, or tutor to read your draft with a pencil in hand, placing a checkmark next to the passages that work well and a question mark next to those that do not. Ask your reader to tell back to you what main point you made and how you supported and developed it. This process might reveal any lack of clarity or indicate gaps in the logic of your draft. Your reader does not have to be an expert English teacher to give you good feedback. If you notice worried frowns (or worse, yawns) as the person reads, you will know that something in your text is puzzling, disconcerting, or boring. Even that simple level of feedback can be valuable.

When you are asked to give feedback to a classmate, read first for ideas and clarity. Don't begin by looking for mistakes. Try to avoid comments that sound like accusations ("You were too vague in paragraph 3"). Instead, use "I" to emphasize your reaction as a reader ("I had a hard time visualizing the scene in paragraph 3").

Here is a sample peer response form that a classmate can use to provide you with feedback. This form is available online for downloading and printing at <college.hmco.com/keys.html>.

---

Draft by _____  Date _____
Response by _____  Date _____

1. What do you see as the writer's main point in this draft?
2. What part of the draft interests you the most? Why?
3. Where do you feel you would like more detail or explanation? Where do you need less?
4. Do you find any parts unclear or confusing? Write questions to the writer, and put a small question mark in pencil in the margin of the paper next to the parts you mean.
5. Give the writer one suggestion that would improve the draft.

---

## **3b** Reading and analyzing your own drafts

Feedback from your peers, instructor, and colleagues and friends is useful, but your own analysis of your work is crucial. Do the following:

- Print your draft out triple-spaced with wide margins, so that you can pencil in changes and new ideas.

- Create distance and space. Put a draft away for a day or two, and then read it again with fresher eyes. Imagine a reader's reaction to your title and your thesis.

- Read your draft aloud. Mark any places where you hesitate and sense something is amiss. Go back to them later.

- Be on the lookout for excessive use of generalizations—*everyone, most people, all human beings, all students/lawyers/politicians,* and so on. Think of specific examples to introduce in their place: *the students in my political science course this semester.*

- Make an outline of what you have written (see **1f**).

- Select the first sentence of each paragraph, and use the Copy and Paste features to move the sequence of sentences into a new file.

Then examine these first sentences. Do they provide a sense of logical progression of ideas? Is there any repetition? What will readers of these first sentences expect each paragraph to contain?

- Save all new drafts and old drafts under different file names, so that you can retrieve older material if you need to. If you use Microsoft Word, use the Tools/Track Changes/Compare Documents features to highlight and examine the differences between drafts.
- Make back-up copies of all your draft files. A computer virus can crash a hard drive.

## **3c** Writing and revising a title

You might have a useful working title as you write, but after you finish writing, brainstorm several titles and pick the one you like best. If titles occur to you as you write, be sure to make a note of them. A good title captures the reader's attention, makes the reader want to read on, and lets the reader know what to expect in the essay.

WORKING TITLE    **Problems in the Fashion Industry**

REVISED TITLE    **Thin and Thinner: How the Fashion Industry Denigrates Women**

## **3d** Editing, proofreading, and using computer tools

Examine your draft for grammar, punctuation, and spelling errors. Often, reading your essay aloud will help you find sentences that are tangled, poorly constructed, or not connected. Looking carefully at every word and its function in a sentence will alert you to grammatical problem areas. Turn to pages 281–292 for help with standard edited English and methods for correcting common errors.

*Computer tools for editing*    Run the *spelling checker* in your word processor to check on spelling throughout your draft. It will flag any word it does not recognize, and it is very good at catching typographical errors, such as *teh* (for *the*) and *responsability* (for *responsibility*). However, it will not identify grammatical errors that affect only spelling, such as missing plural or *-ed* endings. Nor will it find an omitted word or a misspelled word that forms another word, such as *then* (for *than*), *their* (for *there*), or *affect* (for *effect*).

The Word Count feature under Tools in Microsoft Word (see **23a** for Word screens) is handy when you are given a word limit: it provides an immediate, accurate count.

*Grammar checking programs* such as MLA Editor and Grammatik will analyze your sentences and make suggestions about what might need to be fixed, tightened, or polished. They provide observations about simple mechanical matters, such as pointing out that commas and periods need to go inside quotation marks, or they indicate a problem with a sentence such as "Can the mayor wins?" Be aware, though, that these programs cannot take content into account, so their capabilities are limited. Some errors they cannot recognize because they do not "understand" the context. For example, if you wrote "The actors were boring" but meant to write "The actors were bored," the grammar checking programs would not reveal your mistake. Use these programs with great care.

**ESL Note**   Never make a change in your draft at the suggestion of a grammar checking program before verifying that the change is really necessary. A student from Ukraine wrote the grammatically acceptable sentence "What he has is pride." Then, at the suggestion of a grammar checking program, he changed the sentence to "What he has been pride." The program had not recognized the sequence "has is." ■

**Computer tools for designing a document**   For ways to format documents for college, work, or online presentation, see **23–28**.

**Proofreading**   Even after editing carefully and getting as much electronic input as you can, you still need to proofread your final draft to make sure no errors remain.

## KEY POINTS

### Proofreading Tips

1. Make a copy of your manuscript, and read it aloud while a friend examines the original as you read.

2. Use proofreading marks to mark typographical errors (see p. 494).

3. Put a piece of paper under the first line of your text. Move it down line by line as you read to focus your attention on one line at a time.

4. Read the last sentence first, and work backward through your text. This strategy will not help you check for meaning, logic, pronoun reference, fragments, or consistency of verb tenses; but it will focus your attention on the spelling, punctuation, and accuracy of one sentence at a time.

*(Continued)*

*(Continued)*

5. Put your manuscript away for a day or two after you have finished it. Proofread it when the content is not so familiar.

## 3e  Sample student revision

After Brad Thompson wrote the first draft of an essay describing and
analyzing a magazine advertisement for the clothing company DKNY
(Donna Karan New York), he read it aloud to a group of classmates
and took note of their comments. He also received feedback from his
instructor. Here you see Brad's introduction and first descriptive paragraph, with his own annotations for revision. Following that is his
second draft, with some small-scale revisions added by hand. Brad
then went on to write one more draft, making the changes he had
indicated and fine-tuning style, sentence structure, and word choice.

**FIRST DRAFT**

Change title?

DKNY: An Analysis of an Ad

In the September issue of Details, page 13 to be
exact, one will find a rather strikeing advertisement for DKNY clothing. DKNY is power, DKNY is
wealth, DKNY is women, DKNY is stability. And to     *Begin with this?*
think, for the price of a mere overcoat, you too     *Add thesis*
can be all this. I will tell you how.     *Fix fragments*

*frag*  The city (on page one): A dull white light illuminates the gray desolation of downtown manhattan.     *cap*
*frag*  The picture is out of focus. Perhaps another in the     *it shows*
endless series of bad days at the office, perhaps one
too many at the bar? Well, it does look like it could     *cap*
be dawn, maybe you have just woken up to find yourself
on the A train going uptown. The city is a bad place.     *Change you*
It can't quite be seen clearly, it's crooked, like
some sinister shot out of The Third Man. The picture
*Move up to focus*  creates an environment, (an urban Siberia.) What kind
of man could possibly survive in such a place?
*ff*     A DKNY kind of man enters. . . .     *Better transition?*

SECOND DRAFT

Downtown, Killer, New York: Advertising and Power
     DKNY is power, DKNY is wealth, DKNY is women,
DKNY is stability. In the September issue of
<u>Details</u>, ~~page 13 to be exact~~, a ~~rather~~ striking
two-page advertisement for DKNY clothing says all
these things. It illustrates a nightmare world
inhabited by the vast majority of DKNY's target
audience, as well as a survivor of such a world.
DKNY sells the myth of rugged individualism, man
against the wilderness. It offers to all everything it stands for, power, wealth, women, security. All this, for the price of a mere overcoat.
     The first page of the DKNY advertisement pre-
sents an image of the city as an urban Siberia. A
dull white light illuminates the gray desolation of
downtown Manhattan. ~~The picture is out of focus.~~
Perhaps it shows another in the endless series of
bad days at the office, perhaps one too many at the
bar? It could be dawn, just waking up on the A   with people
train headed uptown. The city is a bad place, it
~~can't quite be seen clearly~~. Like some sinister  lc
shot out of <u>The Third Man</u>, with crooked streets
over crooked sewers and serpentine subway tubes.
What kind of man could possibly survive in such a
place?
     Enter the DKNY man, the survivor....

# 4 Writing an Argument and Thinking Critically

When you argue a point, you present your opinions on an issue as
clearly and convincingly as you can. This type of writing is frequently
assigned in courses in the humanities and social sciences. If you are
not assigned a topic from class discussion or reading, choose an issue
that will be interesting for you to write about and for your readers to

read about. Be sure that the issue you choose is one that can be debated. You will probably want to persuade readers to adopt your point of view; but even if they don't, you will want them to acknowledge that your claim rests on solid evidence and that you have good reasons for your position. A written argument is frequently called for outside college, too—in letters to the press or to government agencies or business organizations, in business reports, and in community service.

## **4a** Consider the issue.

Choose an issue that is fresh. Avoid topics such as the death penalty, drug laws, and abortion that have been written about so often that original or interesting arguments are hard to find. Beware of saying that you intend to write about "the importance of family," "the church and morality," or "racial prejudice." Such issues might mean a great deal to you personally, but you will have difficulty structuring a logical argument around them and making a claim that grabs readers' attention.

Brainstorming, reading books, magazines, and newspapers, and browsing on the Internet in search directories, informational sites, or Usenet groups can help you discover novel and timely issues. When you find an interesting issue and your instructor has approved it (if necessary), begin by writing the issue as a question and then making lists of the arguments on both or all sides.

Jennifer Hopper decided to tackle the issue of telemarketing and its impact on society. She began by thinking that she would claim that telemarketing is more harmful than beneficial. Here are her research question and her lists of arguments:

Question: Does telemarketing have more harmful than
beneficial effects on our daily lives?

Harmful Effects
Telemarketers intrude on our privacy.
Some of them prey on the elderly.
Some of their offers are scams.
Telemarketing takes business away from retail stores.

Beneficial Effects
Telemarketing provides buying opportunities for people
  who are disabled and homebound.
It provides jobs, especially in rural areas.

```
The job training that telemarketers receive stresses
   being polite, friendly, and articulate--good qualities.
```

## **4b**    Formulate an arguable claim.

*Making a claim*    The position you take on an issue constitutes your claim or your thesis. A claim should be debatable—for example, "Telemarketing benefits the economy" or "Telemarketers prey on the elderly and the gullible." Neutral statements, which give no hint of the writer's position; facts, which are not arguable; truisms (statements that are obviously true); personal or religious convictions that cannot be disproved; and sweeping generalizations do not provide good claims for an argument, as these examples show:

| | |
|---|---|
| NEUTRAL STATEMENT | **This paper is about standards of beauty in the workplace.** |
| REVISED | **The way we look affects the way we are treated at work and the size of our paychecks.** |
| FACT | *Plessy v. Ferguson*, **a Supreme Court case that supported racial segregation, was overturned in 1954 by** *Brown v. Board of Education of Topeka, Kansas*. |
| REVISED | **The overturning of** *Plessy v. Ferguson* **by** *Brown v. Board of Education* **has not led to significant advances in integrated education.** |
| TRUISM | **Bilingual education has advantages and disadvantages.** |
| REVISED | **A bilingual program is more effective than an immersion program at helping students grasp the basics of science and mathematics.** |
| PERSONAL CONVICTION | **Racism is the worst kind of prejudice.** |
| REVISED | **The best weapon against racism is primary and secondary education.** |
| SWEEPING GENERALIZATION | **Women understand housework.** |
| REVISED | **The publication of a big new guide to housekeeping and its success among both men and women suggest a renewed interest in "the domestic arts."** |

*Changing a claim*   Sometimes you will have an instant reaction to an issue and immediately decide which position you want to take. Other times, you will need to reflect and do research before you take a stand. The statement of your position is your claim or thesis—for example, "Those who refuse to fight in a national war that they consider unjust should—or should not—be punished." Always keep an open mind. Be prepared to find out more about an issue so that you can make an educated claim with concrete support, and be prepared to change your original opinion as you do your research. Jennifer Hopper began her argument paper on one side of the telemarketing debate only to find that her research produced enough convincing evidence to persuade her to change her views — and, of course, her thesis.

*Modifying a claim*   Even if you do not change your position, you will often find yourself modifying your claim as you read, think, and write, making it less all-embracing or less extreme. Here is how one student modified her claim as she worked on an argument paper. She took into account some opposing views, toned down the language, and set limits to her position—not taking on the issue of all the effects a power plant would have but focusing specifically on environmental issues of water, wildlife, and natural beauty.

> <u>Issue</u>: Building a new electrical plant
>
> <u>Audience</u>: General audience
>
> <u>Initial research question</u>: What will be the effects of a Hudson River valley electric power plant on jobs, the local economy, and the environment?

After some research
> <u>Initial claim (working thesis)</u>: A new electric power plant will irreparably damage the environment of the Hudson River valley.

After more brainstorming, discussion, and reading
> <u>Modified claim</u>: Although we need to consider the increased demand for electricity and local economic development, a large power plant on the Hudson River would threaten water quality, wildlife, and natural beauty.

**4c**   Support the claim with reasons and concrete evidence.

*Reasons*   Imagine someone saying to you, "OK. I know your position on this issue, but I disagree with you. Tell me your reasons for making that claim. What data and evidence led you to that conclusion?" State your arguments in support of your claim, and tell why you think what you think. At this point, make a scratch outline listing the claim and your reasons for supporting it. Here is the outline made by the student writing about the power plant.

Claim: Although we need to consider the increased demand for electricity and local economic development, a large power plant on the Hudson River would threaten water quality, wildlife, and natural beauty.

Reasons

1. Discharging heated water into the river can kill fish and animals.

2. Ground water can become polluted, and many nearby homes have wells.

3. Views portrayed by the Hudson River School of painters would be spoiled.

**Concrete evidence**   You need reasons, but reasons are not enough. You also need to include specific evidence that supports, illustrates, and explains your reasons. Imagine a reader saying, after you give one of your reasons, "Tell me even more about why you say that." The details you provide are what will make your essay vivid and persuasive. Add to the outline any items of concrete evidence you will include to illustrate and explain your reasoning. What counts as evidence? Facts, statistics, stories, examples, and testimony from experts can all be used as evidence in support of your reasons.

For example, the student writing on the effects of the power plant decided to include

- facts and figures about water pollution levels and the numbers of fish affected, as well as statistics on emissions;
- examples of ground-water pollution in other parts of the country—what happened, who got sick, what local reactions were;
- accounts of interviews with a representative sample of local residents;
- pictures (downloaded from Web sites) of Hudson River School paintings showing the idyllic landscape.

**ESL Note**   The way arguments are structured and the nature of the evidence regarded as convincing may vary from one culture to another. Looking at newspaper editorials written in your home language and in English will help you discern what differences, if any, exist in the types of evidence used to support an argument. Be sure to consider the readers you will be writing for and the type of evidence they will expect. ■

## **4d** Refute opposing views.

Examine your list of the arguments at odds with your view. Describe the most popular or convincing ones; tell why people take those positions; then show why their reasons are illogical, unimportant, irrelevant, false, self-serving, or at least not as convincing as your own. Be careful to argue logically and rationally. Don't call opposing views "immoral," "ridiculous," or "stupid." Be respectful of your opponents' views, and explain rationally why your views differ from theirs.

## **4e** Identify and involve your audience, and establish common ground.

***Ask who your readers are.***   Consider the readers you are writing for. Assess what they might know, what assumptions they hold, what they need to know, how they can best be convinced to accept your position, and what strategies will persuade them to respect or accept your views.

If you want to argue that a new electric power plant should not be built alongside a major river, you need to consider carefully who your readers are. Electric company workers, the unemployed, and suppliers of industrial equipment and materials, on the one hand, and fishing enthusiasts, environmentalists, and homeowners, on the other, will bring their own assumptions and biases to the argument. Consider and address such biases. If you are writing for a general audience, remember to include background information: the place, the time, the context, the issues. Do not assume that a general reader knows a great deal more than you do. For more on audience, see **1b**.

***Establish common ground.***   Make sure that your arguments are not confrontational. Find ways to point to shared values. Logically refute any arguments that are not valid (**4d**), but in addition, acknowledge when your opponents' arguments *are* valid and work to show why the arguments on your side carry more weight. Try to propose a solution with long-term benefits for everyone. For example, you might acknowledge the importance of generating more electric power and the need for more industry and jobs in a specific area, but you would also show how those goals could be achieved without building a power plant on the proposed river site.

---

### LANGUAGE AND CULTURE

#### Rhetorical Approaches to Involve an Audience

Martin Luther King, Jr., was a master of rhetorical devices to involve his audience, as you can see in this excerpt from his "I Have a Dream" speech to civil rights protesters in 1963.

> We have also come to this hallowed spot to remind America of the fierce urgency of *now*. This is no time to engage in the luxury of cooling off or to take the tranquilizing drug of gradualism. *Now is the time to* make real the promises of democracy. *Now is the time to* rise from the dark and desolate valley of segregation to the sunlit path of racial justice. *Now is the time to* lift our nation from the quicksands of racial injustice to the solid rock of brotherhood. *Now is the time to* make justice a reality for all of God's children.

Getting your listeners or readers to identify with your cause makes them more receptive to the arguments you present and the action you propose.

---

**Use language to involve your audience.** When you are presenting an argument and want to inspire your audience to accept your views, you might wish to employ certain writing strategies to grab readers' attention and drive your point home. These strategies include the use of figurative language ("the tranquilizing drug of gradualism," for instance); clear, direct language; language to establish common ground, such as the inclusive use of *we*; and repetition and parallel structure (see also **40j**).

## **4f** Think critically about your argument, and ask four questions.

Thinking critically does not mean criticizing what you read and hear. It means keeping an open mind and asking probing questions. The readers of arguments, especially, employ their critical thinking capabilities to examine the reasoning a writer uses and to ferret out the writer's assumptions, biases, and lapses in logic. (See **8a** for more on critical reading.) Think of times when you were reading a newspaper or magazine article and exclaimed "What!" and then read the article aloud to your family or friends because the writer's assumptions and biases were so obvious and seemed so misguided. Your readers will be looking for *your* assumptions, biases, and lapses in logic as they read.

*Examine your logic with four questions.* The following four questions, derived from Stephen Toulmin's *The Uses of Argument* (Cambridge UP, 1958), will provide you with a way to examine your own arguments critically.

### KEY POINTS

**Four Questions to Ask about Your Argument**

1. What is your point? (What are you claiming?)
2. What do you have to go on? (What reasons and evidence do you have?)
3. How do you get there? (What assumptions do you rely on to connect your reasons to your claim?)
4. But what could prevent you from getting there? (What can you say after "unless" or "if" to provide exceptions to your assumptions?)

Toulmin provides the following illustration of a simple argument, one not complex enough for an essay but clear enough to show the principles:

1. Harry is probably a British subject.
2. Harry was born in Bermuda.
3. A man born in Bermuda will generally be a British subject . . .
4. . . . unless both his parents were not born in Bermuda or he has become a naturalized American.

*Examine your underlying assumptions.* Pay special attention to examining the assumptions that link a claim to the reasons and to the evidence you provide. Consider whether readers will share those assumptions or whether you need to explain, discuss, and defend them. For example, the claim "Telemarketing should be monitored because it preys on the elderly and the gullible" operates on the assumption that monitoring will catch and reduce abuses. The claim "Telemarketing should be encouraged because it benefits the economy" operates on the assumption that benefit to the economy is an important goal. These different assumptions will appeal to different readers, and some may need to be persuaded of the assumptions before they attempt to accept your claim or the reasons you give for it.

Note that if you claim that "Telemarketing should be encouraged because it is useful," you are saying little more than "Telemarketing is good because it is good." Your reader is certain to object to and reject such circular reasoning. That is why it is important to ask question 3 on page 43, the question that leads you to examine how you get from your evidence to your claim and what assumptions your claim is based on.

## **4g**　Plan the structure of your argument.

Once you have settled on a thesis, main points of support, concrete evidence, and approach to audience, you need to reflect on the best way to present your case. You might choose to present your argument *inductively*—beginning with the data and evidence first and leading the reader to accept your conclusion. You would begin with a hypothesis that you could test: you would list your findings from experimentation, surveys, facts, and/or statistics, and then from the data you have collected you would draw conclusions to support, modify, or reject the hypothesis. This method of argument is often used in the social sciences and scientific fields (see, for example, the APA-style sample paper in section **16**).

Another method, more common in the humanities, is organizing your argument *deductively*—beginning with a claim and then supporting that claim point by point with concrete evidence (**4c**).

Whichever method of presentation you choose, you will also need to decide how and where to deal with opposing views—whether at the beginning, at the end, or point by point throughout your argument.

## **4h**　Avoid flaws in logic.

Faulty logic can make readers mistrust you as a writer. Watch out for these flaws as you write and check your drafts.

***Sweeping generalizations***　Generalizations can sometimes be so broad that they fall into stereotyping: "All British people are stiff and formal" or "The only thing that concerns students is grades."

*Hasty conclusions with inadequate support*   To convince readers of the validity of a generalization, you need to offer more than one personal example. Thoughtful readers can easily spot a hasty conclusion: "My friend Arecelis had a terrible time in a bilingual school. This experience shows that bilingual education has failed."

*Non sequitur*   *Non sequitur* is Latin for "It does not follow." This sentence is a non sequitur: "Maureen Dowd writes so well that she would make a good teacher." The writer does not establish any connection between good writing and good teaching.

*Causal fallacy*   You are guilty of causal fallacy if you assume that one event causes another merely because the second event happens after the first. (The Latin name for this logical flaw is *post hoc, ergo propter hoc:* "after this, therefore because of this.") Example: "The economy collapsed because a new president was elected."

*Ad hominem attack*   *Ad hominem* (Latin for "to the person") refers to appeals to personal considerations rather than to logic or reason. Avoid using arguments that seek to discredit an opinion through personal criticism, such as "The new curriculum should not be adopted, because the administrators who favor it don't even live near the college."

*Circular reasoning*   In an argument based on circular reasoning, the evidence and the conclusion restate each other, thus proving nothing: "That rich man is smart because wealthy people are intelligent."

*False dichotomy or false dilemma*   Either/or arguments reduce complex problems to two simplistic alternatives without exploring them in depth or considering other alternatives. For example, an essay that builds its argument on the assertion "To improve education, the Board can either hire more teachers or build more schools" presents a false dichotomy. Those two options are not the only ways to improve education.

**4i**   Excerpts from an argument paper

Here are the opening four paragraphs of Jennifer Hopper's first draft of her argument paper "The War between the Right to Privacy and Telemarketing," as well as her concluding paragraph.

### OPENING PARAGRAPHS

Approximately twelve years ago, our economy was experiencing a significant slump. Many urban dwellers were out of work. Farm owners were being forced to sell their land. Money woes were on all American minds. Some blamed the President. Others pointed to big business owners. But eventually, the United States managed to escape unscathed from the down-spiraling trend. Coincidentally, another phenomenon hit America at about the same time as the economic upswing--telemarketing.

*Gives background context*

Telemarketing is a relatively new means for companies to sell their wares to American shoppers. Rather than having to wait for consumers to choose to shop in their stores and buy from them, businesses have decided to go straight to the customer. This involves millions of telephone calls from company representatives to households across America every day. The demand for workers to make those calls and the billions of dollars' worth of goods and services sold via the calls have created a booming business for telemarketers (Greenwald).

*Defines term*

*Refers to a one-page source*

Yet every silver lining has its cloud. There has been a substantial outcry from the American public about the irritation of receiving sales calls at home. These objections have led to legislation by Congress, the creation of antitelemarketing Web sites on the Internet, and court battles between private citizens and telemarketing companies (Raisfield). These developments are centered around the issue of Americans' right to privacy at home, and whether telephone solicitations are an intrusion on that privacy.

*Presents one side of issue*

Of course, if this is the ugly side of telemarketing, we must also consider that there is an important bright side. Telemarketing provides

*Presents the other side*

millions of jobs to Americans and has sparked the
growth and development of many otherwise declining
US cities (Greenwald). Although telemarketing can
be a nuisance at times, we cannot ignore its
positive aspects. Telemarketing has proven itself
substantially important to both American workers
and consumers. Therefore, if some individuals find
that telephone solicitations do them more harm
than good, they should address the problem without
compromising the rights of the consumers and
workers who benefit from the industry. In short,
telemarketing cannot be written off as a public
nuisance when it is such a valuable source of
American dollars and provider of goods and services.

Makes claim
and presents
thesis

Reiterates
thesis

**FINAL PARAGRAPH**

It is no longer possible to deem telemarketing
unnecessary and dispensable once we know the
industry's employment numbers and sales revenues.
It has become important and necessary to places
like Omaha and North Dakota, in which many people
need such jobs to keep them from a descent into
poverty. Telemarketing industries are selling
billions of dollars' worth of goods and services
to American consumers every year. Not all these
sales, or even a majority of them, can be the
result of telemarketers supposedly deceiving the
consumer. Many Americans may still not approve of
telemarketing techniques, but they need to fight
the industry from the top down, not from the bottom
up. Telemarketers have just as much of a right to
hold down a job without interference as any other
Americans. Linda Scobee, an Omahan telemarketer,

> expressed this right to one man who seemed to want
> to attack the employees: "He said, 'Why don't you
> get a real job?' and I wanted to say: 'If you'd like
> to send me a check every month to take care of my
> kids, I'll stop.' But I didn't. You know, company
> policy" (Singer 69).

# 5  Writing in All Your Courses

## 5a  Essay exams and short-answer tests

*Essay exams* are an important part of your life as a student. In an examination setting, you have to write quickly and on an assigned topic. Learn how to cope with these tests so that you don't dread them. The advantage of an essay over a multiple-choice test is that you can include in your answer more of the information you have learned. Knowing the material of the course thoroughly will give you a distinct advantage, allowing you to choose the facts and ideas you need and present them clearly.

### KEY POINTS

**How to Approach an Essay Exam**

1. For a content-based essay test, review assigned materials and notes, underline, annotate, summarize, predict questions, and draft some answers.

2. Underline key terms in the assigned questions (see the list on p. 49). Ask for clarification if necessary.

3. Think positively about what you know. Work out a way to highlight the details you know most about. Stretch and relax.

4. Plan your time. Jot down a rough schedule; allow the most time for the questions that are worth the most points. To increase your confidence, answer the easiest question first.

*(Continued)*

*(Continued)*

5. Make a scratch outline (see **1f**) to organize your thoughts. Jot down specific details as evidence for your thesis.

6. Read over your essay, checking for content, logic, and clarity. Make sure you answered the question.

In *short-answer tests,* use your time wisely. So that you know how long you should spend on each question, count the number of questions and divide the number of minutes you have for taking the test by the number of questions (add 1 or 2 to the number you divide by, to give yourself time for editing and proofreading). Then for each answer decide which points are the most important ones to cover in the time you have available. You cannot afford to ramble or waffle in short-answer tests. Get to the point fast, and show what you know.

For essay exams and short-answer tests, always read the questions carefully, and make sure you understand what each question asks you to do. Test writers often use the following verbs:

*analyze:* divide into parts and discuss each part

*argue:* make a claim and point out your reasons

*classify:* organize people, objects, or concepts into groups

*compare:* point out similarities

*contrast:* point out differences

*define:* give the meaning of

*discuss:* state important characteristics and main points

*evaluate:* define criteria for judgment and examine good and bad points, strengths and weaknesses

*explain:* give reasons or make clear by analyzing, defining, contrasting, illustrating, and so on

*illustrate:* give examples from experience and reading

*relate:* point out and discuss connections

## **5b** Writing about literature

Before you begin writing, pay careful attention to the content and form of the work of literature by following the steps listed here.

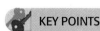

### KEY POINTS

**Preparing to Write about Literature**

1. Consider the type of work (the genre)—drama, novel, short story, biography, sonnet. What do you know about its features? What else have you read within that genre or by that author?

2. Read the work more than once. The first time, read to enjoy and appreciate the work and to form your first impressions. In later readings, read closely and critically.

3. If you own the book you are using, highlight or underline significant passages. Look for patterns, connections, and surprises. Mark only a few places on each page; otherwise, when rereading, you will not know what to pay attention to.

4. Take notes on significant passages in the text, and record your responses to them in a journal (see **1c**). What characters and actions do you relate to best, and why?

5. As you read a short story, novel, or poem, consider who the narrator is (the narrator is the person telling the story, not necessarily the author), what the narrator's background is, what happens, and why.

6. Consider the author's time, history, and motivation, as well as what audience the writer addresses and how different readers are likely to respond to the work.

**Net Note** Consider joining an electronic discussion list for literature. Consult a directory of lists (such as the one at <http://www.n2h2.com/KOVACS>) to find one that fits your interests. ■

*Prose works* As you read novels, short stories, and plays, consider these basic questions for thinking about what you read: What happened? When and where did it happen? Who did what? How were things done? Why? Then extend your inquiry by considering all or some of the following factors in detail:

   *plot:* sequence of events in the work

   *character and character development:* main characters, who they are, how they interact, and if and how they change

   *theme:* main message of the work

   *setting:* time and place of the action and cultural/social context *point of view:* position from which the events are described, such as first or third person narrator (*I/we* or *he/she/they*), biased or reliable, limited or omniscient

*author:* relationship to narrator (same or different person?); relevant facts of author's life

*tone:* attitudes expressed directly or indirectly by the author or narrator

*style:* word choice, sentence length and structure, significant features

*imagery:* effect of figures of speech, such as similes and metaphors (see pp. 51–52 and **33e**)

*symbols:* objects or events with special significance or with hidden meanings

*narrative devices:* foreshadowing, flashback, leitmotif (a recurring theme), alternating points of view, turning point, and dénouement (outcome of plot)

**Poetry**   In addition to using some of the suggestions relating to prose, you can consider the following factors when you analyze a poem.

*stanza:* lines set off as a unit of a poem

*rhyme scheme:* system of end-of-line rhymes that you can identify by assigning letters to similar final sounds—for example, a rhyme scheme for couplets (two-line stanzas), *aa bb cc;* and a rhyme scheme for a sestet (a six-line stanza), *ab ab cc*

*meter:* number and pattern of stressed and unstressed syllables (or *metric feet*) in a line. Common meters are trimeter, tetrameter, and pentameter (three, four, and five metric feet). The following line is written in iambic tetrameter (four metric feet, each with one stressed and one unstressed syllable):

Whŏse woóds / thĕse aŕe / Ĭ thínk / Ĭ knów      —Robert Frost

*foot:* unit (of meter) made up of a specific number of stressed and unstressed syllables

**Figurative language**   The writers of literary works often use figures of speech to create images and intensify effects.

*simile:* a comparison, with two sides stated.

Like as the waves make towards the pebbled shore,
So do our minutes hasten to their end.      —Shakespeare

The weather is like the government, always in the wrong.
                                                          —Jerome K. Jerome

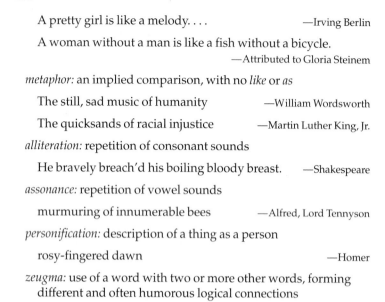

A pretty girl is like a melody. . . .                                    —Irving Berlin

A woman without a man is like a fish without a bicycle.
—Attributed to Gloria Steinem

*metaphor:* an implied comparison, with no *like* or *as*

The still, sad music of humanity                —William Wordsworth

The quicksands of racial injustice              —Martin Luther King, Jr.

*alliteration:* repetition of consonant sounds

He bravely breach'd his boiling bloody breast.      —Shakespeare

*assonance:* repetition of vowel sounds

murmuring of innumerable bees              —Alfred, Lord Tennyson

*personification:* description of a thing as a person

rosy-fingered dawn                                              —Homer

*zeugma:* use of a word with two or more other words, forming
different and often humorous logical connections

The art dealer departed in anger and a Mercedes.

For more on using figurative language in your own writing, see **33e**.

### Five tips for writing about literature

**1.  Consider your reader.**   Are you writing for someone who
knows the work you are writing about? If your professor does not
specify an audience, and if you know that he or she will be the only
person to read the paper, assume a larger audience than this one expert. Think of your reader as someone who has read the work but has
not thought of the issues you have thought of.

**2. Ask questions about the work.**   Narrow your focus from the
broad subject of the work to the specific questions you will ask and
answer about it. (See **1d** on finding a focus.)

- What does the work say and mean? This question may lead to a
line-by-line explication, usually of a short work such as a poem
or of a significant passage from a longer work.

- What elements in the work are significant to understanding it,
and what techniques has the writer used to develop those ele-

ments? These questions lead to an analysis of important points that relate to the theme of the whole work.

- How does this work compare or contrast to one or more other works? This type of question leads you to fit the work you have selected into a larger context. For this approach you will probably have to do more extensive research than would be necessary for explication or analysis of only one text. See **2c** for organizing a comparison and contrast.

**3. Formulate a thesis.**   A thesis is as necessary when you write about literature as when you do other types of college writing. In your repeated readings and in your notes, you need to interpret what you read in light of other works you have read and of your own experience. Use text annotations, notes, and a double-entry journal, as well as other methods of generating ideas, to make a claim (see **1c**). Your aim is to persuade your reader to consider your interpretation. Sample theses:

> W. B. Yeats and James Joyce present radically different perspectives on Ireland.

> Nicholson Baker's work has close links to the author he has written about so admiringly: John Updike.

> The green light in *The Great Gatsby* is not necessarily the guiding image of the novel.

**4. Avoid an emphasis on summary.**   A brief summary of the work might be necessary to orient readers, but the major part of your paper should be an analysis and interpretation of the work, not simply a description or a summary. Readers need to see clearly that the paper is not just a retelling of, for example, the story of *The Great Gatsby* but an explanation of your analysis and opinions of *The Great Gatsby*, organized around a thesis. They also need to understand why you advance this thesis. References to the text should help explain your interpretation.

**5. Turn to the text for evidence—and do so often.**   Offer support for your assertions, especially the debatable ones, by giving examples from the text. Text references are the most convincing evidence you can provide. Summarize, paraphrase, and quote when the exact words are appropriate. Any quotation you include, particularly a long one, should support a point you are making in your essay. Avoid stringing quotations together.

## KEY POINTS

### Common Conventions in Writing about Literature

**Tense**   Use the present tense to discuss works of literature (**41e**).

**Authors' Names**   Use an author's full name the first time you mention it: "Stephen King." Thereafter, and always in parenthetical citations, use only the last name: "King," not "Stephen" and certainly not "Steve." (See **11** for information on citations.)

**Titles of Works**   Underline or italicize the titles of books, journals, and other works published as an entity and not as part of a larger work. Use quotation marks to enclose the titles of short stories, essays, songs, and poems.

**Quotations**   Integrate quotations into your text, and use them for help in making your point (**10d**). Avoid a mere listing and stringing together: "Walker goes on to say. . . . Then Walker states. . . ." Indent long quotations (more than three lines of poetry or four typed lines of prose) ten spaces without using quotation marks (**10c**).

**Citations**   Supply specific references to the literary text under discussion to support your opinions, and cite any references to the work or to secondary sources. (See **9e** for advice on what to cite.) Cite author and page number within your essay for all quotations and references to the work of others; at the end of your paper attach an alphabetical list of works cited. Follow the MLA style of documentation (see **11–13**).

## **5c**  Oral reports

You may be asked to give oral reports or oral presentations in writing courses and in other college courses. Usually you will do some writing as you prepare your talk, and you will deliver your oral report either from a complete manuscript text or from notes.

*Audience*   Consider the background and expectations of your audience. Jot down what you know about your listeners and what stance and tone will best convince them of the validity of your views. For example, what effect do you want to have on the members of your audience? Do you want to inform, persuade, move, or entertain them? What do you know about your listeners' age, gender, background, education, occupation, political affiliation, beliefs, and knowledge of your subject? What do listeners need to know? In a college class, your audience will be your classmates and instructor. It is often desirable to build a sense of community with your audience by asking questions and using the inclusive pronoun *we*.

***Preparation for oral reports*** Making an effective oral presentation is largely a matter of having control over your material, deciding what you want to say, and knowing your subject matter well. Preparation and planning are essential.

---

### KEY POINTS

#### Tips for Preparing an Oral Report

1. Select a topic you are committed to, and decide on a clear focus.

2. Make a few strong points. Back them up with specific details. Have a few points that you can expand on and develop with interesting examples, quotations, and stories.

3. Include signposts and signal phrases to help your audience follow your ideas (*first, next, finally; the most important point is . . .*).

4. Structure your report clearly. Present the organizational framework of your talk along with illustrative materials in handouts, overhead transparencies, PowerPoint slides (see **28**), posters, charts, or other visuals (see **24**).

5. Use short sentences, accessible words, memorable phrases, and natural language. In writing, you can use long sentences with one clause embedded in another, but these are difficult for listeners to follow.

6. You can effectively use repetition much more in an oral report than in a written report. Your audience will appreciate being reminded of the structure of the talk and points you referred to previously.

7. Meet the requirements set for the presentation in terms of time available for preparation, length of presentation (most people read a page of double-spaced text in just over two minutes), and possible questions from the audience.

8. Prepare a strong ending that will have an impact on the audience. Make sure that you conclude. Do not simply stop or trail off.

---

You can make your presentation from a specially prepared manuscript, or you can distill your information to notes, which you can then either memorize or consult as you talk.

*Speaking from a manuscript*  The advantages of speaking from a prepared manuscript are that you can time the presentation exactly and that you will never dry up and wonder what to say next. The disadvantages are that you have to read the text and that reading aloud is not easy, especially if you want to maintain eye contact with your audience. If you prefer to speak from a complete manuscript text, prepare the text for oral presentation:

- Triple-space your text and use a large font.
- When you reach the bottom of a page, begin a new sentence on the next page. Do not start a sentence on one page and finish it on the next.
- Highlight key words in each paragraph so that your eye can pick them out easily.
- Underline words and phrases that you want to stress.
- Use slash marks (/ or //) to remind yourself to pause. Read in sense groups (parts of a sentence that are read as a unit—a phrase or clause, for example—often indicated by a pause when spoken and by punctuation when read). Mark your text at the end of a sense group.
- Number your pages so that you can keep them in the proper sequence.

The following excerpt from a student's text prepared for an oral report shows some distinctive features.

Signpost to structure

Short and direct

    Should men get and take paternity/leave? Of

    course they should. Here's why. / First, everyone

    benefits if fathers have a chance to bond with their

    children—the father, the mother, and most of all,

    the infant. The literature we have read in this

    class tells us that crucial bonding takes place

Question used to draw the audience in

```
between mother and child in the early days after

birth. // But the issue is not only one of personal

need for bonding. It's an issue of social and

gender equity. If women are granted time off from

work and often take it, men should take time off,

too. "But business and industry can't afford it," I     Direct
                                                        quotation

hear you say. Let's look at what it would cost. . . .   Informal
                                                        language
```

***Speaking from notes*** Speaking from notes instead of reading aloud will create a more spontaneous effect. For this method, notes or a key-word outline must be clear and organized:

```
Paternity Leave

1. Children's needs
   Benefits
   Bonding

2. Issue of equity
   Equal treatment for men and women
   Cost
```

Your notes or outline should make reference to specific illustrations and quotations and contain structural signals so that the audience knows when you begin to address a new point. Use notes for a short presentation on a topic that you know very well. You can also use PowerPoint slides (see **28**).

### Practice, practice, practice

- Practice not just once but many times. Try tape-recording yourself, listening to the tape, and asking a friend for comments.

- Speak at a normal speed and at a good volume. Speaking too quickly and too softly is a common mistake.

- Imagine a full audience; use gestures, and practice looking up to make eye contact with people in the audience.

- Beware of filler words and phrases like *OK, you know,* and *like.* Such repeated verbal tics annoy and distract an audience.

- If you use visual aids to outline your talk and provide essential information, check your equipment and practice with it. If you use an overhead projector or PowerPoint slides (see **28**), the font size must be large enough for people at the back of the room to read. Use headings (**23d**) and bulleted lists (**23e**) to make your material clear. When you speak, remember to face the audience and not the projector or screen. Do not provide lengthy or complicated visual aids; otherwise, your audience will be reading them instead of listening to you.

**Delivery**   It is natural to feel some anxiety before the actual presentation, but most people find that their jitters disappear as soon as they begin talking, especially when they are well prepared.

Look frequently at your listeners. Work the room so that you gaze directly at people in all sections of the audience. In *Secrets of Successful Speakers,* Lilly Walters points out that when you look at one person, all the people in a V behind that person will think you are looking at them. Bear in mind that no matter how well prepared a report is, listeners will not respond well if the presenter reads it too rapidly or in a monotone or without looking up and engaging the audience. Remember to smile.

**5d**   Community service writing

Service learning projects link a college to the community. For such projects, students volunteer for community service, often related to the content of a discipline or a particular course. They then must demonstrate to the college instructor what they learned from the service experience. There are three main types of writing for community service projects:

1. writing done initially with the site supervisor to outline the goals, activities, and desired outcomes of the service project

2. writing done during the service work, such as reports to a supervisor, daily records, and summaries of work completed

3. writing done for the college course—usually reflective reports describing the service objectives and the writer's experiences and assessing the success of the project

To reflect fully on the work you do, keep an ongoing journal of your activities, so that you can provide background about the setting and the work and give specific details about the problems you encounter and their solutions. Link your comments to the goals of the project.

The following paragraph is from Joanne L. Soriano's reflective journal. While enrolled in a microbiology course at Kapi'olani Community College in Hawaii, Joanne worked at an arboretum (a place to study trees) propagating endangered plant species.

```
Through Service Learning, I am able to contribute to the
Lyon Arboretum's efforts. I made my first visit on
February 5th, and was taken to their micropropagation
lab. In it, my supervisor, Greg Koob, showed me racks and
racks of test tubes filled with plantlets. They were
either endangered or native Hawaiian, or both. The
endangered ones were clones; in some cases they were
derived from only a few remaining individuals. A major
function of the lab is to perpetuate these species by
growing them in the test tubes and then splitting each
individual into more test tubes as they grow. Thus one
specimen can become hundreds under the right conditions.
They can be planted on the Arboretum's grounds, or sent
to various labs to be studied. I am thrilled to be given
the opportunity to participate in the process.
```

Source: Excerpt from KCC Service Learning at the Lyon Arboretum.

## 5e Laboratory reports

Students write laboratory reports to describe their experiments in social science and science courses. Some instructors provide detailed directions on the format they expect for a lab report. If they do not, use the following guidelines for reports in introductory courses.

The *Publication Manual of the American Psychological Association* (APA) describes a report format that generally is acceptable to college instructors in the sciences as well as the social sciences. The APA author/year style closely resembles the author/year style described in the Council of Biology Editors style manual (*Scientific Style and*

*Format: The CBE Manual for Editors, Authors, and Publishers*) as one of its recommended styles of documentation. (You will find an example of a typical APA-style report of an experimental procedure in **16**.)

For an APA-style lab report, include a title page, a page header on every page, and an abstract (see p. 179). Divide the report into headed sections: Introduction, including the purpose and background of the experiment, your hypothesis, and a review of similar experiments; Materials and Methods (with subheadings such as Apparatus, Participants, and Procedure); Results (include statistical data and explain your tables and figures); Discussion; and Conclusion(s). Include a list of references (see **15–16**) and notes, on separate pages. Finally, attach any tables and figures, such as graphs, drawings, and photographs, on separate pages at the end of your report (see p. 186).

The following passage is from Natasha Williams's lab report on microbial genetics conjugation, written for a college cell biology course. This excerpt shows part of the Discussion section, annotated to point out various conventions of science writing.

---

Discussion

Conjugation involves transfer by appropriate mating types. F+ and Hfr are donor cells with respectively low and high rates of genetic transfer. F- cells are recipients. Contact between the cell types is made by a conjugation bridge called an F pilus extending from the Hfr cell. The donor chromosome appears to be linearly passed through the connecting bridge. Sometimes this transfer is interrupted. The higher the frequency of recombination, the closer the gene is to the beginning of the circular DNA. In this way one can determine the sequence of genes on the chromosome.

Table 1 shows consistently that histidine is the last amino acid coded with the smallest number of recombinants, and arginine is the second to last coded with the next smallest number of recombinants. However, the results obtained for proline and leucine/threonine vary.

| Annotation |
|---|
| Major section heading is centered. |
| Passive construction, common in lab reports |
| Note the use of *one* for general reference. |
| Researcher places Table 1 at end of report and here discusses its details. |

## **5f** Writing in the disciplines

In a biology course, you might be expected to write scientific laboratory reports and to use a style of documentation different from one you learned in an English course. In a music course, another format and still another documentation style might be required.

### LANGUAGE AND CULTURE

#### The Culture of the Academic Disciplines

Each discipline has its own culture and its own expectations of the people who practice in the discipline and write about it. When you take a course in a new discipline, use the following strategies to get acquainted with its ways of thinking and operating.

1. Listen carefully to lectures and discussion; note any specialized vocabulary.

2. Read the assigned textbook, and note the conventions that apply in writing about the field.

3. Subscribe to e-mail discussion lists (**21a**) in the field so that you can see what issues people are concerned about.

4. When given a writing assignment, make sure you read samples of similar types of writing in that discipline.

5. Talk with your instructor about the field, its literature, and readers' expectations.

Find out what way of writing and documenting is expected in each of your courses. Although each one may call for some adaptation of the writing process and for awareness of specific conventions, in general you will engage in familiar activities—planning, drafting, revising, and editing.

You will be aware of the biggest differences when you come to do research and write research papers or accounts of experiments. Follow the conventions of the discipline you are writing in. Consider the following:

- types of data to gather—from primary or secondary sources? (**6b**, item 4)

- sources to consult (**7b, 7c, 7d, 7e**)

- methods of presenting papers (**5c, 13, 16**)
- documentation style to use (see **11–19**)
- terminology specific to the field (**33d**)
- type of language in common use: subjective or objective? (**10e**)

This book contains several samples of or from student papers written in different disciplines: humanities (**3e, 4i, 13, 18d**), social sciences (see **16**), and sciences (**5e, 17e**).

# Doing Research/
# Evaluating Sources

# 6 Research Basics

## 6a What is research, and why do it?

You think you might have West Nile virus, and you try to find out what the symptoms are and the best way to treat them. That's research. You want to buy a digital camera, but you don't know anything about the features, brands, and prices. You order catalogs, talk to salespeople, go to stores, try out cameras, ask friends what they recommend, read consumer magazines, and roam the Web. That's research. You have a bet with a friend that tea contains as much caffeine as coffee, so you go to an encyclopedia or to Ask Jeeves! or Sherlock on the Web and find out you are wrong. That's research, too. And when your English professor asks you to write a paper on the impact of shopping malls on town centers, research helps you do that. You first discover the important issues and then explore, evaluate, and synthesize information about the topic and consider the opinions of various experts who have studied the question in depth. Doing research is finding out as much as possible about an issue, finding good questions to ask, formulating one major research question, and then attempting to find answers to that question. It is a vital part of daily life as well as an essential part of academic and scholarly work.

## 6b The process of writing a research paper: A guide

Use the following strategies for working on a research paper.

*1. Know the requirements, and set a realistic schedule.* Find out what the demands of the assignment are, such as length, due date, information you should include, number and types of sources, documentation style, and manuscript format. Set a week-by-week or day-by-day schedule for the steps in the process. Even if you do not keep to the schedule exactly, it will help organize your time and let you know when you absolutely must move on to the next step.

*2. Establish your topic.* Make sure you understand and answer the assigned question or address the assigned topic. If you select your own topic, check with your instructor to make sure it is appropriate. Narrow the topic so that it is manageable for the number of pages you intend to write. You may have to do a great deal of background reading before you settle on a narrow enough topic (**1d**). The more you know about a topic, the easier it will be for you to find good questions to ask. Make sure, too, to choose a topic that will engage and sustain not only readers' interests but your own. Connect your topic to your own experience whenever possible. Readers recognize a bored writer who is simply going through the motions of writing a paper. If your topic is assigned, make sure you understand the terms used in the assignment (**5a**).

### 3. *Develop your research question and thesis.*  For a full-scale research paper, design a research question that gets at the heart of what you want to discover. The answer you find as you do research is likely to become your thesis.

If you find huge amounts of material on your question and realize that you would have to write a book (or two) to cover it, narrow your question.

QUESTIONS NEEDING FOCUS

a. How important are families? (too broad—important to whom and for what?)

b. What problems does the Internet cause? (too broad—what types of problems? what aspects of the Internet?)

c. What are the treatments for cancer? (too wide ranging—volumes could be and have been written on this)

d. Should prayer be encouraged in schools? (difficult to discuss without relying on personal and religious conviction)

QUESTIONS REVISED TO HAVE GREATER FOCUS

a. In what ways does a stable family environment contribute to an individual's future success?

b. Should Internet controls be established to protect individual privacy?

c. For which types of cancer are the success rates of radiation therapy highest?

d. If prayer is allowed in schools, how can a multicultural policy be maintained?

A research question will give you a sense of direction. Frequently, as you read and take notes, you will have in mind a tentative response to your question. Sometimes that hypothesis will be confirmed. Sometimes, though, your research will reveal issues you did not consider and facts that are new to you, so you will refine, adapt, or even totally change your working thesis (**1e**). If after a few days of research you either cannot find enough material on your topic or discover that all the information is dated, flimsy, or biased, waste no more time. Turn immediately to another topic, and formulate a new research question. (See **8** on evaluating sources.)

### 4. Determine types of research and types of sources.

Decide which of the following will give you the best results; then draw up a plan of action. Allow large blocks of time for research. This work cannot be done in just an hour or two.

**BACKGROUND SOURCES**   Tools such as encyclopedias and general or specialized reference works can help you choose or focus a topic. Because they will provide an overview of the issues involved in a complex topic, they can also help you in formulating a research proposal if you are asked to provide one. Use them only as a way to get into your subject matter and to start your research, but do not rely on them for most of your project. For some specific reference works, see **7b**.

**PRIMARY SOURCES**   Primary sources are the firsthand, raw, or original materials that researchers study and analyze. You can consult historical documents, people's journals and letters, autobiographies, government documents, speeches, and news reports. You can examine works of art, literature, and architecture or watch or listen to performances and programs. You can conduct your own observations or scientific experiments and take extensive field notes.

You can also conduct interviews and use questionnaires. The use of such primary sources can bring an original note to your research and new information to your readers.

*Interviews*   Interview people who have expert knowledge of your topic. Plan a set of interview questions, but do not stick so closely to your script that you fail to follow up on good leads in your respondent's replies. Ask permission to tape-record the interview; otherwise, you will have to take quick and accurate notes, particularly if you want to quote. Check the functioning of your tape recorder beforehand. Make note of the date, time, and place of the interview.

*Questionnaires*   Designing useful questionnaires is tricky, since much depends on the number and sample of respondents you use, the types of questions you ask, and the methods you employ to analyze the data. Embark on questionnaire research only if you have been introduced to the necessary techniques in a college course or have consulted experts in this area.

**SECONDARY SOURCES**   Secondary sources are analytical works that comment on and interpret other works, such as primary sources.

Examples include reviews, discussions, biographies, critical studies, analyses of literary or artistic works or events, and commentaries on current and historical events.

**5. Make copies and keep full and accurate records of sources.**
Record full bibliographical information for every source you consult. For the essential information to record, see **9a**. Download, print, or make photocopies of your source material whenever possible, so that you can annotate and make notes later.

**6. Make precise notes.**   Paraphrase and summarize as often as possible while taking notes. Be sure to use your own words and write down why the information is useful or how you might integrate it into your paper (**9d**). Make sure you copy quotations exactly as they are written (**10c**), with quotation marks. In your notes, record all page numbers of print sources. Copy and save Web addresses.

**7. Establish your thesis.**   Digest your material, and determine your focus. Your paper should not string together what others have said, with no commentary from you. In the humanities, use your research to help yourself form opinions and arrive at conclusions about your topic. Readers want to find *you* and your ideas in your paper (**9f**). Develop a working thesis as soon as you can, and make lists of supporting evidence and specific details from what you know and what you read.

**8. Write drafts.**   Write more than one draft. As with almost all writing for college and beyond, revision is an essential step in the writing process. You should not expect to produce a perfect first draft. Make an outline of each draft to check on the logic of your argument (**3b**).

**9. Acknowledge all your sources.**   Avoid plagiarism by providing information in your text every time you refer to facts you have used or to someone else's words or ideas (**9b, 9e**).

**10. Use quotations appropriately.**   Quote only an author's exact words, making no changes or substitutions. Summaries and paraphrases should not contain chunks from the original source. Quotations should add support to your assertions and claims; they should not be strung together or used to fill space (**10c**).

**11. Prepare a list of works cited.**   Follow a clear and consistent set of conventions (spacing, indentation, names, order, and punctuation of entries) when you prepare a list of works cited (see **12–13** and **15–19**).

**12. Compare your citations with your list.** Make sure that every item on your list appears in your paper and that every work referred to in your paper appears in your list. Use a system of checkmarks in both places as you read a draft.

## 6c Research papers in the disciplines

In addition to the general research guidelines outlined in **6b**, be aware that different disciplines follow different conventions.

### Writing research papers in the humanities and arts

- Consult primary sources, such as original works of literature, or attend original performances, such as plays, films, poetry readings, and concerts.
- Form your own interpretations of works.
- Use secondary sources (works of criticism) only after you have formed your own interpretations and established a basis for evaluating the opinions expressed by others.
- Look for patterns and interpretations supported by evidence, not for one right answer to a problem.
- Use the present tense to refer to what writers have said (*Emerson points out that . . .*).
- Use MLA guidelines (see **11–13**) or *Chicago Manual of Style* (see **18**) for documentation style. Consult with your instructor about whether to use the style for online sources described in *The Columbia Guide to Online Style* (CGOS; see **19**).

### Writing in the social sciences

- Examine the forms and processes that contribute to the construction of society and social institutions.
- Examine research studies in the field, evaluate their methodology, compare and contrast results with those of other experimental procedures, and draw conclusions based on the empirical evidence uncovered.
- Look for accurate, up-to-date information, and evaluate it systematically against stated criteria.
- Use the first person (*I* and *we*) less frequently than in the humanities.
- Use the present perfect tense to refer to what researchers and writers have reported (*Smith's study has shown that . . .*).

- Use the passive voice as appropriate when reporting on scientific and experimental procedures (*The stimulus was repeated* in place of *I repeated the stimulus*).

- Where possible and appropriate, present graphs, charts, and tables in support of your conclusions.

- Use APA documentation style (**14–16**). Consult with your instructor about whether to use *The Columbia Guide to Online Style* (CGOS; see **19**) for citing online sources.

### Writing in the natural sciences and mathematics

- Use primary sources more frequently than secondary sources.

- Avoid personal anecdotes.

- Report firsthand original experiments and calculations.

- Refer to secondary sources in the introductory section of your paper, a section sometimes called "Review of the Literature."

- Use the present perfect tense to refer to what researchers and writers have reported in published works (*Brown has said that . . .*).

- Use the passive voice more frequently than in other types of writing (**42a**).

- Be prepared to write according to a set format, using sections with headings (see Laboratory reports, **5e**).

- Use APA (see **14–16**) or CBE (see **17**) documentation style, or follow specific style manuals in scientific areas. Ask your instructor whether you should use *The Columbia Guide to Online Style* (CGOS; see **19**) for citing online sources.

See **7c** for basic print and online sources to get you started in twenty-four subject areas.

## 7  Searching for Sources

### 7a  Library and Web—a merger

Finding print or online materials is no longer divided into the choice of either going to a library for print materials or turning on a computer to find online sources. You can do your computer search in a library or by accessing a library or database from a remote location by using a password; your search can help you find traditional print materials as well as Internet sources. In addition, a visit to the library will give you access not only to books, print articles, and special collections but also to the library's collection of CD-ROMs and the online databases the library subscribes to. Print materials have accompanying Web sites and links; Web sites provide access to print materials such as newspaper and periodical articles and even complete books. The Web, aptly named, has woven itself into the fabric of our lives.

With access via the Internet to reference works, complete texts, and reliable sources such as databanks of scholarly articles, the Internet can be seen as a virtual library, available at the click of a mouse. The Internet provides both a means of access to what were once seen as traditional print sources and a source of information that exists only online.

Although you can search for and find many useful sources without leaving the computer at your desk or in your college computer lab, don't neglect the resources provided by your library. Apart from giving you access to the world of books, the library can extend your search choices for other resources, too. Get to know your library, its layout, and what its holdings include: What CD-ROMs does it own? What online databases and indexes does it subscribe to? Does it provide online access to the full text of scholarly articles? The greatest resource of all is the reference librarian, who can direct you to valuable sources, a service not available from America Online. Never be afraid to ask for a librarian's help.

Ask yourself where you are likely to find the most appropriate sources for your topic. For tracing historical development or looking back to the past, scholarly articles, books, and primary documents such as diaries, memoirs, and speeches are your best bet. For contemporary political or cultural issues, you will probably search newspapers, magazines, Web sites, and online discussion groups. If in doubt about whether time spent in the library or at your home computer will be more productive for your topic, get advice from your instructor or a reference librarian.

Searching for, evaluating, and recording source information are crucial parts of research. Each is discussed here in sequence, but in reality you will be searching, evaluating, and recording all through the process of writing a research paper. In particular, as you search for sources, be sure to keep full records of the sources you find and may use. See **9a** on how best to do this.

## 7b    Basic reference works, bibliographies, indexes, databases, and Web sites

When you are warned about the dangers of finding irresponsible or trashy material on the Internet, those warnings refer to sources generated for Internet publication, such as individuals' Web pages. But using the Internet as a means to access information can lead you to many sources once viewed as traditional—reference works, books, scholarly articles, newspaper reports, government documents, and so on—as well as to many reputable sources available only online, such as scholarly online journals and professional sites. Check at your library reference desk and on your library's Web page for which scholarly reference works and databases are available to you online and which Web sites might be particularly pertinent to your topic.

***Basic reference works***    The reference section of your college or local library is a good place to gather basic information. Reference books cannot be taken home, so they are in the library at all times. And with more and more reference works being made generally available online, the accessibility of material from a library or home computer increases.

Reference works provide basic factual information and lead to other sources. However, be careful to regard using reference works as a way to start your research, not to complete it. Remember that you need to go beyond them to more specialized and detailed sources for in-depth information and analysis of your topic. (See **7c–f** for details on finding sources other than basic reference works.)

ENCYCLOPEDIAS    Print and online encyclopedias present the broad picture and the most pertinent facts. They do not discuss issues in detail, but they often include bibliographies that lead you to more specialized material. Leading print and online encyclopedias (no charge for use) are *Encyclopaedia Britannica* at <http://www.eb.com> and *Columbia Encyclopedia* at <http://www.bartleby.com>. Specialized encyclopedias cover many fields and include, for example, *Encyclopedia of Psychology, Encyclopedia of the Biological Sciences, Encyclopedia of Asian History, Oxford Companion to English Literature,* and *McGraw-Hill Encyclopedia of Science and Technology.*

COLLECTIONS OF ARTICLES OF TOPICAL INTEREST AND NEWS SUMMARIES    *Opposing Viewpoints* series, *CQ (Congressional Quarterly)* weekly reports, *Facts on File* publications, and *CQ Almanac* are available in print and online by subscription. *Newsbank* provides periodical articles on microfiche, classified under topics such as "Law" and "Education," and *SIRS (Social Issues Resources Series)* appears in print, CD-ROM, and online.

**BIOGRAPHIES** Read accounts of people's lives in biographical works such as *Who's Who, Dictionary of American Biography, Biography Index: A Cumulative Index to Biographic Material in Books and Magazines, Contemporary Authors, Dictionary of Literary Biography, African American Biographies, Chicano Scholars and Writers, Lives of the Painters,* and *American Men and Women of Science.*

**CRITICAL WORKS** Read what scholars have to say about works of art and literature in *Contemporary Literary Criticism* and in *Oxford Companion* volumes (such as *Oxford Companion to Art* and *Oxford Companion to African American Literature*).

**STATISTICS AND GOVERNMENT DOCUMENTS** Among many useful sources are *Statistical Abstract of the United States, Current Index to Statistics, Handbook of Labor Statistics, Occupational Outlook Handbook,* U.S. Census publications (print and online), and *Digest of Educational Statistics.*

**ALMANACS, ATLASES, AND GAZETTEERS** For population statistics and boundary changes, see *The World Almanac, Countries of the World,* or *Information Please.* For locations, descriptions, pronunciation of place names, climate, demography, languages, natural resources, and industry, consult *Columbia-Lippincott Gazetteer of the World* and the CIA *World Factbook,* both of which are available in print and online.

**DICTIONARIES** For etymologies, definitions, and spelling, consult *American Heritage Dictionary of the English Language,* 4th edition (one volume), *Oxford English Dictionary* (multiple volumes—useful for detailed etymologies and usage discussions and examples), *Facts on File* specialized dictionaries, and other specialized dictionaries such as *Dictionary of Literary Terms* and *Dictionary of the Social Sciences.*

## Bibliographies, indexes, databases, and Web sites

**BIBLIOGRAPHIES AND GUIDES** You can find lists of books and articles on a subject in bibliographies such as *Books in Print, Foreign Affairs Bibliography, Political Science Bibliographies, MLA International Bibliography of Books and Articles on the Modern Languages and Literature, Bibliographies in American History, Science and Engineering Literature,* and specialized bibliographies on topics of interest, such as *Homelessness: An Annotated Bibliography* (1993).

**INDEXES AND DATABASES** Databases of articles appearing in periodicals make searching for an article on a specific topic easy. Databases contain publication information and an abstract and sometimes the full text of the article, available for downloading or printing right from your computer. Your library houses print and CD-ROM databases and subscribes to some online databases; others are accessible through online library catalogs or Web links. See **7c** and **7e**.

**WEB SITES FOR RESEARCH IN ACADEMIC AREAS**  Some Web sites contain vast amounts of information and useful links to other sites. Always bookmark any sites you find useful so you can return to them easily. *Examples: The WWW Virtual Library* (covers basic sources in many academic disciplines) at <http://vlib.stanford.edu/Overview.html>; the University of Minnesota *Research Quickstart* site, with basic resources for research by subject at <http://research.lib.umn.edu>; and, for the humanities, *Voice of the Shuttle* at <http://vos.ucsb.edu>.

## 7c   Research resources in twenty-four subject areas

This list of frequently used reference works in print, print and electronic indexes, and Web sites was compiled with the help of nineteen college librarians from seventeen colleges in thirteen states. These resources are particularly useful for giving you background information and for pointing you in the right direction for further research. Browse freely, and remember to ask a librarian for advice if you have trouble finding a source or need a specific piece of information.

**Net Note**   The *Keys for Writers* Web site at <college.hmco.com/keys.html> duplicates and expands this list, keeping it up to date and providing direct links to all the nonsubscription online reference sites. From the *Keys* site, click on an online source in, say, business or engineering, and you will be taken right there. Sources with no URL given may also be available online. Check with your librarian as to the availability of these sources. ■

### Art and architecture
*Oxford Companion to Art*
*Lives of the Painters*
*Dictionary of Art* (known as *Grove*) (print and online)
*Encyclopedia of World Art*
*Arts and Humanities Citation Index*
*Bibliography of the History of Art*
*Contemporary Artists*
*Art Abstracts* (online and CD-ROM)

*Art Index* (online and CD-ROM)
*Avery Index to Architectural Periodicals* (online and CD-ROM)
*The Getty Institute:* <http://www.getty.edu>
*Local and Global Internet Resources for Art Historians and Art History Students:*
   <http://www.wisc.edu/arth/otherresources.html>
*World Wide Arts Resources:* <http://wwar.com>

### Biology
*Encyclopedia of the Biological Sciences*
*Encyclopedia of Bioethics*
*Encyclopedia of Human Biology* (Academic Press)
*Henderson's Dictionary of Biological Terms*
*Biological and Agricultural Sciences Index* (print, online, and CD-ROM)
*Biological Abstracts:* BIOSIS (print, online, and CD-ROM)
*WWW Virtual Library: Biosciences:* <http://mcb.harvard.edu/BioLinks.html>
*Zoological Record: Internet Resource Guide for Zoology* (by BIOSIS):
   <http://www.york.biosis.org/zrdocs/zoolinfo/zoolinfo.htm>
*BiochemLinks:* <http://schmidel.com/bionet.cfm>
*Biolinks:* <http://www.biolinks.com>

### Business
*International Encyclopedia of Business and Management*
*Hoover's Handbook of World Business*
*Encyclopedia of American Business History and Biography*
*Monthly Labor Review*
*Prentice Hall Encyclopedic Dictionary of Business Terms*
*Ward's Business Directory of U.S. Private and Public Companies*
*ABI Inform* (index online and CD-ROM)
*Business Abstracts* (online: full text)
*Business Periodicals Index* (online and CD-ROM)
*Business Dateline* (CD-ROM database of full-text articles from business journals)
*Business and Industry* (*Dialog* database with full texts of articles): <http://
   library.dialog.com/bluesheets/html/bl0009.html>
*Bureau of Labor Statistics:* <http://www.bls.gov>
*MSU-Ciber. International Business Resources on the WWW* (Michigan State
   University): <http://ciber.bus.msu.edu>

### Chemistry
*Kirk-Othmer Encyclopedia of Chemical Technology*
*Ullman's Encyclopedia of Industrial Chemistry*
*CRC Handbook of Chemistry and Physics*
*Beilstein Handbook of Organic Chemistry*
*Macmillan Encyclopedia of Chemistry*
*Encyclopedia of Chemical Terminology*

*Chemical Abstracts* (online and CD-ROM, from the American Chemical Society)
*ChemistryWeb:* <http://www.ssc.ntu.edu.sg:8000/chemweb/htmlj>
*ChemInfo* (Chemical Information Sources): <http://www.indiana
.edu/~cheminfo>
*Chemistry Virtual Library Resources:* <http://www.chem.ucla
.edu/chempointers.html>
*NIST* (National Institute of Standards and Technology) *Webbook:* <http://
webbook.nist.gov> (physical properties for thousands of substances)
*Chemicool Periodic Table:* <http://www-tech.mit.edu/Chemicool/index.html>
*American Chemical Society ChemCenter:* <http://www.chemcenter. org>

## Classics

*Classical Scholarship: An Annotated Bibliography*
*Concise Oxford Companion to Classical Literature*
*Chronology of the Ancient World*
*DCB: Database of Classical Bibliography* (CD-ROM)
*Library of Congress Resources for Greek and Latin Classics:*
<http://lcweb.loc.gov/global/classics/classics.html>
*The Perseus Project:* <http://www.perseus.tufts.edu>
*Internet Classics Archive:* <http://classics.mit.edu>

## Communications and media

*Webster's New World Dictionary of Media and Communications*
*ABC-CLIO Companion to the Media in America*
*International Encyclopedia of Communications*
*ComIndex* (print and CD-ROM index of articles)
*American Communication Association:* <http://www.uark.edu/~aca>
*Kidon Media-Link:* <http://www.kidon.com/media-link/index.shtml>
*News Resource:* <http://newo.com>
*Telecom Information Resources:* <http://china.si.umich.edu/
telecom/telecom-info.html>
*WWW Virtual Library: Communications and Media:* <http://
vlib.org/Communication.html>

## Computer science

*Encyclopedia of Computer Science and Technology*
*Computer Abstracts*
*Microcomputer Abstracts* (online by subscription)
*ACM Guide to Computing Literature* (online and CD-ROM)
*MIT Laboratory for Computer Science:* <http://www.lcs.mit.edu>
*Information Resources for Computer Science:* <http://www.library
.ucsb.edu/subj/computer.html>
*WWW Virtual Library: Computing:* <http://vlib.org/Computing.html>
*Virtual Computer Library:* <http://www.utexas.edu/computer/vcl>

### Economics

*Dictionary of Economics*
*Prentice Hall Encyclopedic Dictionary of Business Terms*
*Econlit* (online by subscription)
*PAIS* (Public Affairs Information Service) database (online and CD-ROM)
*WWW Virtual Library: Resources in Economics:* <http://www.hkkk.fi/
    EconVLib.html>

### Education

*Dictionary of Education*
*International Encyclopedia of Education*
*Encyclopedia of Educational Research*
*Education Index* (online and CD-ROM)
*ERIC* (Educational Resources Information Center; supplies indexes such as
    *Current Index to Journals in Education* and *Resources in Education*):
    <http://www.accesseric.org.81>
*National Center for Education Statistics:* <http://nces.ed.gov>
*Higher Education Research Institute, UCLA:* <http://www.gseis.ucla.edu/
    heri/heri.html>
*Online Educational Resources:* <http://quest.arc.nasa.gov/OER>

### Engineering

*McGraw-Hill Encyclopedia of Engineering*
*Compendex/Engineering Index* (online by subscription)
*Engineering Library at Cornell University:* <http://www.englib.cornell.edu>
*WWW Virtual Library: Engineering:* <http://vlib.org/Engineering.html>

### Ethnic studies

*Historical and Cultural Atlas of African Americans*
*Oxford Companion to African American Literature*
*Encyclopedia of Asian History*
*Chicano Scholars and Writers*
*Harvard Encyclopedia of American Ethnic Groups*
*Native Web:* <http://www.nativeweb.org>
*WWW Virtual Library: Migration and Ethnic Relations:* <http://
    www.ercomer.org/wwwvl>

### Geography

*Encyclopedia of World Geography*
*Companion Encyclopedia of Geography*
*Geographical Abstracts* (online and CD-ROM)
*U.S. Census Bureau: U.S. Gazetteer:* <http://www.census.gov/
    cgi-bin/gazetteer>
*WWW Virtual Library: Geography:* <http://geography.pinetree.org>

## Geology

*Glossary of Geology and Earth Sciences*
*Macmillan Encyclopedia of Earth Sciences*
*New Penguin Dictionary of Geology*
*Encyclopedia of Earth System Science*
*GeoRef* (electronic index produced by American Geological Institute):
    <http://agiweb.org/georef>
*USGS* (United States Geological Survey): <http://www.usgs.gov>
*USGS Library:* <http://www.usgs.gov/library>
*AGI* (American Geological Institute): <http://www.agiweb.org>

## History

*Encyclopedia of American History*
*Dictionary of Medieval History* (Scribner)
*Great Events from History* series
*Horus' Web Links to History Resources:* <http://www.ucr.edu/
    h-gig/horuslinks.html>
*WWW Virtual Library: History Central Catalogue:* <http://
    www.ukans.edu/history/VL>
*Don Mabry's Historical Text Archive:* <http://www.geocities.com/djmabry/
    index.html>

## Linguistics

*Oxford Companion to the English Language* (ed. Tom McArthur)
*Cambridge Encyclopedia of Language* (ed. David Crystal)
*Cambridge Encyclopedia of the English Language* (ed. David Crystal)
*Applied Linguistics WWW Virtual Library:* <http://alt.venus.co.uk/VL/
    AppLingBBK/welcome.html>
*WWW Virtual Library: Linguistics:* <http://www.emich.edu/~linguist/
    www-vl.html>
*Center for Applied Linguistics:* <http://www.cal.org>

## Literature

*Oxford Companion to Contemporary Authors*
*Dictionary of Literary Biography*
*New Cambridge Bibliography of English Literature*
*MLA International Bibliography of Books and Articles on the Modern Languages
    and Literature* (online and CD-ROM)
*Project Bartleby* (complete texts of books no longer in copyright):<http://
    www.bartleby.com>
*Voice of the Shuttle:* <http://vos.ucsb.edu>

## Mathematics and statistics

*HarperCollins Dictionary of Mathematics*
*Statistical Abstract of the United States* (Government Printing Office)

*Mathematical Reviews* (print and online)
*MathSciNet* (index and abstracts of articles): <http://www.ams.org/mathscinet>
*WWW Virtual Library: Statistics:* <http://www.stat.ufl.edu/vlib/statistics.html>
*University of Tennessee Math Archives:* <http://archives.math.utk.edu>

## Music
*New Grove Dictionary of Music and Musicians*
*New Oxford History of Music*
*New Harvard Dictionary of Music*
*Baker's Biographical Dictionary of Musicians*
*Thematic Catalogues in Music: An Annotated Bibliography Including Printed, Manuscript, and In-Preparation Catalogues*
*International Index to Music Periodicals*
*The Music Index* (CD-ROM)
*RILM Abstracts of Musical Literature* (online and CD-ROM)
*WWW Virtual Library: Music:* <http://www.vl-music.com>
*WWW Virtual Library: Classical Music:* <http://www.gprep.pvt.k12.md.us/classical/catalog.html>
*Classical USA:* <http://classicalusa.com>
*Indiana University Worldwide Internet Music Resources:* <http://www.music.indiana.edu/music_resources>

## Philosophy
*Oxford Companion to Philosophy*
*Cambridge Dictionary of Philosophy*
*Philosopher's Index*
*Routledge History of Philosophy*
*American Philosophical Association:* <http://www.udel.edu/apa>
*Philosophy in Cyberspace:* <http://www-personal.monash.edu.au/~dey/phil>
*Guide to Philosophy on the Internet:* <http://www.earlham.edu/~peters/philinks.htm>

## Physics
*Encyclopedia of Physics* (ed. Rita Lerner and George L. Trigg)
*Macmillan Encyclopedia of Physics*
*Physics Abstracts* (online and CD-ROM)
*American Institute of Physics:* <http://www.aip.org>
*American Physical Society:* <http://www.aps.org>
*WWW Virtual Library: Physics:* <http://vlib.org/Physics.html>

## Political science
*Political Handbook of the World* (annual)
*Congressional Quarterly Weekly Reports*

*International Political Science Abstracts*
*American Statistics Index*
*U.S. Census Bureau: The Official Statistics:* <http://www.census.gov>
*The White House:* <http://www.whitehouse.gov>
*United Nations:* <http://www.un.org>
*Political Science Resources on the Web:* <http://www.lib.umich.edu/libhome/
Documents.center/polisci.html>
*PAIS* (Public Affairs Information Service) database (online and CD-ROM)
*THOMAS: Legislative Information on the Internet:* <http://thomas.loc.gov>

## Psychology

*Encyclopedia of Psychology*
*Psychological Abstracts*
*PsycINFO* (online database of abstracts)
*CyberPsychLink:* <http://cctr.umkc.edu/user/dmartin/psych2.html>
*Social Psychology Network, Wesleyan University:* <http://
www.socialpsychology.org>
*American Psychological Association:* <http://www.apa.org>

## Religion

*Anchor Bible Dictionary*
*Encylopedia of the American Religious Experience*
*New Interpreter's Bible*
*Encyclopedia of World Religions*
*Encyclopedia of Religion* (print and CD-ROM)
*Religion Index*
*ATLA Religion Database*
*Wabash Center Guide to Internet Resources for Teaching and Learning in Theology
and Religion:* <http://www.wabashcenter.wabash.edu/Internet/front.htm>
*Academic Info: Religious Studies:* <http://www.academicinfo.net/Religion.html>

## Sociology

*Encyclopedia of Sociology* (ed. Rhonda J. Montgomery)
*Handbook of Sociology* (Neil Smelser)
*Social Sciences Abstracts* (print and online)
*International Encyclopedia of the Social and Behavioral Sciences* (print and online):
<http://www.iebs.com>
*FirstGov* (U.S. government site): <http://firstgov.gov>
*Public Agenda* (public opinion data): <http://www.publicagend.org>
*Statistical Abstract of the United States:* <http://www.census.gov>
*U.S. Census Bureau:* <http://quickfacts.census.gov/qfd>
*Sociological Abstracts:* <http://www.socabs.org>
*CIA Factbook:* <http://www.odci.gov/cia/publications/factbook/index.html>
*Data on the Net:* <http://odwin.ucsd.edu/idata>

**7d** Searching for books and periodical articles in print

*Types of search*   For library catalogs and periodical databases, decide whether to search under *T* (title), *A* (author), *S* (subject), or *K* (keyword). Exact wording and exact spelling are essential for all these searches.

Use keyword searching (**7g**) when searching for material that is electronically stored, whether in a library catalog, on a CD-ROM, in a database, or on a Web page. For subject searching, you need to know the specific subject headings the catalogers used to identify and classify material. Consult a reference source such as *Library of Congress Subject Headings*, or ask a librarian for help. For example, you won't find *cultural identity* or *social identity* in *Library of Congress Subject Headings*, but you can look up *culture* and find a list of thirty-two associated headings, such as "language and culture" and "personality and culture." In addition, these subject headings show related terms, which can suggest ways to narrow or broaden a topic and can help you in other subject searches, particularly in electronic keyword searches. *Bilingualism*, for example, takes you to topics such as "air traffic control," "code-switching," and "language attrition." An entry in a library catalog will appear with the subject descriptors, so if you find one good source, use its subject classifications to search further.

If your college library does not own a book or periodical you want, ask a librarian about interlibrary loan. This option is helpful, of course, only if you begin your search early.

## Books

**CALL NUMBER**   The call number tells you where a book is located in the library stacks (the area where books are shelved). Write this number down immediately if a book looks promising, along with the book's title and author(s) and publication information (**9a**). Many catalogs identify the floor on which the book is located. Write that down to save time later. If a library has open stacks, you will be able to browse through books on a similar topic on the same shelf or on one nearby. In a library with closed stacks, you need the call number to direct a library staff member to locate the book for you. Most college libraries use the Library of Congress classification system, which arranges books according to subject area and often the initial of the author's last name and the date of publication. The Library of Congress call number determines where a book is shelved in the library. The call number for this book, for example, is PE 1408 .R35 2002.

**INFORMATION IN THE CATALOG** The screens of electronic catalogs vary from one system to another, but most screens contain the following information:

- the name of the system you are using;
- the details of your search request and of the search, such as the number of records found;
- the number of pages (or screens) that the record covers;
- a list of commands that the system uses;
- a blinking cursor, where you type the command for what you want to do next.

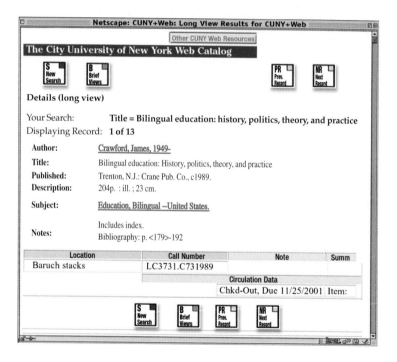

The screen shown here tells you that the book is checked out and gives the date when it is due. It provides all the essential information you will need to document the source at the end of your paper: author, title, place of publication, publisher, and date of publication. In addition, it lets you know the number of pages in the book and shows that the book contains illustrations, a bibliography, and an index—all useful research tools.

Once you find a book that seems to be related to your topic, you do not have to read the whole book to use it for your paper. Learn what you can from the catalog entry; then skim the table of contents, chapter headings, and bibliography. Your best time-saver here is the index. Turn to it immediately, and look up some keywords for your topic. Read the section of the book in which references to your topic appear; take notes; annotate a photocopy of the relevant pages (**9c**). A book's bibliography and references are useful, too. The author has done research, and this can help you in your search. It is a good idea to make a copy of the title page and the page on which the copyright notice appears. If you find nothing remotely connected to your research question, do not cite the book as a resource, even though you looked at it.

**BOOKS IN PRINT AND ALTERNATIVES**   If you want to find a book or to check on bibliographical details, use *Books in Print* (available in print and online). If your library does not subscribe to the online version, you can use the Amazon.com site at <http://www.amazon.com> or any other large commercial online bookseller to look up the details of a book—free.

*Periodical articles*   Find articles in periodicals (works issued periodically, such as scholarly journals, magazines, and newspapers) by using a periodical index. Use electronic indexes for recent works, print indexes for earlier works—especially for works written before 1980. Check which services your library subscribes to and the dates the indexes cover. Indexes may provide abstracts; some, such as *Lexis-Nexis Academic Universe, InfoTrac, OCLC FirstSearch,* and *New York Times Ondisc,* provide the full text of articles. (See also **7b** and **7e** for more on indexes.)

Search methods are similar to those in book searches. If the periodical index does not provide the full text, you will need to find out first whether your library owns the periodical and then in which form it is available: in files, in bound volumes, or in film form with pages shown in a strip (microfilm) or on a sheet (microfiche), which you will need to read with a special machine. The catalog for your library will tell you on the screen which issues are available in your library and in which format and location.

**7e**   Searching for materials available online

The Internet can take you to many sources formerly accessible only if you went to a library and dug through shelves and bound volumes of periodicals. Newspaper and magazine articles from ten years ago, scholarly journal articles, news commentary, statistical information from government agencies—all are available. However, the democratic nature of the Internet means that many Web pages have no editorial control, so although you might find considerable material, much of it could be mindless and inaccurate (**8d**). On the plus side, you will find vast resources, current material, and frequent updates—all without leaving your computer. As you plan your research, consider which of the following Internet resources might be the most appropriate for your topic. A reference librarian can help you decide. And as you do the research, remember to keep track of your sources and record all the necessary information. See **9a** for ways to do this.

**Online library catalogs and home pages of libraries and universities**   The Web gives you access to the online resources of many libraries (actual and virtual) and universities, which are good browsing sites. Some useful sites follow:

- *Library of Congress* at <http://lcweb.loc.gov> provides lists of links (with descriptions) of Internet search tools, as well as access to subject guides, government resources, online library catalogs, and Internet tutorials.

- *LibWeb* at <http://sunsite.berkeley.edu/Libweb> offers information on library holdings in over 100 countries.

- *Smithsonian Institution Libraries* at <http://www.sil.si.edu/newstart.htm> provides a catalog and links to databases and e-journals.

- *New York Public Library* at <http://www.nypl.org/index.html> allows searching of its vast online catalog.

**Online indexes and databases**   Online databases and citation indexes owned or leased by libraries can be accessed in the library itself. Many libraries also make the databases they subscribe to available on the Internet through their home pages. For example, many library sites provide online access to the following:

- databases of abstracts in specific subject areas, such as *ERIC* (for education), *PAIS* (for public affairs), *PsycINFO* (for psychology), and *Sociofile* (for the social sciences);

- databases of full texts of articles published from 1980, such as *InfoTrac: Expanded Academic ASAP* (see **7h** for a sample search), *Lexis-Nexis Academic Universe,* and *OCLC FirstSearch*;

- databases of abstracts of general, nonspecialized magazine articles, such as the Wilson *Readers' Guide to Periodical Literature.*

Frequently, though, access to databases in university library Web sites is limited to enrolled students who have been assigned a password. Check with your college library to see which databases are available online in the library only and which are available on the Web.

***Online magazines and journals***   Online magazines and journals are proliferating. Some examples are *Slate* at <http://www.slate.com>, *Chronicle of Higher Education* at <http://chronicle.com>, *Early Modern Literary Studies* at <http://purl.oclc.org/emls/emlshome.html>, *Postmodern Culture* at <http://jefferson.village.virginia.edu/pmc>, and *Sociological Research Online* at <http://www.socresonline.org.uk>.

Some online journals are available free; some allow you to view only the current issue at no cost. Many, however, require a subscription through your library computer network or a personal subscription.

***Online texts***   Literary texts that are out of copyright and in the public domain are increasingly available online for downloading. The following are useful sites to consult, although the versions of texts you see may not always be authoritative:

- *Project Gutenberg* at <http://www.promo.net/pg/index.html>;
- the University of Virginia's *Electronic Text Center* at <http://etext.lib.virginia.edu>;
- Columbia University's *Project Bartleby* at <http://www.bartleby.com>.

***Online news sites***   The Web sites of major newspapers, magazines, and television networks provide up-to-date news information; some offer archived information but often only to subscribers. See, for example, *The New York Times on the Web* at <http://www.nytimes.com> and *CNN Interactive* at <http://www.cnn.com>.

***Nonprofit research sites***   Many nonprofit sites offer valuable and objective information. See *Public Agenda Online* at <http://www.publicagenda.org> and *American Film Institute* at <http://www.afionline.org>.

***Web pages and hypertext links***   Many universities and research institutes provide information through their own Web home pages, with hypertext links that take you with one click to many other sources. Individual Web pages can provide useful information, too, but need careful evaluation, since anyone can publish anything on the Web (**8d**).

***E-mail discussion lists*** With e-mail, you have access to many discussion groups. Messages go out to a list of people interested in specific topics. Without charge, you can join a list devoted to a topic of your interest (see **21a** for how to join a list and participate in a list). These discussion lists number more than ninety thousand, according to Liszt at <http://www.liszt.com>, a catalog of lists. However, most of the lists are not refereed or monitored, so you have to evaluate carefully any information you find (**8d**). Listserv, Listproc, and Majordomo are the common list programs, accessed through e-mail. The Hypernews tool at <http://www.hypernews.org>, which sponsors independent Web discussions on specific themes (threads), also allows you to read and contribute to the discussions.

***Usenet newsgroups*** Usenet newsgroups are open e-mail discussions on a wide variety of topics, linked under a common address. These newsgroups are different from discussion lists in that you do not have to join a list to read and contribute messages. Newsgroup mailings are not forwarded to your e-mail mailbox; you access them with newsreader programs such as the ones provided by America Online (click on Internet, then on Newsgroups), Netscape Messenger, or Outlook Express or by searching on <http://groups.google.com>. Addresses begin with terms like *rec.* (recreation), *sci.* (science), *soc.culture* (cultural environment in various countries and locations), *biz.* (business), *comp.* (computing), and *alt.* (alternatives—a variety of topics) and then indicate the subject matter: *alt.alien.visitors; biz.comp.accounting; comp.ai.nat-lang; rec.arts.movies.production.* See **21b**.

***Other interactive sources*** Other interactive e-mail sources of information are "buddy lists" such as those offered by America Online, Web forums and bulletin board services provided by business and academic sites, and real-time spaces for interaction such as chat rooms, MUDs (multi-user domains), and MOOs (multi-user domains, object-oriented). However, evaluating the reliability of someone's contribution to interactive discussion can be difficult. See **21b** and **21c**.

**7f**  Online searches and search engines

**URLs** If you already know the Web address (the Uniform Resource Locator, or URL) of a useful site, type it exactly, paying attention to spaces (or, more often, lack of spaces), dots, symbols, and capital or lowercase letters. Just one small slip can ruin your search. If you get a message saying "site not found," check your use of capitals and low-ercase letters (and avoid inserting spaces as you type an address), and try again. You may find that the site is no longer available. See **20d** for more on e-mail and Web addresses.

***Browsers, search engines, meta search engines, subject directo-ries, and virtual libraries*** If you do not know the exact Web site you want, you need to search for the information you need. Some search tools search the whole Web for you; some search selected sites; some search only the first few pages of a document; still others search only a specific site, such as a university library system or a noncom-mercial organization, or they search other search engines (these are called *meta search engines*). Make sure you try all types before you give up on finding information on a topic.

Your Web browser, probably Netscape, Internet Explorer, or AOL, will give you access to search engines and other resources that do for you most of the work of rapidly searching Web sites. Note that the Internet Explorer browser offered through AOL does not have the same capability to access complex sites as a stand-alone version of the browser. You can, however, use AOL as a portal to take you to a full version of Netscape or Internet Explorer. Whichever browser you use, spending time searching (and playing) is the best way to become fa-miliar with reliable search tools, the types of searches they do best, and the system they use for searching. Try out the following:

Excite at <http://www.excite.com> supports searching by con-cept as well as by keyword, so it finds not only documents containing your search terms but also documents related to the idea of the search. When a search retrieves a list of docu-ments, you can look for the document that seems to be what you want, and you can initiate a new search based on the fea-tures that one document exhibits.

AltaVista at <http://www.altavista.com> is a comprehensive search tool using keywords. It is a good tool for serious aca-demic research. Its database is huge, so you need to be precise with your search terms. It indexes millions of Web pages, Usenet groups, and online articles, and it can also search for images, and audio and video files. AltaVista allows you to check the reliability of a site by doing a reverse search to find out what other sites are linking to it.

WebCrawler at <http://www.webcrawler.com>, similar to AltaVista, is sponsored by AOL. Search by keywords or by lists of classified subjects. It lets you search with natural language (such as "symphony orchestra in Norway"), but its number of hits is limited.

MetaCrawler at < http:// www.metacrawler.com> provides a subject directory, and it searches many of the best search engines: AltaVista, Excite, Lycos, Infoseek, Google, WebCrawler, and others.

Google at <http:// www.google.com> searches many search engines and organizes results by the numbers of links to a site.

Yahoo! at <http:// www.yahoo.com> is a subject index and directory of the Web, organized hierarchically. You can keep narrowing down your subjects, or you can also use specific keywords. Such a tool is particularly useful when you are trying to decide what to write about.

Ask Jeeves! at <http:// www.ask.com> responds to a regular question, such as "Does tea contain more caffeine than coffee?"

Deja.com, now at <http:// groups.google.com>, searches Usenet groups by topic and presents its findings in reverse chronology. You will find it difficult to evaluate the credentials of contributors and the accuracy of any information given, but the correspondence gives a sense of the issues people are interested in.

Argus Clearinghouse at <http:// www.clearinghouse.net> provides links to virtual (that is, online) libraries, subject guides, and search engines.

Directory of Scholarly and Professional E-Conferences at <http:// www.n2h2.com/ KOVACS/> includes links to online journals, discussion lists, Usenet groups, and real-time conferencing programs.

Internet Public Library at <http:// www.ipl.org> is run by librarians. It includes a guide to home pages and a Reference Center, which allows you to e-mail a question about a research project to librarians and receive a reply in a few days.

WWW Virtual Library at <http:// vlib.org> is useful for finding sources in a large number of academic disciplines.

Liszt at <http:// www.liszt.com> catalogs over ninety thousand discussion lists.

CataList at <http:// www.lsoft.com/ lists/ listref.html> catalogs discussion lists using Listserv software, which offers Web interface.

## **7g** Keyword searches

Use keywords to search for any material stored electronically—on the Web, in library catalogs, in CD-ROM databases, or in online subscription services. Keyword searching is especially effective for finding material in journal and newspaper articles in databases such as *InfoTrac* and *Lexis-Nexis*, because a computer can search not only titles but also abstracts (when available) or full articles.

Keywords are vital for your Web searches. Spend time thinking of the keywords that best describe what you are looking for. If a search yields thousands of hits, try requiring or prohibiting terms and making terms into phrases (see the Key Points box). If a search yields few hits, try different keywords or combinations of keywords, or try another search engine. In addition, try out variant spellings for names of people and places: *Chaikovsky, Tchaikovsky, Tschaikovsky.*

### KEY POINTS

#### Doing a Keyword Search

1. *Know the search engine's system.* Always use the Search Tips or the Help link to find out how to conduct a search. Search engines vary. Some search for any or all of the words you type in, some need you to indicate whether the words make up a phrase, and some allow you to exclude words or search for alternatives.

2. *Use Boolean terms to narrow or expand a search.* Some searches operate on the Boolean principle, which means that you use the "operators" *AND, OR,* and *NOT* in combination with keywords to define what you want the search to include and exclude. Imagine that you want to find out if and how music can affect intelligence. A search for *music AND intelligence* would find sources in the database that include both the word *music* and the word *intelligence* (the overlap in the circles below).

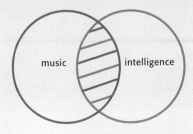

*(Continued)*

*(Continued)*

Parentheses can aid in searches, too. A search for *music AND (intelligence OR learning)* would expand the search. You would find sources in the database that include the word *music* and also the word *intelligence* or the word *learning*.

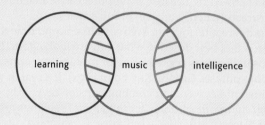

In Boolean searches, *AND* and *NOT* narrow the search: *chicken AND salmonella; dolphins NOT Miami*. *OR* expands the search: *angiogram OR angioplasty*. Not all databases and search engines use this system. MetaCrawler, for instance, asks simply if you want to include *any* or *all* of the search terms or use *all* as a phrase.

3. *Use a wildcard character to truncate a term.* A wildcard allows you to use at the end of a phrase a character that indicates that more letters can be attached. Common wildcard characters are * and ?. The truncated search term *addict** will produce references to *addict, addicts, addiction, addictive,* and so on.

4. *Group words into phrases.* Often, you can use double quotation marks—"Michael Jackson"—or parentheses—(Michael Jackson)—to surround a search term and group the words into a phrase. *Michael Jackson* entered as a term without such quotation marks or parentheses would produce references to other Michaels—Johnson and Jordan, for instance—and to other Jacksons—Stonewall Jackson, Jackson Pollock, and so on.

5. *Learn how to require or prohibit a term.* Many search engines allow you to use a symbol such as + (plus) before a term that must be included in the document indexed; a − (minus) symbol prohibits a term: +"Civil War"−Gettysburg. Some search engines use these symbols in place of the *AND* and *NOT* of Boolean searching.

*(Continued)*

*(Continued)*

6. *Take advantage of the "proximity" search feature if available.*   Some search engines—AltaVista is one—let you indicate when you want your search terms to occur close to each other in the text. Check in the Help or Tips file to determine whether the engine you are using has this feature. Proximity is indicated in various ways in various search engines. *NEAR* or *ADJ* (adjacent) are common: *"Virginia Woolf" NEAR "Bloomsbury group"* would search for the two phrases near each other in the text.

Use the results to help tailor and refine your search. If your search produces only one useful source, look at the terms used in that one source and its subject headings, and search again, using those terms. Above all, be flexible. If your search results in no hits, try again with a different search term or terms. Once you find a promising reference to a source that is not available online in full text, check whether your library owns the book or journal. If your search yields a source available only on microfilm or microfiche, you might need a librarian's help to learn how to use the reading machines and how to make copies.

## **7h**  A sample search

Audrey Fort used print and online sources to write a paper about music and intelligence (see **13** for the complete paper, documented in MLA style). Each search will vary, but the overall process will resemble Audrey's. Choose your sequence to fit your topic, consider different types of sources, and tailor your search to the time you have available.

***Step 1: Topic***   Audrey began with the idea that she wanted to write about music, specifically about the new science that examines the nervous system in relation to music—the new field of neuromusicology. That idea had been suggested to her by a section in the textbook assigned for her music appreciation course.

***Step 2: Research question***   Audrey went to encyclopedias and the *Readers' Guide to Periodical Literature* database of general articles; she read several articles, discussed the issues with her music instructor, and, based on the information she had discovered, formulated some research questions: Does the new field of neuromusicology offer us insights into emotions, behavior, health, and intelligence? Does such scientific application affect our enjoyment of music?

**Step 3: College library catalog for articles and books** Audrey began her research by finding article abstracts in her college library catalog database and finding the print articles in the library in bound volumes or on microfilm. Several of the articles she found were published in newspapers or popular magazines such as *Newsweek* and *Psychology Today*, so she broadened her search to find a scholarly article in *Social Forces*, whose bibliography also led her to books on the topic. (See Audrey's list of works cited in section **13**.)

**Step 4: Online subscription database** Audrey then ran a search on an online database her college subscribed to. In *InfoTrac: Expanded Academic ASAP*, using the keywords *music AND intelligence*, she was able to find abstracts and full-text articles of recent academic studies relating to the earlier print studies she had found in print, and she came across several useful sources (see below and p. 93). She marked three articles to download from the first ten hits of sixty-five hits.

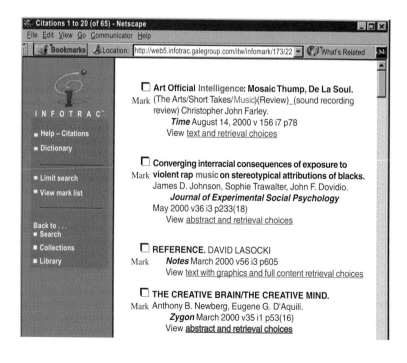

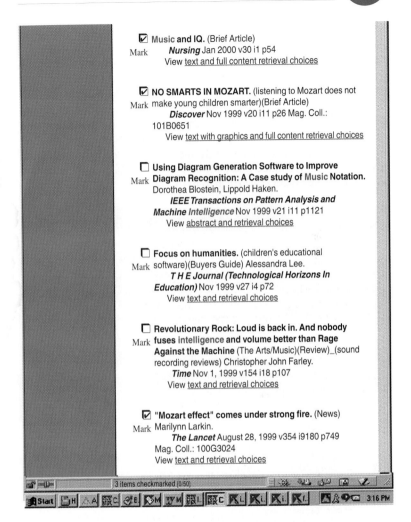

☑ **Music and IQ.** (Brief Article)
Mark    *Nursing* Jan 2000 v30 i1 p54
View text and full content retrieval choices

☑ **NO SMARTS IN MOZART.** (listening to Mozart does not
Mark make young children smarter)(Brief Article)
         *Discover* Nov 1999 v20 i11 p26 Mag. Coll.:
101B0651
         View text with graphics and full content retrieval choices

☐ **Using Diagram Generation Software to Improve
Mark Diagram Recognition: A Case study of Music Notation.**
Dorothea Blostein, Lippold Haken.
         *IEEE Transactions on Pattern Analysis and
Machine Intelligence* Nov 1999 v21 i11 p1121
         View abstract and retrieval choices

☐ **Focus on humanities.** (children's educational
Mark software)(Buyers Guide) Alessandra Lee.
         *T H E Journal (Technological Horizons In
Education)* Nov 1999 v27 i4 p72
         View text and retrieval choices

☐ **Revolutionary Rock: Loud is back. And nobody
Mark fuses intelligence and volume better than Rage
Against the Machine** (The Arts/Music)(Review)_(sound
recording reviews) Christopher John Farley.
         *Time* Nov 1, 1999 v154 i18 p107
         View text and retrieval choices

☑ **"Mozart effect" comes under strong fire.** (News)
Mark Marilynn Larkin.
         *The Lancet* August 28, 1999 v354 i9180 p749
Mag. Coll.: 100G3024
View text and retrieval choices

3 items checkmarked [0/50]

Start    3:16 PM

But after reading the full text of each, she found only one of them (by
Larkin) useful enough to include in her paper. Citation 44 on the extended *InfoTrac* list referred her to an abstract of an article in the journal *Nature*. She located the full text in her college library and decided
to use that source in her paper.

***Step 5: Formation of hypothesis***   Audrey had explored the topic
in enough breadth and depth to understand the issues involved and to
formulate a tentative hypothesis. She wrote her hypothesis as a sentence to guide her future research: *The scientific examination of responses
to music threatens the mystery of music and our enjoyment of it.*

***Step 6: Internet research*** To develop more material for her essay, Audrey turned to two Internet search engines. Using AltaVista, she typed in *neuromusicology + intelligence,* and AltaVista came up with over a million hits. Aghast, Audrey quickly realized that she had put the plus sign only before the last term, not the first. A new search using *+ neuromusicology + intelligence* instructed the search engine to find only documents containing both terms. The result was three hits, as shown below. Audrey knew that the search engines get revenue from advertising, so she wisely ignored the clutter on the screen from the ads and downloaded and printed the third hit, an article in an online journal. She used this article in her paper.

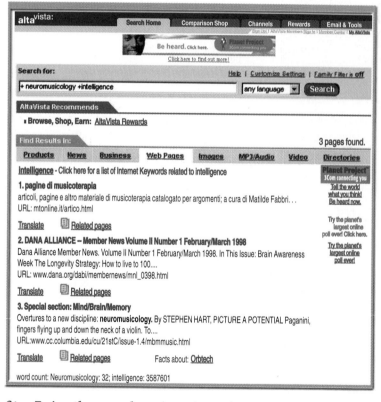

***Step 7: Another search engine*** As an alternative, Audrey began a new search on MetaCrawler. She typed only the two words (this engine requires only the words, with no symbols or connecting words) and hit the button for *all* rather than *any,* telling MetaCrawler to search first for documents containing all the terms listed, then for documents containing one term. This search produced twenty-one results (see the

first few hits below), though some of these were off the track. The Central Intelligence Agency site, produced in response to the search term *intelligence,* obviously would not offer much about music.

Audrey followed some of the promising-looking links. One that both search engines found took her to the Columbia University site of an online journal containing an article by Stephen Hart called "Overtures to a New Discipline: Neuromusicology." Another source found by MetaCrawler was an announcement of a book by Sharlene Habermeyer called *Good Music, Brighter Children.* Audrey decided to include the two references in her paper (see **13**).

Throughout the searches, Audrey made print copies or saved online material, kept a working bibliography (**9a**), evaluated the reliability of sources (**8c, 8d**), and took careful notes. Armed with solid research findings, she was able to confirm her hypothesis—though she later reworded it—and to support it with a great deal of evidence from her sources. She created a scratch outline (**1f**), making note of the specific details gleaned from her research, drafted and revised her paper several times, and turned it in for a grade (see **13**).

## 8 Evaluating Sources

Finding sources is only half the battle. The other half is finding good, relevant sources. How can you tell which sources to use and which to reject? Use the following guidelines.

### 8a    Read critically.

Reading what others write always provides ideas, but not just the ideas you absorb from the page or screen. If you read critically, you will generate ideas of your own as you read. Reading critically does not mean criticizing a writer's views, though it may sometimes include that. Rather, it means reading with an open, questioning mind, examining the writer's assumptions and biases, and scrutinizing the evidence the writer provides.

### KEY POINTS

**Guidelines for Critical Reading**

- Ask questions about the credentials and reputation of the author and the place of publication. What do you learn about the writer's purpose and the audience whom the author is addressing? Make sure you subject any material you find on Web pages to especially careful scrutiny (**8d**).

- Ask questions about the ideas you read. An easy way to do this is to write your annotations in the margin. If you find yourself thinking "But . . ." as you read, go with that sense of doubt, and make a note of what troubles you.

- Be on the lookout for assumptions that may be faulty. If you are reading an article on home schooling and the writer favors home schooling because it avoids subjecting students to violence in schools, the unstated assumption is that all schools are violent places. For more on the logic of argument, see **4f**.

- Make sure the writer's evidence is adequate and accurate. For example, if the writer is making a generalization about all Chinese students based on a study of only three, you have cause to challenge the generalization as resting on inadequate evidence.

*(Continued)*

*(Continued)*

- Note how the writer uses language. Does the writer repeatedly use such phrases as "family values," "right to life," or "democratic freedom" that may signal what values the writer wants to claim? Or does the writer flamboyantly denigrate the views of others with such phrases as "a ridiculous notion" or "laughably inept policies"?

- Be alert for sweeping generalizations, bias, and prejudice: "Women want to stay home and have children." "Men love to spend Sundays watching sports."

Do your reading when you can write—not on the StairMaster™ or while watching TV. Note any questions, objections, or challenges on the page, on Post-it℞ notes, on index cards, in a response file on your computer, or in a double-entry journal (see p. 6). Your critical responses to your reading will provide you with your own ideas for writing.

**8b** **Recognize a scholarly article.**

Learn to distinguish scholarly from nonscholarly articles. A scholarly article is not something you are likely to find in a magazine in a dentist's office. A scholarly article does the following—the first point being the most important:

- refers to the work of other scholars (look for in-text citations and a bibliographical list of works cited, footnotes, or endnotes);

- names the author and usually describes the author's credentials;

- includes notes, references, or a bibliography;

- deals with a serious issue in depth;

- appears in journals that do not include colorful advertisements or eye-catching pictures (a picture of two stunning models is an indication that you are not looking at a scholarly article).

When you read scholarly articles, scan any section headings, read the abstract and any section headed "Summary" or "Conclusions," and skim for the author's main idea to find out whether the article addresses your topic. If you are working on a topic related to current events, you will probably need to consult newspapers, magazines, and online sources as well as or in place of scholarly journals. See **8c** for more on the various types of periodicals, and see the following Web site for more on distinguishing types of periodicals: <http://www.library.cornell.edu/okuref/research/skill20.html>.

## **8c** Evaluate works originating in print.

Before you make detailed notes on a book or an article that began its life in print, be sure it will provide suitable information to help answer your research question.

**Books**   Check the date of publication, notes about the author, table of contents, and index. Skim the preface, introduction, chapter headings, and summaries to give yourself an idea of the information in the book and the book's theoretical basis and perspective. Do not waste time making detailed notes on a book that deals only tangentially with your topic or an out-of-date book (unless your purpose is to discuss and critique its perspective or examine a topic historically). Ask a librarian or your instructor for help in evaluating the appropriateness of sources you discover. If your topic concerns a serious academic issue, readers will expect you to consult books and not limit your references to popular magazines, newspapers, and Internet sources.

**Periodical articles**   Take into account the type of periodical, any organization with which it is affiliated, and the intended audience. Differentiate among the following types of articles (listed in descending order of reliability, with the most reliable first):

- scholarly articles (see **8b**);
- articles, often long, in periodicals for nonspecialist but serious, well-educated readers, such as *New York Review of Books, Atlantic Monthly, Economist, Scientific American,* and *Nation;*
- shorter articles, with sources not identified, in popular magazines for a general audience, such as *Ebony, Time, Newsweek, Parents, Psychology Today,* and *Vogue;*
- articles with dubious sources, written for sensational tabloid magazines, such as *National Enquirer, Globe,* and *Star.*

**Newspaper articles**   The *New York Times, Washington Post,* and *Los Angeles Times,* for example, provide mostly reliable accounts of current events, daily editorial comments, and reviews of books, film, and art. Be aware that most newspapers have political leanings, so reports of and comments on the same event may differ.

## KEY POINTS

### Questions to Evaluate a Print Source

1. *What does the work cover?* It should be long enough and detailed enough to provide adequate information.

2. *How unbiased is the information?* The author, publisher, or periodical should not be affiliated with an organization that has an ax to grind—unless, of course, your topic entails reading critically and making comparisons with other points of view.

3. *How current are the views?* Check the date of publication. The work should be up to date if you need a current perspective.

4. *How reputable are the publisher and author?* The work should be published by a reputable publisher in a source that is academically reliable, not one devoted to gossip, advertising, propaganda, or sensationalism. Check *Books in Print* or *Literary Market Place* for details on publishers. The author should be an authority on the subject. Find out what else the author has written (in *Books in Print* or at <http://www.amazon.com> and what his or her qualifications are as an authority.

## 8d Evaluate sources originating on the Internet.

What makes the Internet so fascinating is that it is wide open, free, and democratic. Anyone can "publish" anything, and thousands or millions can read it. For scholars looking for information and well-presented, informed opinion, however, the Internet can pose a challenge.

If you find an article in a CD-ROM or subscription database (*InfoTrac* or *Lexis-Nexis,* for example), you will know that the article has been published in print, so you can use the criteria for print works (**8c**) to evaluate it. If the article has been published in a reputable periodical, you can assume that it is a valid source for a research paper.

For works devised specifically for the Internet, use the strategies in the Key Points box to help you separate the information from the junk.

**KEY POINTS**

### Developing Your Junk Antennae

1. *Scrutinize the domain name of the URL.* Informational Web pages tend to come from .gov and .edu addresses. Nonprofit organizations (.org) provide interesting mission statements. With .com ("dot com") sources, always assess whether the source is informational or is basically an advertisement or self-promotion.

2. *Check the home page.* Always take the link from a Web site to its home page, if you are not already there. The home page often provides more information about the author, the sponsor, the purpose, and the date of posting.

3. *Assess the originator of an .edu source.* Is the educational institution or a branch of it sponsoring the site? A tilde (~) followed by a name in the URL indicates an individual posting from an academic source. Try to ascertain whether the individual is a faculty member or a student. Increasingly, though, individuals are setting up Web sites under their own domain name (**20d**).

4. *Discover what you can about the author.* Look for a list of credentials, a home page, a résumé, or Web publications. Use the author's name as a search term to see what the author has published on the Internet or who has cited the author.

5. *Investigate the purposes of a Web page author or sponsor.* Objectivity and rationality are not necessarily features of all Web pages. You may come across propaganda, hate sites, individuals purporting to have psychic powers, religious enthusiasts, and extreme political groups. The sponsor of a site may want to persuade, convert, or sell. Go to the home page and to linked sites, and, in addition, note any postal or e-mail address or phone number you can use to get more information about the page and the sponsor. Even if the message is not pointedly biased and extreme, be aware that most authors write from some sense of conviction or purpose. Look for alternative points of view, too.

6. *Evaluate the quality of the writing.* A Web page filled with spelling and grammatical errors should not inspire confidence. If the language has not been checked, the ideas probably haven't been given much time and thought, either. Don't use such a site as a source. Exceptions are discussion lists and Usenet postings. They are written and posted quickly, so even if they contain

*(Continued)*

*(Continued)*

errors, they can also contain useful ideas to stimulate thinking on your topic.

7. *Follow the links.* See whether the links in a site take you to authoritative sources. If the links no longer work (you'll get a 404 message: "Site Not Found"), the home page with the links has not been updated in a while—not a good sign.

8. *Check for dates, updates, ways to respond, and ease of navigation.* A recent date of posting or recent updating, information about the author, ways to reach the author by e-mail, regular mail, or phone, a clearly organized site, easy navigation, and up-to-date links to responsible sites are all indications that the site is well managed and current.

Useful information on evaluating sources is available at a Widener University (Chester, PA) site at <http://www2.widener.edu/Wolfgram-Memorial-Library/webevaluation/webeval.htm> and at a site called *Thinking Critically about World Wide Web Resources* at <http://www.library.ucla.edu/libraries/college/help/critical/index.htm>.

# **9** Recording and Acknowledging Source Material

The need to acknowledge sources is not merely another form of academic pickiness. The nature of research automatically involves the need to acknowledge and document your sources so exactly and so carefully that interested readers will be able to find the exact same source that you found, and find it easily and quickly. In addition, when you acknowledge ideas and words that you found in the works of reputable authors, you bolster your own case. Your readers are far more likely to treat your claim seriously and heed your argument if you show that you can support it with documented evidence, instead of presenting it as something you happened to think of in a random moment or something you heard from a friend. Your readers will be impressed by a judicious use of sources, both those that support your claim and those that run counter to it—which you will, of course, refute. Such an approach reveals a thoroughness that readers find impressive and convincing. From the beginning, then, treat source material as an aid to your argument.

**9a**   Keep track of sources.

From the first steps of your research, keep accurate records of each source. Here's how.

***Know what information to record.***   Record enough appropriate information so that you will be able to make up a list of references in whichever style of documentation you choose. Use the following as a guide for what to record, but be aware that with online sources, especially, much of the information may not be available. Essential information for an online source is the URL and the date on which you access the material. Always note that information.

PRINT BOOK

1. Author(s), editor(s), translator(s)
2. Title and subtitle
3. Publication information: place, publisher, year
4. If necessary, volume number or edition number
5. Call number (see **7d**)

*Hint:* Make a copy of the title page and the copyright page, where the first four items of information are available.

PRINT ARTICLE

1. Author(s), translator(s)
2. Title and subtitle
3. Name of periodical
4. Publication information: volume number, issue number, date, inclusive page numbers of article

*Hint:* Copy the table of contents of the periodical or the anthology.

ELECTRONIC SOURCE

1. Author(s), editor(s), translator(s)
2. Title and subtitle
3. Any print publication information (as for a book or an article, above)
4. Name of site (for example, title of online periodical or Web site, subscription service, or name of discussion list)
5. Electronic publication information, as available (for example, CD-ROM and version number; document number in subscription

service; volume, issue number, and date for online journal; date of online publication or latest update; number of paragraphs, but only if paragraph numbers actually appear on the screen)

6. Compiler or sponsor of site or of CD-ROM
7. Date when you access the source (not for CD-ROM)
8. URL or the keywords you use to get to the site (not for CD-ROM)

*Hint:* Save to disk, e-mail yourself a copy, or print out an online source. The URL will appear on the printout of a Web document, along with the date on which you print the document (the date of access).

*Use the Bookmarks/Favorites feature.* Many search engines have a Bookmarks or Favorites feature that allows you to compile and save a list of useful sites you have visited, so that you can easily revisit them by simply clicking on the bookmark. Bookmarks can be deleted later when you no longer need them. If you work on a networked computer in a lab where you cannot save your work on the hard drive, save your bookmarks to your own bookmark file on a diskette. (In Netscape, go to Bookmarks/Edit Bookmarks/File/Open Bookmark File, and specify the location to save the file.)

You can also keep a bookmark file on the Internet. Try the free service at <http://www.blink.com>.

*Record URL and date of access.* Note that bookmarking will not always last with a long URL, such as URLs of online subscription services. To be safe, also use the Copy and Paste features to copy the URL on your hard drive or diskette, along with the date on which you access the source. As a last resort, copy the URL by hand, but get it exactly right: every letter, symbol, and punctuation mark is important.

*Highlight, copy, and paste.* As you read material on the Web, most reasonably powerful computers allow you to highlight a passage you find, copy it, and then paste it into a file on your own disk. Indicate clearly in your new document that you have included a direct quotation (maybe add the downloaded text in boldface or in a bigger font), and save as much information as you can about the complete document in your working bibliography.

*For all sources, keep full details in a working bibliography.* Choose one way to keep a working bibliography, and be systematic no matter which of the following methods you choose.

- For each source that you use, write a bibliography card containing the relevant information about the source.

- Print out or save to disk the information from the library catalog, online subscription service, or Web site (**7d, 7e**). The Netscape menu provides Page Info, which may give details of the URL, length of document, and date of latest modification. Save this information, and add your date of access.

- Download or print from the *Keys for Writers* Web site at <college.hmco.com/keys.html> the templates for books, articles, and electronic sources, and fill out one for each source you find.

- Keep a computer file for sources. Use the Sort feature to alphabetize sources by last name of author.

- Use research paper software, such as Take Note!™

***Make copies of sources.***    Photocopying print articles and printing or downloading online articles allow you to devote research time to locating relevant sources and taking notes from reference works and books; you can take the copies of articles with you and use them when you are unable to be in the library. A quick way to make a copy of an Internet source is to e-mail it to yourself: in Netscape, go to File/Send Page; in Internet Explorer, use File/Send. As soon as you have time, though, evaluate the usefulness of your copies by highlighting and commenting on relevant sections or by taking notes (**9c, 9d**).

## **9b**    Avoid even the suspicion of plagiarism.

Research and clear documentation open a channel of communication between you and your readers. They learn what your views are and what has influenced those views. They will assume that anything not documented is your original idea and your wording. So if you even accidentally present someone else's actual words or ideas as if they were your own, readers might suspect you of plagiarizing. The word *plagiarize* is derived from a Latin verb meaning "to kidnap," and kidnapping or stealing someone else's ideas and presenting them as your own is regarded as a serious offense in Western academic culture and public life.

Avoiding plagiarism begins with accurate recording and careful management of source material so that you do not end up confused about which parts of your notes contain your ideas and which are derived from the works of others. In the academic world, follow these guidelines to avoid plagiarizing in a paper:

- Never include in your own essay a passage, an identifiable phrase, or an idea that you copied from someone else's work without acknowledging and documenting the source.

- Never use exactly the same sequence of ideas and organization of argument as your source.

- Always put an author's exact words inside quotation marks.

- Always cite the source of any summary or paraphrase. Not only exact words but also ideas need to be credited.

- Never simply substitute synonyms for a few words in the source or move a few words around (see **9d**).

- Never use in your paper long sections that have been written or rewritten by a friend or a tutor.

- Never buy, find, or receive a paper that you turn in as your own work.

Acknowledging your sources gives credit where it is due and also shows how much research you have done. The first step is careful recording of source information and precise note taking (**9c, 9d**). The second step is careful citing of sources in your paper and listing the sources you have used. Sections **11–19** show five different styles of citation and documentation: MLA, APA, CBE, *Chicago,* and CGOS. Once you have recorded the basic information about each source, use whatever documentation style your instructor or discipline requires.

### LANGUAGE AND CULTURE

#### Ownership Rights across Cultures

The Western view takes seriously the ownership of words and text. It respects both the individual as author (and authority) and the originality of the individual's ideas. Copyright laws define and protect the boundaries of intellectual property. However, even the Western world acknowledges that authors imitate and

*(Continued)*

*(Continued)*

borrow from others' work, as Harold Bloom notes in *The Anxiety of Influence*. In some cultures, memorization and the use of classic texts are common in all walks of life. And worldwide, the ownership of language, texts, and ideas is being called into question by the democratic, interactive nature of the Internet. In short, therefore, plagiarism is not something universal and easy to define. In Western academic culture, basic ground rules exist for the "fair use" of another writer's work without payment, but acknowledging the source of borrowed material is always necessary.

Sections **9c–f** provide strategies for avoiding plagiarism.

## 9c  Annotate and take careful notes.

Photocopying and printing from online sources make a source text available for you to annotate. You can interact with the author's ideas, asking questions, writing comments, and jotting down your own ideas. On page 107 is an excerpt from an article on the American Civil Liberties Union's Web site that student Martin Matos found online, printed, and annotated. This article helped him narrow his topic from "free speech" (too broad) to "students' rights to free speech."

Annotating is useful for comments, observations, and questions. You also will need to make notes when you do not have a copy that you can write on or when you want to summarize, paraphrase, and make detailed connections to other ideas and other sources. Write notes on the computer, on legal pads, in notebooks, or on index cards—whatever works best for you. Index cards—each card with a heading and only one note—offer the advantage of flexibility: you can shuffle and reorder them to fit the organization of your paper. In your notes, always include the author's name, a short version of the title of the work, and any relevant page number(s) whenever you summarize, paraphrase, or quote. Include full bibliographical information in your working bibliography. (See **9d** for Martin's summary of the ACLU article.) Then when you start to write your paper, you will have at your fingertips all the information necessary for a citation.

American Civil Liberties Union
**Freedom Network**

### ACLU Urges Boston School to Annul Suspension of Creative Student

*Check on previous attitudes to free speech*

**FOR IMMEDIATE RELEASE**
**Thursday, April 27, 2000**

*Public or private school? Does it make a difference?*

BOSTON, MA -- When Boston Latin Academy suspended Charles Carithers for writing a vivid horror story as assigned by his English teacher, the school not only violated the rights of the student, but violated the principles of free expression which the school should be jealously guarding, the American Civil Liberties Union of Massachusetts said today.

*What was the exact assignment?*

According to the ACLU, Carithers was so successful in fulfilling the writing assignment that he frightened his English teacher. Instead of getting a high grade for his effort, he got suspended because the teacher "took it personally." *What did CC write? It's odd the author doesn't say.*

"What kind of message does it send to students when they are punished based upon the content of their work, when creative, vivid writing becomes the basis for suspension?" said ACLU of Massachusetts executive director John Roberts. "What message does it send students when they must learn to temper their work for fear of retribution from those who are charged to teach them creative composition?" *The ACLU is reporting this, so they are not likely to mention opposing viewpoints. Any articles or letters in the press?*

The ACLU of Massachusetts is calling upon Superintendent Payzant to intercede in the Boston Latin incident by annulling the suspension of Carithers and issuing a clear statement articulating the principles of free expression that could help restore integrity to the Boston school system and protect students from future punishment based upon the content of their academic work.

"If the English teacher cannot handle expressive writing, then such assignments should not be made, or better yet, perhaps the teacher should seek another line of work," Roberts said. *A strong statement*

**Net Note** If you write notes on your computer and download passages from online sources into your notes by using the Copy and Paste features, use a different font or boldface type for any copied material and insert quotation marks along with an author/page citation, so that you are not later misled into thinking the ideas you noted are your own. ■

 **9d** Differentiate summary, paraphrase, and quotation—but integrate and cite them all.

*Summary* Summaries are useful for giving your reader basic information about the work you are discussing. To summarize a source or a passage in a source, select only the main points as the author presents them, without your own commentary or interpretation. Be brief, and use your own words at all times. To ensure that you use your own words, do not have the original source in front of you as you write. Read, understand, and then put the passage away before writing your summary. If you find that you must include some particularly apt words from the original source, put them in quotation marks.

Use summaries in your research paper to let readers know the gist of the most important sources you find. When you include a summary in a paper, introduce the author or the work to indicate where your summary begins. At the end of the summary, give the page numbers you are summarizing. Do not include page numbers if you are summarizing the complete work or summarizing an online source; instead, indicate where your summary ends (see **10f**). When you write your paper, provide full documentation of the source in the list of works cited at the end.

As Martin Matos was working on his essay on students' rights to free speech, he recorded on an index card for his working bibliography the following entry on the article excerpt in **9c**:

"ACLU Urges Boston School to Annul
    Suspension of Creative Student."

ACLU Freedom Network. 27 Apr. 2000.
24 July 2000 <http://www.aclu.org>.

He then wrote this summary in a computer file he labeled "creativity and free speech":

Summary of ACLU Press Release: "ACLU Urges Boston School"

An ACLU press release reports that the Massachusetts ACLU has opposed the suspension of a student for writing an assigned essay that was creative enough to frighten his teacher. For the ACLU, it is an issue of civil rights and free speech. The executive director has criticized the teacher and has demanded the student be reinstated; he also calls upon the superintendent of schools to affirm all students' rights to free speech so that punishments of this kind will no longer be meted out.

*Paraphrase*    When you need more details than a summary provides, paraphrasing provides a tool. A paraphrase is similar in length to the original material—maybe somewhat longer. In a paraphrase, present the details of the author's argument and logic, but be very careful not to use the author's exact words or sentence structure.

### KEY POINTS

**How to Paraphrase**

1. Keep the source out of sight as you write a paraphrase, so you will not be tempted to use any of the sentence patterns or phrases of the original.

2. Do not substitute synonyms for some or most of the words in an author's passage. This practice will result in plagiarism.

3. Use your own sentence structure as well as your own words. Your writing will be regarded as plagiarized if it resembles the original too closely in sentence structure as well as in wording.

4. Do not comment or interpret: just tell readers the ideas that the author of your source presents.

5. Check your text against the original source to avoid inadvertent plagiarism.

6. Cite the author (and page number if a print source) as the source of the ideas, introduce and integrate the paraphrase, and provide full documentation.

When Michelle Guerra was writing a paper on the English-only controversy (whether languages other than English should be banned in schools, government offices, and publications) and looking for the history of the issue, she came across the following source.

ORIGINAL SOURCE

If any language group, Spanish or other, chooses to maintain its language, there is precious little that we can do about it, legally or otherwise, and still maintain that we are a free country. We cannot legislate the language of the home, the street, the bar, the club, unless we are willing to set up a cadre of language police who will ticket and arrest us if we speak something other than English.

—James C. Stalker, "Official English or English Only," *English Journal* 77 (Mar. 1988): 21.

You can use common words and expressions (such as *language, street,* or *free country*) and recognized technical terms (such as *language group*) without quotation marks. But if you use longer or more unusual expressions from the source ("cadre of language police"), always enclose them in quotation marks. Michelle's first attempt at paraphrase is not exactly the same as the original, but it is too close for comfort.

### PARAPHRASE TOO SIMILAR TO THE ORIGINAL

As Stalker points out, if any group of languages, Greek or other, decides to keep its language, there is not much any of us can do, with laws or not, and still claim to be a free country. We cannot pass legislation about the language we speak at home, on the street, or in restaurants, unless we also want to have a group of special police who will take us off to jail if they hear us not speaking English (21).

Michelle cites the page number of the source, using the MLA style of parenthetical documentation. Documentation, however, is not a guarantee against plagiarism. Michelle's wording and sentence structure follow the original too closely.

Michelle then revised the paraphrase by keeping the ideas of the original but using different wording and sentence structure.

### REVISED PARAPHRASE

Stalker points out that in a democracy like the United States, people of all ethnic and language backgrounds are always free to speak their own language without any interference. It is not feasible to have laws against the uses of a language because it certainly would not be possible to make police enforce such laws in homes, on the streets, and in public places (21).

*Quotation*   When an author says something in a particularly clever or dramatic way, you may want to quote his or her words directly. Highlight or make a note of quotations that could be useful in your paper; make sure that you repeat words and punctuation exactly as in the original. If you are downloading information and writing notes on a computer, you can use a different font size or style—such as large or bold type—to download the passage from the source and put it within quotation marks. Then you will see at a glance which words are not yours when you cut and paste them into your essay. See **10c** and **10d** on including quotations in your paper.

## **9e** Know what to cite.

When you refer to a source in your work, carefully cite and document it. Systematically provide information about the author, title, publication data, page numbers, Internet address, dates—whatever is available (see **9a** for the information you need to collect). You provide such documentation so that your readers can locate the sources and read them for further information. (See Part 3 and Part 4 for guides to specific systems of documentation.) You also document sources so that there will be no question about which words and ideas are yours and which belong to other people.

### KEY POINTS

**What to Cite**

1. All facts, statistics, and pieces of information unless they are common knowledge and are accessible in many sources
2. Exact words from your source, enclosed in quotation marks
3. Somebody else's ideas and opinions, even if you restate them in your own words in a summary or paraphrase
4. Each sentence in a long paraphrase (if it is not clear that all the sentences paraphrase the same original source)

Note how James Stalker, in his article "Official English or English Only," does not quote directly but still cites the source of the specialized facts:

By 1745 there were approximately 45,000 German speakers in the colonies, and by 1790 there were some 200,000, nine per cent of the population (Anderson 80).

Citation is not necessary for facts regarded as common knowledge, such as the dates of the Civil War; facts available in many sources, such as authors' birth and death dates and chronological events; or allusions to folk tales that have been handed down through the ages. When you are in doubt about whether a fact is common knowledge, cite your source.

**Net Note**  The Internet is democratic in its approach to knowledge; information there is plentiful, readily available, and free. The Internet's interactive nature means that issues get discussed and worked over by many people (look at an online discussion group or Usenet newsgroup to see examples), so ideas are often generated by collaboration with others. In addition, the information out there is constantly changing. The source material you find today might disappear by tomorrow. The bounty, collaborative nature, and flux of online information mean that you have to be especially careful as you do Internet research and record information. Again, when in doubt, even if you are using information from a discussion list to which you have contributed, always keep a copy of the source, and cite your source in your essay (**9a**). ■

## 9f  Put yourself in your paper—and synthesize.

As you gather information and take notes, always remember to relate your notes to your research question and working thesis. All the notes on your source materials should contribute something to the issue you are researching. As you read and prepare to summarize, paraphrase, or record a quotation, ask yourself, "Why am I telling my readers this? How does it relate to my topic?" Those questions should determine the type of notes you take. Then, when you review your notes later, consider what you know about the authors and whether you share their perspectives on the issue and find their evidence convincing.List the ideas and arguments that emerge from your research, and group various authors' contributions according to the points they make.

Never get so involved in your mountains of notes and copies of sources that you include everything you have read and string it all together. Large amounts of information are no substitute for a thesis with relevant support. Leave plenty of time to read through your notes, think about what you have read, connect with the material, form responses to it, take into account new ideas and opposing arguments, and find connections among the facts and the ideas your sources offer. Avoid sitting down to write a paper at the last minute, surrounded by library books or stacks of photocopies. In this scenario, you might be tempted to lift material, and you will produce a lifeless paper. Remember that the paper is to be *your* work, not a collection of other people's words, and that your identity as the writer should be evident.

Plan and write a paper that is driven not by the sources you have consulted but by your perspectives on the issue, and illustrate those perspectives with points from your source materials. To avoid producing an essay that reads like a serial listing of summaries ("X says this. She goes on to say . . . Y states . . . Z also says . . ."), spend time reviewing your notes and synthesizing what you find into a coherent and convincing statement of what you know and believe. Do the following:

- Make lists of good ideas your sources raise about your topic.

- Look for the connections among those ideas: comparisons and contrasts.

- Find links in content, examples, and statistics.

- Note connections between the information in your sources and what you know from your own experience.

If you do this, you will take control of your material instead of letting it take control of you.

## 10 Using and Integrating Sources in Your Documented Papers

### 10a Get mileage out of your sources.

You have done hours, days, maybe weeks of research. You have found useful sources. You have a working bibliography and masses of photocopies, printouts, and notes. You have worked hard to analyze and synthesize all your material. You have made a scratch outline. Now comes the time to write.

Let readers know about the sources that support your point effectively. Don't mention the author of an influential book or a long, important article just once and in parentheses. Let readers know why this source adds weight to your case. Tell about the expert's credentials, affiliation, and experience. Tell what the author does in the work you are citing. A brief summary of the work might also be useful to provide context for the author's remarks and opinions. Your paper should never be a stringing together of sources ("Crabbe says this." "Tyger says that."). Show readers that they should be impressed by the heavyweight opinions and facts you present.

**10b**  Introduce source material.

When you provide a summary, paraphrase, or quotation to support one of the points in your paper, set up the context. Don't drop in the material as if it came from nowhere. Think about how to introduce and integrate the material into the structure of your paper.

If you quote a complete sentence, or if you paraphrase or summarize a section of another work, prepare readers for your summary, paraphrase, or quotation by mentioning the author's name in an introductory phrase. In your first reference to the work, give the author's full name. To further orient readers, you can also provide the title of the work or a brief statement of the author's expertise or credentials and thesis. Here are some useful ways to introduce source material:

| | |
|---|---|
| X has pointed out that | According to X, |
| X has made it clear that | As X insists, |
| X explains that | In 1999, X, the vice president of |
| X suggests that | the corporation, declared |

The introductory verbs *say* and *write* are clear and direct. For occasional variety, though, use verbs that offer shades of meaning, such as *acknowledge, agree, argue, ask, assert, believe, claim, comment, contend, declare, deny, emphasize, insist, note, observe, point out, propose, speculate, suggest.*

**10c**  Know what, when, and how to quote.

Readers should immediately realize why you quote a particular passage and what the quotation contributes to the ideas you want to convey. They should also learn who said the words you are quoting and, if the source is a print source, on which page of the original work the quotation appears. Then they can look up the author's name in the list of works cited at the end of your paper and find out exactly where you found the quotation.

The Modern Language Association (MLA) format for citing a quotation from an article by one author is illustrated in this section and in Part 3. See Part 4 for examples of citations of other types of sources in APA and other styles of documentation.

***Deciding what and when to quote***  Quote when you use the words of a well-known authority or when the words are particularly striking. Quote only when the original words express the exact point you want to make and express it succinctly and well. Otherwise, paraphrase. When you consider quoting, ask yourself: Which point of mine does the quotation illustrate? Why am I considering quoting this particular passage? Why should this particular passage be quoted rather than paraphrased? What do I need to tell my readers about the author of the quotation?

*Quoting the exact words of the original*  Any words you use from a source must be enclosed in quotation marks and quoted exactly as they appear in the original, with the same punctuation marks and capital letters. Do not change pronouns or tenses to fit your own purpose unless you enclose the changes in square brackets (see below).

To understand how to deal with quotations in your paper, consider this article Martin Matos found (available both in print and online) and the quotations he used as he was working on his paper on students' rights to free speech.

### Suspense and Suspension

Late last month, Charles Carithers got an English assignment: Write "a vivid horror story" about a mysterious person in the community who had a "shocking" secret in his past. So the 11th-grader at Boston Latin Academy, a competitive-admissions public school, wrote about a student athlete (which he is) who went after his English teacher with a chain saw.

The teacher saw details that hit too close to home. Charles got a three-day suspension. The school is defending the action, and Charles's mother is appealing it.

In the current climate of jitters in schools across the United States, chainsaw murders might not be the best topic for an essay. But assignments that open the door to writing about chainsaw murders might not be all that inspired, either. Adults can say that they weren't as prone to writing about such gore in their day, or that horror is more effective when less crudely rendered. But high-schoolers don't think like adults—and they are routinely doused with ridiculously crude and gory films like *Scream* (1, 2, and 3) and *I Know What You Did Last Summer*, all of which Charles said he pondered as he created his opus. (As did perhaps a peer—not suspended—whose protagonist murdered children and cut them up for fertilizer.)

It seems like a "teachable moment" that engendered a hard-line response. And such debacles happen across the US. Why no open discussion of what's acceptable? Or specifics: a horror story, children, but no guns or chain saws allowed. Or, show me the difference between horror and tension.

Assignments can't be created in a cultural vacuum—and no one should expect the results to be, either.

—Amelia Newcomb, "Suspense and Suspension," *Christian Science Monitor,* 2 May 2000: 13

***Quoting part of a sentence***　You can make sure that quotations make a point and are not just dropped in your essay if you integrate parts of quoted sentences into your own sentences. When it is obvious that parts of the quoted sentence have been omitted, you do not need to use ellipsis dots.

```
Reporter Amelia Newcomb wonders about the influence of
"ridiculously crude and gory films."
```

***Omitting words in the middle of a quotation***　If you omit as irrelevant to your purpose any words or passages from the middle of a quotation, signal the omission with ellipsis marks, three dots separated by spaces. To follow MLA style, place the three dots within square brackets to indicate that the ellipsis is not part of the original text. See **51e** for information on brackets and **51g** for ellipsis dots.

```
According to Newcomb, a high school teacher asked stu-
dents to write about a "mysterious person [. . .] who had a
'shocking' secret in his past."
```

***Omitting words at the end of a quotation***　If you omit the end of the source's sentence at the end of your own sentence, and your sentence is not followed by a page citation, signal the omission with three ellipsis dots within brackets, followed by the sentence period—four dots in all—and then the closing quotation marks.

```
With resignation, Newcomb concedes that "such
debacles happen [. . .]."
```

If you include a page citation for a print source, place it after the closing quotation marks and before the final sentence period.

```
With resignation, Newcomb concedes that "such
debacles happen [. . .]" (13).
```

Also use three dots within brackets if you omit a complete sentence (or more). Use a line of dots for an omitted line of poetry (**51g**).

*Adding or changing words*    If you add to a quotation any comments or explanations in your own words, or if you change a word in the quotation to fit it grammatically into your sentence, enclose the added or changed material in brackets (**51e**). Generally, however, it is preferable to rephrase your sentence, because bracketed words and phrases make sentences difficult to read.

AWKWARD    **Newcomb wonders whether we as adults were not "as prone to writing about such gore [in a high school essay assignment] in [our] day."**

REVISED    **Newcomb wonders whether we as adults were not "as prone to writing about such gore" in our high school essays.**

*Quoting longer passages*    If you quote more than three lines of poetry or four typed lines of prose, do not use quotation marks. Instead, begin the quotation on a new line and indent the quotation one inch or ten spaces from the left margin in MLA style, or indent it five spaces from the left margin if you are using APA style. Double-space throughout. Do not indent from the right margin. You can establish the context for a long quotation and integrate it effectively into your text if you state the point that you want to make and name the author of the quotation in your introductory statement.

Author mentioned in introductory statement

```
Newcomb lays some blame on the teacher and uses sentence
fragments to make a strong point about the way the
teacher neglected to discuss the specifics of the
assignment:
```

```
        It seems like a "teachable moment" that
        engendered a hard-line response. And
        such debacles happen across the US. Why
        no open discussion of what's acceptable?
        Or specifics: a horror story, children,
        but no guns or chain saws allowed. Or show
        me the difference between horror and
        tension. (13)
```

Quotation indented 10 spaces

No quotation marks at beginning or end of indented quotation

Page citation (only for a print source) after period

*Note:* After a long indented quotation, put the period before the parenthetical citation.

*Avoiding a string of quotations* Use quotations, especially long ones, sparingly, and only when they bolster your argument. Readers do not want to read snippets from the works of other writers. They want your analysis of your sources, and they are interested in the conclusions you draw from your research.

**10d** Fit a quotation into your sentence.

When you quote, use the exact words of the original, and make sure that those exact words do not disrupt the flow of your sentence and send it in another direction.

| | |
|---|---|
| A BAD FIT | Newcomb says that a teacher suspending a student for writing a gory essay, "such debacles happen across the US." |
| A BETTER FIT | Newcomb says that the teacher who suspended a student was influenced by the contemporary climate since "such debacles happen across the US." |
| A BAD FIT | I wonder if Newcomb is biased when she claims that some "assignments that open the door to writing about chainsaw murders." |
| A BETTER FIT | I wonder if Newcomb is biased when she claims that some "assignments [. . .] open the door to writing about chainsaw murders." |

**10e** Checklist: Using quotations

Examine a draft of your paper, and ask questions about each quotation you have included.

**KEY POINTS**

**Using Quotations: A Checklist**

1. Why do you want to include this quotation? How does it support a point you have made?

2. What is particularly remarkable about this quotation? Would a paraphrase be better?

*(Continued)*

*(Continued)*

3. Does what you have enclosed in quotation marks exactly match the words and punctuation of the original?

4. Have you told your readers the name of the author of the quotation?

5. Have you included the page number of the quotation from a print source?

6. How have you integrated the quotation into your own passage? Will readers know whom you are quoting and why?

7. What verb have you used to introduce the quotation?

8. Are there any places where you string quotations together, one after another? If so, revise. Look for quotation marks closing and then immediately opening again. Also look for phrases such as "X goes on to say . . ."; "X also says . . ."; "X then says. . . ."

9. Have you indented quotations longer than four lines of type and omitted quotation marks?

10. Have you used long quotations sparingly?

## **10f** Indicate the boundaries of a citation.

Naming an author or title in your text tells readers that you are citing ideas from a source, and citing a page number at the end of a summary or paraphrase lets them know where your citation ends. However, for one-page print articles and for Internet sources, a page citation is not necessary, so indicating where your comments about a source end is harder to do. You always need to indicate clearly where your summary or paraphrase ends and where your own comments take over. Convey the shift to readers by commenting on the source in a way that clearly announces a statement of your own views. Use expressions such as *it follows that, X's explanation shows that, as a result, evidently, obviously,* or *clearly* to signal the shift.

### UNCLEAR CITATION BOUNDARY

According to a Sony page on the Web, the company has decided to release <u>Mozart Makes You Smarter</u> as a cassette on the strength of research indicating that listening to Mozart improves IQ. The products show the ingenuity of

commercial enterprise while taking the researchers' conclusions in new directions.

[Does only the first sentence refer to material on the Web page, or
do both sentences?]

#### REVISED CITATION, WITH SOURCE BOUNDARY INDICATED

According to a Sony page on the Web, the company has
decided to release Mozart Makes You Smarter as a cassette
on the strength of research indicating that listening to
Mozart improves IQ. Clearly, Sony's plan demonstrates the
ingenuity of commercial enterprise, but it cannot reflect
what the researchers intended when they published their
conclusions.

Another way to indicate the end of your citation is to include the
author's or authors' name(s) at the end of the citation instead of (or
even in addition to) introducing the citation with the name.

#### UNCLEAR CITATION BOUNDARY

For people who hate shopping, Web shopping may be the
perfect solution. Jerome and Taylor's exploration of
"holiday hell" reminds us that we get more choice from
online vendors than we do when we browse at our local
mall because the online sellers, unlike mall owners, do
not have to rent space to display their goods. In addition, one can buy almost anything online, from CDs,
cassettes, and books to cars and real estate.

#### REVISED CITATION, WITH SOURCE BOUNDARY INDICATED

For people who hate shopping, Web shopping may be the
perfect solution. An article exploring the "holiday hell"
of shopping reminds us that we get more choice from online vendors than we do when we browse at our local mall
because the online sellers, unlike mall owners, do not
have to rent space to display their goods (Jerome and
Taylor). In addition, one can buy almost anything online,
from CDs, cassettes, and books to cars and real estate.

# MLA Documentation

## AT A GLANCE:  INDEX OF MLA STYLE FEATURES

You need to document the sources of your information, not only in research papers but also in shorter essays in which you mention only a few books, articles, or other sources to illustrate a point or support your case. Sections **11–13** provide information on the system commonly used to document sources in the humanities, the Modern Language Association (MLA) system, as recommended in Joseph Gibaldi, *MLA Handbook for Writers of Research Papers,* 5th ed. (New York: MLA, 1999), in Joseph Gibaldi, *MLA Style Manual,* 2nd ed. (New York: MLA, 1998), and on the MLA Web site (http://www.mla.org).

## 11 Citing Sources, MLA Style

Be accurate and consistent when you follow any documentation style. With the MLA style of citing author and page number, learn the basic principles (**11a**), and use the detailed examples in **11b** and **12** for help with citations and links to the list of references. Do not try to rely on memory; instead, always look up instructions and follow examples.

### 11a Two basic features of MLA style

**KEY POINTS**

**Two Basic Features of MLA Style**

1. *In the text of your paper,* include at least *two* pieces of information each time you cite a source:

   the last name(s) of the author (or authors);

   the page number(s) where the information is located, unless the source is online or only one page long.
   Do not include the abbreviation "p." (or "pp.") or the word *page* (or *pages*). See **11b** for examples.

2. *At the end of your paper,* include a list, alphabetized by authors' last names, of all the sources you refer to in the paper. Begin the list on a new page, and title it "Works Cited." See **12**.

## **11b** MLA author/page style for in-text citations

For all MLA in-text citations, identify the author and page number, if available. The first time you mention an author (or authors) in your text, give the full name and, if useful to your readers, a brief statement about credentials. (Thereafter, use the author's last name.) At the end of your text sentence, give only the page number(s) (no "p.," "pp.," or word *page*) in parentheses, followed by the sentence period. Cite inclusive page numbers as follows: 35–36; 257–58; 100–01; 305–06; 299–300.

### *A. One author, named in your introductory phrase*

```
                        ┌─ author ─┐
The sociologist Ruth Sidel's interviews with young women
                                         ┌─ quotation ─
provide examples of what Sidel sees as the "impossible
         ┌─── page number
dream" (19).──period
```

When a quotation ends the sentence, as above, close the quotation marks before the parentheses, and place the sentence period after the parentheses. See **12c**, item 1, to see how this work appears in a works-cited list. (Note that this rule differs from the one for undocumented writing, which calls for a period *before* the closing quotation marks.)

When a quotation includes a question mark or an exclamation point, also include a period after the citation:

```
                                      question mark
                                      /
Mrs. Bridge wonders, "Is my daughter mine?"
              period
              /
(Connell 135).
```

### *B. Author not named in your text*   If you do not mention the author while introducing the reference, include the author's last name in the parentheses before the page number, with no comma between them.

```
Many young women, from all races and classes, have taken
on the idea of the American Dream, however difficult it
                         author and page
                         ┌─ numbers ─┐
might be for them to achieve it (Sidel 19-20).
```

**C. Two or more authors**   For a work with two or three authors, include all the names, either in your text sentence or in parentheses.

```
(Lakoff and Johnson 42)
(Hare, Moran, and Koepke 226-28)
```

For a work with four or more authors, use only the first author's last name followed by "et al." (*Et alii* means "and others.") See **12c**, item 2.

```
Some researchers have established a close link between
success at work and the pleasure derived from community
service (Bellah et al. 196-99).
```

**D. Author with more than one work cited**   You can include the author and title of the work in your text sentence.

```
Alice Walker, in her book In Search of Our Mothers' Gardens,
describes revisiting her past to discover more about
Flannery O'Connor (43-59).
```

If you do not mention the author in your text, include in your parenthetical reference the author's last name, followed by a comma, an abbreviated form of the title, and the page number.

```
O'Connor's house still stands and is looked after by a
```

comma — abbreviated title — page number
```
caretaker (Walker, In Search 57).
```

**E. Work in an anthology**   Cite the author of the included or reprinted work (not the editor of the anthology) and the page number in the anthology. The entry in the works-cited list will include the title of the article, its inclusive page numbers, and full bibliographical details for the anthology: title, editor(s), place of publication, publisher, date. See **12c**, items 5 and 6, for examples.

```
Des Pres asserts that "heroism is not necessarily a
romantic notion" (20).
```

**F. Work cited indirectly in another source**   Use "qtd. in" (for "quoted in") in your parenthetical citation, followed by the last name of the author of the source in which you find the reference (the indirect source) and the page number where the reference appears. List the indirect source in your list of works cited. In the following example, Smith would be included in the list of works cited, not Britton.

```
We generate words unconsciously, without thinking about
them; they appear, as James Britton says, "at the point
of utterance" (qtd. in Smith 108).
```

**G. Reference to an entire work and not to one specific page** If you are referring not to a quotation or idea on one specific page, but rather to an idea that is central to the work as a whole, use the author's name alone. Include the work in your works-cited list.

```
We can learn from diaries about people's everyday lives
and the worlds they create (Mallon).
```

**H. One-page work** If an article is only one page long, cite the author's name alone; include the page number in your works-cited list (**12d**, item 22).

**I. No author or editor named** In your text sentence, give the complete title to refer to the work. In parentheses, use a short title to refer to the work. See **12c**, item 8, for the works-cited list entries.

```
According to Weather, one way to estimate the Fahrenheit
temperature is to count the number of times a cricket
chirps in 14 seconds and add 40 (18).
```

```
Increasing evidence shows that glucosamine relieves the
symptoms of arthritis (PDR Family Guide 242).
```

**J. Electronic and Internet sources** Electronic database material and Internet sources, which appear on a screen, have no stable page numbers that apply across systems or when printed. If your source as it appears on the screen includes no text divisions, numbered pages, or numbered paragraphs, simply provide the author's name. In the first mention, establish the authority of your source. If no author's name is given, refer to the title.

```
Science writer Stephen Hart describes how researchers
Edward Taub and Thomas Ebert conclude that for musicians,
practicing "remaps the brain."
```
Online source has no numbered pages or paragraphs.

With no page number to indicate the end of a citation, be careful to define where your citation ends and your own commentary takes over. See **10f** for more on defining the boundaries of a citation.

If possible, locate online material by the internal headings of the source (for example, *introduction, chapter, section*). Give paragraph numbers only if they are supplied in the source (use the abbreviation "par." or "pars."). And then include the total number of numbered paragraphs in your works-cited list (see **12e**, item 35).

> Hatchuel discusses how film editing "can change points of view and turn objectivity into subjectivity" (par. 6).
>
> Film editing provides us with different perceptions of reality (Hatchuel, par. 6).

To cite an online source with no author, give the title of the Web page or the posting. Then begin your works-cited entry with the name of the site (see **12e**, item 40).

> A list of frequently asked questions about documentation and up-to-date instructions on how to cite online sources in MLA style can be found on the association's Web site (<u>Modern Language Association</u>).

**K. Other nonprint sources**   For radio or TV programs, interviews, live performances, films, computer software, recordings, and other nonprint sources, include only the title or author (or, in some cases, the interviewer, interviewee, director, performer, or producer, and so on, corresponding to the first element of the information you provide in the entry in your list of works cited). See **12f**, item 58.

> Some writers and directors can take a lesson from seeing what <u>Copenhagen</u> does with three chairs and three actors talking about physics.
>
> It takes an extraordinary director to make a success from three chairs and three actors talking about physics (Blakemore).

**L. Work by a corporation or some other organization**   Give the complete name of the organization in the introductory passage, or give a shortened form in parentheses. (See **12c**, item 9.)

> ┌──────────── full name ────────────┐
> The College Entrance Examination Board (CEEB) assures students that the test "better reflects the type of work you will do when you get to college" (4).

```
Students are assured that the tasks on the SAT closely
resemble the tasks they will be expected to perform in
college (College Board 4).
```
shortened name

**M. Two authors with the same last name**   Include each author's first initial, or the whole first name if the authors' initials are the same.

```
A writer can be seen as both "author" and "secretary" and
the two roles can be seen as competitive (F. Smith 19).
```

**N. Multivolume work**   Indicate the volume number, followed by a colon, a space, and the page number. List the number of volumes in your works-cited list. (See **12c**, item 11.)

```
Barr and Feigenbaum note that "the concept of translation
from one language to another by machine is older than the
computer itself" (1: 233).
```

**O. More than one work in a citation**   Separate two or more works with semicolons. Avoid making a parenthetical citation so long that it disrupts the flow of your text.

```
The links between a name and ancestry have occupied many
writers and researchers (Waters 65; Antin 188).
```

**P. Lecture, speech, or personal communication such as a letter, an interview, e-mail, or a conversation**   In your text, give the name of the lecturer or person you communicated with. In your works-cited list, list the type of communication after the author or title. (See **12e**, items 48 and 52.)

```
According to George Kane, a vice president of Blackboard
Inc., online courses are more convenient, and often less
expensive, than courses in actual classrooms.
```

**Q. Classic works of literature**   Include information so readers may locate material in whatever edition they are using.

**FOR A NOVEL**   Give the chapter number as well as the page number in the edition you used: (104; ch. 3).

**FOR A POEM**   Give line numbers, not page numbers: (lines 62–73). Subsequent line references can omit the word *lines.* Include up to three lines of poetry sequentially in your text, separated by a slash with a space on each side ( / ) (see **51f**). For four or more lines of poetry, begin on a new line, indent the whole passage ten spaces from the left, double-space throughout, and omit quotation marks from the beginning and end of the passages (see **10c**).

**FOR CLASSIC POEMS, SUCH AS THE *ILIAD***   Give the book or part number, followed by line numbers, not page numbers: (8.21–25).

**FOR A VERSE PLAY**   Give act, scene, and line numbers, using arabic numerals: (`Tempest` 4.1.156–58).

**R. *The Bible***   Give book, chapter, and verse(s) in your text—Genesis 27.29—or abbreviate the book in a parenthetical citation (Gen. 27.29). Do not underline the title of a book in the Bible or the word *Bible* itself. Include an entry in your works-cited list only if you do not use the King James Version as your source.

**S. *Two or more sequential references to the same work***   If you rely on several quotations from the same page within one of your paragraphs, one parenthetical reference after the last quotation is enough, but make sure that no quotations from other works intervene. If you are paraphrasing from and referring to one work several times in a paragraph, mention the author in your introductory phrase; cite the page number at the end of a paraphrase and again if you paraphrase from a different page. Make it clear to a reader where paraphrase ends and your own comments take over (**10f**).

**T. *A long quotation***   See **10c** for MLA format for quotations of four or more lines.

**11c**   Footnotes and endnotes

With the MLA parenthetical style of documentation, use a footnote (at the bottom of the page) or an endnote (on a separate numbered page at the end of the paper before the works-cited list) only for notes giving supplementary information that clarifies a point you make. You might use a note to refer to several supplementary bibliographical sources or to provide a comment that is interesting but not essential to your argument. Indicate a note with a raised number (superscript) in your text, after the word or sentence your note refers to. Begin the first line of each note one-half inch (or five spaces) from the left margin. Do not indent subsequent lines of the same note. Double-space endnotes. Single-space within each footnote, but double-space between notes.

NOTE NUMBER IN TEXT

```
Ethics have become an important part of many writing classes.¹
```

CONTENT ENDNOTE

five spaces ———— raised number followed by space

```
¹ For additional discussion of ethics in the
classroom, see Stotsky 799-806; Knoblauch 15-21; Bizzell
663-67; Friend 560-66.
```

The *MLA Handbook* also describes a system of footnotes or endnotes as an alternative to parenthetical documentation of references. This style is similar to the footnote and endnote style described in *The Chicago Manual of Style* (see **18**).

## 12 The MLA List of Works Cited

The references you make in your text to sources are very brief—usually only the author's last name and a page number—so they allow readers to continue reading without interruption. For complete information about the source, readers can use your brief in-text citation as a guide to the full bibliographical reference in the list of works cited at the end of your paper.

### 12a Guidelines for the MLA list of works cited

Before you begin to prepare your list, familiarize yourself with the basic features of MLA style. (For an example of a works-cited list, see pp. 157–58).

**KEY POINTS**

**Setting Up the MLA List of Works Cited**

1. *What to list*   List only works you actually cited in the text of your paper, not works you read but did not mention, unless your instructor requires you to include all the works you consulted as well as those mentioned in your text.

*(Continued)*

*(Continued)*

2. *Format of the list*    Begin the list on a new numbered page after the last page of the paper or any endnotes. Center the heading (Works Cited) without quotation marks, underlining, or a period. Double-space throughout the list.

3. *Organization*    Do not number the entries. List works alphabetically by author's last name. Begin each entry with the author's name, last name first (or the corporate name or the title of the work if no author is stated). Omit titles ("Dr.") or degrees, but include a suffix like "Jr." or a Roman numeral, as in "Patterson, Peter, III." Use normal order—first name first—for the names of authors after the first name. List works with no stated author by the first main word of each entry (**12d**, item 26).

4. *Indentation*    To help readers find an author's name and to clearly differentiate one entry from another, indent all lines of each entry, except the first, one-half inch (or five spaces). A word processor can provide these "hanging indents" (**23a**).

   **Net Note**    If you intend to publish on the Internet, it is often preferable to use no indentation at all (HTML does not support hanging indents well). Instead, follow each bibliographical entry with a line space.    ■

5. *Periods*    Separate the main parts of each entry—author, title, publishing information—with a period, followed by one space.

6. *Capitals*    Capitalize all words in titles of books and articles except *a, an, the,* coordinating conjunctions, *to* in an infinitive, and prepositions (such as *in, to, for, with, without, against*) unless they begin or end the title or subtitle.

7. *Underlining or italics*    Underline the titles of books and the names of journals and magazines as in the examples in this section. You may use italics instead if your instructor approves and if your printer makes a clear distinction from regular type.

   **Net Note**    If you write for publication on a World Wide Web site, avoid underlining titles of books and journals, because underlining is a signal for a hypertext link. Use italics, or consult your instructor or editor. For e-mail publication, use _ and _ before and after the text you would normally underline (**57b**).    ■

*(Continued)*

*(Continued)*

8. *Month* When citing articles in journals, newspapers, and magazines, abbreviate all months except May, June, and July.

9. *Publisher* Use a short form of the name of book publishers (*Random,* not *Random House; Columbia UP,* not *Columbia University Press*). For place of publication when more than one office is mentioned, list only the first city mentioned on the title page.

10. *Page numbers* Give inclusive page numbers for articles and sections of books. Do not use "p." ("pp.") or the word *page* (or *pages*) before page numbers in any reference. For page citations over 100 and sharing the same first number, use only the last two digits for the second number (for instance, 683–89, but 798–805). For an unpaginated work, write "n. pag."

## **12b** Order of entries in the list of works cited

*Alphabetical order* Alphabetize entries in the list by authors' last names. Note the following:

- Alphabetize by the exact letters in the spelling: *MacKay* precedes *McHam.*

- Let a shorter name precede a longer name beginning with the same letters: *Linden, Ronald* precedes *Lindenmayer, Arnold.*

- With last names using a prefix such as *le, du, di, del,* and *des,* alphabetize by the prefix: *Le Beau, Bryan F.*

- When *de* occurs with French names of one syllable, alphabetize under *d: De Jean, Denise.* Otherwise, alphabetize by last name: *Maupassant, Guy de.*

- Alphabetize by the first element of a hyphenated name: *Sackville-West, Victoria.*

- Alphabetize by the last name when the author uses two names without a hyphen: *Thomas, Elizabeth Marshall.*

For a work with no author named, alphabetize by the first word in the title other than *A, An,* or *The* (see **12c**, item 8, and **12d**, item 26).

***Several works by the same author(s)*** For all entries after the first, replace the name(s) of the author(s) with three hyphens followed by a period, and alphabetize according to the first significant word in the title. If an author serves as an editor or translator, put a comma after the three hyphens, followed by the appropriate abbreviation ("ed." or "trans."). If, however, the author has coauthors, repeat all authors' names in full and put the coauthored entry after all the single-name entries for the author.

Goleman, Daniel. Vital Lies, Simple Truths. New York:
    Simon, 1996.

---. Working with Emotional Intelligence. New York: Bantam,
    2000.

Goleman, Daniel, Paul Kaufman, and Michael L. Ray. "The Art of
    Creativity." Psychology Today Mar./Apr. 1992: 40-47.

***Authors with the same last name*** Alphabetize by first names: *Smith, Adam* precedes *Smith, Frank*.

**12c** Sample MLA entries: print books and parts of books

On the title page of a book and on the copyright page, you will find the information you need for an entry. Use the most recent copyright date. Use a shortened form of the publisher's name; usually one word is sufficient: *Houghton* (not *Houghton Mifflin*); *Basic* (not *Basic Books*). For university presses, use the abbreviations "U" and "P" (no periods).

## 1. Basic form for a book with one author

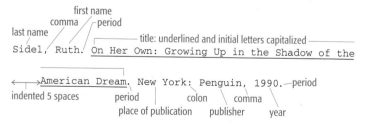

## 2. Book with two or more authors
Use authors' names in the order in which they appear in the book. Separate the names with commas. Reverse the order of only the first author's name.

second author's name
comma          not reversed

Lakoff, George, and Mark Johnson. <u>Metaphors We Live By</u>.

Chicago: U of Chicago P, 1980.

For a work with four or more authors, either list all the names or use only the first author's name followed by "et al." (Latin for "and others").

Bellah, Robert N., et al. <u>Habits of the Heart:</u>

<u>Individualism and Commitment in American Life</u>.

Berkeley: U of California P, 1985.

**3. Edited book** Use the abbreviation "ed." or "eds.," preceded by a comma, after the name(s) of the editor or editors.

Gates, Henry Louis, Jr., ed. <u>Classic Slave Narratives</u>. New

York: NAL, 1987.

For a work with four or more editors, use only the name of the first, followed by a comma and "et al."

**4. Author and editor** When an editor has prepared an author's work for publication, list the book under the author's name if you cite the author's work. Then, in your listing, include the name(s) of the editor or editors after the title, introduced by "Ed." for one or more editors. "Ed." here stands for "edited by."

author of letters                    name of editor

Bishop, Elizabeth. <u>One Art: Letters</u>. Ed. Robert Giroux.

New York: Farrar, 1994.

If you cite a section written by the editor, such as a chapter introduction or a note, list the source under the name of the editor.

name of editor   editor                    author of letters

Giroux, Robert, ed. <u>One Art: Letters</u>. By Elizabeth Bishop.

New York: Farrar, 1994.

**5. One work in an anthology (original or reprinted)** For a work included in an anthology, first list the author and title of the included work. Follow this with the title of the anthology, the name of the editor(s), publication information (place, publisher, date) for the anthology, and then, after the period, the pages in the anthology covered by the work you refer to.

author of article
┌── or chapter ──┐
Des Pres, Terrence. "Poetry and Politics." The Writer

means            name of editor
"edited by"  ┌── of anthology ──┐
in Our World. Ed. Reginald Gibbons. Boston:

Atlantic Monthly, 1986. 17-29.
inclusive page numbers of article or chapter

Naylor, Gloria. "The Meanings of a Word." Language Awareness.

8th ed. Ed. Paul Escholz, Alfred Rosa, and Virginia

Clark. Boston: Bedford, 2000. 272-75.

If the work in the anthology is a reprint of a previously published scholarly article, supply the complete information for both the original publication and the reprint in the anthology.

Gates, Henry Louis, Jr. "The Fire Last Time." New Republic

1 June 1992: 37-43. Rpt. in Contemporary Literary

Criticism. Ed. Jeffrey W. Hunter. Vol. 127. Detroit:

Gale, 2000. 113-19.

**6. More than one work in an anthology, cross-referenced** If you refer to more than one work from the same anthology, list the anthology separately, and list each essay with a cross-reference to the anthology. Alphabetize in the usual way, as in the following examples.

title of
┌── author of article ──┐   ┌── article in anthology ──┐
Des Pres, Terrence. "Poetry and Politics." Gibbons

17-29.                                    editor of anthology
page numbers of article

┌── editor of anthology ──┐        ┌── title of anthology ──┐
Gibbons, Reginald, ed. The Writer in Our World. Boston:

Atlantic Monthly, 1986.

┌── author of article ──┐    ┌── title of article in anthology ──┐
Walcott, Derek. "A Colonial's-Eye View of America."

editor of anthology   page numbers of article
Gibbons 73-77.

**7. Reference book** For a well-known reference book, give only the edition number and the year of publication. When articles in an encyclopedia are arranged alphabetically, omit page numbers.

"Multiculturalism." Columbia Encyclopedia. 6th ed. 2000.

**8. Book with no author named**   Put the title first. Do not consider the words *A, An,* and *The* when alphabetizing the entries. The following entries would be alphabetized under *P* and *W*.

The PDR Family Guide to Natural Medicines and Healing
      Therapies. New York: Three Rivers-Random, 1999.

Weather. New York: Discovery-Random, 1999.

**9. Book by a corporation or some other organization**   Alphabetize by the name of the corporate author. If the publisher is the same as the author, include the name again as publisher.

College Entrance Examination Board. Index of Majors and
      Graduate Degrees 2000. New York: College Entrance
      Examination Board, 1999.

**10. Translated book**   After the title, include "Trans." followed by the name of the translator, first name first.

Grass, Günter. Novemberland: Selected Poems, 1956-1993.
      Trans. Michael Hamburger. San Diego: Harcourt, 1996.

**11. Multivolume work**   If you refer to more than one volume of a multivolume work, indicate the number of volumes (abbreviated "vols.") after the title.

Barr, Avon, and Edward A. Feigenbaum, eds. The Handbook of
      Artificial Intelligence. 4 vols. Reading: Addison, 1981-86.

If you refer to only one volume of a work, limit the information in the entry to that one volume.

Feigenbaum, Edward A., and Paul R. Cohen, eds. The Handbook of
      Artificial Intelligence. Vol. 3. Reading: Addison, 1985.

**12. Book in a series**   Give the name of the series after the book title.

Connor, Ulla. Contrastive Rhetoric: Cross-Cultural
      Aspects of Second Language Writing. Cambridge Applied
      Linguistics Series. New York: Cambridge UP, 1996.

**13. Book published under publisher's imprint**   State the names of both the imprint (the publisher within a larger publishing enterprise) and the larger publishing house, separated by a hyphen.

Richards, Thomas. The Meaning of Star Trek. New York:
      Anchor-Doubleday, 1999.

**14. *Foreword, preface, introduction, or afterword*** List the name of the author of the book element cited, followed by the name of the element, with no quotation marks. Give the title of the work; then use "By" to introduce the name of the author of the book (first name first). After the publication information, give inclusive page numbers for the book element cited.

```
Hemenway, Robert. Introduction. Dust Tracks on a Road:
    An Autobiography. By Zora Neale Hurston. Urbana:
    U of Illinois P, 1984. ix-xxxix.
```

**15. *Republished book*** After the title, give the original date of publication. Then cite information about the current publication.

```
Walker, Alice. The Color Purple. 1982. New York: Pocket, 1985.
```

**16. *Edition after the first*** After the title, give the edition number, using the abbreviation "ed."

```
Raimes, Ann. Keys for Writers. 3rd ed. Boston: Houghton, 2002.
```

**17. *Book title including a title*** Do not underline a book title that is part of the source title. (However, if the title of a short work, such as a poem or short story, is part of the source title, enclose it in quotation marks.)

```
Hays, Kevin J., ed. The Critical Response to Herman
                    book title not
                    ┌underlined┐
        Melville's Moby Dick. Westport: Greenwood, 1994.
```

**18. *Government publication*** If no author is named, begin the entry with the name of the federal, state, or local government, followed by the agency.

```
United States. Department of Labor. Occupational Outlook
    Handbook 1999-2000. Indianapolis: JIST, 1999.
```

**19. *Dissertation*** For an unpublished dissertation, follow the title (in quotation marks) with "Diss." and the university and date.

```
Hidalgo, Stephen Paul. "Vietnam War Poetry: A Genre of
    Witness." Diss. U of Notre Dame, 1995.
```

Cite a published dissertation as you would a book, with place of publication, publisher, and date, but also include dissertation information after the title (for example, "Diss. U of California, 1998.").

If the dissertation is published by University Microfilms International (UMI), underline the title and include "Ann Arbor: UMI," the date, and the order number at the end of the entry.

Diaz-Greenberg, Rosario. The Emergence of Voice in Latino
     High School Students. Diss. U of San Francisco. 1996.
     Ann Arbor: UMI, 1996. 9611612.

If you cite an abstract published in *Dissertation Abstracts International*, give the relevant volume number and page number.

Hidalgo, Stephen Paul. "Vietnam War Poetry: A Genre of Witness."
     Diss. U of Notre Dame, 1995. DAI 56 (1995): 0931A.

## 12d Sample MLA entries: print articles

The conventions for listing print articles depend on whether the articles appear in newspapers, popular magazines, or scholarly journals. For distinguishing scholarly journals from other periodicals, see **8b**. In all cases, omit from your citation any introductory *A, An,* or *The* in the name of a newspaper, magazine, or scholarly journal.

**20. Article in a scholarly journal: pages numbered consecutively through each volume** For journals with consecutive pagination through a volume (for example, the first issue of volume 1 ends with page 174, and the second issue of volume 1 begins with page 175), give only the volume number and year.

Korotayev, Andrey, and Dmitri Bondarenko. "Polygyny and
     Democracy: A Cross-Cultural Comparison." Cross-
     Cultural Research 34 (2000): 190-206.

**21. Article in a scholarly journal: each issue paged separately** For journals in which each issue begins with page 1, include the issue number after the volume number, separated from the volume number by a period.

Ginat, Rami. "The Soviet Union and the Syrian Ba'th Regime:
     From Hesitation to *Rapprochement*." Middle Eastern
     Studies 36.2 (2000): 150-71.

**22. Article in a magazine** For a magazine published every week or biweekly, give the complete date (day, month, and year, in that order, with no commas between them). For a monthly or bimonthly magazine, give only the month and year (see item 61). In either case, do not include volume and issue numbers. If the article is on only one page, give that page number. If the article covers two or more consecutive pages, list inclusive page numbers.

```
Naughton, Keith. "Bring on the Junk Food." Newsweek 10 July
     2000: 44.

Cooper, Marc. "Arizona: The New Border War." Nation 17 July
     2000: 20-24.
```

**23. Article in a newspaper** Omit an initial *The* in a newspaper title. Include the date after the newspaper title. For a newspaper that uses letters to designate sections, give the letter before the page number: "A23." For a numbered section, write, for example, "sec. 2: 23." See **12e**, item 37, for the online version of the article below.

```
Navarro, Mireya. "Bricks, Mortar, and Coalition Building."
     New York Times 13 July 2001: A1+.
```

**24. Article that skips pages** When an article does not appear on consecutive pages (the one by Gladwell begins on p. 68, runs to 72, and skips to p. 84), give only the first page number followed by a plus sign.

```
Gladwell, Malcolm. "The New-Boy Network." New Yorker 29 May
     2000: 68+.
```

**25. Review** Begin with the name of the reviewer and the title of the review article, if these are available. After "Rev. of," provide the title and author of the work reviewed, followed by publication information for the periodical in which the review appears.

```
Annan, Gabriele. "Close to the Edge." Rev. of Mr. Phillips,
     by John Lanchester. New York Review of Books 29 June
     2000: 18-19.
```

**26. Unsigned editorial or article** Begin with the title. For an editorial, include the label "Editorial" after the title. In alphabetizing, ignore an initial *A, An,* or *The.*

```
"Air-Traveler Abuse." Editorial. Washington Post 25 July
     2000: A22.
```

**27. Letter to the editor** Write "Letter" or "Reply to letter of . . ." after the name of the author.

```
Goldstone, Richard J. Letter. Wall Street Journal 7 July
     2000: A13.
```

**28. Abstract in an abstracts journal**   For abstracts of articles, provide exact information for the original work and add information about your source for the abstract: the title of the abstract journal, volume number, year, and item number or page number. (For dissertation abstracts, see **12c**, item 19.)

Van Dyke, Jan. "Gender and Success in the American Dance World."
    Women's Studies International Forum 19 (1996): 535-43.
    Studies on Women Abstracts 15 (1997): item 97W/081.

**29. Article on microform (microfilm and microfiche)**   To cite sources that are neither in hard copy nor in electronic form, provide as much print publication information as is available along with the name of the microfilm or microfiche and any identifying features. Many newspaper and magazine articles published before 1980 are available only in microfiche or microfilm, so you will need to use this medium for historical research. However, be aware that such collections may be incomplete and difficult to read and duplicate clearly.

"War with Japan." Editorial. New York Times 8 Dec. 1941:
    22. UMI University Microfilms.

Savage, David. "Indecency on Internet Faces High Court
    Test." Los Angeles Times 16 Mar. 1997. Newsbank: Law
    (1997): fiche 34, grid A6.

**12e**   Sample MLA entries: Internet and other electronic sources

**30. Internet and other electronic sources: general requirements**
With the fast pace of change in the electronic world, standards are continually evolving for citing sources. For updated information on citing Internet sources, refer to the MLA Web site at <http://www.mla.org>.

   With whatever system of documentation you use, the basic question you need to ask is "What information does my reader need in order to access the same site and find the same information I found?" Internet sites vary in the amount of information they provide, and with some you need to go to the home page or search the site to find information. Scroll to the end of a page—the date of posting often lurks there. Netscape's View/Page Info sometimes provides a date. For all of your sources, you *must* provide the date when you found the material (your date of access) and the URL.

**KEY POINTS**

### Citing Internet Sources

1. *Information to include*  As a general rule, follow this pattern, including as much of the information as is relevant and available to you:
   - author(s);
   - title of work;
   - print publication information;
   - title of online site, project, journal, or database, underlined;
   - online publication information: date of latest update, volume and issue number of online journal, name of online service, sponsor of site, or discussion list;
   - date when you accessed the site;
   - electronic address (URL).

   For specific examples, see **12e**, items 31–49.

2. *Dates*  The last date in your source reference, immediately before the URL or keywords, should be the date when you accessed the material. Two dates might appear next to each other in a source reference, as in **12e**, items 36, 37, and 43, but both are necessary: the first, the date when the work was posted or updated electronically; the second, the date when you found the material.

3. *URL*  Break a URL for a new line only after a slash. Never insert a hyphen into a Web address (a URL), and never split a protocol (for example, http://) across lines. When using MLA style, enclose a URL in angle brackets (< >).

4. *Page numbers only for print version*  Include in your citation the page numbers for any print version of the source. For the electronic version, include page or paragraph numbers of the on-screen version *only* if they are indicated on the screen. Usually they are not, so the page numbers on your printout of a source would not necessarily correspond to the page numbers on other printouts. When no page or paragraph information for the online version appears on the screen, include no page numbers in your list of references. For how to cite unpaged online material in your text, see **11b**, item J. See also **10f** on how to indicate where your citation ends.

5. *Permissions*  Request permission to use any graphics or e-mail postings you include in your paper, especially if you intend to post your paper on a Web site. Make this request via e-mail.

Internet Sources

KeyTab®

Bookmark • Margin • Notecard

### 31. Work in an online database or subscription service

Libraries subscribe to large information services and databases (such as *InfoTrac, First Search, EBSCO, SilverPlatter, Dialog, SIRS,* and *Lexis-Nexis*) to gain access to extensive databases of online articles, as well as to specialized databases (such as *ERIC, New York Times Online, Contemporary Literary Criticism,* and *PsycINFO*). You can use these databases to gain access to abstracts and full texts of thousands of articles. When you link to a database in this way, look to see if the URL of the database is displayed in the location toolbar of your browser. If it is, after details of author, title, and any print publication information, give the name of the database, the library that subscribes to the service, any article access number, your own date of access, and the URL of the entry page of the database.

```
Lowe, Michelle S. "Britain's Regional Shopping Centres:
                    ┌── print publication information ──┐
     New Urban Forms?" Urban Studies 37.2 (2000).
     ┌────────── name of database ──────────┐   ┌── library subscriber ──
     InfoTrac: Expanded Academic ASAP. City University of
     ─────────────────────────────────┘  access number    date of access
     New York Libraries. Article A61862666. 14 Jan. 2001
     <http://web5.infotrac.galegroup.com>.
```

If the service provider provides a direct link to a licensed database without displaying the URL of the accessed database, give the name of the database, the name of the subscription service or library, and your date of access. Specify any path or keywords that you used to access the source.

```
"Parthenon." The Columbia Encyclopedia Online. 6th ed. 2000.
     America Online. 12 July 2000. Keywords: Reference/
     Encyclopedias/Encyclopedia.com/Bartleby.com/Columbia
     Encyclopedia 6th ed.

Verdon, Mary E., and Leonard H. Sigel. "Recognition and
     Management of Lyme Disease." American Family Physician,
     56.2 (1997). NOAH (New York Online Access to Health).
     Brooklyn Public Library, Brooklyn, NY. 13 Sept. 2000.
     Path: Health topics; Lyme disease; Diagnosis and
     symptoms.
```

### 32. Online book or text

Give whatever is available of the following: author, title, editor or translator (if applicable), print publication information, electronic publication information and date, date of access, and complete electronic address (URL).

```
                                              print publication
         ──── author ────    ──────── title of work ────────  ── information ──
Darwin, Charles. The Voyage of the Beagle. London: John
```

```
                                       date of electronic
         ──────────────  ── title of database ──  ── publication ──
Murray, 1859. Oxford Text Archive. 28 Mar. 2000.
```

```
         ──────────────────── name of sponsor of site ────────────────────
Arts and Humanities Data Service, Oxford University
```

```
                               date of
         ────────────────────  ── access ──  ──────────
Computing Services. 31 May 2000 <http://
```

```
electronic address enclosed
  ── in angle brackets ──
ota.ahds.ac.uk>.
```

### 33. *Online poem*

```
── author ──    ── title of poem ──    ── print source ──
Levine, Philip. "What Work Is." What Work Is.
```

```
          print publication
         ──── information ────    ──────── title of database ────────
New York: Knopf, 1991. Internet Poetry Archive.
```

```
date of electronic              sponsor                date of
  ── updating ──       ──────── of site ────────      ── access ──
4 Apr. 2000. U of North Carolina P. 31 May 2000
```

```
                       electronic address (URL)
         ──────── enclosed in angle brackets ────────
<http://metalab.unc.edu/ipa/levine/work.html>.
```

### 34. *Article in a reference database*

```
── title of article ──           ──────── title of database ────────
"Bloomsbury group." Encyclopaedia Britannica Online.
```

```
     version      date of electronic
  ── number ──    ── update ──        ──────── sponsor ────────
Vers. 99.1. 7 July 2000. Encyclopaedia Britannica.
```

```
          date of
         ── access ──
10 July 2000 <http://www.eb.com:180>.
```

### 35. *Article in an online journal or newsletter*   Give the author, title of article, title of journal, volume and issue numbers, and date of issue. Include page or the number of paragraphs only if pages or paragraphs are numbered in the source, as they are for the first example below. End with date of access and electronic address.

```
      author                         title of article
Hatchuel, Sarah. "Leading the Gaze: From Showing to

    Telling in Kenneth Branagh's Henry V and Hamlet."
```

```
                   name of              volume and    date of online
                 online journal         issue number   publication
    Early Modern Literary Studies 6.1 (2000):
```

```
number of paragraphs         date of
(numbered in the text)       access
    22 pars. 13 July 2000 <http://www.shu.ac.uk/emls/06-1/

    hatchbra.htm>.
```

```
      author                 title of article
Hart, Stephen. "Overtures to a New Discipline:
```

```
                            title of
                          online journal   volume and issue numbers
    Neuromusicology." 21st Century 1.4 (July 1996).
                                           date of
                                        electronic publication
  no numbered pages or paragraphs
  3 Nov. 2000 <http://www.columbia.edu/cu/21stC/
   date of
    access

    issue-1.4/mbmmusic.html>.
```

### 36. Article in an online magazine

```
Mendelsohn, Jennifer. "Seven Habits of Highly Effective
    Rags." Slate 8 June 2000. 14 June 2000 <http://
    Slate.msn.com/keepingtabs/00-06-08/keepingtabs.asp>.
```

### 37. Article in an online newspaper

```
Plate, Tom. "The Costs of a Ludicrous 'Defense.'"
    Los Angeles Times: LATimes.com. 12 July 2000. 13 July
    2000 <http://www.latimes.com/news/comment/20000712/
    t000065479.html>.
```

```
Navarro, Mireya. "Bricks, Mortar, and Coalition Building."
    New York Times 13 July 2000: A1+. New York Times on
    the Web 13 July 2000. 13 July 2000 <http://nytimes
    .com/library/national/race/071300navarro-houston.html>.
```

### 38. Review, editorial, abstract, or letter in an online publication

After author and title, identify the type of text: "Letter," "Editorial," "Abstract," or "Rev. of . . . by . . ." (see **12d**, items 25–28). Continue with details of the electronic source.

## 39. *Scholarly project*

```
          title of                                date of electronic
   ┌ scholarly project ┐    ┌──────── editor ───────┐  ┌─ publication ─┐   sponsor
   Perseus Project. Ed. Gregory Crane. 3 June 2000. Tufts U.
```
```
        ┌ date of access ┐
        8 Jan. 2001 <http://www.perseus.tufts.edu>.
```

## 40. *Professional site*

```
                                         date of
   ┌──────── title of professional site ────────┐  ┌─ update ─┐   ┌──────── sponsor ────────┐
   Modern Language Association. May 2000. Modern Language
```
```
   ┌────────────────────────────────────────┐  ┌─ date of access ─┐
   Association of America. 30 Aug. 2000
   <http://www.mla.org>.
```

**41. Linked site**   If you connect to one site from another, include "Lkd." (linked from) after the details of the source you cite, followed by the title of the document you originally accessed (in italics or underlined), along with any additional details necessary for linking. Follow this with the date of access and the URL.

```
"Morisot, Berthe." WebMuseum, Paris (30 Dec. 1995). Lkd.
    AntePodium Links, at "Gender Studies" and "Canadian
    Women's Studies Online." 15 June 2000 <http://
    www.ruw.ac.nz/atp>.
```

**42. Personal Web page**   If the personal Web page has a title, supply it, underlined. Otherwise, use the designation "Home page."

```
                              date of      personal site with
                           ┌─ update ─┐   ┌─ no title ─┐
   Kuechler, Manfred. 12 Jan. 2000. Home page. 7 July 2000
       <http://maxweber.hunter.cuny.edu/socio/faculty/
       kuech.html>.
```

**43. Online posting in a discussion list, Web forum, bulletin board service, Usenet, or HyperNews**   Give the author's name, title of document (as written in the subject line), the label "Online posting," and the date of posting. Follow this with the name of the forum, date of access, and URL or address of discussion list. For a Usenet newsgroup, give the name and address of the group, beginning with the prefix "news:".

```
                                    title of
                      ┌──────────── posting ──────────────┐
Kramer, Wayne. "'Crossing Over' on Ifilm.com." Online

              date of                    name of
           ┌── posting ──┐         ┌───── forum ──────────┐
    posting. 28 Apr. 2000. LatinoLink Bulletin Board:

                           date of
    ┌──────────────────┐ ┌── access ──┐ ┌── URL ──┐
    Criminal Justice. 14 June 2000 <http://

    ┌──────────────────┐
    boards.latinolink.com>.
```

```
  Fontana, Richard. "Origin of 'Yo!'" Online posting.
           date of           date of          name of Usenet
        ┌── posting ──┐   ┌── access ──┐   ┌── discussion group ──┐
        10 July 2000. 12 July 2000 <news:alt.usage.english>.
```

```
Peckham, Irvin. "Class origins." Online posting.
                  name of discussion list      address of discussion list
        1 May 2000. WPA-L. 6 May 2000 <WPA-L@asu.edu>.
```

To make it easier for readers to find the posting, refer whenever possible to one stored in the list's archives or available in HyperNews:

```
Peckham, Irvin. "Class origins." Online posting. 1 May 2000.
        WPA-L Archives. 13 July 2000 <http://lists.asu.edu>.
```

```
Lang, Tom. "Writing in the First Person." Online posting.
        17 Aug. 1998. CBE Forum: HyperNews. 14 July 2000
        <http://www.hypernews.org>.
```

To cite a forwarded document in an online posting, include author, title, and date, followed by "Fwd. by" and the name of the person forwarding the document. End with "Online posting," the date of the forwarding, the name of the discussion group, date of access, and address of the discussion list.

```
Feng, Clarence. "VBS Kakworm." 14 June 2000. Fwd. by Jim
        Barry. Online posting. 14 June 2000. Hunter-1.
        17 June 2000 <hunter-1@shiva.hunter.cuny.edu>.
```

**44. *Synchronous communication*** When citing a source from a chat room, a MUD (multi-user domain), or a MOO (multi-user domain, object-oriented), give the name of the person speaking or posting information, the type of event, title, date, forum, date of access, and electronic address. Refer to archived material whenever possible.

```
Delker, Natalie. Vertical file. "Cyborg Bibliography." Nov.
     1997. LinguaMOO. 9 Jan. 1998 <http://
     lingua.utdallas.edu:7000/4125>.
```

### 45. Work of art online

```
Kelly, Ellsworth. Sculpture for a Large Wall. 1957. Museum of
     Modern Art, New York. 13 July 2000 <http://www.moma.org/
     docs/collection/paintsculpt/recent/c467.htm>.
```

### 46. Television and radio programs online

```
Black, Louis, and John Butler. "Live Town Hall: Austin, Texas.
     High-Tech Haven or Paradise Lost?" Changing Face of
     America: Talk of the Nation. National Public Radio.
     30 Mar. 2000. NPR Online. 27 July 2000 <http://
     www.npr.org/programs/totn/000330.cfoa.html>.
```

### 47. Film or film clip online

```
Clinton, Bill. Address to California Institute of Technology on
     Science and Technology. 21 Jan. 2000. Caltech. 27 July 2000
     <http://www.caltech.edu/events/PresVisit-MCP-LAN.ram>.
```

### 48. Personal e-mail message   Treat this form like a letter.

```
Kane, George. "New developments." E-mail to the author.
     23 Feb. 2001.
```

### 49. Other Internet sources   Identify online interviews, maps, charts, sound recordings, cartoons, and advertisements as you would sources that are not online (see **12f**), with the addition of electronic publication information, date of access, and the URL.

### 50. Electronic source medium not known   When you use a computer network to access information, you may not know whether the material is on the library's hard drive or on CD-ROM. In such a case, use the word *Electronic* for the medium, and give the name and sponsor of the network, followed by your date of access.

```
"Renaissance." 1996. Concise Columbia Electronic Encyclopedia.
     Electronic. ColumbiaNet. Columbia U. 18 July 2000.
```

### 51. CD-ROM   Cite material from a CD-ROM published as a single edition (that is, with no regular updating) in the same way you cite a book, but after the title add the medium of publication and any version or release number.

Keats, John. "To Autumn." <u>Columbia Granger's World of Poetry</u>.
    CD-ROM. Rel. 3. New York: Columbia UP, 1999.

To cite an updated database on CD-ROM, include any print publication information, the name of the database, the label "CD-ROM," the name of the producer or distributor, and the electronic publication date.

Dowd, Maureen. "Spite or Art?" <u>New York Times</u> 23 Apr. 2000:
    11. <u>New York Times Ondisc</u>. CD-ROM. UMI-ProQuest. 2000.

## **12f** Sample MLA entries: other sources

### *52. Lecture, speech, letter, personal communication, or interview*
For a lecture or speech, give the author and title, if known. For a presentation with no title, include a label such as "Lecture" or "Address" after the name of the speaker. Also give the name of any organizing sponsor, the venue, and the date.

Alexander, Meena. Lecture. Hunter College, New York. 15 Apr. 2001.

For a letter that you received, include the phrase "Letter to the author" after the name of the letter writer. For an interview that you conducted, indicate the type of interview ("Personal interview," "Telephone interview").

Rogan, Helen. Letter to the author. 3 Feb. 2001.

Gingold, Alfred. Telephone interview. 5 May 2001.

Cite a published letter as you would cite a work in an anthology. After the name of the author, include any title the editor gives the letter and the date. Add the page numbers for the letter at the end of the citation.

Bishop, Elizabeth. "To Robert Lowell." 26 Nov. 1951. <u>One Art:</u>
    <u>Letters</u>. Ed. Robert Giroux. New York: Farrar, 1994. 224-26.

### *53. Published or broadcast interview*
For print, radio, or TV interviews that have no title, include the label "Interview" after the name of the person interviewed, followed by the bibliographical information for the source.

Bloom, Harold. Interview. <u>Charlie Rose</u>. PBS. WNET, New York.
    11 July 2000.

### *54. Map or chart*
Underline the title of the map or chart, and include the designation after that title.

<u>Auvergne/Limousin</u>. Map. Paris: Michelin, 1996.

**55. Film or video**  List the title, director, performers, and any other pertinent information. End with the name of the distributor and the year of distribution.

Sunshine. Dir. Istvan Szabo. Perf. Ralph Fiennes. Paramount,
     2000.

When you cite a videocassette or DVD, include also the medium, the name of the distributor, and the date of the recording.

Casablanca. Dir. Michael Curtiz. Perf. Humphrey Bogart and
     Ingrid Bergman. Turner, 1943. DVD. MGM, 1998.

**56. Television or radio program**  Give the title of the program; any pertinent information about performers, writer, narrator, or director; the network; and the local station and date of broadcast.

Storms of the Century. Narr. Stacey Keach. Savage Planet.
     PBS. WNET, New York. 9 July 2000.

**57. Sound recording**  List the composer or author, the title of the work, the names of artists, the production company, and the date. If the medium is not a compact disc, indicate the medium, such as "Audiocassette," before the name of the production company.

Scarlatti, Domenico. Keyboard Sonatas. Andras Schiff,
     piano. London, 1989.

Walker, Alice. Interview with Kay Bonetti. Audiocassette.
     Columbia: American Audio Prose Library, 1981.

**58. Live performance**  Give the title of the play, the author, pertinent information about the director and performers, the theater, the location, and the date of performance. If you are citing an individual's role in the work, begin your citation with the person's name.

Copenhagen. By Michael Frayn. Dir. Michael Blakemore. Perf.
     Philip Bosco. Royale Theater, New York. 16 May 2000.

Blakemore, Michael, dir. Copenhagen. By Michael Frayn. Perf.
     Philip Bosco. Royale Theater, New York. 16 May 2000.

**59. Work of art, slide, or photograph**  List the name of the artist, the title of the work (underlined), the name of the museum, gallery, or owner, and the city.

Johns, Jasper. Racing Thoughts. Whitney Museum of American
     Art, New York.

For a photograph in a book, give complete publication information, including the page number on which the photograph appears.

```
Johns, Jasper. Racing Thoughts. Whitney Museum of American
     Art, New York. The American Century: Art and Culture
     1950-2000. By Lisa Phillips. New York: Norton, 1999. 311.
```

For a slide in a collection, include the slide number: "Slide 17," for example.

**60. Cartoon**   After the cartoonist's name and the title (if any) of the cartoon, add the label "Cartoon." Follow this with the usual information about the source, and give the page number.

```
Chast, Roz. "When Hell Freezes Over." Cartoon. New Yorker
     15 Sept. 1997: 56.
```

**61. Advertisement**   Give the name of the product or company, followed by the label "Advertisement" and publication information. If a page is not numbered, write "n. pag."

```
Zeroknowledge.com. Advertisement. Wired July 2000: 82-83.
```

**62. Legal case**   Give the name of the case with no underlining or quotation marks. Also give the volume number, name, and page of the law report, the name of the court, and the year.

volume   United States   court deciding case:
number   Law Report      US Supreme Court

Roe v. Wade. 410 U.S. 209. U.S. Sup. Ct. 1973.

page number cited                     year of decision

However, if you mention the case in your text, underline it.

```
Chief Justice Burger, in his concurring statement on the
Roe v. Wade decision (209), noted that . . .
```

## 13   Sample Documented Paper: MLA Style

Section **7h** shows how Audrey Fort did research for a paper examining music, emotions, and intelligence. Here is her completed, revised paper, with citations for all the sources she used and a corresponding works-cited list. (If your instructor requires a separate title page, see **25c** or ask for guidelines.)

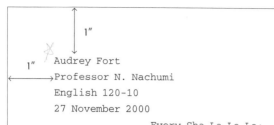

1″

½″

Fort 1

1″

Audrey Fort

Professor N. Nachumi

English 120-10

27 November 2000

Every Sha La La La:

Music as Mystery or Manipulation

Title: centered, not underlined

No extra space below title

"I haven't understood a bar of music in my life, but I have felt it" (qtd. in Peter 350). These words were spoken by Igor Stravinsky, who composed some of the most complex and sophisticated music of the twentieth century. If the great Stravinsky can accept the elusive nature of music and still love it, why can't we? Why are we analyzing it to try to make it useful?

Writer uses an indirect source.

Double-spaced throughout

Writer poses questions.

Paragraph indent ½″ or 5 spaces

Ours is an age of information--an age that wishes to conquer all the mysteries of the human brain. Today there is a growing trend to study music's effects on our emotions, behavior, health, and intelligence. Journalist Alex Ross reports how the relatively new field of neuromusicology (the science of the nervous system and its responses to music) has been developed to experiment with music as a tool and to shape it to the needs of society. Observations like these let us know that we are on the threshold of seeing music in a whole new way and using music to achieve measurable changes in behavior. However, this new approach carries dangers, and once we go in this direction, there can be no turning back. How far do we want to go in our study of musical science? What effects will it have on our listening pleasure?

Writer cites source of idea. Page number unnecessary for electronic source.

Thesis: writer states her opinion of neuro-musicology.

Writer asks questions she hopes to answer in essay.

A short history lesson reveals that there has long been an awareness that music affects us, even if the reasons are not clear. Around 900 B.C., David (later King David) played the harp

1″

Fort 2

"to cure Saul's derangement" (Gonzalez-Crussi 69). Perhaps he was one of the first music therapists. The positive influence of music may have also saved Beethoven's life in the early nineteenth century. In a letter, the now famous "Heiligenstadt Testament," Beethoven credits music with keeping him alive: "I would have ended my life--it was only my art that held me back" (qtd. in Kamien 159).

Writer quotes exact words; cites author and page number.

In modern times, an interesting story about monks who still use medieval Gregorian chants also demonstrates the power of music over well-being. Marilyn Ferguson tells how monks deprived of chanting time grew sluggish and tired and required more sleep. French physician Alfred Tamatis, interested in chanting and its effects on mental health, was called in to observe the monks and discovered that after being put back on their chanting schedule, they soon felt energetic again, working more and sleeping less (168). The restorative powers of chanting have kept this sacred practice alive for centuries.

Writer names author.

Writer gives page number in Ferguson's book.

Music can thus have a positive influence on emotions and behavior, but perhaps it can have a negative effect on them as well. This is where neuromusicology may step in to save the day. If a connection between music and depression could be established, then the benefits of this science would be twofold: it would give psychologists another tool to help untangle the web of depression, and it might help those vulnerable to depression understand what triggers the blues.

Writer recognizes benefits of neuro-musicology.

Country music, for example, apparently tugs hard on the heartstrings. A study by researchers Stack and Gundlach has examined the link between country music and suicide rates in forty-nine cities:

Writer gives an example.

Writer introduces source of quotation.

Fort 3

1" or
10 spaces

> Country music is hypothesized to nurture a
> suicidal mood through its concerns with
> problems common in the suicidal
> population, such as marital discord,
> alcohol abuse, and alienation from work.
> The results [. . .] show that the greater
> the airtime devoted to country music, the
> greater the white suicide rate. The effect
> is independent of divorce, southernness,
> poverty, and gun availability. (211)

The researchers found in their study that "the
greater the percentage of radio time devoted to
country music, the higher the incidence of white
suicide" (215). (Their study does not reveal a
similar relationship for black suicide.) With
links established between country music and
suicidal depression, further clinical studies could
be useful. Perhaps just listening to an uplifting
radio station would be beneficial to people at risk
of suicide.

Not only does music affect our emotions, but it
can also manipulate them. Muzak, according to
psychologist Anne Rosenfeld, is artificially
"programmed to manipulate our feelings and
behavior" (56). Muzak is omnipresent; supermarkets
use that subtle overhead encouragement to relax
people and induce buying. Muzak's impact on
industrial behavior, too, is strong: it has led to
a 17 percent increase in a factory's productivity,
a 13.5 percent increase in clerical performance
for workers in an office, and a 58 percent reduc-
tion in personnel turnover among one airline's
reservation employees (Rosenfeld 56). With the
production of percentages like these,
neuromusicologists may soon be highly sought

**Writer sets off a long quotation.**

**Writer omits passage from source.**

**Writer gives page number after period in a long quotation.**

**Writer puts sentence period after citation.**

**Writer comments on quotations.**

**Transition to new topic: manipulation**

**Writer cites statistics in support of point.**

**Writer comments on the statistics.**

Fort 4

after. Many businesses would benefit financially from increased efficiency, and if staff morale were improved, disruptive turnover would be lessened. On the negative side, we would live in a sterile musical world, bombarded with Muzak engineered to create desired behavior. We would be manipulated into working harder and buying against our will.

Writer reinforces point about manipulation.

However, the presence of music might have good effects on learning processes. Certainly, America's schools need help. A controversial 1993 study grabbed attention when it determined that "listening to Mozart actually makes you smarter" (Ross). Researchers Rauscher, Shaw, and Ky report that they had 36 college students listen to ten minutes of Mozart piano music. Immediately afterward, the students were given tests of spatial reasoning. Scores were a mean of eight to nine points higher than the scores the subjects received after listening to a "relaxation tape." The effect, however, was temporary, and whether the students liked Mozart or not made no difference in their test scores. Physiological arousal was ruled out because pulse rates remained the same throughout the testing. Why Mozart? One theory reported in a popular weekly magazine is that "the intricate musical structures may resonate in the brain's dense web, lubricating a flow of neurons" (Ramo).

Research report is only one page long.

Ross article is one page long, so no page number is necessary.

In addition, 1999 duplications of the 1993 study by researchers at Harvard University (Chabris et al.) and Appalachian State University (Steele, Bass, and Crook) find no evidence of the so-called Mozart effect on reasoning ability. Undaunted, Rauscher and Shaw stand by their results (Larkin), and continue to publish

Fort 5

research--nine papers in 1999 alone, which they claim as "dramatically successful research" (Research into the Mozart Effect).

The consequences of these developments could be that what was once a basic pleasure, an aesthetic, social, and sensual delight, threatens to become a new technology. Neuromusicology, according to science writer Stephen Hart, is being hailed and promoted as a "new discipline"; practice is no longer the boring chore we all thought it was but is seen as something that "remaps the brain" (Hart). This technology is spawning a range of products: the Symposium on Foundations of Musicology at the University of Ghent in June 1997; the Sony recording and Web site called Mozart Makes You Smarter; two 1999 books promising brighter children through music (Shaw; Habermeyer); and the establishment of the Music-Intelligence-Neural-Development (M.I.N.D.) Institute, with its Web site devoted to Research into the Mozart Effect and Education. The consequences could be that what we listen to and where we listen to it will be specifically designated to create an intended result. Mozart will become the "composer who gives you an edge on the SATs" (Ross), and his superb piano music will become the Muzak of learning institutions. The private world of music that has the power to move us in a highly personal way will be force-fed to us by researchers proud of themselves for unlocking the mystery of music.

The beauty of music lies in its mystery, and to dissect music's impact ignores its mystery. Many of us will prefer enjoying our favorite Beethoven symphony or love songs by Whitney Houston to hearing about the connections psychologists have seen in them.

*Writer returns to thesis.*

*The Internet source has no numbered pages or paragraphs.*

*Writer integrates a quotation and makes a strong point.*

*Writer returns to thesis in her conclusion.*

Fort 6

Works Cited

Chabris, Christopher F., et al. "Prelude or Requiem
for the 'Mozart effect'?" Abstract. Nature 26
Aug. 1999: 826-28. PsycINFO. WebSPIRS
SilverPlatter. City University of New York
Libraries. Article 1999-11328-001. 7 Nov. 2000
<http://webspirs4.silverplatter.com:8500/cuny>.

Ferguson, Marilyn. Pragmagic. New York: Pocket,
1990.

Gonzalez-Crussi, Frank. "Hearing Pleasures."
Health Mar. 1989: 65+.

Habermeyer, Sharlene. Good Music, Brighter
Children. Rocklin: Prima, 1999.

Hart, Stephen. "Overtures to a New Discipline:
Neuromusicology." 21st Century 1.4 (1996).
3 Nov. 2000 <http://www.columbia.edu/cu/
21stC/issue-1.4/mbmmusic.html>.

Kamien, Roger. Music: An Appreciation. New York:
McGraw, 1994.

Larkin, Marilynn. "'Mozart Effect' Comes under Strong
Fire." Lancet 28 Aug. 1999: 749. InfoTrac:
Expanded Academic ASAP. City University of New
York Libraries. Article A55942471.1 Nov. 2000
<http://web4.infotrac.galegroup.com>.

Mozart Makes You Smarter. 26 June 2000. Sony
Classical. 8 Nov. 2000 <http://
www.sonyclassical.com/music/66245/index.html>.

Peter, Laurence J. Peter's Quotations. New York:
Bantam, 1977.

Ramo, Joshua Cooper. "Music Soothes the Savage
Brain: Listening to Mozart Improves
Intelligence Test Scores." Newsweek 25 Oct.
1993: 51. Lexis-Nexis Academic Universe. City
University of New York Libraries. 8 Nov. 2000
<http://web.lexis-nexis.com/universe>.

Title:
centered,
not
underlined

Article is
from a
subscription
database.

Entries are
alphabetized.

Article is not
on consecu-
tive pages.

Online
journal
article has
no page
numbers.

½" or
5 spaces

Web site:
commercial

Rauscher, Frances H., Gordon L. Shaw, and
    Katherine N. Ky. "Music and Spatial Task
    Performance." Nature 14 Oct. 1993: 611.
Research into the Mozart Effect and Education.
    M.I.N.D. Institute. 25 Oct. 2000. 11 Nov. 2000
    <http://www.mindinst.org>.
Rosenfeld, Anne H. "Music, the Beautiful Disturber."
    Psychology Today Dec. 1985: 48+.
Ross, Alex. "Listening to Prozac . . . Er, Mozart."
    New York Times 28 Aug. 1994, sec. 2: 23.
    New York Times Ondisc. CD-ROM. UMI-ProQuest.
    1994.
Shaw, Gordon L. Keeping Mozart in Mind. San Diego:
    Academic-Harcourt, 1999.
Stack, Steven, and Jim Gundlach. "The Effect of
    Country Music on Suicide." Social Forces 71.1
    (1992): 211-18.
Steele, Kenneth M., Karen E. Bass, and Melissa D.
    Crook. "The Mystery of the Mozart Effect:
    Failure to Replicate." Psychological Science
    10.4 (1999): 366-69.
Symposium on "Foundations of Neuromusicology." 13
    June 1997. FWO Research Society on Foundations
    of Music Research. 11 Nov. 2000 <http://
    next.rug.ac.be/ nfwo/meeting3.html>.

Web site:
professional

Material
is on
CD-ROM.

Article
spans
consecutive
pages.

Web site:
professional

# APA, CBE, Chicago, *and* CGOS Documentation

# AT A GLANCE: INDEX OF APA STYLE FEATURES

Sample APA Entries:

### Print Books (15d), 169

### Print Articles (15e), 172

### Internet and Other Electronic Sources (15f), 174

### Other Sources (15g), 177

---

In Part 4 you will find descriptions of documentation systems other than the MLA system. Sections **14, 15,** and **16** focus on the style recommended for the social sciences by the *Publication Manual of the American Psychological Association,* 5th ed. (Washington, DC: Amer. Psychological Assn., 2001), and on the Web site for the APA *Publication Manual* at <www.apastyle.org>. A student's paper written in APA style is presented in section **16.** Section **17** describes the citation-sequence style recommended by the Council of Biology Editors (CBE). Section **18** describes the endnote and footnote style recommended in *The Chicago Manual of Style,* 14th ed. (Chicago: U of Chicago P, 1993), for writing in the humanities; it is sometimes used as an alternative to MLA style. Section **19** outlines the system recommended in *The Columbia Guide to Online Style* (New York: Columbia UP, 1998) and at <http://www.columbia.edu/cu/cup/cgos> for citing online sources in the humanities and sciences.

## 14 Citing Sources, APA Style

### 14a Two basic features of APA style

**KEY POINTS**

**Two Basic Features of APA Style**

1. *In the text of your paper,* include at least two pieces of information each time you cite a source:

   the last name(s) of the author (or authors);

   the year of publication.

2. *At the end of your paper,* include on a new numbered page a list entitled "References," double-spaced and arranged alphabetically by authors' last names, followed by initials of first and other names, the date in parentheses, and other bibliographical information. See **15** for the information to include in an APA-style reference list.

### 14b APA author/year style for in-text citations

**A. One author** If you mention the author's last name in your own sentence, include the year in parentheses directly after the author's name.

```
 author     year
   /         /
Wilson (1994) has described in detail his fascination
with insects.
```

(See **15d**, item 1, to see how this work appears in a reference list.)

If you do not name the author in your sentence, include both the name and the year, separated by a comma, in parentheses.

```
The role of the Educational Testing Service (ETS) in
designing, evaluating, and promoting the test has been
harshly criticized (Owen, 1985).
                    author comma  year
```

If you use a direct quotation, include in parentheses the abbreviation "p." or "pp." followed by a space and the page number(s). Separate items within parentheses with commas.

```
Memories are built "around a small collection of
dominating images" (Wilson, 1994, p. 5).
                        comma  comma  page number
                                     with a quotation
```

**B. More than one author**   For a work by two authors, name both in the order in which their names appear on the work. Within parentheses, use an ampersand (&) between the names, in place of *and*.

```
Kanazawa and Still (2000) in their analysis of a large
set of data show that the statistical likelihood of being
divorced increases if one is male and a secondary school
teacher or college professor.

Analysis of a large set of data shows that the statisti-
cal likelihood of being divorced increases if one is male
and a secondary school teacher or college professor
(Kanazawa & Still, 2000).
 ampersand in parentheses
```

(See **15e**, item 13, to see how this work appears in a reference list.)

For a work with three to five authors or editors, identify all of them the first time you mention the work. In later references, use only the first author's name followed by "et al." (for "and others") in place of the other names.

```
Jordan, Kaplan, Miller, Stiver, and Surrey (1991) have
examined the idea of self.

Increasingly, the self is viewed as connected to other
human beings (Jordan et al., 1991).
```

(See **15d**, item 2, to see how this work appears in a reference list.)

For six or more authors, use the name of the first author followed by "et al." both for the first mention and in a parenthetical citation.

**C. Author with more than one work published in one year** Identify each work with a lowercase letter after the date: (Zamel, 1997a, 1997b). Separate the dates with a comma. The reference list will contain the corresponding letters after the dates of each work. (See **15b** for how to order the entries in the list of references.)

**D. Work in an anthology** In your text, refer to the author of the work, not to the editor of the anthology. In the reference list, give the author's name, title of the work, and bibliographical details about the anthology, such as the editor, title, publisher, and date (**15d**, item 4).

```
Seegmiller (1993) has provided an incisive analysis of
the relationship between pregnancy and culture.
```

**E. Work cited indirectly, in a secondary source** Give the author or title of the original work preceded by "as cited in" to indicate that you are referring to a work mentioned in the work of another author. List the secondary source in your list of references. In the following example, *Smith* will appear in the list of references; *Britton* will not.

```
The words we use simply appear, as Britton says, "at the
point of utterance" (as cited in Smith, 1982, p. 108).
```

**F. An entire work or an idea in a work** Use only an author and a year to refer to a complete work; for a paraphrase or a comment on a specific idea, a page number is not required but is recommended.

**G. No author named** In your text, use the complete title if it is short (capitalizing major words) or a few words for the title in parentheses, along with the year of publication.

```
According to Weather (1999), one way to estimate the
Fahrenheit temperature is to count the number of times a
cricket chirps in 14 seconds and add 40.
```

```
Increasing evidence shows that glucosamine relieves the
symptoms of arthritis (The PDR Family Guide, 1999).
```

(See **15d**, item 5, to see how the latter work is listed.)

**H. Electronic or other Internet source** Give author, if available, or title, followed by the year of electronic publication or of the most recent update. Also provide the date on which you access the material. Be wary of citing e-mail messages (personal, bulletin board, discussion list, or Usenet group) as these are not peer reviewed or easily retrievable. If you need to cite an e-mail message, cite from an archived list whenever possible (see examples **15f**, item 30); otherwise, cite the message in your text as a personal communication (**14b**, item O), but do not include it in your list of references.

**I. Entire Web site** Give the complete URL in the text of your paper. Do not list the site in your list of references.

```
Research on the "Mozart effect" has generated an institute
with a Web site providing links to research studies
(http://www.mindinst.org).
```

**J. Nonprint source**   For a film, television or radio broadcast, recording, or other nonprint source, include in your citation the name of the originator or main contributor (such as the writer, interviewer, director, performer, or producer) or an abbreviated title if the originator is not identified, along with the year of publication—for example, "(Morris, 1993)." (See **15g**, item 32, to see how this work appears in a reference list.)

**K. Work by a corporation or some other organization**   In the initial citation, use the organization's full name; in subsequent references, use an abbreviation if one exists.

```
One of the defenders of the appropriateness of the SAT
                       ┌────────── first mention: full name ──────────┐
is its creator, the College Entrance Examination Board

(CEEB). The claim is that "the SAT has been changed
                       abbreviation in citation
because education has changed" (CEEB, 1993, p. 4).
```

**L. Two authors with the same last name**   Include the authors' initials, even if the publication dates of their works differ.

```
F. Smith (1982) has often described a writer as having
two competitive roles: author and secretary.
```

(For the order of entries in the list of references, see **15b**.)

**M. Multivolume work**   In your citation, give the publication date of the volume you are citing: (Barr & Feigenbaum, 1982). If you refer to more than one volume, give inclusive dates for all the volumes you cite: (Barr & Feigenbaum, 1981–1986). (See **15d**, item 8, to see how this work appears in a reference list.)

**N. More than one work in a citation**   List the sources in alphabetical order, separated by semicolons. List works by the same author chronologically (earliest source first) or by the letters *a*, *b*, and so on, if the works were published in the same year.

```
Criticisms of large-scale educational testing abound
(Crouse & Trusheim, 1988; Nairn, 1978, 1980; Raimes,
1990a, 1990b; Sacks 2000).
```

*O. Personal communication, such as a conversation, a letter, e-mail, an unarchived electronic discussion group, or an interview* Mention these only in your paper; do not include them in your list of references. Give the last name and initial(s) of the author of the communication and the exact date of posting.

```
According to Dr. C. S. Apstein, Boston University School
of Medicine, research in heart disease is critical to the
well-being of society today (personal communication,
January 7, 2001).
```

*P. A classic work* If the date of publication of a classic work is not known, use in your citation "n.d." for "no date." If you use a translation, give the year of the translation, preceded by "trans." You do not need a reference list entry for the Bible or ancient classic works. Just give information about book and line numbers in your text.

*Q. Long quotation* If you quote more than forty words of prose, do not enclose the quotation in quotation marks. Start the quotation on a new line, and indent the whole quotation half an inch or five spaces from the left margin. Double-space the quotation.

**14c** Notes

In APA style, you can use content notes to amplify information in your text. Number notes consecutively with superscript numerals. After the list of references, attach a separate page containing your numbered notes and headed "Footnotes." Include all important information in your text, not in footnotes. Use notes sparingly.

## 15 The APA List of References

**15a** Guidelines for the APA list of references

The APA *Publication Manual* and Web site provide guidelines for submitting professional papers for publication, and many instructors ask students to follow those guidelines to prepare them for advanced work. This section follows APA guidelines. Check with your instructor, however, as to specific course requirements for the reference list. See **15c** for a discussion of format and indentation.

**KEY POINTS**

**Setting Up the APA List of References**

1. *What to list* List only the works you cited (quoted, summarized, paraphrased, or commented on) in the text of your paper, not everything you read.

2. *Format* Start the list on a new numbered page after the last page of text or notes. Center the heading "References," without quotation marks, not underlined or italicized, and with no period following it. Double-space throughout the list.

3. *Organization* List the works alphabetically, by last names of primary authors. Do not number the entries. Begin each entry with the author's name, last name first, followed by an initial or initials. Give any authors' names after the first in the same inverted form, separated by commas. Do not use "et al." List works with no author by title, alphabetized by the first main word.

4. *Date* Put the year in parentheses after the authors' names. For journals, magazines, and newspapers, include also month and day, but do not abbreviate the names of the months.

5. *Periods* Use a period and one space to separate the main parts of each entry.

6. *Indentation* Use hanging indents. See **15c**.

7. *Capitals* In titles of books and articles, capitalize only the first word of the title or subtitle and any proper nouns or adjectives.

8. *Italics* Italicize the titles of books, but do not italicize or use quotation marks around the titles of articles. For magazines and journals, italicize the publication name, the volume number, and the comma. Italicize the names of newspapers.

9. *Page numbers* Give inclusive page numbers for articles and sections of books, using complete page spans ("251–259"). Use the abbreviation "p." or "pp." only for newspaper articles and sections (such as chapters) of books.

10. *Publisher* Do not abbreviate the name of the publisher. Give state (abbreviated) as well as city except for major cities.

**15b** Order of entries in the reference list

*Alphabetical order*   Alphabetize letter by letter. Treat *Mac* and *Mc* literally, by letter.

MacKay, M.          D'Agostino, S.
McCarthy, T.        De Cesare, P.
McKay, K.           De Curtis, A.

A shorter name precedes a longer name beginning with the same letters, whatever the first initial: *Black, T.* precedes *Blackman, R.*

For a work with no known author, list by the first word in the title other than *A, An,* or *The.*

Alphabetize numerals according to their spelling: 5 ("five") will precede 2 ("two").

*Several works by the same author*   List the author's name in each entry. Arrange entries chronologically from past to present. Entries published in the same year should be arranged alphabetically by title and distinguished with lowercase letters after the date (*a, b,* and so on). Note that entries for one author precede entries by that author but written with coauthors.

Goleman, D. (1996a, July 16). Forget money; nothing can buy
     happiness, some researchers say. *The New York Times,*
     p. C1.
Goleman, D. (1996b). *Vital lies, simple truths.*
     New York: Simon & Schuster.
Goleman, D. (2000). *Working with emotional intelligence.*
     New York: Bantam.
Goleman, D., Kaufman, P., & Ray, M. L. (1992, March-April).
     The art of creativity. *Psychology Today, 25,* 40-47.

*Authors with the same last name*   List alphabetically by first initial: *Smith, A.* precedes *Smith, F.*

**15c** Format and indentation

*Underlining or italics?*   The fifth edition of the APA *Publication Manual* includes instructions that "take advantage of the nearly universal use of sophisticated word processors." It now recommends that authors use italics in place of underlining to represent text that would eventually be converted to italics in print.

*Use hanging indents in the list of references.* The new APA guidelines specify hanging indents for manuscript and final copy. A hanging indent sets the first line of each item in the reference list at the left margin, with subsequent lines of the entry indented five spaces or one-half inch.

```
Klein, D. F. (1995). Response to Rothman and Michels on
     placebo-controlled clinical trials. Psychiatric
     Annals, 25, 401-403.
Rothman, K. F., & Michels, K. D. (1994). The continuing
     unethical use of placebo controls. New England Journal
     of Medicine, 331, 394-398.
```

However, the fifth edition of the *Publication Manual* also notes that if a word-processing program makes it difficult to achieve a hanging indent, then a paragraph indent (first line of entry indented five spaces) is acceptable. In either case, the usage should be consistent throughout.

**15d** Sample APA entries: print books and parts of books

*1. Book with one author*  You will find the information you need on the title page and the copyright page of the book. Use the most recent copyright date. Include both the city and the state of publication if the name of the city is not familiar. Give the publisher's name in a short but intelligible form, spelling out *University* and *Press* but omitting *Co.* and *Inc.*

```
       last name   initials    periods
                             /   year in parentheses
          comma    /     /       title and period italicized
             \     |    /    period
   Wilson, E. O. (1994). Naturalist. Washington:
         Island Press.              place of    colon
         publisher   final period   publication
```

*2. Book with two or more authors*  List all authors' names in the order in which they appear on the book's title page. Reverse the order of each name: last name first, followed by initials. Do not use "et al." Separate all names with commas, and insert an ampersand (&) before the last name.

all names reversed

Jordan, J. V., Kaplan, A. G., Miller, J. B., Stiver,

indented
5 spaces    ampersand

I. P., & Surrey, J. L. (1991). *Women's growth in
connection: Writings from the Stone Center*. New
York: Guilford Press.

### 3. Edited book   Use "Ed." or "Eds." for one or more editors, in parentheses.

Denmark, F., & Paludi, M. (Eds.). (1993). *Psychology of
women: A handbook of issues and theories*. Westport,
CT: Greenwood Press.

### 4. Work in an anthology or reference book   List the author, date of publication of the edited book, and title of the work. Follow this with "In" and the names of the editors (not inverted), the title of the book, and the page numbers (preceded by "pp.") of the work in parentheses. End with the place of publication and the publisher. If you cite more than one article in an edited work, include full bibliographical details in each entry.

names of editors
not reversed

Seegmiller, B. (1993). Pregnancy. In F. Denmark &

M. Paludi (Eds.), *Psychology of women: A handbook of
issues and theories* (pp. 437-474). Westport, CT:
Greenwood Press.

For a well-known reference book with unsigned alphabetical entries, give only the edition number and year of publication. When articles are arranged alphabetically in an encyclopedia, omit page numbers.

Multiculturalism. (2000). In *Columbia Encyclopedia* (6th ed.).

### 5. Book with no author named   Put the title first. Ignore *A, An,* and *The* when alphabetizing. Alphabetize the following under *P.*

*The PDR family guide to natural medicines and healing
therapies*. (1999). New York: Three Rivers-Random House.

**6. *Book by a corporation or some other organization***   Give the name of the corporate author first. If the publisher is the same as the author, write "Author" for the name of the publisher.

```
College Entrance Examination Board. (1999). Index of majors
     and graduate degrees 2000. New York: Author.
```

**7. *Translated book***   In parentheses after the title of the work, give the initials and last name of the translator, followed by a comma and "Trans."

```
Jung, C. G. (1960). On the nature of the psyche
```
    name of translator not reversed
```
     (R. F. C. Hull, Trans.). Princeton, NJ: Princeton
     University Press.
```

**8. *Multivolume work***   When you refer to several volumes in a work of more than one volume, give the number of volumes after the title, in parentheses. The date should indicate the range of years of publication, when appropriate.

```
Barr, A., & Feigenbaum, E. A. (1981–1986). The handbook of
     artificial intelligence (Vols. 1-4). Reading, MA:
     Addison-Wesley.
```

**9. *Foreword, preface, introduction, or afterword***   List the name of the author of the book element cited. Follow the date with the name of the element, the title of the book, and, in parentheses, the page numbers on which the element appears.

```
Weiss, B. (Ed.). (1982). Introduction. American education and
     the European immigrant, 1840-1940 (pp. xi-xxviii).
     Urbana, IL: University of Illinois Press.
```

**10. *Republished book***   After the author's name, give the most recent date of publication. At the end, in parentheses add "Original work published" and the date. In your text citation, give both dates: (Smith, 1793/1976).

```
Smith, A. (1976). An inquiry into the nature and causes of
     the wealth of nations. Chicago: University of Chicago
     Press. (Original work published 1793)
```

**11. *Technical report***   If the report has a number, state it in parentheses after the title.

```
Breland, H. M., & Jones, R. J. (1982). Perceptions of writing
    skill (Rep. No. 82-4). New York: College Entrance
    Examination Board.
```

**12. Dissertation or abstract** For a manuscript source, give the university and year of the dissertation and the volume and page numbers of *DAI*.

```
Salzberg, A. (1992). Behavioral phenomena of homeless women
    in San Diego county (Doctoral dissertation, United
    States International University, 1992). Dissertation
    Abstracts International, 52, 4482.
```

For a microfilm source, also include in parentheses at the end of the entry the university microfilm number. For a CD-ROM source, include "CD-ROM" after the title. Then name the electronic source of the information and the *DAI* number.

**15e** Sample APA entries: print articles

**13. Article in a scholarly journal: pages numbered consecutively through each volume** Give only the volume number and year for journals with consecutive pagination through a volume (for example, the first issue of volume 1 ends on page 174, and the second issue of volume 1 begins on page 175). Italicize the volume number and the following comma as well as the title of the journal. Do not use "p." or "pp." with page numbers. Do not abbreviate months. For the title of an article, use capital letters only for the first word of the title and subtitle (if any) and for proper nouns. See **8b** on recognizing a scholarly journal.

no quotation marks around
┌──── article title ────
```
Kanazawa, S., & Still, M. C. (2000). Teaching may be
```
journal title, volume number,
┌─ and commas italicized ─
```
hazardous to your marriage. Evolution and Human
```

```
Behavior, 21, 185-190.
```
no "p." or "pp." before page numbers

**14. Article in a scholarly journal: each issue paged separately** For journals in which each issue begins with page 1, include the issue number—in parentheses but not in italics—immediately after the volume number.

```
Ginat, R. (2000). The Soviet Union and the Syrian Ba'th
     regime: From hesitation to rapprochement. Middle
     Eastern Studies, 36(2), 150-171.
```
                              issue number not in italics

**15. Article in a magazine**   Include the year and month or month and day of publication in parentheses. Italicize the magazine title, the volume number, and the comma that follows; then give the page number or numbers.

```
                         year,
                    ┌── month, day ──┐
Naughton, K. (2000, July 10). Bring on the junk food.
     Newsweek, 136, 44.
```
                    volume number included and italicized

**16. Article in a newspaper**   In parentheses, include the month and day of the newspaper after the year. Give the section letter or number before the page, where applicable. Use "p." and "pp." with page numbers. Do not omit *The* from the title of a newspaper.

```
Navarro, M. (2000, July 13). Bricks, mortar, and coalition
     building. The New York Times, pp. A1, A16-17.
```

**17. Article that skips pages**   When an article appears on discontinuous pages, give all the page numbers, separated by commas, as in item 16, above.

**18. Review**   After the title of the review article, add in brackets a description of the work reviewed and identify the medium: book, film, or video, for example.

```
Weatherall, D. J. (2000, June 18). No panaceas [Review of the
     book The elusive magic bullet: The search for the
     perfect drug]. The Times Literary Supplement, p. 32.
```

**19. Unsigned editorial or article**   For a work with no author named, begin the listing with the title; for an editorial, add the label "Editorial" in brackets.

```
Air-traveler abuse [Editorial]. (2000, July 25). The
     Washington Post, p. A22.
```

**20. Letter to the editor**   Put the label "Letter to the editor" in brackets after the date or the title of the letter, if it has one.

```
Goldstone, R. J. (2000, July 7). [Letter to the editor].
    The Wall Street Journal, p. A13.
```

## **15f** Sample APA entries: Internet and other electronic sources

The American Psychological Association supplements the fifth edition of its *Publication Manual* with a style Web site (http://www.apastyle.org) offering examples, periodic updates, tips, and the opportunity to ask questions. The version posted on August 3, 2001, advises providing as many of the following elements as you can when citing Internet and electronic sources.

- name of author(s), if available
- date of work ("n.d" if no date is available)
- title of work (article, report, Web document or site, abstract, subject line of e-mail message), with additional necessary information added in brackets: [*letter to the editor, data file,* etc.]
- print publication information (such as name of journal, volume number, page numbers)
- a retrieval statement containing the date you retrieved the information (month, day, year, with comma after day and after year) and the name of the database or the Internet address (URL) of the specific document you refer to, not just the home page.
- a period at the end of the entry—but no period if the entry ends with a URL.

The URL must be exact. Use the Copy function to copy it from the address window in your browser (making sure you have turned off automatic hyphenation: (Tools/Language/Hyphenation), and then use the Paste function to paste the URL into your document.

**21. Work in an electronic database**   Many universities, libraries, and organizational Web sites subscribe to large searchable databases, such as *InfoTrac, EBSCO, Lexis-Nexis,* OCLC, *SilverPlatter, WilsonWeb, Dialog,* and *SIRS.* These databases provide access to large numbers of published, scholarly abstracts and full-text articles. In addition, available both online and on CD-ROM are specialized databases such as *ERIC, New York Times Online, PsycINFO,* and *PAIS* (Public Affairs Information Service). However or wherever you access a source from an electronic database, cite it as follows:

Goldstein, B. S. C., & Harris, K. C. (2000). Consultant
    practices in two heterogeneous Latino schools. *The
    School Psychology Review, 29,* 368-377. Retrieved August
    2, 2001, from WilsonWeb Education Full Text database.

If an item number or accession number is provided, you have the option of including it at the end in parentheses. With the item number, the above entry would end like this:

Retrieved August 2, 2001, from WilsonWeb Education Full
    Text database (0279-6015).

## 22. Newpaper article retrieved from database or Web site

Newspaper articles, as well as journal articles, are often available from several sources, in several databases and in a variety of formats, such as on CD-ROM, in a university online subscription database, or on a Web site. The two examples below show references to the same article, accessed first via an online database and then via a CD-ROM.

Wade, N. (2000, May 9). Scientists decode Down syndrome
    chromosome. *The New York Times,* p. F4. Retrieved
    September 18, 2000, from Lexis-Nexis Academic Universe
    database.

Wade, N. (2000, May 9). Scientists decode Down syndrome
    chromosome. *The New York Times,* p. F4. Retrieved
    September 18, 2000, from UMI ProQuest database.

The following example shows a newspaper article accessed from a Web site:

Blakeslee, S. (2001, August 2). Study says surgery tops
    drugs in epilepsy. *The New York Times.* Retrieved August
    6, 2001, from http://www.nytimes.com

## 23. Online abstract

For an abstract retrieved from a database or from a Web site, begin the retrieval statement with the words "Abstract retrieved" followed by the date and the name of the database or the URL of the Web site.

Zadra, A., & Donderi, D. C. (2000, May). Nightmares and bad
    dreams: Their prevalence and relationship to well-
    being. *Journal of Abnormal Psychology, 109,* 273-281.

```
Abstract retrieved July 17, 2000, from http://
www.apa.org/journals/abn/500ab.html#11
```

**24. Online article, based on a print source**   If you read a print article in electronic form, unchanged from the original and with no addtional commentary, cite the article as you would a print article, with the addition of [Electronic version] after the title of the article. If information such as page numbers or figures are missing or if the document may have additions or alterations, give full retrieval information:

```
Jones, C. C., & Meredith, W. (2000, June). Developmental
    paths of psychological health from early adolescence to
    later adulthood. Psychology and Aging, 15, 351-360.
    Retrieved July 17, 2000, from http://www.apa.org/
    journals/pag/pag152351.html
```

**25. Article in an online journal, no print source**

```
Holtzworth-Munroe, A. (2000, June). Domestic violence:
    Combining scientific inquiry and advocacy [10
    paragraphs]. Prevention & Treatment, 3. Retrieved July
    18, 2000, from http://journals.apa.org/prevention/
    volume3/pre0030022c.html
```

**26. Article in an online site, no author identified**

```
Gold medal awards. (2000, September). APA Monitor, 31(8).
    Retrieved September 11, 2000, from http://www.apa.org/
    monitor/apfnews.html
```

**27. Entire Web site**   Give the complete URL in the text of your paper, not in your list of references. For an example see **14b**, item I.

**28. Document on a Web site, no author identified**   Italicize the title of the document (the Web page). Alphabetize by the first major word of the title.

```
APAStyle.org: Electronic references. (2001, August 3).
    Retrieved August 5,2001, from http://www.apastyle.org/
    elecref.html
```

### 29. Document on a university or government agency site
Italicize the title of the document. In the retrieval statement, give the name of the university or government agency (and the department or division if it is named). Follow this with a colon and the URL.

```
McClintock, R. (2000, September 20). Cities, youth, and tech-
    nology: Toward a pedagogy of autonomy. Retrieved July 18,
    2001, from Columbia University, Institute for Learning
    Technologies Web site: http://www.ilt.columbia.edu/
    publications/cities/cyt.html
```

### 30. E-mail and contributions to electronic mailing lists
Make sure that you cite only scholarly e-mail messages. Cite a personal e-mail message in the body of your text as "personal communication," and do not include it in your list of references (see **14b**, item O). For messages posted to discussion lists and newsgroups, put the following information in your list entry, but only if the list maintains archives:

Name of author or authors. (Date of posting: year, month, day). Subject line or "thread" of message [message number, if available]. Message posted to [electronic address of newsgroup or discussion group]

```
Gracey, D. (2001, April 6). Monetary systems and a sound
    economy [Msg 54]. Message posted to http://
    groups.yahoo.com/group/ermail/message/54
```

```
Fontana, R. (2000, July 10). Origin of "Yo!" Message posted to
    news:alt.usage.english
```

Whenever possible, cite an archived version of a message:

```
Peckham, I. (2000, May 1). Class origins. Message posted
    to WPA-L eletronic mailing list, archived at http://
    lists.asu.edu
```

### 15g Sample APA entries: other sources

### 31. Personal communication (letter, telephone conversation, or interview)
Cite a personal communication only in your text. (See **14b**, item O.) Do not include it in your list of references.

### 32. Film, recording, or video Identify the medium in brackets after the title.

```
Morris, E. (Director). (1993). A brief history of time
     [Video]. Hollywood: Paramount.
```

### 33. Television or radio program

```
Keach, S. (Narrator). (2000, July 9). Storms of the century.
     New York: WNET.
```

## 16 Sample Documented Paper: APA Style

The paper that follows was written for a college course in experimental psychology. Check with your instructor to see whether your title page should strictly follow APA guidelines, as this one does, or whether it should be modified to include the course name, instructor's name, and date.

TITLE PAGE

Running head and page number on every page

5 spaces

Absolute Auditory Thresholds ↔ 1 ⟷

1" margin

Running head: ABSOLUTE AUDITORY THRESHOLDS

Absolute Auditory Thresholds
in College Students
Todd Kray
Hunter College of the City University of
New York

Centered title, writer's name, and writer's affiliation

APA ABSTRACT PAGE

Absolute Auditory Thresholds      2

Heading centered

Abstract

Seventeen college students participated in an auditory experiment, collecting data while working in pairs. In the experiment, absolute auditory thresholds were established and compared to "normal" thresholds. This study discusses details and plots results on two graphs for one pair of students: one 20-year-old female, and one 37-year-old male. While results paralleled the "norm" at many frequencies (125Hz, 250Hz, 500Hz, 1000Hz, 2KHz, 4KHz, and 8KHz), strong evidence for high frequency loss was discovered for the older of the two participants. Environmental conditions and subject fatigue were also seen to be influences on determining auditory thresholds.

Passive voice common in accounts of research

Results summarized

**TEXT FOLLOWS ABSTRACT**

Absolute Auditory Thresholds
in College Students

1″ margin

For decades, the branch of psychophysics known as psychoacoustics has concerned itself with the minimum amount of Sound Pressure Level (SPL) required for detection by the human ear. An early landmark study by Sivian and White (1933) examined loudness thresholds by measuring minimum audible field (MAF) and minimal audible pressure (MAP) and found that the ear was not as sensitive as had been reported in earlier studies by Wien (as cited in Sivian & White, 1933). Parker and Schneider (1980) tested Fechner's and Weber's laws, both of which concern themselves with measuring changes in physical intensity and the psychological experiences of those changes (Ansburg, 2000) and determined that loudness is a power function of intensity, which was consistent with Fechner's assumption.

An experiment was designed to utilize the method of limits, which establishes the absolute sensitivity (threshold) for a particular sound, to test auditory thresholds in college students and compare them to the "norm." Each threshold is determined by presenting the tone at a sound level well above threshold, then lessening it in discrete intervals until the tone is no longer perceived by the participant (Gelfand, 1981). The present study predicts that, according to Gelfand's (1981) summary of the research on normal hearing, college students' thresholds would be described as "normal."

Title centered, not underlined

Date after citation

Ampersand within parentheses

Author and year in parentheses

Hypothesis

Absolute Auditory Thresholds      4

Method

Subheading
italicized

*Participants*

Main
heading
centered

Seventeen college students in an introductory
experimental psychology course participated in the
experiment. The median age of the 5 males and 12
females was 24, with ages ranging from 20 to 37
years old. None of the participants claimed to be
aware of any significant hearing loss, and none
claimed to have ever participated in this or a
similar experiment before. All appeared to be in
good overall physical and mental condition, though
no formal testing was done in these areas.

Details of
participants

*Apparatus*

Specialized
equipment
described

Pure tones were generated by a B&K waveform
generator. The intensity of the tones was
controlled by a Hewlett-Packard 350D attenuator.
Tones were gated on and off by a push-button-
controlled, light-dependent resistor. This
provided for a gradual "ramping" on and off of
sound. The tones were presented to the subject
through a pair of Koss PRO/99 headphones. The
headphones were calibrated at all test frequencies
on a Kemar dummy head with a 6 cc coupler.

Passive voice
common in
description of
experiment

*Procedure*

Participants worked in pairs to run and
participate in the experiment. In each pair, one
participant controlled the waveform generator and
attenuator while the other faced away from the tester
toward the wall. Participants had been instructed
to choose an order of frequencies prior to taking
the test. They then administered the tests to
each other, trading "roles" after one block of
attenuated tones for each frequency was completed.

Absolute Auditory Thresholds    5

On the first day of testing, the method of limits
was utilized to determine a baseline threshold for
each frequency. Seven frequencies were generated:
125Hz, 250Hz, 500Hz, 1000Hz, 2KHz, 4KHz, and 8KHz.

The tests were administered in small cubicles
that were quiet but not soundproof. Participants
had been instructed to use their "good ear." Tones
were heard monophonically, through one side of the
headphones.

Eight blocks were run for each frequency, 4
ascending and 4 descending, in a semirandomized
order determined by the experimenter to help insure
accurate responses rather than the participant
being able to "guess it out." Participants were
instructed to say "yes" after each audible tone for
a descending block, until they could no longer hear
the tone, at which point they would say "no" and
that particular block would end. For an ascending
block, participants were to say "no" for each
ascending tone that they could not hear, until
the first tone they heard, at which point they
would say "yes" and that block would be complete.
Each response was recorded on a sheet of paper by
the experimenter, handwritten.

Results

For this pair of participants, 2 audiograms were
plotted to display dB SPL (decibel sound pressure
level) thresholds for Subject A and Subject B.
Threshold ranges for the subjects in one pair were
quite different from each other. Subject A's ranged
from 5.9 dB to 39.3 dB (Fig. 1); Subject B's ranged
from 2.7 dB to 26.6 dB (Fig. 2), resulting in a more
"normal" curve than the one for Subject A.

Details of
procedure

Main
heading
centered

Reference to
figures at
end of paper

Absolute Auditory Thresholds    6

## Discussion

Subject B's absolute threshold levels somewhat resemble those of "normal" hearing, as reported by Gelfand (1981) with a peculiar loss of sensitivity at 2 KHz and extreme sensitivity at 8 KHz. While loss of sensitivity is not uncommon for those who have had prolonged exposure to loud sounds, such as listening to a Walkman being played at the maximum level or attending rock concerts frequently, it seems odd that Subject B, who claimed not to possess these conditions, would experience a loss of sensitivity at 2 KHz, particularly at age 20. In the light of that, it seems even stranger that Subject B would have sensitivity greater than the norm at both 4KHz and 8KHz. However, the fact that both subjects had elevated thresholds at 2KHz could lead to the suspicion of faulty apparatus.

Subject A seems to be a classic example of somebody who would be prone to loss of sensitivity at higher frequencies. He had constant exposure to loud sounds as a result of over 2 decades spent playing in rock bands, frequently attending rock concerts, wearing a Walkman often in his youth, working in extremely loud nightclubs, and working in recording studios. In addition, he is currently 37 years old and may be experiencing the first symptoms of Presbyacusia--hearing loss at high frequencies due to aging. Subject A showed an extreme loss of sensitivity at 2 KHz (again, apparatus could be at fault here) and the loss at 4 KHz seems real when compared to Gelfand's (1981) norm.

Auditory testing over the years has provided us with no easy answers regarding absolute threshold.

Results evaluated with respect to hypothesis

Unusual results analyzed

Causes of results considered

Details of causes

Many of the articles cited in this study provide more questions than conclusions. Sivian and White (1933) inquired as to whether ear sensitivity was determined by the actual physiological construction of the ear or if air as a transmitter was responsible. It would be helpful to test for this in the future.

The tests themselves are problematic as well. It is easy to wind up with a masked threshold if thresholds are not measured in absolute silence-- not always an easy condition to create. Even under the best conditions that could be achieved in this experiment, demand characteristics and experimenter effects were unavoidable. The dial of the attenuator clicked loudly when turned, providing very definite clues that attenuation levels were being changed. In addition, the test, which took several hours to complete, caused subjects to feel fatigued and restless, making it difficult to concentrate at times.

Despite these hurdles, the experiment produced reasonable estimates for absolute auditory thresholds for college students and a reasonable estimate for a person experiencing symptoms of high-frequency loss due to abuse to the ear in the form of prolonged and excessive exposure to high volume.

Study related to prior research

Future research suggested

Problems with research procedures discussed

Results related to hypothesis

New page for references, double-spaced

Absolute Auditory Thresholds 8

References

Organized alphabetically

Ansburg, P. (2000, April 24). *Fechner's law* [Lecture notes]. Retrieved March 15, 2001, from http://clem.mscd.edu/~ansburg/sensationperception/splecchpt2.htm

Gelfand, S. A. (1981). *Hearing: An introduction to psychological and physiological acoustics.* New York: Marcel Dekker.

Parker, S., & Schneider, B. (1980). Loudness and loudness discrimination. *Perception and Psychophysics, 28,* 398-406.

Sivian, L. J., & White, S. D. (1933). Minimum audible sound fields. *The Journal of the Acoustical Society of America, 4,* 288-321.

Year in parentheses after author

Hanging indents (see **15c**)

Italics extend through volume number and commas

Absolute Auditory Thresholds 9

Figure Captions

*Figure 1.* Comparison of thresholds for "normal" and Sub. A.

*Figure 2.* Comparison of thresholds for "normal" and Sub. B.

Figure 1

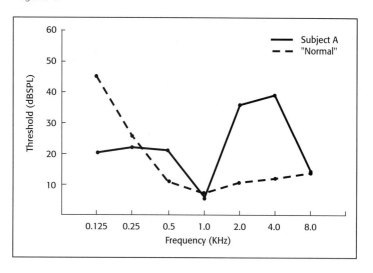

Figure 2

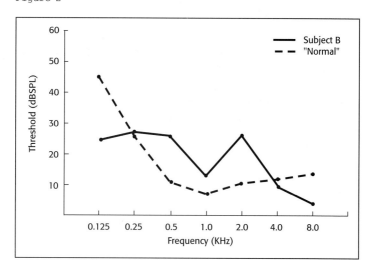

# 17 The CBE Style of Documentation in the Sciences and Mathematics

This section outlines the documentation style recommended by the Council of Biology Editors (CBE)—recently renamed "Council of Science Editors"—for all scientific disciplines in *Scientific Style and Format: The CBE Manual for Authors, Editors, and Publishers*, 6th ed. (New York: Cambridge UP, 1994). The *CBE Manual* recommends two systems of documentation, one an author/year system similar to the APA system, the other a citation-sequence system that numbers and lists sources in the order in which they are mentioned in the paper. Sections **17a**, **17b**, and **17c** give details for using the latter system.

## 17a Two basic features of CBE citation-sequence style

Always check with your instructor about documentation style guidelines. Some may not specify one particular style but will ask you to select one and use it consistently. For CBE citation-sequence style, follow the guidelines below.

### KEY POINTS

**Two Basic Features of CBE Citation-Sequence Style**

1. *In the text of your paper,* number each reference with a superscript in a smaller size than the type for the text, or place the reference number on the line within parentheses. Numbers run sequentially through your paper.

2. *At the end of your paper,* list the references by number, in the order in which you cite them in your paper. Do not alphabetize the entries. Begin the list on a new page, and title it "References" (see **17e**).

## 17b CBE in-text citations

Use superscript numbers to refer readers to the list of references at the end of your paper.

superscript number
```
One summary of studies of the life span of the fruit fly[1]
has shown....
```

Refer to more than one entry in the reference list as follows:

```
Two studies of the life span of the fruit fly1,2 have
shown that. . . .
```

```
Several studies of the life span of the fruit fly1-4 have
shown that. . . .
```

For the listed entries that the superscript numbers refer to, see **17e**.

## **17c** Guidelines for the CBE list of references

**KEY POINTS**

### Setting Up the CBE List of References

1. After the last page of your paper, attach the list of references, headed "References" or "Cited References."

2. Number the works consecutively in the order in which you mention them in your paper. Invert all authors' names, and use the initials of first and middle names. Use no punctuation between last names and initials, and leave no space between initials.

3. Begin each entry with the note number followed by a period and a space. Do not indent the first line of each entry; indent subsequent lines to align beneath the first letter on the previous line.

4. Do not underline or use quotation marks for the titles of articles, books, or journals and other periodicals.

5. Abbreviate titles of journals and organizations.

6. Use a period between major divisions of each entry.

7. Use a semicolon and a space between the name of the publisher and the publication date of a book. Use a semicolon with no space between the date and the volume number of a journal.

8. For books, give the total number of pages, followed by a space and "p." For journal articles, give inclusive page spans, using digits in the second number that are *not* included in the first: 135–6; 287–93; 500–1.

**17d** Examples of entries in a CBE sequential list of references

### Book with one author

no punctuation ┌── title not underlined, only first word capitalized ──┐

initials    2. Finch CE. Longevity, senescence and the genome.
with no              abbreviated        semicolon
periods         ┌─ publishing terms ─┐      number of pages in book
between     Chicago: Univ Chicago Pr; 1990. 922 p.

### Book with two or more authors

all authors'
┌──── names inverted ────┐
8. Ferrini AF, Ferrini RL. Health in the later years.
   2nd ed. Dubuque (IA): Brown & Benchmark; 1993.   470 p.
                              semicolon after publisher

### Article in a scholarly journal

1. Kowald A, Kirkwood TB. Explaining fruit fly longevity.
            no spaces in information
            ┌── about journal ──┐
   Science 1993;260:1664-5.
            volume number

In a journal paginated by issue, include the issue number in parentheses after the volume number.

### Newspaper or magazine article

6. Altman LK. Study prompts call to halt a routine eye
   operation. NY Times 1995 Feb 22;Sect C:10.

### Article with no author named   Begin with "[Anonymous]."

### Editorial   After the title, insert "[editorial]."

### Audiovisual materials   Begin the entry with the title, followed by the medium in brackets. Then include the author (if known), producer, place, publisher, and date. Include a description, such as number of cassettes, length, color or black and white, and accompanying material. End with a statement of availability, if necessary.

7. AIDS in Africa: living with a time bomb [videocassette].
   Princeton: Films for the Humanities and Sciences; 1991.
   33 min, sound, color, 1/2 in.

*Electronic journal article with a print source*   Cite as for a print journal article, and include the type of medium in brackets after the journal title. Include an availability statement and the access date.

10. Jones, CC, Meredith, W. Developmental paths of psychological health from early adolescence to later adulthood. Psych and Aging [serial online], 2000;15(2): 351-360. Available from: URL: http://www.apa.org/ journals/pag/pag152351.html. Accessed 2000 Sep 19.

*Electronic journal article with no print source*

9. Holtzworth-Munroe, A. Domestic violence: Combining scientific inquiry and advocacy. Prev and Treatment [serial online], 2000;3. Available from: URL: http:// journals.apa.org/prevention/volume3/pre0030022c.html. Accessed 2000 Aug 18.

**17e** Sample CBE list of references

The following list of references for a paper on "Research Findings and Disputes about Fruit Fly Longevity" uses the CBE sequential numbering system. Note the use of abbreviations and punctuation.

                    Fruit fly longevity    17
                      References
   1. Kowald A, Kirkwood TB. Explaining fruit fly
      longevity. Science 1993;260:1664-5.
   2. Finch CE. Longevity, senescence and the genome.
      Chicago: Univ Chicago Pr; 1990. 922 p.
   3. Carey JR, Liedo P, Orozco D, Vaupel JW. Slowing
      of mortality rates at older ages in large medfly
      cohorts. Science 1992;258:457.
   4. Skrecky D. Fly longevity database [online
      posting] 1997 June 19. Available from:
      URL: http://www.cryonet.org/archive/8339.
      Accessed 2001 Jan 14.

> 5. Muller H-G, Wang J-L, Capra WB, Liedo P, Carey JR. Early mortality surge in protein-deprived females causes reversal of sex differential of life expectancy in Mediterranean fruit flies. Proc of the Nat Acad of Sci of the US [online] 1997 Mar 18;94. Available from InfoTrac Searchbank: Expanded Academic ASAP: URL: http://web4.infotrac.galegroup.com. Accessed 2001 Jan 11.

## 18 *Chicago Manual of Style:* A System of Endnotes or Footnotes

As an alternative to an author/year citation style similar to the APA system, *The Chicago Manual of Style*, 14th ed. (Chicago: U of Chicago P, 1993), describes a system in which sources are documented in footnotes or, preferably, endnotes. This system is used widely in the humanities, especially in history, art history, literature, and the arts. For a *Chicago*-style paper, include an unnumbered title page, and number the first page of your text as page "2."

### **18a** Two basic features of *Chicago* endnotes

**KEY POINTS**

**Two Basic Features of *Chicago* Endnotes**

1. Place a superscript numeral at the end of the quotation or the sentence in which you mention source material; place the number after all punctuation marks except a dash.

2. List all endnotes, double-spaced, on a separate numbered page at the end of the paper, and number the notes sequentially, as they appear in your paper.

## **18b** In-text citations and notes

Use the following format, and number your notes sequentially.

> George Eliot thought that <u>Eliot</u> was a "good, mouth-filling, easy to pronounce word."[5]

### *First note for a source*

author's name ——— in normal order ———

title underlined, all ——— important words capitalized ———

5. Margaret Crompton, <u>George Eliot: The Woman</u>

comma page number
(London: Cox and Wyman, 1960), 123.

### *Second reference to the same source, immediately following the first*    Use "Ibid." (Latin *ibidem*, meaning "in the same place") only to refer to exactly the same author and work as in the previous reference. All the details except the page number should correspond to the previous citation.

> 6. Ibid., 127.

However, avoid a series of "ibid." notes. Instead, place page references within your text: *As Crompton points out (127),* . . .

### *Any subsequent reference to the same source*

> 14. Crompton, 124.

## **18c** Guidelines for *Chicago* endnotes

### KEY POINTS

#### Setting Up *Chicago* Endnotes

1. In the list of endnotes, place each number on the line (not as a superscript), followed by a period and one space.
2. Indent the first line of each entry three or five spaces. Double-space the notes.
3. Use the author's full name, not inverted, followed by a comma and the title of the work. Underline book titles (or use an italic font), and put quotation marks around article titles.

*(Continued)*

*(Continued)*

4. Capitalize all words in the titles of books and articles except *a, an, the,* coordinating conjunctions, *to* in an infinitive, and prepositions. Capitalize any word that begins or ends a title or subtitle.

5. Follow a book title with publishing information in parentheses followed by a comma and the page number(s), with no "p." or "pp." Follow an article title with the journal or newspaper name and pertinent publication information (volume, issue, date, page numbers). Do not abbreviate months.

6. Separate major parts of the citation with commas, not periods.

## **18d** Examples of *Chicago* notes

### *Book with one author*

9. Judith Thurman, Isak Dinesen: The Life of a Storyteller (New York: St. Martin's Press, 1982), 80.

### *Book with two or more authors*

7. George Lakoff and Mark Johnson, Metaphors We Live By (Chicago: University of Chicago Press, 1980), 22.

For a book with more than three authors, use only the name of the first author followed by "et al." (for "and others").

### *Book with no author named*

5. The Chicago Manual of Style, 14th ed. (Chicago: University of Chicago Press, 1993), 369.

### *Article in an edited volume*

14. Terrence Des Pres, "Poetry and Politics," in The Writer in Our World, ed. Reginald Gibbons (Boston: Atlantic Monthly Press, 1986), 25.

### *Article in a scholarly journal*

25. William W. Cook, "Writing in the Spaces Left," College Composition and Communication 44 (1993): 21.

When each issue of a journal is paged separately, include the issue number after the volume number: "83, no. 5 (1989): 16."

*Article in a magazine or newspaper* Include the month for monthly magazines and the date for weekly magazines and newspapers.

> 9. Marc Cooper, "Arizona: The New Border War," <u>Nation</u>, 17 July 2000, 22.

### *Film, filmstrip, slides, or videocassette*

> 13. <u>Citizen Kane</u>, prod., written, and dir. Orson Welles, 119 min., RKO, 1941, film.

*Online source* After any available print information, give the date of online posting, if any; the name of the database, if any; the URL and other retrieval information; and the date you accessed the material.

> 9. Geoffrey Bent, "Vermeer's Hapless Peer," <u>North American Review</u> 282 (1997), InfoTrac: Expanded Academic ASAP <http://web4.infotrac.galegroup.com> (8 January 2001).

## **18e** Sample *Chicago* endnotes and bibliography page

Check whether your instructor wants you to include a list of works cited or a bibliography of works consulted in addition to notes. The bibliography begins on a new, numbered page after the endnotes. List entries alphabetically, by authors' last names. Include full names, inverted, not just initials. Indent all lines three or five spaces except the first line of each entry. Double-space throughout. Separate the major parts of each entry with a period and one space. Excerpts of the endnotes and bibliography from a student's paper on the seventeenth-century Dutch painter Pieter de Hooch follow.

---

                                        Quinones    15
                            Notes
        1. Peter Sutton, <u>Pieter de Hooch: Complete
    Edition, with a Catalogue Raisonné</u> (Ithaca, N.Y.:
    Cornell University Press, 1980), 44.
        2. Wayne E. Franits, "The Depiction of Servants
    in Some Paintings by Pieter de Hooch,"
    <u>Zeitschrift für</u> Kunstgeschichte 52 (1989): 560.

---

Quinones    16

Bibliography

Bent, Geoffrey. "Vermeer's Hapless Peer." North
    American Review 282 (1997). InfoTrac: Expanded
    Academic ASAP <http://web4.infotrac.galegroup
    .com> (8 January 2001).

Botton, Alain de. "Domestic Bliss: Pieter de Hooch
    Exhibition." New Statesman, 9 October 1998:
    34–5.

Franits, Wayne E. "The Depiction of Servants in
    Some Paintings by Pieter de Hooch."
    Zeitschrift für Kunstgeschichte 52 (1989):
    559–66.

Glueck, Grace. "A Loving Home Life, Right Down to the
    Nits." New York Times, 8 January 1999, E40.

Sutton, Peter. Pieter de Hooch: Complete Edition,
    with a Catalogue Raisonné. Ithaca, N.Y.:
    Cornell University Press, 1980.

## **19** CGOS Style for Online Sources

Your instructor may refer you to Janice Walker and Todd Taylor's book *The Columbia Guide to Online Style* (New York: Columbia UP, 1998) for formats to use when you are citing online sources in the humanities or sciences, especially when a specific style manual is not up-to-date with its recommendations on citing Internet sources. CGOS provides full details, and regular updates are available at <http://www.columbia.edu. cu.cup.cgos>.

CGOS recommends indenting all but the first line of each entry in lists of works cited in the humanities and the sciences. However, if you publish a paper online, such hanging indents may cause problems, and it may be preferable to use no indentation at all and instead separate entries with a line of space. Check with your instructor.

## **19a** Two basic features of CGOS humanities style

The CGOS style for the humanities is based on the MLA style but differs in its recommendations for citing online material.

---

 **KEY POINTS**

**Two Basic Features of CGOS Humanities Style**

1. Use MLA style to cite the source in your text, giving page or paragraph numbers for online sources only if these are provided in the online site. They rarely are, however.

   ▶ **Science writer Stephen Hart claims that neuromusicology is being hailed as a "new discipline."**

   ▶ **Neuromusicology is being hailed as a "new discipline" (Hart).**

2. In your list of works cited, follow MLA style to include information about authors and titles and any basic print information, and then include information about the online source. Include whatever is available of the following items in the order indicated, each item ending with a period. Use italics (as shown below) in place of underlining if you post your paper online.

   > Last name of author, first name. "Title of document." Print publication information for book or article in MLA style. *Title of complete work or Web site*. Any version number, volume or issue number, access number. Date of online posting or update. URL (date of access).

   You can omit the URL if the database is licensed and access is limited to a specific library or institution.

---

## **19b** Sample entries in CGOS humanities style

In a works-cited list in print, titles would be underlined, not italicized. But in online documents, underlining is reserved for links, so italics for titles are preferable.

### Article in an online database

Lowe, Michelle S. "Britain's Regional Shopping Centres: New
  Urban Forms?" *Urban Studies* 37 (Feb. 2000). *InfoTrac:*
  *Expanded Academic ASAP*. Article A61862666.
  http://web5.infotrac.galegroup.com (14 Jan. 2001).

### Article in an online journal

Hart, Stephen. "Overtures to a New Discipline:
  Neuromusicology." *21st Century* 1:4 (1996). http://
  www.columbia.edu/cu/21stC/issue-1.4/mbmmusic.html
  (3 Nov. 2000).

### Online posting to a discussion group

Kramer, Wayne. "'Crossing Over' on Ifilm.com." 28 Apr.
  2000. *LatinoLink Bulletin Board: Criminal Justice*.
  http://boards.latinolink.com (14 Jun. 2000).

## **19c**   Two basic features of CGOS scientific style

**KEY POINTS**

**Two Basic Features of CGOS Scientific Style**

1. As with APA style, in your text give the author's name and date
of online publication:

 ▶ **Analysis of a large set of data shows that the statistical**
  **likelihood of being divorced increases if one is male and a**
  **secondary school teacher or college professor (Kanazawa**
  **& Still, 2000).**

2. Follow APA style for the list of references. Include whatever is
available of the following information in the order indicated,
ending each part with a period.

  Author's last name, initial(s). (Date of online publication).
  Title of online work. Any print publication information.
  *Title of complete work, online service, or site* (with any version,
  volume, issue number(s)). URL (date of access).

You can omit the URL if the database is a licensed database and
access is limited to a specific library or institution.

**19d**   Sample entries in CGOS scientific style

### *Article from an online database*

Lowe, M. S. (2000, February). "Britain's regional shop-
     ping centres: New urban forms?" *Urban Studies 37.2.*
     *InfoTrac: Expanded Academic ASAP* (Article A61862666).
     http://web5.infotrac.galegroup.com (14 Jan. 2001).

### *Article in an online journal*

Holtzworth-Munroe, A. (2000, June). Domestic violence:
     Combining scientific inquiry and advocacy. *Prevention*
     *and Treatment 3* (Article 22). http://journals.apa.org/
     prevention/volume3/pre0030022c.html (12 Sep. 2000).

# Technology:
## For Communication,
## Document Design, and Work

When we write, wherever we write, we deal increasingly with technology. We use computers to write online and communicate over the Web. We use word processing software to design college and work documents. Design operations that used to be so time-consuming with a typewriter, such as inserting headers and footers, inserting tables and graphs, and including illustrations, can now be done more swiftly and accurately. And when we need to edit or "cut and paste" material within a document, we rarely resort to white-out, rubber cement, press-on correction tape, Scotch tape, and scissors; for the most part, we revise on the computer. Not only in college are technology and writing closely intertwined. Technology plays so vital a role in the world of work that we can hardly imagine working without spreadsheets, word processing, e-mail, presentation slides, and Web sites. Part 5 takes a twenty-first-century approach, acknowledging the role of new technology in the writing process.

## ONLINE COMMUNICATION

Online communication can reach one reader or millions of readers. It can be one-to-one in e-mail correspondence; messages that reach a large, interested audience through networks and discussion lists; or documents displayed on the World Wide Web and available around the world. Sections **20**, **21**, and **22** deal with this spread.

## 20  E-mail

### 20a  Writing for online readers

Writing for a computer screen differs from writing for the printed page. Particularly when you post messages on e-mail discussion lists and bulletin boards, pay careful attention to the following.

*Length*   Be brief, and state your main points clearly at the start. One screen holds about 250 words, and online readers do not want to scroll repeatedly to find out what you are saying. In the business world, e-mail messages are used to speed communication, so their length should be tailored to the content and purpose of the message.

*Links*   When you provide links to other relevant documents, place them at the end of your message. That way, you will not tempt readers to click on a link and leave your message (often called a "posting") before they finish reading it.

*Attachments and graphics*   Writing online entails not just a linear progression of text but attachments to e-mail in the form of text or audio files, Web pages, graphics, even greeting cards. On the Web we are exposed to color, flashing and moving images, and many elements that may appear distracting. Always consider how attachments and graphics will add to your message and help you make a point (see **20e**).

## **20b** E-mail style and mechanics

*Format*   Some e-mail programs can handle all kinds of formatting, giving you choices of fonts, colors, columns, and graphics; other programs cannot. Also, some readers may deliberately restrict the capabilities of their e-mail program as a protection against viruses. If you send messages as plain text, not HTML (hypertext markup language), all readers will be able to read your messages, but you will not be able to include graphics. To send plain text messages in Netscape Communicator, go to Preferences/Formatting to set the option, and in Microsoft Outlook Express, go to Tools/Options/Send.

*Formal vs. informal style*   Considering your audience and your readers' expectations is as important in writing online as in writing on paper. Because of the spread of e-mail into business and other organizations, e-mail is no longer considered only an informal means of communication. It is often businesslike and serious, even when writers use contracted forms (*isn't, can't*) and a conversational tone. Use slang, abbreviations such as *BTW* ("by the way") and *BCNU* ("be seeing you"), and sideways "smileys" such as :-) and :-( only when you are absolutely certain that your readers expect and understand them.

E-mail offers a quick and efficient means of transporting a document. Edit your e-mail before sending if you are writing to people whom you do not know well and whom you want to take your ideas seriously—for example, your boss, business associates, or the anonymous subscribers to a discussion list. If you own your own computer with an e-mail program that includes a spelling checker and word processing capability, then your e-mails can always be edited. If you use an e-mail program such as Pine, or if you use a Web interface and not an e-mail client such as Eudora or Outlook Express, consider writing your e-mail document on a word processor, revising and editing it for clarity, and then uploading it into an e-mail system to send it. Such a strategy is also useful if your college restricts the amount of time you can spend online.

*Subject heading*    Subscribers to a list and regular e-mail correspondents are likely to receive a great deal of mail every day. Be clear and concise when composing a subject heading, so readers will know at a glance what your message is about.

*Line length and paragraph length*    Choose a line of 50 to 60 characters to make your text easy to read. Keep paragraphs short and manageable, so readers can take in the information at a glance. Use numbered or bulleted lists to present a sequence of points as brief items that are readily seen and absorbed.

*Spelling*    Many e-mail programs (such as Eudora, AOL, and Netscape Messenger) include spelling checkers. Although you may not bother using these tools on a quick message to a friend, do use a spelling checker in postings that go out to many readers.

*Mechanics*    E-mail programs do not always support the text features of word processors, so you might not be able to underline, vary your font and type size, or use boldface or italic type. Even if your system has all the features, they might not carry over from one system to another but instead get stripped out by the time your reader receives the message. Make sure your words themselves carry the meaning you intend. Do not rely on the mechanics of printing. See section **57** for more on punctuation and text features to use when writing online.

*Caution and tact*    Be careful about what you say and how you say it. Sarcasm and attempts at humor can misfire. Criticism can hurt. A reader can easily forward your message to another person or to an entire list—even though that reader is not supposed to do so without your permission first.

*Flames*    Sometimes a writer fires off a message full of anger and name-calling. Such a message is called a *flame*. Avoid flaming. If someone flames you, do not get drawn into battle.

*Signing off*    Always put your name and e-mail address at the end of your online message. It is not always obvious from an e-mail address who you are. Construct a "signature file," which will appear automatically at the end of every message you send. Find out how to do this from the help menu of your e-mail program.

 **20c** Netiquette

Letters written on paper and sent through the mail, reviews, reports, and arguments follow cultural conventions for their construction and presentation. The electronic culture, too, has its own conventions, often referred to as *netiquette* (meaning [Inter]*net etiquette*).

---

**KEY POINTS**

**A Twelve-Step Netiquette Quick Reference**

**Access Rules**

1. Always learn and follow the acceptable use policy (AUP) set by your college or Internet service provider.

2. Don't tie up computers in public labs with game playing when other people need to work and are waiting for a terminal.

**E-mail Rules**

3. Always end your message with your name and e-mail address.

4. Always include a subject heading.

5. Forward a message only if it is appropriate and if doing so will not harm the reputation of the writer. If in doubt, get permission from the original sender to forward the message.

6. Quote judiciously from an original message that you reply to. Do not automatically include the complete message in your reply.

7. Take reasonable care with your punctuation and spelling, and don't write in uppercase letters, SINCE DOING SO LOOKS AS IF YOU ARE SHOUTING.

**Research and Citation Rules**

8. If you quote e-mail in a paper, an article, or an online essay, try to get permission from the writer you are quoting.

9. Always give proper credit for anything you use or find on the Internet.

10. Make sure you give all the information needed for others to go to a source you have cited.

*(Continued)*

*(Continued)*

**Honesty and Decorum Rules**

11. Never use shareware (software available to the public at low prices and paid for on the honor system) without paying the fee for it.

12. If you get flamed (see p. 203), do not flame in return. Stay cool and respond with wit and good humor. Doing so will make you look cool and make the flamer look bad.

Adapted from Nick Carbone, *Writing Online: A Student's Guide to the Internet and World Wide Web*, 3rd ed. (Boston: Houghton, 2000), inside front cover.

**20d** Online addresses

In online addresses, pay attention to accuracy of punctuation and capital letters. Both matter; one slip can invalidate an address and cause you great frustration.

*E-mail addresses* An e-mail address consists of the user's name, the @ sign, then the name of the domain (the host computer). The last element of the domain name identifies the type of site or the country of origin. There are never any spaces between any of the parts. Many addresses are case-sensitive, so use capital and lowercase letters accurately.

name of organization
user name      Houghton Mifflin Company
▶ **Tom_Cutler@hmco.com**
type of site (commercial)

WHAT THE ENDINGS OF SOME ONLINE ADDRESSES MEAN

| | |
|---|---|
| .edu educational site | .org noncommercial organization |
| .com commercial site | .ca Canada |
| .mil military site | .cn China |
| .gov government site | .uk United Kingdom |

When you include an e-mail address in your own text, italicize it or, if writing online, enclose it in angle brackets:

▶ **Please send mail to** *Tom_Cutler@hmco.com* **after May 1.**

▶ **Please send mail to <Tom_Cutler@hmco.com>.**

*Internet site addresses* Each Web or other Internet address (known as a URL—uniform resource locator) begins with what is called a protocol tag (such as http:// or ftp://). Web addresses frequently contain www. (for World Wide Web) followed by the name of the server and type of organization, each separated by a dot (.), with no spaces anywhere in the address. The domain name ends with a suffix that indicates the type of site.

protocol ——— domain ———
▶ **http://college.hmco.com**
Houghton Mifflin Company        commercial site

Often a reference to a more specific linked site is added in a directory path after a single slash in the address:

protocol ——— domain ——— ——— path ———
▶ **http://college.hmco.com/products.html**

A tilde (~) in a Web address signals that the page is initiated by an individual or department in a larger institution:

protocol ——— domain ——— —— path ——
▶ **http://www.polsci.uiowa.edu/~liu.html**

Individuals can also have their own domain names, as in <http://www.stephenking.com>.

Web addresses are often very long. Copy them exactly, or, better still, use the Select, Copy, and Paste functions to avoid a slip. When you include a URL in a piece of writing, italicize it or enclose it in angle brackets. In an MLA-style works-cited list, use angle brackets to enclose all electronic addresses. If you need to spread an address over two lines, break it after a slash (MLA style) or before a period. Whichever style you follow, be consistent.

▶ **Recent press releases are available at <http:// www.whitehouse.gov>.**

[Shows break after the protocol slashes]

▶ **The *Internet TESL Journal* provides grammar quizzes for ESL students at <http://www.aitech.ac.jp/~iteslj/quizzes/ grammar.html>.**

[Shows break after a slash]

▶ **The ESL Help Center is at <http://www.eslcafe .com/help/>.**

[Shows break before a period]

If you want to copy, paste, and link to a URL that is split into two lines as the preceding examples are, you will need to splice the address together again into one line.

## 20e Attachments to e-mail documents

Most e-mail programs allow you to send your own text files and Web pages as attachments to your e-mail so that your readers can open them, view them, and easily file them if necessary. Suppose you want to send an essay draft to your instructor. You can do so by using the Edit/Select All and Copy commands in your word processor and then simply using Paste to insert the document into your e-mail. This method guarantees delivery, but most formatting and typographical features may be lost. An alternative is to use the attachment option in your e-mail program and simply attach the name and location of the file you want to send. First, however, you have to ensure that your word processing program is compatible with your recipient's. If it is not, you may subject a reader to a page of incomprehensible symbols. Try saving and attaching your own document in RTF (rich text format) or in HTML (hypertext markup language) to avoid issues of incompatible programs and alarming gobbledygook on the screen (though RTF files saved on a Mac may not open in Windows).

*Note:* Attachments can harbor computer viruses, so always be cautious about opening any attachments to an e-mail message. Open attachments only from known senders, and keep your antivirus software up-to-date.

## 21 Online Discussions

The Web provides many forums for you to not only find information but enter discussions with others and make your own contributions. Since many of the groups and forums are not moderated or refereed in any way, you must always be careful about evaluating the reliability of a source of information, but any discussion group can be valuable not only for the information it provides but also for the ideas that emerge as participants discuss an issue and tease out its complexities.

## 21a E-mail discussion lists

Are you interested in Peter Gabriel, the St. Louis Cardinals, bonsai, beagle puppies, orchids, the Argentine tango, the Battle of Antietam, writing across the curriculum? Thousands of e-mail discussion groups exist—some public, some private. The administrators of even a public list may screen potential subscribers carefully even though generally there is no fee for subscribing. Private lists and professionally moderated lists, especially those with a technical focus, can be reliable sources of factual information and informed opinion. Use Liszt at <http://www.liszt.com> or CataList at <http://www.lsoft.com/lists/listref.html> to find public lists that cover a topic you are interested in. To participate in an e-mail list, you need only an e-mail address and a mail program.

When you join an e-mail list (discussion group), all the messages posted are sent automatically to the e-mail accounts of all those who have registered as "subscribers." Lists are managed by specific software programs, such as Listserv, Listproc, and Majordomo, which have similar but not identical procedures. See <http://www.webcom.com/impulse/list.html> for a brief summary of the main commands for all three management programs. And see <http://maxweber.hunter.cuny .edu/eres/docs/eres/SOC325.22_KUECHLER/ho-lists.htm> for a step-by-step demonstration, with screen shots, of how to subscribe to a list. Use the following general guidelines for participating in lists.

**KEY POINTS**

**Guidelines for Participating in Mailing Lists**

1. A list has two addresses: the *posting* address (to send messages to all subscribers) and the *subscription* address (to send commands about managing your subscription). To differentiate between them, think of the difference between sending a letter to the editor of a printed newspaper for publication and sending a note to the circulation manager about a vacation suspension of your subscription.

2. Use the subscription address (not the posting address) to subscribe, suspend, or unsubscribe to a list (or make any changes in your subscription details). Leave the subject line blank, and include no signature or signature file in the message section—just the command to the list software. Follow the list's directions for the commands. The wording must be exact.

*(Continued)*

*(Continued)*

### EXAMPLES OF "SUBSCRIBE" REQUESTS TO TWO SUBSCRIPTION ADDRESSES

| To: listserv@lists.asu.edu<br>  Sub wpa-l Dolly Parton | To: majordomo@shiva.hunter<br>  .cuny.edu<br><br>  subscribe hunter-l Dolly Parton<br>  <dparton@hejira.hunter<br>  .cuny.edu> |
|---|---|

### EXAMPLES OF THE CORRESPONDING POSTING ADDRESSES

| To: wpa-l@asu.edu | To: hunter-l@shiva.hunter<br>  .cuny.edu |
|---|---|

3. Make a folder in your e-mail program for the list's instructions and messages you want to save. It is especially important to keep a copy of the list instructions, sent to you automatically after you subscribe, so that you know, for instance, if you can suspend mail during vacations and, if so, which command to use.

4. Lurk before you post! Spend time reading and browsing in the list or the list archives (Web archives are easier to use—look for a list that provides them) to learn the conventions and the types of topics before you start sending messages to everyone on the list.

5. Manage the volume of mail. A mailing list may generate 30, 100, or more messages a day, so after a few days away, you may feel overwhelmed. Use the options the list provides to select—for example, Nomail, Digest, or Index. Nomail temporarily suspends the sending of messages to your mailbox; Digest allows you to get only one bundle of mail every day; Index simply lists the messages once a day and you retrieve the ones you want to read. However, not all options are available for all lists.

6. If you want to reply only to the sender of a message, do not send your message to the whole list. A Reply command will sometimes prompt you to say whom you want to include in your reply. Some lists offer a default recipient—either the individual poster or the whole list. Make sure you know who will actually receive your message. Don't complain to Manuel about Al's views and then by mistake send your reply to the whole list, including Al.

7. Avoid sending a message like "I agree" to the many subscribers to the list. Make your postings substantive and considerate, so subscribers find them worth reading.

*(Continued)*

*(Continued)*

8. Do not forward a posting from one list to another unless you ask the sender for permission.

## 21b Usenet groups, Web forums, and bulletin boards

In addition to e-mail lists that require registering for a subscription and deliver postings directly to a subscriber's e-mail address, you can contribute to online discussion forums where anyone can read and post messages. Such forums are known by several different names—newsgroup, Web forum, bulletin board—and differences exist in the software managing them.

***Usenet groups*** The oldest system of bulletin boards started in 1979—long before the Internet and the Web became popular—and is known as Usenet ("user network"). Today tens of thousands of newsgroups cover every imaginable topic.

**NAMES** Newsgroup names begin with identifiers such as *rec.* (recreation), *sci.* (science), *comp.* (computing), *biz.* (business), and *alt.* (alternatives—a wide variety of topics). These tags give a rough indication of the subject matter: *alt.alien.visitors; alt.English.usage; biz.com.accounting; comp.ai.nat-lang; rec.arts.movies.production.*

**NEWSREADER ACCESS** Usenet newsgroups can be accessed via a newsreader (now often bundled with a Web browser or a mail program), which connects to a special news server at your Internet service provider (ISP) or your college. In AOL, for instance, go to Internet/Newsgroups/Add to find newsgroups you can access.

**WEB ACCESS** Some special Web sites offer access to newsgroups via a user-friendly Web interface. One of the best of these sites is at <http://groups.google.com>. There you can use a search engine to search for subjects and keywords that interest you, and you can read recent postings. Postings are organized by "threads" consisting of the first introduction of a new topic and responses pertinent to that topic.

**A CAUTIONARY NOTE** However you access newsgroups, keep in mind that postings stay posted for only a limited time, no control whatsoever exists over the postings, and you are likely to come across postings that offend your political, religious, or humanitarian beliefs. Usenet is anarchy. Nobody is in charge.

*Web forums, chat pages, and bulletin boards* Some restricted, some open to anyone, Web forums (also called chat pages) and bulletin boards are attached to Web pages and provide the opportunity for interaction and debate on topics pertinent to the page. Carlsbad Caverns National Park at <http://www.carlsbad.caverns.national-park.com/wwwboard/carlchat.htm> and many other national parks provide such forums (see below). Bulletin boards are often attached to course Web pages or to writing center sites, so that students and instructor can post queries and comments and respond to messages. For an example, see page 9 and the Colorado State University site at <http://www.colostate.edu/Depts/WritingCenter/ceilidh/wcenter/forum.htm>.

---

**Carlsbad Caverns National Park Chat Page**

Hall of Giants - NPS Photo

Press "**Reload or Refresh**" when you post a message to ensure that it was posted

[ Post Message ] [ FAQ ]

- **Two 13yr olds and me.... 40.** - Mrs. DTkz *16:39:34 8/02/100* (1)
  **carlsbad** - wesstex *23:36:33 8/03/100* (0)
- **entryfees** - kassylee *13:21:09 7/31/100* (1)
  **Re: Answers** - Utahtea *09:02:02 8/01/100* (0)
- **Entryfees** - kassylee *13:18:39 7/31/100* (0)
- **entryfees** - kassylee *13:17:32 7/31/100* (0)
- **admition** - kassylee *18:49:27 7/30/100* (0)
- **Carlsbad** - Stevie *10:50:51 7/23/100* (1)
  **None needed** - Paul Rabe *19:48:55 7/28/100* (0)
- **Iceberg Rock Explosion** - Deborah *16:55:01 7/19/00* (0)
- **Make plans now for third annual International Bat Festival** - Rick LoBello *23:18:17 7/16/100* (0)
- **ineedinformation** - carlos *17:38:24 7/15/100* (1)
  **Check this URL** - Paul Rabe *10/06/50 7/22/100* (0)
- **passes for national park** - JOHN KIM *11:19:01 7/07/100* (1)
  **Re: passes for national park** - Utahtea *17:05:44 7/07/100* (0)

---

## 21c Chat rooms, MOOs, and MUDs

None of the discussions in the forums described in **21a** and **21b** take place in real time. For all of them, you post a message, and then later, when someone logs on and takes the time to write, you may get a response.

Chat rooms and buddy lists, in contrast, operate in real time. Cable News Network, for instance, offers chat rooms to discuss CNN programs. A college writing center may offer to set up a chat room where a tutor can discuss an essay online with a student (see Colorado State University's site at <http://writing.colostate.edu/sndpaper/discuss.htm>).

MUDs (multi-user domains) and MOOs (multi-user domains, object oriented) are often accessed through a Telnet protocol at <telnet://>, but more and more are now accessible via the Web. They provide and describe real-time settings and spaces for interaction and role-playing. Conversations get going when a MOO or MUD is set up for a specific time on a topic, so that it can be a virtual community for a specific purpose. You can find a partial listing of MOOs at <http://www.csun.edu/~hceng028/#moo-list> and at <http://moo.domain.du.org:8000> (log in as WebGhost Viewer and click on MooList). A catalog of MUDs is available at <http://www.mudconnect.com>. Visit and learn the basic commands and conventions before you enter an ongoing conversation, such as always typing *&join* to ask if you may join in. See <http://www.hunter.cuny.edu/ieli/moo-cmd.html> for more on MOO commands. Abbreviations such as *ttyl* ("talk to you later") and *irl* ("in real life") are commonly used in MOOs.

## 21d Distance learning programs

Distance learning programs frequently make use of bulletin boards and real-life chat rooms where you can "meet" other enrolled students and discuss reading assignments or posted papers. For these programs, as for all e-mail discussions, the rules of netiquette apply (**20c**). You may never meet the students enrolled with you in the course, but you still need to be courteous and respectful of their views. In a distance learning situation, you may be asked to work collaboratively on some assignments. For more on collaborative writing, see **1h**; for more on peer review, see **3a**.

## 22 Web Site Design

### 22a The nature of hypertext

When we read a printed document, we read mainly from beginning to end, though we may do some skimming and scanning and peek at the end of a murder mystery to see whether the butler actually did it.

Basically, though, reading print is a linear process, as one word follows another, one idea follows another, one paragraph follows another. In contrast, when we read HTML-created documents in e-mail or on the Web, we can follow the links. Even in an e-mail message from a friend, we may read only a line or two and then come across an underlined or highlighted hyperlink (or *hotlink*) that with one click takes us to another document, with its own hotlinks, anywhere on the Internet. This kind of online reading is not linear; rather, it is associative and digressive. Often we start reading a Web page and then half an hour later, after following interesting links, we find ourselves pages and pages away and wonder how we got there.

## **22b** Tools for Web site design

The language commonly used for Web site design is HTML (hypertext markup language). Other languages are available for advanced Web pages. In HTML files, the visible text is supplemented by specific instructions, known as "tags," that are enclosed in angle brackets (< . . . >). However, if the sight of such tags and the often rather messy-looking "source code" makes you shudder, you can begin by using a program that creates the underlying HTML tags automatically (this is like driving a car without knowing or caring what the carburetor does). Recent versions of word processing programs can automatically convert a document and save it as an HTML file. Or you can use a WYSIWYG ("what you see is what you get") HTML editor such as Netscape Composer, Microsoft FrontPage, or—if you go high end—Adobe GoLive or Dreamweaver. All of them have the ability to insert links and graphics very easily without your inserting special codes—the programmers did the work for you, sparing you the immediate need to learn HTML. Many universities offer students home pages with their e-mail accounts and run workshops on Web page design.

Once you are no longer a beginner and want to do complex operations, then you will need to know how to fine-tune commands to get the look exactly right. The learning curve for HTML is steep initially, but people get the hang of it quite quickly. One good resource for HTML is the National Center for Supercomputing Applications (NCSA) Beginner's Guide at <http://www.ncsa.uiuc.edu/General/Internet/WWW/HTMLPrimer.html>. Another way to become familiar with HTML is to look at a document on the screen and then see how the effects are achieved and what codes have been used. You can start by finding a page of text and links and then going to View/(Page) Source to find out the HTML structure of the page. Be aware that some Web pages are subdivided into "frames"; if you want, you can display each frame separately in a new window and refer to it by its own URL. Note, though, that Web usability expert Jakob Nielsen has advised, "Frames: just say no."

## 22c Planning and organizing a Web site

Though the terms are often used rather loosely, a "Web page" can be viewed in a single window (though some scrolling may be necessary) whereas a "Web site" consists of a number of interrelated (linked) Web pages. Allison Marsh (pp. 217–18) has a Web site that consists of one start page, three second-level pages (university and professional information, personal information, and e-mail), and many third-level pages. In addition, many pages are subdivided into frames (her "side frame" is decorative and is used on more than one page). You will generate one page at a time, but you should start by considering the following:

- What is your purpose? What content do you want to provide? What message do you want to get across?

- Who do you think will visit your site? What will your visitors expect?

- How do you want to structure the site? How will visitors navigate around the site?

- How much maintenance will the site need (updating links and content, for example)?

Then draw a site map—that is, a flow chart that shows the logic of how the different parts of the site relate to each other.

Decide if you want to use single pages or pages divided into frames. Keep in mind that the way Web pages are displayed on a visitor's screen depends much on the size and setup of the visitor's monitor and the type, version, and setup of the browser he or she uses. What may look terrific on your own station may look messy on the station of a visitor, or—worse yet—parts of your page may not display at all. Basic HTML gives you only limited control of how your pages display on other stations. Therefore, keep your start (home) page simple, think twice before using nonstandard features (Javascripts, Java applets, and so on), and make sure that all links to the other pages within your own site and to external sites are easily recognizable and clearly indicate what content they lead to.

Allison Marsh's home page (p. 217) clearly links to three other pages within her site, which in turn link to other pages, internally and externally. Here is her site map for the first levels of her site.

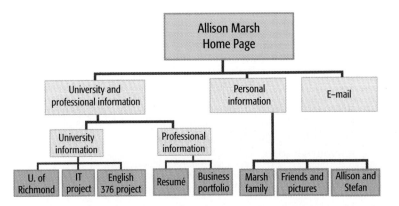

 **KEY POINTS**

**Web Site Design Guidelines**

- Keep pages short—as a general rule, no more than 2–3 screens.
- Set your own monitor to a resolution not higher than $800 \times 600$, and make sure all the text is visible on your screen without horizontal scrolling.
- Keep sentences short and direct.
- Break text into short passages.
- Use headings, and provide internal links to the headings.
- Use visuals—such as pictures, diagrams, photographs, graphs, clip art, or animations—to enhance and illustrate ideas. Graphics should offer more than a distraction. Pay attention to the file size of such add-ons. It is often possible to reduce the file size significantly with only a minimal loss of image quality.
- Choose descriptive text or images as "anchors" for links. Check on their reliability and keep them up-to-date.
- Use color and background patterns judiciously. Blue type on a black swirling background may look interesting, but it can be difficult to read.

*(Continued)*

*(Continued)*

- Keep the site uncluttered for ease of navigation.
- Include relevant navigational links from each page of your site to other pages, such as the home page. Consider the use of a "navigation bar" that appears on each page of your site.
- If you download and use text and graphics in your own site, ask for permission and acknowledge the fact that you received permission to use the material. Also, provide full documentation for your sources.
- Include your own e-mail address for comments and questions about your site. State the date of the last page update.
- Do not include personal information, such as your home address and telephone number.

## **22e** Useful resources

A writing handbook cannot cover many of the intricate details of Web site preparation. For more complete coverage, consult the following:

- Johndan Johnson-Eilola, *Designing Effective Web Sites: A Concise Guide* (Boston: Houghton Mifflin, 2001);
- Jakob Nielsen, *Designing Web Usability* (Indianapolis: New Riders, 1999);
- Jennifer Niederst, *Web Design in a Nutshell* (Cambridge: O'Reilly, 1999);
- <http://builder.cnet.com/Graphics/CTips/ss06.html> for a series of useful Web page design tips;
- Web design instructions by Tim Berners-Lee at <http://www.w3.org/Provider/Style/Introduction.html>;
- Library of Congress Resource Page linking to sites dealing with HTML at <http://lcweb.loc.gov/global/html.html>.

## **22f** Sample student Web site

Here are three pages of the site designed by Allison Marsh, University of Richmond, Richmond, Virginia at <http://www.student.richmond.edu/2001/amarsh/public_html/>.

**HOME PAGE**

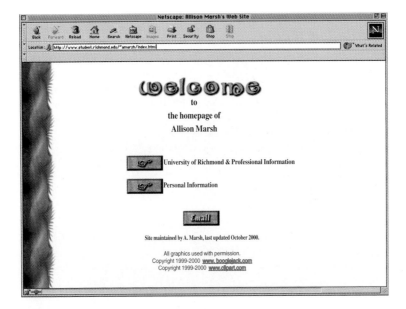

**LINK FROM "UNIVERSITY OF RICHMOND & PROFESSIONAL INFORMATION"**

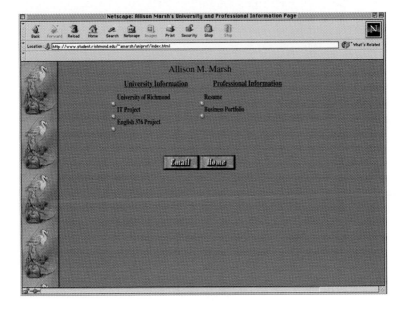

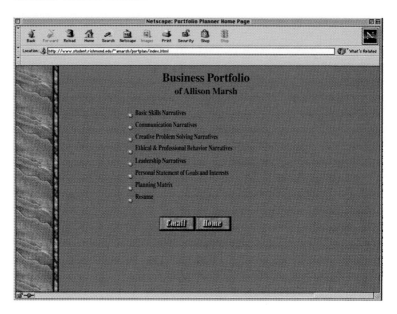

# DOCUMENT DESIGN

## 23 Tools and Design Features

Designing documents for college or business, in hard copy or online, involves many decisions. Make use of the technology your word processor provides as you consider page size, margins, typefaces, spacing, color, indentations, headings, lists, columns, boxes, headers or footers, and page numbering. The most important point to consider as you ponder these options is readability. What features will get your ideas across clearly in an attractive, inviting document?

**23a** Word processing tools for designing your document

Use the following screen capture of a Microsoft® Word 2000 (9.0) screen to find out what formatting tools are at your fingertips, though be aware that the appearance of the toolbars may differ according to the installation. In addition, earlier versions of Word and other word processing programs may vary in the capabilities they offer.

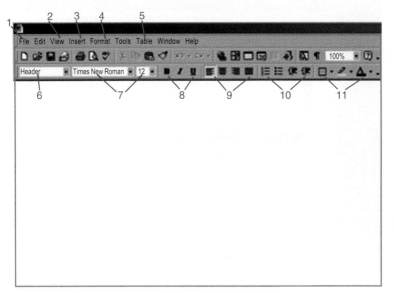

**1. File/Page Setup** Set page size, paper orientation, margins, and layout (page selection for headers and footers, line numbering, and so on). Do this before you start your document, or select all (Edit/Select All) or a portion of your document to set. (You may want to change the margins after you have written part or all of your document.) Print Preview shows what your pages will look like before you actually print.

**2. View/Header and Footer** By opening the View menu (see p. 220), you will be able to select the Header/Footer option. The toolbar allows you to (a) include a page number along with any text; (b) include the date and time; (c) toggle between the choice of headers or footers. Headers and footers will adjust automatically to any changes in the pagination of your document. You type the information once only, and it appears in the place you specify on every page.

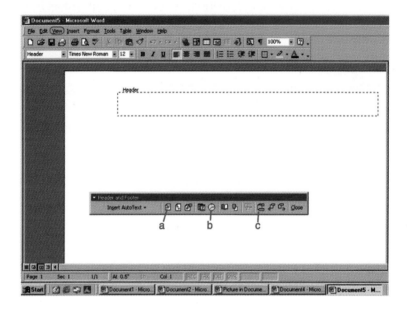

**3. Insert/Page Numbers** Use this command if you want only page numbers and no additional text in your header or footer. Select whether you want the page number to appear on the first page or not.

From the Insert menu, you can also insert date and time, a comment, a symbol such as ✔, a footnote, caption, a cross-reference, clip art, charts, pictures, and hyperlinks.

**4. Format** This feature takes you to menus for changing the font (typeface), style, and size as well as using superscripts (useful for *Chicago Manual of Style* citations). The Paragraph function provides options for line spacing and indenting (see p. 221 for how to set the special command for the hanging indents used in an MLA list of works cited). Here you can also make changes in Borders and Shading, Columns, and Bullets and Numbering for lists. You can also change a word or whole section of text from capital letters to lower-case or vice versa (Change Case).

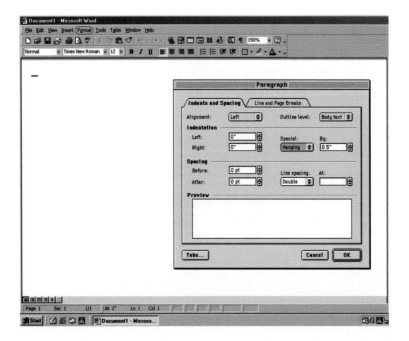

**5. Table**   Design and insert your own table with this feature.

**6. Style**   Here you can select Normal, Heading, or Envelope style.

**7. Font and Font Size**   You can select a typeface and size here or via Format/Font.

**8. Font Style**   You can select text and make it bold, italic, or underlined here or via Format/Font.

**9. Text Alignment**   This is useful for centering a title or heading. Otherwise use left alignment. Do not use Align Right or Justify for college essays.

**10. Lists and Indenting**   These buttons provide shortcuts for making a numbered or bulleted list and changing indentations.

**11. Borders, Highlighting, Font Color**   These buttons provide options for borders of paragraphs, tables, table cells, and graphics; highlighting text in a choice of colors; and selecting a font color.

## **23b**    Typeface options

Select your fonts (typefaces) with care. Don't overdo the varieties. The business text *Contemporary Business Communication,* 4th edition, by Scot Ober (Boston: Houghton, 2001) recommends the following typefaces in business correspondence, and the recommendation extends to college essays in hard copy:

- Times Roman, 12-point size, for the body of the text (This is a *serif* font, with little strokes—serifs—at the top and bottom of individual characters: Times Roman)

- Arial or some other *sans serif* font for captions and headings (The word *sans* is French for "without"; a sans serif font does not have the little strokes at the top and bottom of the characters.)

- Courier (This is an alternative if you want the typewriter look, with all characters the same width.)

Avoid excessive and unnecessary use of ornamental fonts such as *Coronet* and *Brush Script*. Note that if you are designing a Web page or an online communication, browsers cannot always read the more unusual fonts. For the body of your text, stick to 10- to 12-point type. Use larger type only for headings and subheadings in business, technical, or Web documents. Do not increase font size to achieve a required page length. You will convey desperation, and you will certainly not fool your instructor.

*Note:* MLA and APA guidelines do not recommend typeface changes or bold type for titles and main headings.

## **23c**    Color

Color printers and online publication have made the production of documents a much more jazzy enterprise than was possible until just recently. You can include graphs and illustrations in color, and you can highlight headings or parts of your text by using a different color typeface. However, simplicity and readability should prevail. Use color only when its use will enhance your message. Certainly, in the design of business reports, newsletters, brochures, and Web pages, color can play an important and eye-catching role (see **22**). But for college essays, the leading style manuals ignore the use of color.

## 23d Headings

Headings divide running text into helpful chunks and give readers a sense of your document's structure. Main divisions are marked by first-level headings, subdivisions by second-level and third-level headings. In the heading structure of section **24**, for example, the main heading is "Visuals," and the subheadings are "Tables," "Charts and graphs," and "Illustrations, clip art, and Web graphics." Generally speaking, you should use at least two subheadings—not just one.

For headings, bear in mind the following recommendations:

- Decide on the position of each level of heading: centered, flush left (aligned at the left with the edge of your text), or indented five spaces?

- Decide on typeface features for each level: bold, capital, underlined, italic, different size, color?

- Keep headings clear, brief, and parallel in grammatical form (for instance, all commands: "Set Up Sales Strategies"; all beginning with -*ing* words: "Setting Up Sales Strategies"; or all noun-plus-modifier phrases: "Sales Strategies").

See the APA paper in **16** for the use of headings and subheadings.

## 23e Lists

Technical reports often contain lists. Decide whether to use numbers, dashes, or bullets to set off the items in a list (see **23a**, item 4). Introduce the list with a sentence ending in a colon (see **23d** for an example). Items in the list should be parallel in grammatical form (all commands, all -*ing* phrases, all noun phrases, for example; see **40j**) and should not end with a period unless the listed items are complete sentences.

## 24 Visuals

The technology of scanners, photocopiers, digital cameras, and downloaded Web images provides the means to make documents more functional and more attractive by allowing the inclusion of visual material. Frequently, when you are dealing with complicated data, the best way to get information across to readers is to display it visually. Read, for example, the following:

In twenty-three years (1976–1999), the percentage of all wealth in the US owned by the richest 10% of the population rose from 49% to 73%.

A graph serves to illustrate the same data in a much more attention-grabbing way (see Figure 1, below). Such graphs are not easy to create, but they are available in abundance in print and on Web sites (the one reproduced here appeared in an advertisement in the *New York Times*).

**FIGURE 1  Where Do You Sit?**

Source: Chuck Collins and Felice Yeskel, *Economic Apartheid in America: A Primer on Economic Inequality and Insecurity*, The New Press, 2000. Reprinted by permission of TomPaine.com, The New Press, and United for a Fair Economy. Illustration © United for a Fair Economy (http://www.ufenet.org).

In a college essay read only by your classmates and instructor, cite the source of any borrowed visuals you include. If you intend to publish your work in print or online in any forum, you must also get permission from the originator of the material before you use it and cite it.

Computer software and word processing programs make it easy for you to create your own tables and graphs to accompany your written text.

**KEY POINTS**

**On Using Visuals**

1. Decide which type of visual presentation best fits your data and where visuals are to be placed—in text or in an appendix.

2. If you place a visual in your text, introduce it and discuss it fully before readers come across it. Do not just make a perfunctory comment like "The results are significant, as seen in Table 2." In your discussion, indicate where the visual appears ("In the graph below" or "In the pie graph on page 8"), and carefully interpret or analyze the visual for readers, using it as an aid that supports your points, not as something that can stand alone.

3. Give each visual a title; number each visual if you use more than one of the same type; and credit the source.

## 24a Tables

Tables are useful for presenting data in columns and rows. They can be created easily with word processing programs (see **23a**, item 5).

**TABLE 1   Percent of U.S. Households with Internet Access by Education of Householder, 1998 and 2000***

|  | December 1998 | August 2000 | Point Change | Expansion Rate |
|---|---|---|---|---|
| Less than high school | 5.0 | 11.7 | 6.7 | **134.0** |
| High school graduate | 16.3 | 29.9 | 13.6 | **83.4** |
| Some college | 30.2 | 49.0 | **18.8** | **62.3** |
| College graduate | 46.8 | 64.0 | **17.2** | 36.8 |
| Postgraduate | 53.0 | 69.9 | **16.9** | 31.9 |

*Note: **Bold** indicates above the average 15.3 point change and 58.4 percent expansion rate. Data from U.S. Department of Commerce, using U.S. Bureau of the Census Current Population Survey supplements.

Source: *Falling through the Net: Toward Digital Inclusion. A Report on Americans' Access to Technology Tools,* Oct. 2000. National Telecommunications and Information Administration, Table 1-2 <http://www.ntia.doc.gov/ntiahome/fttn00/charts00.html#t31> (27 November 2000).

## **24b** Charts and graphs

Charts and graphs come in many forms and are useful for presenting data and comparisons of data. Many software products allow you to produce charts and graphs easily, and even standard word processing software gives you several ways to present your numbers in visual form. In Microsoft Word 2000, for example, go to Insert/Picture/Chart, and in the Chart screen go to Chart/Chart Type. You will be able to select a type of chart and enter your own details, such as title, labels for axes, numbers, and data labels.

*Simple line graph* Use a line graph to show changes over time. Figure 2 has a clear caption, is self-explanatory, and states the source of the data.

**FIGURE 2   Growing Freshman Stress (% frequently overwhelmed)***

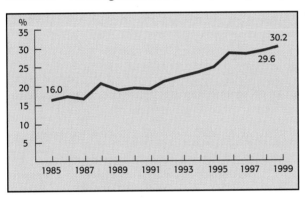

*Data from 261,217 college students.
Source: L. J. Sax et al., *An Overview of the 1999 Freshman Norms*, Los Angeles, Higher Education Research Institute, UCLA, 1999 <http://www.gseis.ucla.edu/heri/executive.htm> (28 November 2000).

KEY POINTS

**Using Charts and Graphs**

- Use a chart or graph only to help make a point.
- Set up a chart or graph so that it is self-contained and self-explanatory.

*(Continued)*

*(Continued)*

- Make sure that the items on the axis of a graph are proportionately spaced.
- Always provide a clear caption.
- Use precise wording, and place labels directly on the graph.
- Provide any necessary details about the sample population studied and the time. You may need to give this information in a footnote below the chart or graph.
- Always give details about the source of the information if the data are not your own.

*Comparative line graph* Line graphs such as Figure 3 are especially useful for showing comparisons of sets of data over time.

**FIGURE 3   High School Grade Inflation***

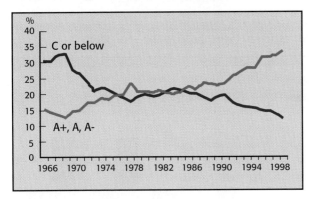

*Data from 261,217 college students.
Source: L. J. Sax et al., *An Overview of the 1999 Freshman Norms*, Los Angeles, Higher Education Research Institute, UCLA, 1999 <http://www.gseis.ucla.edu/heri/executive.htm> (28 November 2000).

*Pie graph* Use a pie graph (or pie chart) to show how fractions and percentages relate to one another and make up a whole. The pie chart shown in Figure 4 displays the results of a survey in a sociology course. Note that it is important to provide information about the number of respondents (N =  ), especially with a small local survey, so that percentage figures can be put into perspective.

**FIGURE 4    Start of Regular Computer Use: Hunter College Sociology Students**

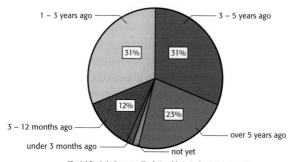

"Social Statistics" course (Prof. Kuechler), Spring 2000, N = 52

Source: Manfred Kuechler, Dept. of Sociology, Hunter College <http://maxweber .hunter.cuny.edu/eres/docs/eres/SOC241.00_KUECHLER/hw4-fb.htm> (7 August 2000).

*Bar graph*    A bar graph (or bar chart) is useful to show comparisons and correlations and to highlight differences among groups. The bar graph shown in Figure 5 represents the data in Table 1 (p. 225). The graph makes the differences immediately obvious.

**FIGURE 5    Percent of U.S. Households with Internet Access by Education of Householder, 1998 and 2000**

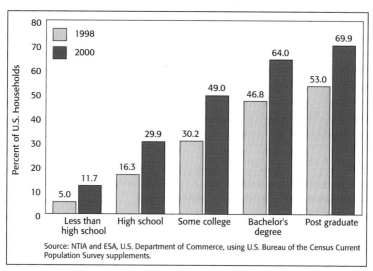

Source: NTIA and ESA, U.S. Department of Commerce, using U.S. Bureau of the Census Current Population Survey supplements.

Source: *Falling through the Net: Toward Digital Inclusion. A Report on Americans' Access to Technology Tools*, Oct. 2000, National Telecommunications and Information Administration, Figure 1-8 <http://www.ntia.doc.gov/ntiahome/ fttn00/charts00.html#f11> (28 November 2000).

A bar graph can also be presented horizontally, which makes it easier to attach the labels to the bars. Figure 6 presents the same data from the sociology course survey as the pie chart in Figure 4.

**FIGURE 6** **Start of Regular Computer Use: Hunter College Sociology Students**

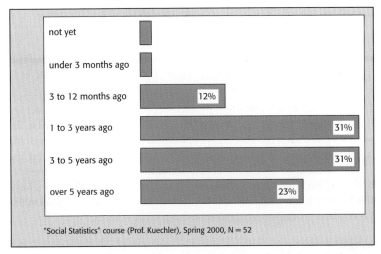

"Social Statistics" course (Prof. Kuechler), Spring 2000, N = 52

Source: Manfred Kuechler, Dept. of Sociology, Hunter College, 695 Park Avenue, New York, NY 10021 <http://maxweber.hunter.cuny.edu/eres/docs/eres/ SOC241.00–KUECHLER/hw-fb.htm> (7 August 2000).

## 24c  Illustrations, clip art, and Web graphics

Your computer software provides many standard images (clip art) and photographs that you can use free in your documents, without any copyright concerns. In Microsoft Word, for instance, find the clip art at Insert/Picture. Some Web sites offer free images to download: try <http://www.clipart.com> for free graphics and links to other clip art sites. Other useful sites are <http://www.screamdesign.com>, <http://angelfire.lycos.com/doc/graphics.html>, and <http://www .barrysclipart.com>. AltaVista also lets you search for specific images: <http://www.altavista.com/cgi-bin/query?pg=q&stype=simage>.

Sophisticated and original graphics are usually copyrighted, so if you intend to use an image in a document that you post on the Web or make available in print, you need not only to download the image and cite the source, but also to get permission from the creator to use and disseminate it. For a college paper, you may want to include an illustration you find on the Web, such as a map or an illustration from an online encyclopedia. You can do so without getting permission, but you must cite the source. Do not include graphics just because you find them and like them. A graphic should add to and supplement your text, not merely provide a decorative touch. If your document is to be posted on the Web, readers who have slow Internet connections or videocards may find it time-consuming or even impossible to download elaborate images, so keep images small and simple.

## 25 College Essay Formats

Perhaps you are wondering why this section refers to *formats* and not just to *a format* for college essays. The plural is necessary because the various pundits of manuscript preparation (such as the authors of the MLA, APA, and CBE manuals, the *Chicago Manual of Style,* and the *Columbia Guide to Online Style*) provide different sets of recommendations and because various disciplines and individual instructors have their own preferences. Whichever format you use, make sure you use your word processor's functions to help with your design.

### 25a Designing for page or screen

A major format consideration is the destination of your document: will you be presenting your essay on paper (hard copy), e-mailing it (to your instructor and/or classmates), or posting it on the Web? You will need to think of a hard-copy document in a linear way—readers will progress methodically from beginning to end, and information must fit in logically with the whole. For a Web posting, in contrast, hotlinks (electronic links to other Web sites) in your essay can do the work of descriptive and substantive footnotes, references to sources, and examples of external evidence. An essay prepared for Web posting also needs internal divisions, each with an internal link so readers can go directly to a specific section.

The design of a document is, therefore, a very real issue, for college essays as well as for business communications.

### 25b Guidelines for college essays (hard copy)

The Key Points box provides basic guidelines for preparing your essay on paper, whichever style guide you follow. See **23a** for using the formatting tools on your word processor.

**KEY POINTS**

**Guidelines for College Essay Format**

| | |
|---|---|
| Paper | White bond, unlined, $8\frac{1}{2}'' \times 11''$; not erasable or onionskin paper. Separate computer fanfold paper, and remove the strips. Clip or staple the pages. |
| Print | Always use dark black printing ink. |
| Margins | 1" all around. Lines not aligned on right. |
| Space between lines | Uniformly double-spaced. |
| Spaces after a period, question mark, or exclamation point | Most style manuals suggest one space. Your instructor may prefer two in the text of your essay. |
| Type font and size | Use a standard type font (such as Times New Roman or Courier), not a font that looks like handwriting. Select a regular size of 10 to 12 points. |
| Page numbers | Put in the top right margin. Use arabic numerals with no period (see p. 232). (See p. 232 for MLA format.) |
| Paragraphing | Indent $\frac{1}{2}''$ (5 spaces) from the left. |
| Title and identification | On the first page or on a separate title page. See **25c**. |
| Parentheses for sources cited | For MLA and APA style, give source information in parentheses for any written source you refer to or quote, including the textbook for your course (for an electronic source, give author only); then add at the end a list of works cited (see **11, 12, 14, 15**). |

## 25c  Title and identification of essay

Sometimes instructors prefer a title page. Sometimes they prefer you to include the identification material on the first page of the essay.

*Title and identification on the first page*   The following sample of part of a first page shows one format for identifying a paper and giving it a title. The MLA recommends this format for papers in the humanities.

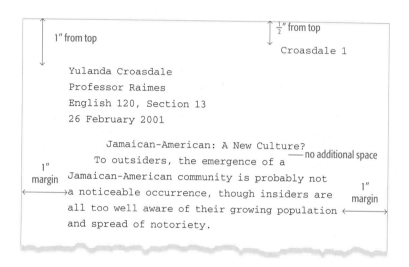

At the top of subsequent pages, write the page number in the upper right corner, preceded by your last name. No period or parentheses accompany the page number. See **23a**, item 2, on creating the page header in a word processing program.

*Title and identification on a separate title page*   In the humanities, include a title page only if your instructor requires one. On the title page include the following, all double-spaced.

*Title:* Centered, about one-third of the way down the page. Do not enclose the title in quotation marks, do not underline it, and do not put a period at the end.

*Name:* Centered, after the word *by,* centered on a separate line.

*Course information:* Course and section, instructor, and date, each centered on a new line, either directly below your name or at the bottom of the title page.

For the social sciences (APA style), see the sample title page in **16**.

## **25d** Portfolio presentation

Selecting work to include in a portfolio gives you an opportunity to review your progress over time and to assess which pieces of writing best reflect your abilities and interests. Choose pieces that indicate both the range of topics covered in the course (or in your course of study) and the types of writing you have done. To show readers that you are able to produce more than one type of writing, include pieces on different topics, written for different purposes. Number and date drafts, clip or staple all drafts and final copy together, and to each separate package in your portfolio add a cover sheet describing the contents of the package (for example, "In-class essay" or "Documented paper with three prior drafts"). Include a brief cover letter to introduce the material and yourself. Finally, pay special attention to accuracy and mechanics. Your semester grade may depend on the few pieces of writing that you select to be evaluated, so make sure that the ones you include are carefully edited and well presented.

## THE WORK WORLD

Communication in the work world frequently revolves around technology: telephones, faxes, computers, e-mail, presentational software, and spreadsheets. In business, knowing how to prepare documents for the screen and the page is a valuable skill whether you are applying for a job or communicating with colleagues and clients.

## **26** Résumés and Letters of Application

## **26a** How to write a résumé

Résumés can be delivered on paper, on the Web, or via e-mail. Designs differ, and no one format works for everyone. However, in all formats you need to convey to a prospective employer what you have accomplished and when, providing details of your education, work experience, honors or awards, interests, and special skills. Above all, you need to show that your qualifications and experience make you suitable for the job you are applying for.

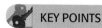

---

**KEY POINTS**

**Writing a Résumé**

1. Decide how to present your résumé: on paper, on the Web, or via e-mail.

2. For a hard-copy version, print on standard-size paper of good quality, white or off-white.

3. Use headings to indicate the main sections.

4. For a hard-copy version, highlight section headings and important information with boldface, italics, bullets, indentation, or different fonts. Use a clear, simple design. Do not use overly elaborate fonts or design features.

5. Keep your résumé to one page, if possible. Do not include extraneous information to add length.

6. Include information and experience relevant to the job you are applying for. Use reverse chronological order (begin with your most recent work experience and education).

7. Proofread your résumé several times, and ask someone else to examine it carefully as well. Make sure it contains no errors.

8. Accompany your print résumé with a cover letter.

---

*Note:* Microsoft Word provides résumé templates that set up headings for you—a useful guide.

## 26b Sample print or Web page résumé

Notice how Kenny Liu organized his résumé (see p. 235) into clear divisions, using bold capitalized headings, and separated the sections with space. He designed the résumé both for hard copy and for posting in HTML format on his Web page.

**KENNY LIU**
15 Maple Street
Iowa City, IA 52240
(319) 624-7918
E-mail *KLiu@mercury.aol.com*

---

**POSITION DESIRED**
- Public policy administration with city or state agency

**EDUCATION**
- University of Iowa, Iowa City, IA     1998–2001
  Bachelor of Science Degree in
  Political Science     May 2001
  Major average: 3.8
- Central Connecticut State University,
  New Britain, CT     1997–98
  Cumulative average: 3.4/4.0

**WORK EXPERIENCE**
- Worked as cook and waiter,
  Paul Revere's Pizza, Iowa City, IA     2000–01
- Worked with foreign students in Peer
  Counseling Office, University of Iowa     1999–2001
- Assisted with record keeping: New     Summer 1998
  Britain Department of Child Welfare

**ACTIVITIES AND INTERESTS**
- Served as chair, Debating Society, 2000–01
- Produced promotional video on immigrants' use of
  social services in Iowa City, 2000
  Won campus prize for video production, 2000
- Poetry; photography; film and video production

**SPECIAL SKILLS**
- Word processing: 55 wpm
- Computer: Familiar with Microsoft Word and Excel
  and with World Wide Web, WIN2000, HTML, and C
- Bilingual: Chinese (Cantonese) and English

**REFERENCES**
- Upon request and on file at Placement Office,
  University of Iowa, Iowa City, IA 52242

Further details and an online résumé can be found on my
home page at <http://www.polsci.uiowa.edu/~liu.html>.

## 26c The scannable or e-mail résumé

Companies often scan the print résumés they receive to establish a database of prospective employees. They can then use a keyword search to find suitable candidates from those in the database. You may need to e-mail your résumé to a prospective employer. In this case, adapt your print résumé to make it easy for users to read and scan. You do not need to limit the length of a scannable or e-mail résumé.

### KEY POINTS

#### Preparing a Scannable or E-mail Résumé

- Check any prospective employer's Web site to find its emphasis and important keywords.

- Use nouns as résumé keywords to enable prospective employers to do effective keyword searches (use "educational programmer," for example, rather than "designed educational programs").

- Use a standard typeface, 10 to 12 points, and for an e-mail document use "text-only" or ASCII.

- Avoid italics and underlining.

- Use a line length of fewer than 70 characters.

- Avoid marked lists, or change bullets to + (plus signs) or to * (asterisks).

- Begin each line at the left margin.

- Do not include any decorative vertical or horizontal lines or borders.

- Consult the Web site for the division of employment and training in your state.

- E-mail yourself or a friend a copy of your résumé (both as an attachment and within the body of a message) before you send it, so that you can verify the formatting.

- If you feel it is necessary, attach a note saying that a formatted version is available in hard copy, and send one as a backup.

- For further advice and examples of online résumés, consult the Résumé Writing Center at <http://jobsearchtech.about.com>.

## 26d Sample e-mail or scannable résumé

Here are examples of some changes Kenny Liu made to the beginning of his résumé to make it electronically accessible:

```
KENNY LIU          ——— not bold, not centered
15 Maple Street
Iowa City, IA 52240
(319) 624-7918
E-mail Kliu@mercury.aol.com          ——— not italic
                              ——— no horizontal line separator
                              work experience emphasized by placing it
                                              before "Education"
WORK EXPERIENCE
**1999–2001 Foreign student counselor, Peer
Counseling, University of Iowa          ——— nouns instead of verbs
**Summer 1998 Office intern and record-keeper, New
Britain Department of Child Welfare
```

*text aligned at left* (label pointing to left margin)

*asterisks in place of bullets* (label pointing to the asterisks)

## 26e Cover letter and sample

Accompany your print or e-mail résumé with a cover letter that explains what position you are applying for and why you are a good candidate for the position. Find out as much as you can about the potential employer and type of work; then, in your letter, emphasize the connections between your experience and the requirements for the job. Let the employer see that you understand the type of person he or she is looking for. Tell the employer when you will be available for an interview, and provide information about when, where, and how you can be contacted. As with the résumé itself, proofread the letter carefully.

The following cover letter by Kenny Liu is written in the modified block format, with return address, date, closing phrase, and signature placed at the right. (See **27c** for more on formatting business letters.) Kenny sent the letter along with a hard-copy version of his résumé, and he also e-mailed the online version of his résumé with a brief note attached explaining that a formatted version would arrive in the mail.

Return
address
and date
at right

15 Maple Street
Iowa City, IA 52240
April 9, 2001

Mr. M. Garcia
Pluzynski Associates Inc.
26 West 17th Street
New York, NY 10011

Dear Mr. Garcia:

**Identifies where he heard of job and why he is a good candidate**

I am applying for the position of advertising coordinator that you advertised in the New York Times on Sunday, April 8, 2001. I think you would find in me the "versatile and energetic individual" you seek.

As you will see from the enclosed résumé, I am about to graduate from the University of Iowa with a major in political science. My extracurricular activities have included counseling foreign students, running a debating society, and producing a video. Your involvement in public service announcements and in outreach to the immigrant community ties in with my past activities, and my experience with video and photography could be useful in an advertising setting.

**Matches his skills to those described in the ad**

**Tells when he is available for an interview and how he can be reached**

I am available for an interview during the last week of April, when I will be in New York, or at any other time convenient for you. You can reach me at (319) 624-7918 or at KLiu@mercury.aol.com.

Thank you for considering me for a position with your firm. I look forward to hearing from you.

**Thanks employer for considering him**

**Closing phrase and signature at right**

Sincerely yours,

Kenny Liu

Kenny Liu

## 27 Business Letters and Memos

### 27a Features of a business letter

A good business letter usually has the following qualities:

1. It is brief.
2. It clearly conveys to the reader information and expectations for action or response.
3. It lets the reader know how he or she will benefit from or be affected by the proposal or suggestion.
4. It is polite.
5. It is written in relatively formal language.
6. It contains no errors.

**LANGUAGE AND CULTURE**

**Business Letters across Cultures**

Basic features of business letters vary from culture to culture. Business letters in English avoid both flowery language and references to religion, elements that are viewed favorably in some other cultures. Do not assume that there are universal conventions. When writing cross-cultural business letters, follow these suggestions:

1. Use a formal style; address correspondents by title and family name.
2. If possible, learn about the writing conventions of your correspondent's culture.
3. Use clear language and summary to get your point across.
4. Avoid humor; it may fall flat and could offend.

### 27b Sample business letter

The sample letter on page 240 uses a block format, with all parts aligned at the left. This format is commonly used with business stationery. See **26e** for a sample of an alternative business letter format.

15 Maple Street
Iowa City, IA 52240          ]——— Return address
17 January 2001             ——— Date

Dr. Paula Chernow
Dean of Students            Name and
University of Iowa      ——— inside address
Iowa City, IA 52242         (see p. 214)

Dear Dr. Chernow:      ——— Salutation
                           with colon

**Block style, paragraph not indented**

I am writing to you in my capacity as chair of
the Debating Society on campus. We are hoping to
make a trip during the spring break to York
University in Toronto, Canada, to meet York's
team in a debating contest. (The invitation is
enclosed.) You will probably agree with us that the
trip will not only benefit the students involved,
but also pave the way for future events and enhance
the University's reputation. We would, therefore, like
to ask your permission to raise funds for the trip by
selling pizza slices in the main lobby of the student
union building every weekday from 11:30 a.m. to 2:00 p.m.
for three weeks, beginning on Monday, 19 February 2001.

**No justification at right margin**

**Single-spaced**

We propose to set up a table in the southwest corner
of the lobby, adjacent to the bulletin boards. The
pizza will be delivered to us by Paul Revere's
Pizza. The manager of that restaurant has agreed
to supply us with a microwave oven, paper and
plastic goods, and large trash disposal drums. He
will also provide the pizza at cost. We should be
able to realize a profit of 35 cents on each slice.

**Double-spacing between major blocks of letter**

Because we must make arrangements by February 7,
would you please let me know of your decision by
February 1? In the meantime, if you would like more
details, please call me at 624-7918, or e-mail me
at KLiu@mercury.aol.com.

**Suggests followup**

Sincerely yours,

*Kenny Liu*

Kenny Liu                  ——— Typed name

Enc.              ——— Materials enclosed

## **27c** Technical requirements of a business letter

*Paper and page numbering*   Use 8½" × 11" white unlined paper. If your letter is longer than one page, number the pages beginning with page 2 in the top right margin.

*Spacing*   Type single-spaced, on one side of the page only, and double-space between paragraphs. Double-space below the date, the inside address, and the salutation. Double-space between the last line of the letter and the closing. Quadruple-space between the closing and the typed name of the writer, and then double space to *Enc.* or *cc:* (indicating that you are enclosing materials or are sending a copy to another person).

*Left and right margins*   The sample letter in **27b** uses a block format: the return address, inside address, salutation, paragraphs, closing, and signature begin at the left margin. The right margin should not be justified; it should be ragged (with lines of unequal length) to avoid awkward gaps in the spacing between words. The modified block format (shown in the sample letter in **26e**) places the return address and date, closing, and signature on the right.

*Return address*   If you are not using business letterhead, give your address as the return address, followed by the date. Do not include your name with the address. (If you are using business letterhead on which an address is printed, you do not have to write a return address.)

*Inside address*   The inside address gives the name, title, and complete address of the person you are writing to. With a word processing program and certain printers, you can use this part of the letter for addressing the envelope.

*Salutation*   In the salutation, mention the recipient's name if you know it, with the appropriate title (*Dr., Professor, Mr., Ms.*), or just the recipient's title (*Dear Sales Manager*). If you are writing to a company or institution, use a more general term of address (*Dear Sir or Madam*) or the name of the company or institution (*Dear Gateway 2000*). Use a colon after the salutation in a business letter.

*Closing phrase and signature*   Capitalize only the first word of a closing phrase, such as *Yours truly* or *Sincerely yours*. Type your name four lines below the closing phrase (omitting *Mr.* or *Ms.*). If you have a title (*Supervisor, Manager*), type it underneath your name. Between the closing phrase and your typed name, sign your name in ink.

***Other information***    Indicate whether you have enclosed materials with the letter (*Enc.*) and to whom you have sent copies (*cc: Ms. Amy Ray*). The abbreviation *cc:* used to refer to *carbon copy* but now refers to *courtesy copy* or *computer copy*. You may, however, use a single *c:* followed by a name or names, to indicate who besides your addressee is receiving the letter.

***The envelope***    Choose an envelope that fits your letter folded from bottom to top in thirds. Use your computer's addressing capability to place the name, title, and full address of the recipient in the middle of the envelope, and your own name and address in the top left-hand corner. Remember to include ZIP codes. Word processing programs include a function (Tools) that allows you to create labels for envelopes.

**Net Note**    Businesses frequently use e-mail to conduct correspondence. In a business letter sent by e-mail, be just as careful about style, editing, and proofreading as you would be in a hard-copy version. You do not want to be seen as someone who litters correspondence with grammatical errors. Your mistakes may only be typographical errors. But how will the recipient know that?    ■

## **27d** Basic features of a memo

A memo (from the Latin *memorandum,* meaning "to be remembered") is a message from one person to someone else within an organization. It can be sent on paper or by e-mail. A memo usually reports briefly on an action, raises a question, or asks permission to follow a course of action. It addresses a specific question or issue in a quick, focused way, conveying information in clear paragraphs or numbered points.

Begin a memo with headings such as *To, From, Date,* and *Subject;* such headings are frequently capitalized and in boldface type. In the first sentence, tell readers what your point is. Then briefly explain, giving reasons or details. Single-space the memo. If your message is long, divide it into short paragraphs, or include numbered or bulleted lists and headings (see **23d** and **23e**) to organize and draw attention to essential points. Many computer programs provide a standard program for memo format. The design and headings are provided; all you do is fill in what you want to say.

**27e** Sample memo

---

TO:      All personnel
FROM:    Harold Moore, Vice President *HM*
DATE:    May 20, 2001
SUBJECT: Summer hours

Summer hours will begin on July 2 and end on
August 31.

On Fridays throughout this period, the
workday will be 8:30 a.m. to 12:30 p.m.

For security reasons, staff members who work after
12:30 p.m. on Fridays will be asked to sign out as
they leave the building.

Enjoy your extended weekends!

jrr


cc: Irwin Weinstein, President

*Margin notes:*
- Important information at beginning
- Short paragraphs in a memo
- Initials of person who typed the memo
- Courtesy copy to

---

# 28 Business Presentations: PowerPoint and Other Tools

When you have to give an oral presentation in a college or business setting, a useful tool is presentation software such as Microsoft® PowerPoint, in its Office suite of programs, or Corel Presentations. These programs allow you to create and save slides to accompany your oral presentation. For general guidelines for oral presentations, see **5c**.

## 28a The value of a multimedia presentation

Using a tool like PowerPoint to prepare a presentation gives you access to organizing tools. As the name suggests, PowerPoint forces you to think of your main points and organize them. Preparing slides that illustrate the format and logic of your talk helps you separate the main points from the supporting details and examples, and the slides keep you focused as you give your presentation. Your audience follows your ideas not only because you have established a clear principle of organization, but also because the slide on the presentation screen reminds them of where you are in your talk, what point you are addressing, and how that points fits into your total scheme. Presentation software also allows you to include sound, music, and movie clips to illustrate and drive home the points you want to make.

## 28b Preparation

The illustration below shows a PowerPoint screen (Office 2000, 9.0), with its choices of format for a slide: you can select anything from a title slide, a bulleted list, a table, a graph, text and graph, an organization chart, clip art, and text, to a blank screen. Toolbars provide you with the means to insert your content into the slide you choose: text, line drawing, line types, shapes, and color. Additional toolbars make it possible to insert a graph, clip art, and animation effects, such as a text line dropping in from the top, flying in, appearing one letter at a time, flashing, or sliding across from one side.

The slides you prepare can be used as a basis for overhead transparencies or 35 mm slides, as handouts, or as outlines for the audience or yourself. But the best use of the slides is direct projection from the computer on to a large screen.

You can import material from Word and Excel into a PowerPoint slide. PowerPoint comes with a self-paced tutorial, too.

Screen shot reprinted by permission from Microsoft Corporation.

## 28c Presentation

A computer with your PowerPoint slides can be connected to a screen for your presentation. Once you have prepared, sorted, and saved your slides, you can access them with a click. A slide can diagram the structure of your talk or provide material to support the points you make.

A PowerPoint specialist has advised, "If you have something to show, use PowerPoint." *Show* is the important word. Do not expect your audience to read a lot of text. PowerPoint is not for writing paragraphs and essays. It's for getting and keeping the audience's attention with the main points and illustrative details. Outlines, bulleted points, tables, pie charts, and graphs are what PowerPoint does well. See also **24a** and **24b**.

## 28d Sample slides

The PowerPoint slides shown here were prepared by New York City agencies. The first, designed by a member of the Municipal Water Finance Authority in February 2000, outlines three major points to be covered by a presentation and discussion, along with an illustrative map to orient the audience and accompany the presentation. The second, part of a presentation on employment in the public sector given in May 2000 by the chief economist at the New York City Office

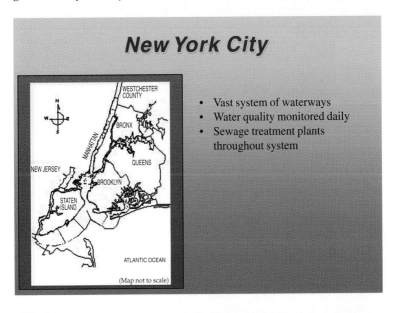

of Management and Budget, shows complex data illustrating how government employees and budget analysts fare in an earnings comparison.

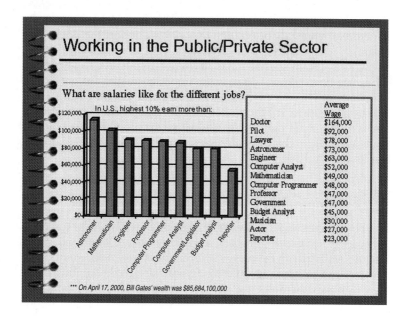

# PART 6

## Style

# THE FIVE C'S OF STYLE

# AN INDIVIDUAL VOICE

Sometimes, even when ideas are well organized, readers suffer from the so-called MEGO reaction to a piece of writing—"My Eyes Glaze Over." The readers are bored by wordiness, flatness, inappropriate word choice, clichés, and sentences constructed without interesting variations. Working on sentence structure and style can help prevent that glazing over.

With acknowledgment to Joseph Williams's *Style: Ten Lessons in Clarity and Grace*, 6th ed. (Reading, MA: Addison, 1999), sections **29–33** examine five anti-MEGO strategies, called here the "Five C's of Style": cut, check for action, connect, commit, and choose your words. Sections **34–36** present some stylistic options and tips.

## THE FIVE C'S OF STYLE

Consider these points when you are examining a draft.

### KEY POINTS

**Style: A Checklist for Revision**

1. Do any parts seem wordy or repetitive? Make your writing concise. Cut what you can. (See **29**.)

2. Are any sentences flat because of an unnecessary *there is* or *there are*, too many prepositional phrases (**37d**), or passive voice verbs? If so, ask "Who's doing what?" and revise. (See **30**.)

3. Do any passages seem jumpy, disconnected, and not easy to follow? Have you used coordination and subordination effectively? Aim for coherence and make clear connections. (See **31**.)

4. Do any passages seem weak and apologetic? Commit to critical thinking, to a point of view, and to confident language. (See **32**.)

5. Could any of your words baffle, bore, or offend a reader? Choose exact, concrete words, and eliminate clichés and language that is biased, inappropriate, or stuffy. (See **33**.)

6. Have you used a style-check program and exercised caution in taking its suggestions? Computer style-check programs alert you to such problems as possibly wordy phrases, repetition, clichés, sexist language, and colloquial usage. However, often they are not attuned to the subtleties of language and grammar. Never simply accept a suggestion as accurate.

## 29 The First C: Cut

You can improve most of your writing if you focus on stating your ideas succinctly. Examine your writing for unnecessary ideas, sentences, phrases, and individual words. Sometimes you may be tempted to pad your work to fill an assigned number of pages. However, work on filling pages with substantive information and commentary, not with empty words.

### 29a Cut repetition and wordiness.

Say something only once and in the best place.

▶ The Lilly Library ~~contains many rare books. The books in~~

~~the library are~~ carefully preserved. ~~The library also houses~~
    many rare books and manuscripts
~~a manuscript collection.~~

           director of
▶ Steven Spielberg, ~~who has directed~~ the movie ~~that has been~~ described as the best war movie ever made, ~~is someone who~~ knows many politicians.

▶ California residents voted to abolish bilingual education.
~~The main reason for their voting to abolish bilingual~~
        because
~~education was that~~ many children were being placed

indiscriminately into programs and kept there too long.

If your draft says something like "As the first paragraph states" or "As previously stated," beware. Such phrases probably indicate that you have repeated yourself.

### 29b Cut formulaic phrases.

Writers sometimes use formulaic phrases in a first draft to keep the writing process going. In revision, these wordy phrases should come out or be replaced with shorter or more concise expressions.

| FORMULAIC | CONCISE |
|---|---|
| at the present time | now |
| at this point in time | |
| in this day and age | |
| in today's society | |
| because of the fact that | because |
| due to the fact that | |
| are of the opinion that | believe |
| have the ability to | can |
| in spite of the fact that | although, despite |
| last but not least | finally |
| prior to | before |
| concerning the matter of | about |

**29c** As appropriate, cut references to your intentions.

In writing for the social sciences or sciences, the main goal is usually to provide information. State, therefore, how you intend to structure your argument, and then summarize that structure again at the end of the essay—that is, present a plan of your organization at both the beginning and the end of the essay.

In the humanities, readers want to read about your topic and usually are not interested in explanations of your thinking process and plan of organization. Eliminate references to the organization of your text and your own planning, such as *In this essay, I intend to prove . . .* or *In the next few paragraphs, I hope to show . . .* or *In conclusion, I have demonstrated . . .* or *What I want to say here is . . . .*

**29d** Cut redundant words and phrases.

Trim words that simply repeat an idea expressed by another word in the same phrase: *basic* essentials, *true* facts, circle *around*, cooperate *together*, *final* completion, return *again*, refer *back*, *advance* planning, consensus *of opinion*, *free* gift. Also edit redundant pairs: *various and sundry*, *hopes and desires*, *each and every*.

▶ The task took ~~diligence and~~ perseverance.

▶ He gave his Web page a background ~~in a yellow color~~. [yellow]

▶ His surgeon ~~is a doctor with~~ a great deal of clinical experience. [has]

## 30 The Second C: Check for Action

As a general rule, use vigorous sentences with vivid, expressive verbs. Avoid bland forms of the verb *be (be, am, is, are, was, were, being, been)* or verbs in the passive voice (see **42**).

### 30a Ask "Who's doing what?" about subject and verb.

Let the subject of your sentence perform the action, and use expressive verbs.

WORDY **The mayor's approval of the new law was due to voters' suspicion of the concealment of campaign funds by his deputy.**

This sentence contains three abstract nouns *(approval, suspicion,* and *concealment)* formed from verbs *(approve, suspect,* and *conceal),* as well as five prepositional phrases: *of the new law, due to voters' suspicion, of the concealment, of campaign funds,* and *by his deputy.*

| WHO'S DOING WHAT? | |
| --- | --- |
| SUBJECT | VERB |
| the mayor | approved |
| the voters | suspected |
| his deputy | had concealed |

REVISED **The mayor approved the new law because voters suspected that his deputy had concealed campaign funds.**

### 30b Use caution in beginning a sentence with *there* or *it*.

For a lean, direct style, rewrite sentences in which *there* or *it* occupies the subject position (as in *there is, there were, it is, it was*). Revise by using verbs that describe an action and subjects that perform the action.

WORDY **There was a discussion of the health care system by the politicians.** [Who's doing what?]

REVISED **The politicians discussed the health care system.**

WORDY **There is a big gate guarding the entrance to the park.**

REVISED **A big gate guards the entrance to the park.**

WORDY      **It is a fact that Arnold is proudly displaying a new tattoo.**

REVISED      **Arnold is proudly displaying a new tattoo.**

Use the Search function of your computer to find all instances in your draft of *it is, there is,* and *there are* in the initial position in a clause. If you find a filler subject with little purpose, revise.

### **30c** Avoid unnecessary passive voice constructions.

The *passive voice* tells what is done to the grammatical subject of a clause ("The turkey *was cooked* too long"). Extensive use of the passive voice makes your style dull and wordy. When you can, replace it with active voice verbs.

PASSIVE      **The problem will be discussed thoroughly by the committee.**

ACTIVE      **The committee will discuss the problem thoroughly.**

If you are studying in the social sciences or sciences, where readers are primarily interested in procedures and results, not in who developed or produced them, the frequent use of passive voice constructions may seem natural—for example, in lab reports and experiments, you will read *The rats were fed* instead of *The researchers fed the rats.* For acceptable uses of the passive voice, see **31a** and **42**.

## **31** The Third C: Connect

In coherent pieces of writing, information that has been mentioned before is linked to new information in a smooth flow, not in a series of grasshopper-like jumps. Connect ideas clearly for maximum coherence.

### **31a** Use consistent subjects and topic chains for coherence.

Readers expect to be able to connect the ideas beginning a sentence with what they have already read. From one sentence to the next, avoid jarring and unnecessary shifts from one subject to another. Let your subjects form a topic chain.

JARRING SHIFT    *Memoirs* **are becoming increasingly popular.** *Readers*
**of all ages are finding them appealing.**

TOPIC CHAIN    *Memoirs* **are becoming increasingly popular.** *They*
**appeal to readers of all ages.**

In the revised version, the subject of the second sentence, *they,* refers to the subject of the previous sentence, *memoirs;* the new information about "readers of all ages" comes at the end, where it receives more emphasis (**31b**).

Examine your writing for awkward topic switches. Note that preserving a topic chain may mean using the passive voice, as in the last sentence of the next revision (see also **42d**).

FREQUENT TOPIC SWITCHES    **I have lived all my life in Brooklyn, New York.** *Park*
*Slope* **is a neighborhood that has many different ethnic**
**cultures.** *Harmony* **exists among the people, even**
**though it does not in many other Brooklyn neighbor-**
**hoods.** *Many articles in the press* **have praised the Slope**
**for its ethnic variety.**

REVISED WITH TOPIC CHAIN    *Many different ethnic cultures* **flourish in Park Slope,**
**Brooklyn, where I have lived all my life.** *These different*
*cultures* **live together harmoniously, even though they**
**do not in many other Brooklyn neighborhoods. In fact,**
*the ethnic variety* **of the Slope has often been praised in**
**the press.**

## **31b** Put new information at the end of a sentence for emphasis.

If you preserve a topic chain of old information, new information will come at the end of a sentence. Make your sentences end on a strong and interesting note, one that you want to emphasize. This technique helps keep the flow of your ideas moving smoothly. Don't let a sentence trail off weakly.

WEAK ENDING    **Women often feel silenced by men, according to one**
**researcher.**

REVISED    **According to one researcher, women often feel**
**silenced by men.**

**31c** Explore options for connecting ideas: coordination, subordination, and transitions.

When you write sentences containing two or more clauses (**37e**), consider where you want to place the emphasis.

*Coordination*    You give two or more clauses equal emphasis when you connect them with one of the following coordinating conjunctions: *and, but, or, nor, so, for,* or *yet* (see **37b**). (For more on clauses, see **34c** and **37e**.)

▶ **The bus trip was long. The seats seemed more uncomfortable with every mile.**

┌── independent clause ──┐        ┌── independent clause ──┐
▶ **The bus trip was long, and the seats seemed more**

**uncomfortable with every mile.**

*Subordination*    When you use subordinating conjunctions (**37e**) such as *when, if,* or *because* to connect clauses, you give one idea more importance by putting it in the independent clause (**34c**).

▶ **We cannot now end our differences. At least we can help make the world safe for diversity.** [Two sentences with equal importance]

┌──────── dependent clause ────────┐   ┌
▶ **If we cannot now end our differences, at least we can help**

┌──────── independent clause ────────┐
**make the world safe for diversity.**            —John F. Kennedy

[Two clauses connected by *if*; emphasis on the independent clause at the end of the sentence]

*Transitional expressions*    Use words such as *however, therefore,* and *nevertheless* (known as *conjunctive adverbs;* see **37b**) and phrases such as *as a result, in addition,* and *on the other hand* to signal the logical connection between independent clauses (for a list of transitional expressions, see **2d**). A transitional expression can move around in its own clause—yet another stylistic option for you to consider.

▶ **He made a lot of money; however, his humble roots were always evident.**

▶ He made a lot of money; his humble roots, however, were always evident.

The Key Points box summarizes the available connecting options.

**KEY POINTS**

**Options for Connecting Clauses**

| COORDINATING CONJUNCTION | TRANSITIONAL EXPRESSION | SUBORDINATING CONJUNCTION |
|---|---|---|
| and (addition) | also, further, furthermore, moreover, in addition | |
| but, yet (contrast) | however, nevertheless, on the other hand | although, even though, whereas, while |
| or, nor (alternative) | instead, otherwise, alternatively | unless |
| so, for (result) | therefore, as a result, hence, consequently, thus, accordingly, then | because, as, since, so/such ... that, now that, once |

The following examples illustrate some options.

▶ Brillo pads work well. I don't give them as gifts.

▶ Brillo pads work well, but I don't give them as gifts.

▶ Although Brillo pads work well, I don't give them as gifts.

▶ Brillo pads work well; however, I don't give them as gifts.

▶ Brillo pads work well; I, however, don't give them as gifts.

Make your choice by deciding what you want to emphasize and seeing what structures you used in nearby sentences. If, for example, you used *however* in the immediately preceding sentence, choose some other option for expressing contrasting ideas. Notice how subordinating a different idea can change your meaning and emphasis.

▶ Although I don't give Brillo pads as gifts, they work well.

*Avoiding excessive coordination or subordination*  Too much of any one stylistic feature will become tedious to readers.

| | |
|---|---|
| EXCESSIVE COORDINATION WITH *AND* | I grew up in a large family, and we lived on a small farm, and every day I had to get up early and do farm work, and I would spend a lot of time cleaning out the stables, and then I would be exhausted in the evening, and I never had the energy to read. |
| REVISED | Because I grew up in a large family on a small farm, every day I had to get up early to do farm work, mostly cleaning out the stables. I would be so exhausted in the evening that I never had the energy to read. |
| EXCESSIVE SUBORDINATION | Because the report was weak and poorly written, our boss, who wanted to impress the company president by showing her how efficient his division was, to gain prestige in the company, decided, despite the fact that work projects were piling up, that he would rewrite the report over the weekend. |
| REVISED | Because the report was weak and poorly written, our boss decided to rewrite it over the weekend, despite the fact that work projects were piling up. He wanted to impress the company president by showing her how efficient his division was; that was his way of gaining prestige. |

**31d** Perhaps begin a sentence with *and* or *but*.

Occasionally, writers choose to start a sentence with *and* or *but*, either for stylistic effect or to make a close connection to a previous, already long sentence:

▶ **You can have wealth concentrated in the hands of a few, or democracy. But you cannot have both.**   —Justice Louis Brandeis

Writers and teachers who consider *and* and *but* conjunctions to be used to join two or more independent clauses within a sentence may frown when they see these words starting a sentence. Nevertheless, examples of this usage can be found in literature from the tenth century onward. If you do use *and* or *but* to begin a sentence, do so sparingly and when you aim for a special effect. And, given the difference of opinion on this usage, check with your instructor, too.

## 31e Connect paragraphs.

Just as readers appreciate a smooth flow of information from sentence to sentence, they also look for transitions—word bridges—to move them from paragraph to paragraph. A new paragraph signals a shift in topic, but careful readers will look for words and phrases—transitions—that tell them *how* a new paragraph relates to the paragraph that precedes it. Provide your readers with steppingstones; don't ask them to leap over chasms.

### KEY POINTS

**A Checklist for Connecting Paragraphs**

1. Read your draft aloud. When you finish a paragraph, make a note of the point you made in the paragraph. Then, check your notes for the flow of ideas and logic.

2. Refer to the main idea of the previous paragraph as you begin a new paragraph. After a paragraph on retirement, the next paragraph could begin like this, moving from the idea of retirement to saving: *Retirement is not the only reason for saving. Saving also provides a nest egg for the unexpected and the pleasurable.*

3. Use adjectives like *this* and *these* to provide a link. After a paragraph discussing urban planning proposals, the next paragraph might begin like this: *These proposals will help. However, . . .*

4. Use transitions such as *also, too, in addition, however, therefore,* and *as a result* to signal the logical connection between ideas (**2d**).

# 32 The Fourth C: Commit

Readers of academic prose in English usually expect writers to analyze and question their sources, to commit to an informed and interesting point of view (not necessarily to the dominant view), and to provide convincing reasons why that view is valid. For writers, commitment means researching and considering an issue, assuming a critical stance, taking a position, and persuasively supporting that position (**4a–4f**).

## **32a** Commit to critical thinking.

Critical thinking does not mean criticizing negatively. It means examining and analyzing information with an open mind. Whether you are writing a business analysis, an essay about literature, or a persuasive argument, committing to critical thinking is a necessary first step.

Develop a system of inquiry. Do not assume that because something is in print, it is accurate. A system of inquiry will lead you to use certain stylistic features in your writing: questions, reflective statements about the position of authors you read, and statements that point out an alternative view (introduced with transitional phrases such as *but, however, on the other hand,* and *this also indicates that . . .*). When you think critically, your writing takes on your own voice, your own stance. It becomes engaged and vital, a reflection of your thinking rather than a regurgitation of others' opinions. Following are suggestions to help you develop a style reflecting critical thinking skills.

*Write journal entries.*   When you read or research an issue, keep a journal of your responses to what you read. There, in your own ungraded writing, you can write summaries, make inferences, ask questions, challenge views, and reflect on the opinions of others.

*Observe details.*   In your journal entries, e-mails, letters, conversations, and papers, develop your skill in observing and remembering details: the names of characters in a novel, the author of a magazine article, the main points in a lecture, and so on.

*Ask questions.*   In spoken discussion, in the margins of books or articles, or in your journal, ask questions. Interact with ideas. As—or after—you read an article or listen to a lecture, write questions that you would like to see answered about the specific content covered. When confronting new information, ask yourself these questions:

What do I need to know to understand this information fully?

Where does this information come from?

What are the author's purpose and bias?

What evidence does the author provide? Do I find that evidence convincing?

How does this information fit with what I already know?

What else do I need to ask?

*Look for assumptions and bias.* Writers often work to establish common ground with their readers. When you read, determine what that common ground is. What audience is the writer writing for? Is the writer presenting facts or opinions? What does the writer assume about the reader? Do you accept the writer's assumptions? See **4e.**

*Understand other viewpoints, and consider alternatives.* If you read an argument that you disagree with, do not automatically reject it or write it off as ridiculous. Try to understand why the writer holds the opinion, what the writer's background is, and what audience the writer is writing for. Such reflection can lead to concessive statements (those that yield to, grant, or acknowledge an opposing position) in your writing, such as "The author explains why he holds this view, and he does so convincingly for the small segment of the population he addresses. However, ..."

*Analyze and evaluate arguments.* Analyze how writers present information. If they classify information, do their categories cover all the material? If they compare and contrast, are their points solid or stretched? If they speculate about cause and effect, do they do a thorough job? Similarly, when you write and revise, consider your own presentation of information, and anticipate and address any objections or questions readers might have. As you evaluate other writers' logic, watch for flaws in your own logic, and construct your arguments with care. For more on critical thinking and critical reading, see **4f** and **8a.**

## **32b** Commit to a point of view.

Your background reading, critical thinking, and drafting will help you discover and decide upon a perspective and thesis that seem correct to you (**1e**). Once you have made those decisions, commit to that point of view. When you are trying to persuade readers to accept your point of view, avoid the ambivalence and indecisiveness evident in words and phrases like *maybe, perhaps, it could be, it might seem,* and *it would appear.* Aim for language that reflects accountability and commitment: *as a result, consequently, of course, believe, need, demand, should, must.* Use the language of commitment, however, only after thoroughly researching your topic and satisfying yourself that the evidence is convincing.

**32c** Commit to a confident stance.

Convey to readers an attitude of confidence in your own abilities and judgment. Readers will not be impressed by apologies. One student ended an essay draft this way:

Too
APOLOGETIC
> I hope I have conveyed something about our cultural differences. I would like my reader to note that this is just my view, even if a unique one. Room for errors and prejudices should be provided. The lack of a total overview, which would take more time and expertise, should also be taken into account.

If you really have not done an adequate job of making and supporting a point, try to gather more information to improve the draft instead of adding apologetic notes. The student writer revised the ending after reading **2e** on conclusions.

REVISED
VERSION
> The stories I have told and the examples I have given come from my own experience, but they illustrate clearly the idea that in one place and at one time, cultural differences did not have to separate people but could bring them closer together. A diverse, multicultural society holds many potential benefits for all its members.

 **33 The Fifth C: Choose Your Words**

Word choice, or *diction,* contributes a great deal to the effect your writing has on your readers. Do not give readers puzzles to solve.

**33a** Word choice checklist

 **KEY POINTS**

**Word Choice: A Checklist for Revision**

1. Underline words whose meaning or spelling you want to check and words that you might want to replace. Then spend some time with a dictionary and a thesaurus. **(33b)**

*(Continued)*

*(Continued)*

2. Look for words that might not convey exactly what you mean (*thrifty* vs. *stingy,* for example), and look for vague words. (**33c**)

3. Check figurative language for appropriateness, think about where a simile (a comparison) might help convey your meaning, and find original substitutes for any clichés. (**33e, 33g**)

4. Check for tone, level of formality, and the appropriateness of any colloquial, regional, ethnic, or specialized work terms. (**33d**)

5. Check for gender bias in your use of *he* and *she* and other words that show gender. (**33f**)

6. Look for language that might exclude or offend (such as *normal* to mean people similar to you). Build community with your readers by eliminating disrespectful or stereotyping terms referring to race, place, age, politics, religion, abilities, or sexual orientation. (**33f**)

## **33b** Use a dictionary and a thesaurus.

A good dictionary contains a wealth of information—spelling and definitions, syllable breaks, pronunciation, grammatical functions and features, word forms, etymology (word origins and historical development), usage, synonyms (words of similar meaning), and antonyms (words of opposite meaning). The following dictionary entry from *The American Heritage Dictionary of the English Language,* 4th ed., shows how much information is available. A "Usage Note" after this entry endorses using "She graduated from Yale in 1998" but notes that "She graduated Yale in 1998" was unacceptable to 77 percent of a usage panel.

Use a dictionary to learn or confirm the *denotation*—the basic meaning—of a word. Some words that appear similar are not interchangeable. For example, *respectable* has a meaning very different from *respectful; emigrant* and *immigrant* have different meanings; and so do *defuse* and *diffuse, uninterested* and *disinterested,* and *principal* and *principle.*

A thesaurus is useful when you want to find alternatives to words that you know. Exercise caution, however, to make sure that the word you choose fits your context. Suppose you use the word *privacy* a few

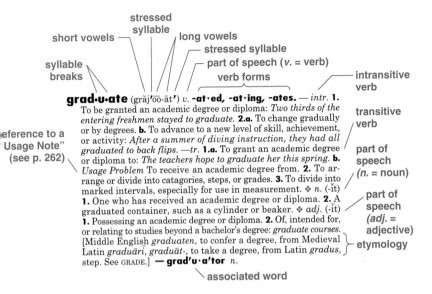

short vowels

stressed syllable

long vowels

stressed syllable

part of speech (*v.* = verb)

verb forms

intransitive verb

syllable breaks

transitive verb

reference to a "Usage Note" (see p. 262)

part of speech (*n.* = noun)

part of speech (*adj.* = adjective)

etymology

associated word

**grad·u·ate** (grăj'ōō-āt') *v.* **-at·ed, -at·ing, -ates.** — *intr.* **1.** To be granted an academic degree or diploma: *Two thirds of the entering freshmen stayed to graduate.* **2.a.** To change gradually or by degrees. **b.** To advance to a new level of skill, achievement, or activity: *After a summer of diving instruction, they had all graduated to back flips.* —*tr.* **1.a.** To grant an academic degree or diploma to: *The teachers hope to graduate her this spring.* **b.** *Usage Problem* To receive an academic degree from. **2.** To arrange or divide into catagories, steps, or grades. **3.** To divide into marked intervals, especially for use in measurement. ❖ *n.* (-ĭt) **1.** One who has received an academic degree or diploma. **2.** A graduated container, such as a cylinder or beaker. ❖ *adj.* (-ĭt) **1.** Possessing an academic degree or diploma. **2.** Of, intended for, or relating to studies beyond a bachelor's degree: *graduate courses.* [Middle English *graduaten,* to confer a degree, from Medieval Latin *graduāri, graduāt-,* to take a degree, from Latin *gradus,* step. See GRADE.] — **grad'u·a'tor** *n.*

times and want an alternative in the sentence "She values the privacy of her own home." You could consult a thesaurus. The following entry, from Barbara Ann Kipfer, *Roget's Twenty-first Century Thesaurus,* provides synonyms listed alphabetically:

> **privacy** *n.* aloofness, clandestineness, concealment, confidentiality, isolation, one's space, penetralia, privateness, quiet, retirement, retreat, seclusion, separateness, separation, sequestration, solitude.

The word *aloofness* would not work as a replacement for *privacy* in the example sentence. *Seclusion* would probably be the best choice, but the thesaurus has no way of letting you know that. Using a thesaurus along with a dictionary allows you to find the exact word or words you need. You might, in the end, want to use two words to convey your meaning: *She values the* safety *and* seclusion *of her own home.*

Thesaurus programs attached to word processing programs typically offer lists of synonyms but little guidance on *connotation*—the meaning associated with a word beyond its literal definition. Always check a word in a dictionary.

**33C** Use exact words and connotations.

When you write, use words that convey exactly the meaning you intend. Two words that have similar dictionary definitions (*denotation*) can also have additional positive or negative implications and emotional overtones (*connotation*). Readers will not get the impression you intend if you describe a person as *lazy* when you mean *relaxed*.

Select words with appropriate connotations. Hurricanes *devastate* neighborhoods; construction workers *demolish* buildings. Writing "Construction workers devastated the building" would be inappropriate. Note how word choice can affect meaning:

VERSION 1    **The crowd consisted of young couples holding their children's hands, students in well-worn clothes, and activist politicians, all voicing support of their cause.**

VERSION 2    **The mob consisted of hard-faced workers dragging children by the hand, students in leather jackets and ragged jeans, and militant politicians, all howling about their cause.**

Some words do little more than fill space because they are so vague. Words such as the following signal the need for revision: *area, aspect, certain, circumstance, factor, kind, manner, nature, seem, situation, thing.*

VAGUE    **Our perceptions of women's roles differ as we enter new *areas*. The girl in Kincaid's story did many *things* that are commonly seen as women's work.**

REVISED    **Our perceptions of women's roles differ as we learn more from what we *see, hear, read, and experience*. The girl in Kincaid's story did many *household chores* that are commonly seen as women's work. She washed the clothes, cooked, swept the floor, and set the table.**

Some words are abstract and general; other words are concrete and specific. Notice the increasing concreteness and specificity in this list: *tool, cutting instrument, knife, penknife*. If you do not move away from the general and abstract, you will give readers too much imaginative leeway. "Her grandmother was shocked by the clothing she bought" leaves a great deal to readers' imaginations. What kind of clothing do you mean: a low-necked dress, high-heeled platform shoes, and black fishnet stockings, or a conservative navy blue wool suit? Choose words that convey exact images and precise information.

**33d** Monitor tone and use of the language of speech, region, and workplace.

*Tone and level of formality*   The words and structures you choose convey a tone. They reveal a great deal about you and your attitude toward your readers and your topic. Readers sense your tone when they read your work and say it sounds, for example, humorous, serious, friendly, sincere, stuffy, critical, aggressive, sarcastic, respectful, or deferential. For most academic writing, aim for a serious and sincere tone. Avoid sarcasm, street talk, and name-calling. Note that the synonyms of the italicized words listed below convey different attitudes and different degrees of formality:

> *child:* kid, offspring, progeny
>
> *friend:* pal, buddy, chum, mate, brother / sister, comrade
>
> *jail:* slammer, cooler, prison, correctional institution
>
> *angry:* ticked off, furious, mad, fuming, wrathful
>
> *computer expert:* geek, hacker, techie, programmer
>
> *threatening:* spooky, scary, eerie, menacing

Some of these words—*kid, pal, slammer, ticked off, geek, spooky*—are so informal that they would rarely if ever be appropriate in formal academic writing or business letters, though they would raise no eyebrows in journalism, advertising, or e-mail. Overuse of the formal words—*progeny, comrade, wrathful*—on the other hand, could produce a tone that suggests a stuffy, pedantic attitude (see **33g**).

*The language of speech*   In a formal college essay, avoid colloquial language and slang. Do not enclose a slang expression in quotation marks to signal to readers that you know it is inappropriate. Instead, revise to reach an appropriate level of formality.

> disgusting
> ▶ The working conditions were "~~gross.~~"
>
> affects me powerfully
> ▶ The sound of sirens ~~gets to me.~~
>
> defendant
> ▶ The jury returned the verdict that the ~~guy~~ was guilty.

In formal writing, avoid colloquial words and expressions, such as *folks, guy, OK, okay, pretty good, hassle, kind of interesting/nice, too big of a deal, a lot of, lots of, a ways away, no-brainer.*

*Regional and ethnic language*   Use regional and ethnic dialects in your writing only when you are quoting someone directly (*"Your car needs fixed,"* the mechanic grunted.) or you know that readers will understand why you are using a nonstandard phrase. See the Language and Culture box below.

myself
▶ I bought ~~me~~ a camcorder.

                                              any attention
▶ He vowed that he wouldn't pay them ~~no never mind~~.

   have been
▶ They'~~re~~ here three years already.

               be able to
▶ She used to ~~could~~ run two miles, but now she's out of shape.

*The language of the workplace*   People engaged in most areas of specialized work and study use technical words that outsiders perceive as jargon. A sportswriter writing about baseball will refer to *balks, twinight double-headers, ERAs, brushbacks,* and *crooked numbers.* A linguist writing about language for an audience of linguists will use terms like *phonemics, sociolinguistics, semantics, kinesics,* and *suprasegmentals.* If you know that your audience is familiar with the technical vocabulary of a field, specialized language is acceptable. Try to avoid jargon when writing for a more general audience; if you must use technical terms, provide definitions that will make sense to your audience.

### LANGUAGE AND CULTURE

#### Formal Tone and Informal Dialogue

Note how Paule Marshall uses standard English for the narrative thread of her story, while reproducing the father's Barbadian dialect and idioms in the conversation:

> She should have leaped up and pirouetted and joined his happiness. But a strange uneasiness kept her seated with her knees drawn tight against her chest. She asked cautiously, "You mean we're rich?"
> "We ain rich but we got land."
> "Is it a lot?"
> "Two acres almost. I know the piece of ground good. You could throw down I-don-know-what on it and it would grow. And we gon gave a house there—just like the white people own. A house to end all house!"

*(Continued)*

(*Continued*)

"Are you gonna tell Mother?"

His smile faltered and failed; his eyes closed in a kind of weariness. "How you mean? I got to tell she, nuh."

"Whaddya think she's gonna say?"

"How I could know? Years back I could tell but not any more."

She turned away from the pain darkening his eyes.

—Paule Marshall, *Brown Girl, Brownstones*

**33e** Use figurative language for effect, but use it sparingly.

Figures of speech can enhance your writing and add to imaginative descriptions. Particularly useful are similes and metaphors. A *simile* is a comparison in which both sides are stated explicitly and linked by the word *like* or *as*. A *metaphor* is an implied comparison in which the two sides are indirectly compared. When figurative language is overused, however, it becomes tedious and contrived.

### Simile: an explicit comparison with both sides stated

▶ America is *not like a blanket*—one piece of unbroken cloth, the same color, the same texture, the same size. America is more *like a quilt*—many pieces, many colors, many sizes, all woven and held together by a common thread.  —Rev. Jesse Jackson

▶ [Matt Drudge] is *like a kind of digital Robin Hood* among a corrupt and venal press.  —Joshua Quittner

### Metaphor: an implied comparison, *without* like *or* as

▶ A foolish consistency is the hobgoblin of little minds.
—Ralph Waldo Emerson

▶ Some television programs are so much chewing gum for the eyes.
—John Mason Brown

### Mixed metaphors  Take care not to mix metaphors.

▶ As she walked onto the tennis court, she was ready to sink or swim. [Swimming on a tennis court?]

▶ **He is a snake in the grass with his head in the clouds.**

[The two metaphors clash.]

▶ **He was a whirlwind of activity, trumpeting defiance whenever anyone crossed swords with any of his ideas.**

[The three metaphors—*whirlwind, trumpet, crossed swords*—obscure rather than illuminate.]

For more on figurative language in literature, see **5b**.

## 33f Avoid biased and exclusionary language.

You cannot avoid writing from perspectives and backgrounds that you know about, but you can avoid divisive terms that reinforce stereotypes or belittle other people. Be sensitive to differences. Consider the feelings of members of the opposite sex, minorities (now sometimes called "world majorities"), and special-interest groups. Do not emphasize differences by separating society into *we* (people like you) and *they* or *these people* (people different from you). Use *we* only to be truly inclusive of yourself and all your readers. Be aware, too, of terms that are likely to offend. You don't have to be excessive in your zeal to be PC ("politically correct"), using *underachieve* for *fail*, or *vertically challenged* for *short*, but do your best to avoid alienating readers.

*Gender* The writer of the following sentence edited to avoid gender bias in the perception of women's roles and achievements.

    Andrea
▶ ~~Mrs. John~~ Harrison, ~~married to a real estate tycoon and~~ ~~herself the bubbly, blonde~~ chief executive of a successful computer company, has expanded the business overseas.

Choice of words can reveal gender bias, too.

| AVOID | USE |
|---|---|
| actress | actor |
| authoress | author |
| chairman | chairperson |
| female astronaut | astronaut |
| forefathers | ancestors |
| foreman | supervisor |
| mailman | mail carrier |
| male nurse | nurse |

| | |
|---|---|
| man, mankind (meaning any human being) | person, people, our species, human beings, humanity |
| manmade | synthetic |
| policeman, policewoman | police officer |
| salesman | sales representative, salesclerk |
| veterans and their wives | veterans and their spouses |

When using pronouns, too, avoid the stereotyping that occurs by assigning gender roles to professions. See **44e**.

*or she*
▶ Before a surgeon can operate, he must know every detail of the patient's history.

Often it is best to avoid the *he-or-she* issue by recasting the sentence or using plural nouns and pronouns.

▶ Before operating, a surgeon must know every detail of the patient's history

▶ Before surgeons can operate, they must know every detail of the patient's history.

At times when the singular form is preferable, consider using *he* in one section of your manuscript and *she* in another, as long as you do not alternate within a paragraph. See **44e** for more on pronouns, gender, and the use of *he or she*.

*Race*   Mention a person's race only when it is relevant. If you write "Attending the meeting were three doctors and an Asian computer programmer," you reveal more about your own stereotypes than you do about the meeting. In general, use the names that people prefer for their racial or ethnic affiliation. *The Columbia Guide to Standard American English* advises: "It is good manners (and therefore good usage) to call people only by the names they wish to be called." Consider, for example, that *black* and *African American* are preferred terms; *Native American* is preferred to *American Indian*; *Asian* is preferred to *Oriental*.

*Place*   Avoid stereotyping people according to where they come from. Some British people may be stiff and formal, but not all are. Not all Germans eat sausage and drink beer; not all North Americans carry cameras and wear plaid shorts.

Be careful, too, with the way you refer to countries and continents. The Americas include both North and South America, so you need to make the distinction. England, Scotland, Wales, and Northern

Ireland make up Great Britain, or the United Kingdom. In addition, shifts in world politics and national borders have resulted in the re-naming of many countries: *Burma* is now *Myanmar; Ceylon* is *Sri Lanka; Rhodesia* is now *Zimbabwe; Czechoslovakia* has been divided into the *Czech Republic* and *Slovakia.* Check a current atlas or almanac.

*Age and condition*   Avoid derogatory or condescending terms as-sociated with age. Refer to a person's age or condition neutrally, if at all: not "a well-preserved little old lady" but "a woman in her eight-ies"; not "an immature sixteen-year-old" but simply "a teenager."

*Politics*   Words referring to politics are full of connotations. Con-sider, for instance, the positive and negative connotations of *liberal* and *conservative* in various election campaigns. Take care when you use words like *radical, left-wing, right-wing,* and *moderate.* How do you want readers to interpret them? Are you identifying with one group and implicitly criticizing other groups?

*Religion*   An old edition of an encyclopedia referred to "devout Catholics" and "fanatical Muslims." The new edition refers to both Catholics and Muslims as "devout," thus eliminating biased lan-guage. Examine your use of the following: words that sound deroga-tory or exclusionary, such as *cult* or *fundamentalist;* expressions, such as *these people,* that emphasize difference; and even the word *we* when it implies that all your readers share your beliefs.

*Health and abilities*   Avoid expressions like *confined to a wheelchair* and *AIDS victim,* so as not to focus on difference and disability. Instead, write *someone who uses a wheelchair* and *person with AIDS.* Do not unnecessarily draw attention to a disability or an illness.

*Sexual orientation*   Mention a person's sexual orientation only if the information is relevant in context. To write that someone accused of stock market fraud was "defended by a homosexual lawyer" would be to provide gratuitous information. The sexual orientation of the at-torney might be more relevant in a case involving discrimination against homosexuals. Since you may not know the sexual orientation of your readers, do not assume it is the same as your own.

*The word* **normal**   Be especially careful about using the word *nor-mal* when referring to your own health, ability, or sexual orientation. Some readers might justifiably find that usage offensive.

## **33g** Avoid tired expressions (clichés) and pretentious language.

*Avoid clichés.*   *Clichés* are tired, overly familiar expressions such as *hit the nail on the head, crystal clear, better late than never,* and *easier said than done.* They never contribute anything fresh or original. Avoid or eliminate them as you revise your early drafts.

▶ *Last but not least,* the article sends an important message.

▶ My main ambition in life is not to make a fortune, since I know that, as they say, *"money is the root of all evil."*

▶ For Baldwin, the problem never *reared its ugly head* until one dreadful night in New Jersey.

*Distinguish the formal from the stuffy.*   Formal does not mean stuffy and pretentious. Writing in a formal situation does not require you to use obscure words and long sentences. Clear, direct expression can be formal. Pretentious language makes reading difficult, as the following example shows:

▶ When a female of the species ascertains that a male with whom she is acquainted exhibits considerable desire to extend their acquaintance, that female customarily will first engage in protracted discussion with her close confidantes.

Simplify your writing if you find sentences like that in your draft. Here are some words to watch out for:

| STUFFY | DIRECT | STUFFY | DIRECT |
|---|---|---|---|
| ascertain | find out | optimal | best |
| commence | begin | prior to | before |
| deceased | dead | purchase | buy |
| endeavor | try | reside | live |
| finalize | finish | terminate | end |
| implement | carry out | utilize | use |

*Avoid euphemisms.*   *Euphemisms* are expressions that try to conceal a forthright meaning and make the concept seem more delicate, such as *change of life* for *menopause* or *downsized* for *fired.* Because euphemisms often sound evasive or are unclear, avoid them in favor of direct language. Similarly, avoid *doublespeak* (evasive expressions that seek to conceal the truth, such as *incendiary device* for *bomb*). Examples of such language are easy to find in advertising, business, politics, and some reporting. Do not equate formality with these roundabout expressions.

> bribes
> ▶ The building's owners offered the inspectors many ~~financial incentives~~ to overlook code violations.

## AN INDIVIDUAL VOICE

The 5 C's of style will help you develop a style that will serve you well in college and the business world. The more you write, the more you will develop your own voice as you strive for variety, rhythm, and specific effects. The next three sections focus on sentence variety and on observing and learning from other writers. In the concluding section are some tips to help you review your drafts for style.

## 34 Sentence Variety

### 34a Sentence length

Readers appreciate variety, so aim for a mix of long and short sentences. If your editing program can print out your text in a series of single numbered sentences, you will easily be able to examine the length and structure of each sentence. Academic writing need not consist solely of long, heavyweight sentences. Short sentences interspersed among longer ones can have a dramatic effect.

This passage from a student memoir demonstrates the use of short sentences to great effect:

When I started high school and Afros became the rage, I immediately decided to get one. Now at that time, I had a head full of long, thick, kinky hair, which my mother had cultivated for years. When she said to me, "Cut it or perm it," she never for one minute believed I would do either. I cut it. She fainted.

—Denise Dejean, student

### 34b Statements, questions, commands, and exclamations

*Declarative* sentences make statements, *interrogative* sentences ask questions, *imperative* sentences give commands, and *exclamatory* sentences express surprise or some other strong emotion. Most of the sentences in your college writing will be declarative, though an occasional question is useful to draw readers into thinking about your topic. An occasional exclamatory sentence can be powerful, too, although exclamation points rarely appear in academic writing.

When you are writing an argument and want to persuade readers to act or to agree with you, you may feel tempted to write commands:

▶ **We need to help the homeless. Contribute money, lobby your local politicians, and volunteer your time. Remember that homelessness is often the result of an accident.**

Your argument will be more persuasive, however, if you make your points without directly addressing your readers and telling them what to do.

## **34c** Types of sentences

Vary the structure of your sentences throughout any piece of writing. Aim for a mix of simple, compound, complex, and compound-complex sentences.

A *simple sentence* contains one independent clause.

▶ **Kara raised her hand.**

A *compound sentence* contains two or more independent clauses connected with one or more coordinating conjunctions *(and, but, or, nor, so, for, yet)*, or with a semicolon alone, or with a semicolon and a transitional expression (**2d**).

┌─independent clause─┐ ┌─────independent clause─────┐
▶ **She raised her hand, and the whole class was surprised.**

┌─independent clause─┐ ┌─independent clause─┐
▶ **She raised her hand, but nobody else responded.**

┌─independent clause─┐ ┌────independent clause────┐
▶ **She raised her hand; the whole class was surprised.**

┌─independent clause─┐ ┌────independent clause────┐
▶ **She raised her hand; as a result, the whole class was surprised.**

A *complex sentence* contains an independent clause and one or more dependent clauses (**37e**).

┌────dependent clause────┐ ┌────independent clause────┐
▶ **When she raised her hand, the whole class was surprised.**

┌────independent clause────┐ ┌────dependent clause────┐
▶ **The whole class was surprised when she raised her hand.**

A *compound-complex sentence* contains at least two independent clauses and at least one dependent clause.

```
      ┌───── dependent clause ─────┐  ┌───── independent clause ─────┐
```
► **When she raised her hand, the whole class was surprised, and**
```
      ┌───── independent clause ─────┐  ┌───── dependent clause ─────┐
```
**the professor waited eagerly as she began to speak.**

## **34d** Inverted word order

Sometimes, inverted word order—switching from the usual subject-then-verb order—will help you achieve coherence, consistent subjects, emphasis, or a smooth transition:

```
                      V    ┌──── S ────┐
```
► **Next to the river runs a superhighway.**
```
            V   S   V
```
► **Never have I been so tired.**
```
            V   ┌─ S ─┐      V
```
► **Not only does the novel entertain, but it also raises our awareness of poverty.**
```
            V   S
```
► **So eager was I to win that I set off before the starter's gun.**
```
            V   ┌─S─┐        V
```
► **Rarely has a poem achieved such a grasp on the times.**

## **34e** Sentence beginnings

Consider using some of these variations to begin a sentence, but remember that beginning with the subject will always be clear and direct for readers. Any of the following beginnings repeated too often will seem like a stylistic tic and will annoy or bore readers.

### *Begin with a dependent clause or a condensed clause.*

```
      ┌────────────── dependent clause ──────────────┐
```
► **While my friends were waiting for the movie to begin, they ate three tubs of popcorn.**
```
      ┌───── clause condensed to a phrase ─────┐
```
► **While waiting for the movie to begin, my friends ate three tubs of popcorn.**

### *Begin with a participle or an adjective.*   A sentence can begin with a participle or an adjective if the word is in a phrase that refers to the subject of the independent clause. (See **37d** and **40c**.)

*-ing* participle
▶ **Waiting for the movie to begin, my friends ate popcorn.**

past participle
▶ **Forced to work late, they ordered a pepperoni pizza.**

adjective
▶ **Aware of the problems, they nevertheless decided to continue.**

*Begin with a prepositional phrase.*

┌ prepositional phrase ┐
▶ **With immense joy, we watched our team win the pennant.**

You can also occasionally use inverted word order after a preposi-tional phrase (**34d, 37c, 43d**).

┌────── prepositional phrase ──────┐ verb ┌────── subject ──────┐
▶ **At the end of my block stands a deserted building.**

## 35 Writers' Voices: A Nonfiction Style Sampler

Here are a few samples of clear, effective style in a variety of nonfiction contexts. The first passage is from the *Chicago Manual of Style FAQ (and not so FAQ)* Web site for Frequently Asked Questions at <http://www.press.uchicago.edu/Misc/Chicago/cmosfaq.html>. Note how a response to an anonymously posed question ("Should the word 'pre-dewatering' be hyphenated?") takes on a chatty and direct voice and even offers engaging humor, particularly with the use of the word *grumpy*:

> If what you want to say is "before dewatering," then you can use the word "before." If you are tempted to say "pre-" because you want to use the phrase to modify another noun (e.g., in the pre-dewatering period), then you can rephrase to avoid the problem (in the period before dewatering).
>
> If you were to write back and tell me that this word is standard parlance in some technical field, it would make me grumpy, but I would tell you that *Chicago* style is to close up all prefixes unless confusion would result.

In the next example, novelist Philip Roth recalls his parents' rela-tionship after his father retired:

His obsessive stubbornness—his stubborn obsessiveness—had very nearly driven my mother to a breakdown in her final years: since his retirement at the age of sixty-three, her once spirited, housewifely independence had been all but extinguished by his anxious, overbearing bossiness. For years he had believed he was married to perfection, and for years he wasn't far wrong— my mother was one of those devoted daughters of Jewish immigrants who raised housekeeping in America to a great art. (Don't talk to anyone in my family about cleaning—we saw cleaning in its heyday.) But then my father retired from one of the Metropolitan Life's big South Jersey offices, where he'd been managing a staff of fifty-two people, and the efficient, clear-cut division of labor that had done so much to define their marriage as a success gradually began to be obliterated—by him. He had nothing to do and she had everything to do—and that wouldn't do. "You know what I am now?" he told me sadly on his sixty-fifth birthday. "I'm Bessie's husband." And by neither temperament nor training was he suited to be that alone. So...he settled down to become Bessie's boss—only my mother happened not to need a boss, having been her own since her single-handed establishment of a first-class domestic-management and mothering company back in 1927, when my brother was born.

—Philip Roth, *Patrimony: A True Story*

In a book review, Robert Pinsky describes Roth as a "master of narrative of a definite kind—fast, accurate, free and deeply unpoetic" (*New York Times* 6 Jan. 1991) and comments on the passage quoted above:

Such telling is a marvel of artful wit and vigor. Almost mathematical dual balances support the passage, from the doubling game of the first six words through "spirited, housewifely" played against "anxious, overbearing" and twinned repetitions like "For years...for years" or—right there in mid-gag— "about cleaning...we saw cleaning," up to where the pair "nothing to do"/"everything to do" is capped by the tripled repetition of "that wouldn't do," just before the dialogue.

But that structure of braced formal balances is like a roadbed of analytical intelligence to bear the driving, vernacular onrush of American language, the confident terms "bossiness," "wasn't far wrong," "heyday," "big South Jersey offices," "settled down," "single-handed," these phrases all in the same dirt-simple key as Herman Roth's question that splashes against the grid of balanced phrases: *"You know what I am now?"* Abstract intelligence in the structure, vernacular sureness in the texture: those are the means by which Mr. Roth makes so very much happen in sentences that do not look—in fact are *not*—especially graceful.

—Robert Pinsky, "Letting Go"

Philip Roth shows that style is not necessarily associated with exalted topics and flowery language. Another writer, Nicholson Baker, also writes about everyday life and activities and helps us see them in a new light by providing minute details. Here he makes us realize what reading a newspaper in its original form entails by putting us in the reader's position, making us remember how we read a newspaper, and providing an image of microfilm reading that contrasts with the immediacy of reading a newspaper:

The size of newspapers is indispensable to our experience of their content. The newspaper reader proceeds nonlinearly, not as he would holding a typical book but circling around the opened double-page spread, perhaps clockwise, or counterclockwise, moving his whole head as well as his eyes, guided by island landmarks like photos and ads. Even the papers that have no pictures at all have a visual exorbitance that a microfilm's image (which one observer in the seventies likened to "kissing through a pane of glass") subverts and trivializes.

—Nicholson Baker, "Deadline"

Baker relishes words that provide a detailed description. He is not averse to inventing a word for humorous effect, such as when he describes reading microfilm as an "ocular and *neckular* ordeal." Working on style means experimenting and finding language that captures what you intend and pleases your readers.

## 36 Style Tips

As you write and revise, keep in mind the five C's of style. For a final quick review of your style, read your draft aloud and use these tips.

1. Consider your purpose and the style your readers will expect. Don't work on developing a figurative style for short stories and then continue to use it in business communications or e-mail.

Choose a style as you choose your clothes: the right outfit for the occasion. The following sentence, part of an e-mail message to the author of this book from a technical adviser in response to a question about sending an e-mail message, is decidedly overdressed and stuffed with bureaucratic nothings: "It has been a pleasure assisting you. It is my hope that the information provided would be of great help with regards to your concern."

2. Be clear and straightforward. Don't search for the big words or the obscure turn of phrase.

3. Details and descriptions are interesting, but don't overload your writing with adjectives and adverbs: *The perky little red-haired twin sat languidly in the comfortable, overstuffed green-striped armchair and bit enthusiastically into a red and yellow, fleshy, overripe peach.* Such prose is as overripe as the peach.

4. Avoid intensifying adverbs such as *very, really, extremely, terribly,* and *enormously.* Find a stronger word to use in place of the two words, such as *terrified* in place of *extremely scared.*

5. Put your verbs to work:

   Noт    **In Baker's *The Mezzanine,* one footnote is about perforation.**

   Bυт    **In Baker's *The Mezzanine,* one footnote celebrates perforation.**

6. Use to best advantage the parts of a sentence that carry the most weight: the subject, the verb, the ending.

   Noт    **Speed is a feature of the new Jaguar manufactured in Germany.**

   Bυт    **The new Jaguar manufactured in Germany roars past other cars.**

7. Focus on rhythm, not rules. Heed the advice of *The New York Times Manual of Style and Usage*: "One measure of skill is exceptions, not rules." Keep in mind this remark by novelist Ford Madox Ford: "Carefully examined, a good—an interesting—style will be found to consist in a constant succession of tiny, unobservable surprises." Ask yourself how you can provide pleasant surprises for your readers.

# PART 7

## Common
## Sentence Problems

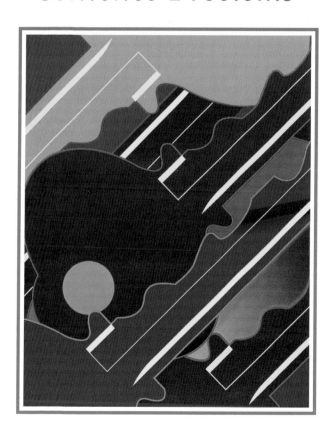

# PART 7     Common Sentence Problems

**37** **Top Ten Problems and Basic Grammar Review**

*The American Heritage Dictionary* (4th ed.) defines *Standard English* as "the variety of English that is generally acknowledged as the model for the speech and writing of educated speakers." It is the type of English that readers expect in the academic and business worlds. If you are accustomed to speaking some other varieties of English in your different communities, you have probably learned how to "switch codes"—that is, to move from a local dialect into Standard English—whenever the occasion demands it. Knowing how to make your writing conform to the conventions of Standard English whenever the audience and the occasion call for it is also a good practice.

This section first shows you ten common problems facing all writers of Standard English sentences. You can use the list to test yourself and as a checklist for your own writing. Cross-references in parentheses direct you to detailed discussions in sections **38–46**. If you feel you need to brush up on the grammatical conventions of Standard English, turn to sections **37b–37e** for a review of basic principles and common terminology. You might also find the Glossary of Grammatical Terms (see **66**) helpful if class discussion uses terms you are not entirely familiar with. Computer grammar checkers may alert you to possible grammar problems. However, they have not reached a high level of linguistic sophistication, so you need to weigh whatever they suggest and not automatically act on every suggestion.

## **37a** Top ten sentence problems

*1. Phrase fragments*   To be complete, a sentence must have both a subject and a verb. A phrase fragment lacks a subject, a verb, or both. Identify phrase fragments, and edit to attach them to a sentence that contains a subject and a verb (**38a**).

▶ She never talks about her inner feelings, ~~Her feelings~~ of fear or of joy.

*2. Clause fragments*   A dependent clause must always be connected to an independent clause. If you begin a sentence with *when, because, although,* or some other subordinating conjunction, connect that clause to an independent clause (**38b**).

▶ The play failed, ~~Because~~ because it received three bad reviews.

*3. Run-on sentences and comma splices*   Separate or revise independent clauses that are connected incorrectly (see **39**).

▶ He trained hard, ~~he~~ He never considered the strain.

▶ The city is lively; the restaurants and clubs are open late.

▶ The film has been released; however, it has not come to our theater.

**4. *Fuzzy syntax*** Look for sentences that might make readers say "Huh?," sentences that begin in one way but end in another, mixing constructions (**40a**). Readers should be able to tell clearly who (or what) is doing what (**30a**).

> ▶ In ~~the~~ essay "Notes of a Native Son"~~by~~ James Baldwin
> discusses . . .

*(edits: "his" inserted above "the"; "by" deleted; comma inserted after "Son")*

**5. *Wrong verb forms*** Be sure to use standard verb forms. Avoid nonstandard forms, such as *brung, has went, should of went, have being noticed, have drank* (**41a**).

**6. *Tense shifts*** Avoid flip-flopping between past and present time (**41h**).

> ▶ Foote ~~wrote~~ about Shiloh and describes its aftermath.

*(edit: "writes" above "wrote")*

**7. *Lack of subject-verb agreement*** A singular third person subject (*he, she, it,* or a singular noun) takes a singular verb, with an *-s* ending in the present tense (**43a**); a plural subject takes a plural verb. Check carefully for verbs with *-s* endings. Look for and edit nonstandard forms.

> ▶ the owner ~~have~~        ▶ the author suggest
>
> *(has)*                      *(s)*
>
> ▶ she ~~don't~~             ▶ It pose a problem.
>
> *(doesn't)*                  *(s)*

> ▶ The students in the class likes peer response.
>
> *(s)*

**8. *Faulty pronoun case and reference*** Check that subject and object pronouns are correct (**44a**), and avoid ambiguous or unclear pronoun references (**44c**).

> ▶ ~~Me and my sister~~ went to Florida.
>
> *(My sister and I)*

> ▶ The incident in the story reminds me of my mother and ~~I~~.
>
> *(me)*

> ▶ When Dean and George crossed the border with two
> friends, ~~they~~ searched all the luggage.
>
> *(customs officers)*

**9. *Adjective/adverb confusion*** Use the right forms of adjectives and adverbs in the right places (**45a–45c**).

▶ They did ~~good~~ in the playoffs.
      *well*

▶ They managed to compete ~~real~~ well in the playoffs.
      *really*

**10. *Double negatives*** Double negatives can be vibrant in speech and are customary in some dialects, but avoid them in formal writing (**45g**).

▶ They don't have ~~no~~ problems with that.
      *any*

▶ He ~~can't~~ hardly wait.
      *can*

## **37b** Parts of speech

Words are traditionally classified into eight categories called *parts of speech*. See the Glossary of Grammatical Terms (**66**) for further definitions and examples.

### KEY POINTS

#### Using the Parts of Speech

**Nouns** Words that name a person, place, thing, or concept—*teacher, valley, furniture, Hinduism*—are called nouns. When you use a noun, determine the following: Is it a proper noun, requiring a capital letter? Does it have a plural form? If so, are you using the singular or plural form? See **60a** ESL.

**Pronouns** Words that are substitutes for a noun, a noun phrase, or another pronoun—*she, his, those, themselves, whom, whoever, anyone*—are called pronouns. When you use a pronoun, determine the following: What word or words in the sentence does the pronoun refer to? Does the pronoun refer to a noun or pronoun that is singular or plural? See **43h**, **43i**, **43j**, **44a**, **44h**, and **46a**.

**Verbs** Words that tell what a person, place, thing, or concept does or is—*smile, throw, think, seem, become, be*—are called verbs. Verbs change form to refer to present or past time. Every clause needs a

*(Continued)*

*(Continued)*

verb. When you use a verb, determine the following: What time does the verb refer to? What auxiliary or modal verbs are needed? Is the subject of the verb singular or plural? Is the verb in the active voice or passive voice? What are the five forms of the verb (*sing, sings, singing, sang, sung*), and are you using the correct form? For more on verbs, see **41**, **42**, and **43**.

**Adjectives**   Words that describe nouns—*purple, beautiful, big*—are called adjectives. An adjective can precede a noun (*purple boots*) or follow a linking verb: *Her boots are purple.* Also functioning as adjectives (before a noun) are *a, an,* and *the,* as well as many pronouns: *a cabbage, an allegory, their shoes.* For more on adjectives, see **45**.

**Adverbs**   Words that provide information about verbs, adjectives, adverbs, or clauses are called adverbs. Many but not all adverbs end in *-ly: efficiently, undoubtedly.* Adverbs provide information about "how" or "when": *very, well, sometimes, often, soon.* Conjunctive adverbs—*however, therefore, furthermore*—make connections between independent clauses. See also **2d** and **45**.

**Conjunctions**   Words that connect single words, phrases, and clauses are called conjunctions. Coordinating conjunctions—*and, but, or, nor, so, for, yet*—connect ideas of equal importance. Subordinating conjunctions—*because, if, when, although,* for instance—make one clause dependent on another. Consider the meaning before using a conjunction. See **31c** and **37e**.

**Prepositions**   Words used before nouns and pronouns to form phrases that convey relationships such as of time and space (*in the poem, throughout the day, behind her, without a doubt, for you*) are called prepositions. Prepositional phrases are often idiomatic: *on occasion, in love.* To understand their use and meaning, consult a good dictionary. See also **63** ESL.

**Interjections**   Words that express emotion and can stand alone—*Ha! Wow! Ugh! Ouch! Say!*—are called interjections. Use them only in informal writing.

**37c**   Common sentence patterns

A sentence in English usually consists of a *subject* (the person or thing doing the action) and a *predicate* (a comment or assertion about that subject). A subject can be a word, a phrase, a clause, or a combination.

A predicate must always include a verb. Note that a subject may consist of a head word (a simple subject) along with its modifiers.

subject predicate
▶ **He left.**

simple subject — complete subject — verb
▶ **The *boss* of the successful new computer company *left* the**

— predicate —
**elegantly furnished conference room.**

Here are some common sentence patterns, with different types of predicates (described in brackets):

***Subject + [Verb]*** The basic pattern for a sentence in English is a simple subject followed by a verb: S +V.

S   V
▶ **Babies cry.**

Even when additional elements appear, the subject and verb maintain their key positions.

simple subject
— S — — V —
▶ **All the *babies* in the hospital nursery *are crying*.**

**ESL Note** Not all languages require a subject and a verb. English requires both. See **38c** and **62a** ESL. ■

***Subject + [Verb + Direct Object]*** The direct object completes the meaning of the verb.

— S — V   DO
▶ **Many people wear glasses.**

In that sentence, the direct object (DO) completes the meaning of the verb by telling what many people wear. Verbs that take a direct object are known as *transitive verbs.*

— S —
▶ **The *artist* who lives in the large apartment on the sixth floor**

V   — DO —
***owns* five cute Weimaraner *puppies*.**

*Intransitive verbs,* such as *cry, lie* (meaning "recline"), *sit,* and *rise,* do not take a direct object.

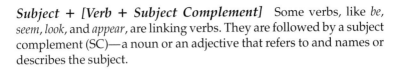
*Subject + [Verb + Subject Complement]*  Some verbs, like *be*, *seem*, *look*, and *appear*, are linking verbs. They are followed by a subject complement (SC)—a noun or an adjective that refers to and names or describes the subject.

         ┌─────── S ───────┐   V   SC
▶ The *players* on the visiting team look fit.

*Subject + [Verb + Indirect Object + Direct Object]*  Verbs such as *give*, *send*, and *offer* can be followed by an indirect object, naming the person or thing to whom or for whom the action of the verb takes place, and by a direct object (**62c** ESL).

    ┌──────── S ────────┐   V   ┌──── IO ────┐   ┌──── DO ────┐
▶ The *director* of the play *gave* his leading *lady* one exquisite *rose*.

*Subject + [Verb + Direct Object + Object Complement]*  The object complement (OC) refers to and renames or describes the direct object.

   S    V   ┌──── DO ────┐   ┌──── OC ────┐
▶ They named the football *star Rookie* of the Year.

*[Verb +]*  A command is the only type of sentence that has an implied rather than a stated subject. The subject of a command is always *you*.

       V
▶ [You] Leave me alone!

*[Verb] + Subject: inverted word order*  In Standard English sentences, the verb precedes the subject only in specific contexts—usually in questions and after *here* and *there*. Here are the patterns that you are most likely to read or use in your writing:

  V   S                          V        S
▶ Is she ambitious?        ▶ Here comes the rain.

       V      S
▶ There were hundreds of people at the rally.

Inverted word order is also used after *never*, *seldom*, *rarely*, *not only*, and phrases used initially for emphasis (see **34d**).

         V    S    V
▶ Rarely have we seen such a spectacle.

                 V   ┌──── S ────┐
▶ Next to the church stands a dilapidated barn.

## **37d** Phrases

A group of words that lacks a subject, a verb, or both is a *phrase.* A phrase cannot be punctuated as a sentence. Phrases perform a number of grammatical functions.

### *Noun phrases*

```
            ┌───────── noun phrase as subject ─────────┐
```
▶ **An elegant sequined evening gown was on sale.**

```
              ┌───────── noun phrase as object ─────────┐
```
▶ **She bought an elegant sequined evening gown.**

```
                  ┌───── appositive noun phrase (47d)─────┐
```
▶ **Her latest purchase, an elegant sequined evening gown, now hangs in her closet.**

*Verb phrases*    A verb phrase consists of all the words that together make up the complete verb of a clause. (A *complete* verb indicates time—when the action mentioned in the sentence takes place; see **41a** and **41c**).

```
              ┌── verb phrase (complete verb) ──┐
```
▶ **That embarrassing letter should have been destroyed years ago.**

*Verbal phrases*    Some phrases begin with parts of verbs. These parts of verbs (called *verbals*) never form a complete verb. Verbals are the present participle (*-ing*), the past participle (*-ed*), or the infinitive form of a verb. *A participle phrase* can never stand alone as a sentence.

```
        ┌───────── past participle phrase ─────────┐
```
▶ **Frightened by her own loud heartbeat, she tried to stay calm.**

```
        ┌── past participle phrase ──┐
```
▶ **Noises heard from afar seem louder at night.**

```
        ┌── -ing participle phrase ──┐
```
▶ **Hurrying across the grass, she heard a loud crash.**

A *participle phrase* at the beginning of a sentence must always describe the subject; otherwise, it is a dangling modifier (**40c**), as in *Hurrying across the grass, a loud crash startled her.* (The *crash* was not hurrying; *she* was.)

An *-ing* phrase can function as a noun. When it does, it is known as a *gerund*.

```
   ┌── -ing noun phrase (subject) ──┐
```
▶ **The blaring of a car horn made her angry.**

```
            -ing noun phrase
          ┌──── (object) ────┐
```
▶ **He enjoys singing in the rain.**

An *infinitive phrase* (*to* + verb) performs various functions.

```
   ┌──── (subject) ────┐
```
▶ **To return to Beijing was her dream.**

```
   ┌──── (adverb) ────┐
```
▶ **To return to Beijing, she took a job as an English teacher.**

```
            ┌──── (adjective) ────┐
```
▶ **She had a plan to return to Beijing.**

*Prepositional phrases*   A prepositional phrase consists of a preposition and a noun or pronoun, called the *object* of the preposition. Prepositional phrases usually function as adjectives or adverbs.

```
 prepositional phrase        prepositional phrase      prepositional phrase
  ┌── (adverb) ──┐            ┌── (adjective) ──┐        ┌── (adverb) ──┐
```
▶ **Without fail, the eerie music from the park began at midnight.**

*Absolute phrases*   An absolute phrase begins with a noun phrase followed by a verbal or a prepositional phrase. It contains no verb form that indicates tense. An absolute phrase modifies a whole sentence and is set off from the rest of the sentence by a comma.

```
              ┌─ absolute phrase, modifying the whole sentence ─┐
```
▶ **She stood in suspense, the clanging noises growing louder.**

```
      absolute phrase,
  ┌─ modifying the whole sentence ─┐
```
▶ **Her thoughts in turmoil, she decided to consult a lawyer.**

**ESL Note**   A phrase beginning with an adjective modifies a noun or pronoun and comes after the noun or pronoun it modifies (**62b** ESL).

```
      phrase used as an adjective after a noun, not before
  ┌────────────────────────────────┐
```
▶ **The person responsible for the profits refused to take credit.**   ■

## **37e**  Clauses

Clauses either stand alone (*independent*) or depend on another clause for their full meaning. A *dependent clause* must be part of a sentence containing an independent clause.

*Independent clauses*   An independent clause is a group of words that contains at least a subject and a verb and can be punctuated as a sentence when standing alone. In each sentence you write, the predicate should include a complete verb and make a comment or assertion about the subject. (For commands, see **37c**.)

| SUBJECT | PREDICATE |
|---|---|
| Eyesight | *deteriorates.* |
| Many people | *wear* glasses. |
| Audre Lorde | *is* a poet. |
| Lorde's poems and essays | *make* one think. |

A subject can also be a verb form used as a noun (an -*ing* participle [gerund] or an infinitive) or a dependent clause.

| SUBJECT | PREDICATE |
|---|---|
| -*ing* form (gerund) | |
| Winning | *is* not everything. |
| infinitive phrase | |
| To do one's best | *is* more important. |
| dependent clause | |
| How the players train | *makes* all the difference. |

**CONNECTING INDEPENDENT CLAUSES: COORDINATION**   Use a coordinating conjunction—*and, but, or, nor, so, for, yet*—usually preceded by a comma, to connect two independent clauses in one sentence (**31c**.)

▶ **Thomas Wolfe's manuscript was 1,100 pages, but his editor cut it substantially.**

*Dependent clauses*   A dependent (or subordinate) clause contains a subject and a predicate but cannot stand alone. A clause beginning with a subordinating conjunction, such as *if, when, because, although, since, who, which, that,* or *whether,* needs to be attached to an independent clause. The idea in a dependent clause is subordinate to the idea in the independent clause.

A sentence can contain any number of independent and dependent clauses, but it must always contain at least one independent clause. Never punctuate a dependent clause alone as a sentence (see **38**).

**CONNECTING CLAUSES BY SUBORDINATION**   By attaching a dependent clause to an independent clause—using *subordination*—you provide information about the relationship between clauses.

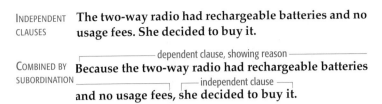

INDEPENDENT CLAUSES **The two-way radio had rechargeable batteries and no usage fees. She decided to buy it.**

COMBINED BY SUBORDINATION

dependent clause, showing reason

**Because the two-way radio had rechargeable batteries**

independent clause

**and no usage fees, she decided to buy it.**

Dependent clauses fall into three types, according to their role in a sentence.

**DEPENDENT ADVERB CLAUSES** Adverb clauses provide information about the verbs, adjectives, or adverbs in an independent clause. They answer questions such as *when, how, where, why, for what purpose,* and *to what extent,* and they express logical relationships between ideas. Adverb clauses begin with subordinating conjunctions.

SUBORDINATING CONJUNCTIONS

*time:* when, whenever, until, till, before, after, while, once, as soon as, as long as

*place:* where, wherever

*cause:* because, as, since

*condition:* if, even if, unless, provided that

*contrast:* although, though, even though, whereas, while

*comparison:* than, as, as if, as though

*purpose:* so that, in order that

*result:* so . . . that, such . . . that

As a general rule, if the dependent clause precedes the independent clause, use a comma to separate the two clauses.

dependent clause    comma  independent clause
▶ **If you send that memo, the columnist will be angry.**

Ordinarily, no comma is needed when the dependent clause follows the independent clause.

▶ **The columnist will be angry if you send that memo.**

However, when the dependent clause is nonrestrictive (that is, adds information that contrasts rather than modifies and limits), it is set off with a comma (**47d**).

▶ **My boss prefers phone calls, whereas I like e-mail.**

**DEPENDENT ADJECTIVE CLAUSES** Adjective clauses (also called *relative clauses*; see **46**) provide information about nouns or pronouns. The subordinating words that introduce adjective clauses are relative pronouns, such as *who, whom, whose, which,* and *that.*

── adjective (relative) clause ──
▶ The kick **that brought the crowd to its feet** broke the impasse.

── adjective (relative) clause ──
▶ The soccer player **whose head is bowed** missed a kick.

**DEPENDENT NOUN CLAUSES** A noun clause functions like a noun in a sentence. Noun clauses are introduced by subordinating words such as *what, that, when, why, how, whatever, who, whom, whoever,* and *whomever.* (A clause that you can replace with the pronoun *something* or *someone* is a noun clause.)

noun clause
── = *something* ──
▶ He wants to know **what he should do.**

── noun clause = *something* ──
▶ The fans wish **that the match could be replayed.**

── noun clause = *someone* ──
▶ **Whoever scores a goal** will be a hero.

## 38 Sentence Fragments

A fragment is a group of words incorrectly punctuated as if it were a complete sentence. Usually you can fix a fragment by connecting it to a closely related sentence in your text.

**KEY POINTS**

### The Requirements of a Sentence

To be complete, a sentence (other than a command) must contain the following:

1. A subject
          They were arguing
   ▶ They drove for six days. ~~Arguing~~ all the way.

*(Continued)*

*(Continued)*

2. A complete verb

                           *were*

▶ We watched the rehearsal. The jugglers‸practicing for four hours.

3. An independent clause    *because*

▶ The spectators shrieked, ~~Because~~ the race was so close.

Advertisers and writers occasionally use fragments deliberately for a crisp, immediate effect: "What a luxury should be." "Sleek lines." "Efficient in rain, sleet, and snow." "A magnificent film." However, you should identify and correct them in your formal writing.

## **38a** Identifying and correcting a phrase fragment

A phrase is a group of words that lacks a subject, a verb, or both (**37d**). A phrase fragment is a phrase incorrectly punctuated as if it were a complete sentence.

                             ——— fragment: infinitive phrase ———

▶ He wanted to make a point. To prove to everyone that he was capable.

                           ——— fragment: *-ing* participle phrase ———

▶ Althea works every evening. Just trying to keep up with her boss's demands.

                           ——— fragment: past participle phrase ———

▶ Ralph talked for hours. Elated by the company's success.

                           fragment: prepositional phrase

▶ They kept dialing the boss's phone number. With no luck.

                         ——— fragment: noun phrase (appositive) ———

▶ A prize was awarded to Ed. The best worker in the company.

                           fragment: noun phrase

▶ Nature held many attractions for Thoreau. First, the solitude.

*Methods of correcting a phrase fragment*

1. Attach the phrase to a nearby independent clause.

▶ He wanted to make a point, <s>To</s> ^to^ prove to everyone that he was capable.   [Simply remove the period and capital letter.]

▶ A prize was awarded to Ed, <s>The</s> ^the^ best worker in the company.

[Use a comma before an appositive phrase, and remove the capital letter.]

2. Change the phrase to an independent clause.

▶ Althea works every evening. ^She is just^ <s>Just</s> trying to keep up with her boss's demands.   [Add a subject and a complete verb.]

▶ Nature held many attractions for Thoreau. First, ^he valued^ the solitude. [Add a subject and a verb.]

3. Rewrite the whole passage.

▶ Ralph <s>talked for hours. Elated</s> ^was so^ ^elated^ by the company's success ^that he talked for hours^

[Make the fragment into a clause, and connect it to another clause with a subordinating word—in this case, one showing a result.]

## **38b**  Identifying and correcting a dependent clause fragment

A dependent clause beginning with a subordinating word (p. 291) such as *because, if, unless, when, whenever, while, although, that, which,* or *who* (or with a question word such as *how, what,* or *why*) cannot stand alone. It must be attached to an independent clause.

▶ The family set out for a new country. <u>A country in which they</u>
┌──────── fragment ────────

could practice their culture and religion.

▶ Lars had always wanted to be a stand-up comic. <u>Because he</u>
┌──────── fragment ────────┐
liked to make people laugh.

▶ Rosa often talks about her relationship with her parents.
┌──────── fragment ────────┐
How she grew up following her family's values.

## *Methods of correcting a dependent clause fragment*

1. Connect the dependent clause to an independent clause (and delete any unnecessary repetition).

   ▶ The family set out for a new country~~/ A country~~ in which they could practice their culture and religion.

   ▶ Rosa often talks about her relationship with her parents~~,~~

       *and how*
   ~~How~~ she grew up following her family's values.

2. Delete the subordinating conjunction (see the list on p. 291). The dependent clause then becomes an independent clause, which can stand alone.

          *He*
   ▶ Lars had always wanted to be a stand-up comic. ~~Because he~~ liked to make people laugh.

*Note:* A subordinating conjunction at the beginning of a sentence does not always signal a fragment. A correctly punctuated sentence may begin with a subordinating conjunction introducing a dependent clause, as long as the sentence also contains an independent clause.

    subordinating conjunction             comma
        ——— dependent clause ———    ——— independent clause ———
▶ When the circus arrives in town, the elephants parade along

the main street.

**38c** Identifying and correcting a fragment with a missing verb or verb part

Every sentence must contain a complete verb in an independent clause. A word group that is punctuated like a sentence but lacks a verb or has an incomplete verb is a fragment. A complete verb is a verb that shows tense (see **41a** and **41c**).

               ——— fragment: incomplete verb ———
▶ Overcrowding is a problem. Too many people living in one area.

               ┌ fragment: missing verb ┐
▶ The candidate explained his proposal. A plan for off-street

parking.

*Methods of correcting*   Supply all necessary verb forms, or recast the sentence.

▶ Overcrowding is a problem. Too many people ^are living in one area.

▶ Overcrowding is a problem, ^with too ~~Too~~ many people living in one area.

▶ The candidate explained his ~~proposal. A~~ plan for off-street parking.

▶ The candidate explained his proposal. ^He emphasized a A plan for off-street parking.

**38d**   Identifying and correcting a fragment with a missing subject

Unless it is a command with the implied subject *you*, a word group appearing without a subject is a fragment.

▶ The commuters were staring hopefully down the track. Just

⌐———— fragment: missing subject ————⌐
wanted to get to work on time.

*Methods of correcting*

1.  Include an appropriate subject to form an independent clause.

    ▶ The commuters were staring hopefully down the track. ^They just ~~Just~~ wanted to get to work on time.

**ESL Note**   Never omit an *it* subject in a clause. If you do, the clause becomes a fragment.

▶ The essay won a prize because ^it was so well researched. ■

2.  Turn the fragment into an *-ing* participle phrase, and attach it to the independent clause.

    ▶ The commuters were staring hopefully down the track. ^just wanting ~~Just wanted~~ to get to work on time.

**38e** Identifying and correcting a fragment with only one part of a compound predicate

A compound predicate (one with two parts joined by *and, but, or,* or *nor*) should not be split into two sentences. If you write a sentence with one subject and a compound predicate, both parts of the predicate must appear in the same sentence.

▶ After an hour, the dancers changed partners. And adapted to a

◖──── fragment ────◗

different type of music.   [The compound predicate is "*changed* partners and *adapted* to a different type of music."]

*Method of correcting*   Correct the fragment by removing the period and capital letter.

▶ After an hour, the dancers changed partners. ~~And~~ adapted to a
    *and*
different type of music.

**38f** Using fragments intentionally

Fragments are used frequently in advertisements to keep the text short. In academic writing, writers sometimes use a fragment intentionally for emphasis after a question, as an exclamation, or at a point of transition.

▶ Is this unease what Kincaid intends? Maybe.

When you are writing academic papers in college, use intentional fragments sparingly, if at all. Readers of your academic writing might not realize when a fragment is intentional.

## 39  Run-ons and Comma Splices

**39a** Identifying run-on (or fused) sentences and comma splices

If two independent clauses run together without any punctuation be-tween them, the error is called a *run-on sentence* or *fused sentence*. If only a comma appears between them with no coordinating conjunc-tion, the error is called a *comma splice*. A comma splice error also occurs when a comma and a transitional expression join two independent clauses. (See **2d**, **31c**, and **47e** on transitional expressions.) As with fragments, you will find comma splices and run-ons used in advertising and other writing for stylistic effect.

comma splice for stylistic effect

▶ It's not that I'm afraid to die, I just don't want to be there when
it happens. —Woody Allen, *Without Feathers*

However, in formal academic writing, prefer more conventional punctuation.

RUN-ON (FUSED) SENTENCES

——— independent clause ———┐ ┌——— independent clause ———┐
▶ My mother's name is Marta my father's name is George.

┌— independent clause —┐ ┌———— independent clause ————┐
▶ Success is their goal happiness comes a close second.

COMMA SPLICES

comma not sufficient
┌——— independent clause ———┐ │ ┌— independent clause —┐
▶ The train picked up speed, the scenery flashed by.

comma not sufficient
┌——— independent clause ———┐ │ ┌——— independent clause ———
▶ Salmon swim upstream, they leap over huge dams to reach

their destination.

┌——————— independent clause ———————┐ comma not sufficient
▶ Some parents support bilingual education, however, many

transitional expression

┌——— independent clause ———┐
oppose it vociferously.

**39b** Correcting run-on sentences and comma splices

You can correct run-ons and comma splices in the following five ways.
Select the one that works best for the sentence you are editing.

*Method 1* Separate the independent clauses into individual sentences
with a period (or question mark or exclamation point, if required).

Happiness
▶ Success is their goal ~~happiness~~ comes a close second.
        ^

They
▶ Beavers cut down trees with their teeth, ~~they~~ use the trees for
                                        ^
food and shelter.

*Method 2*   Separate the independent clauses with a semicolon if the clauses are joined by a transitional expression or if their ideas are closely related.

▶ Some parents support bilingual education;however, many oppose it vociferously.

▶ The hummingbird is amazing;its wings beat fifty to seventy-five times per second.

*Method 3*   Separate the independent clauses with a comma and a coordinating conjunction (*and, but, or, nor, so, for, yet*).

▶ My mother's name is Marta, andmy father's name is George.

▶ Woodpeckers look for insects in trees,butthey do not intentionally destroy live trees.

*Method 4*   Make one clause dependent by adding a subordinating conjunction (see the list on p. 291).

▶ Whenever the ~~The~~ beavers dammed up the river, the rise in the water level destroyed the trees.

▶ The scenery flashed bywhenthe train picked up speed.

*Method 5*   Make one clause a phrase beginning with an *-ing* participle, and attach the phrase to the remaining independent clause.

▶ Salmon swim upstream, leaping ~~they leap~~ over huge dams to reach their destination.

## 40 Sentence Snarls

Sentences with structural inconsistencies make readers pause to untangle the meaning. This section points out how to avoid or edit common snarls.

**40a**   Avoid fuzzy syntax.

Revise sentences that begin in one way and then veer off the track, departing from the original structure. When you mix constructions, make faulty comparisons, or tangle your syntax (sentence structure), you confuse readers. Pay special attention to sentences beginning with *by -ing*, or *when -ing*.

> Some
> ▶ ~~With some~~ professors who never give grades like to write comments.   [Who are the people who "like to write comments"? The prepositional phrase *with some professors* cannot serve as the subject of the sentence.]

MIXED CONSTRUCTION | **When wanting to take on a greater role in business might lead a woman to adopt new personality traits.**
[The reader gets to the verb *might lead* without knowing what the subject is.]

POSSIBLE REVISIONS | **When wanting to take on a greater role in business, a woman might adopt new personality traits.**
[This version provides a grammatical subject—*woman*—for the independent clause.]

**Wanting to take on a greater role in business might lead a woman to adopt new personality traits.**
[This version deletes the preposition *By* and eliminates the prepositional phrase; now the *-ing* phrase functions as the subject of *might lead*.]

When you make comparisons, be sure to tell readers clearly what you are comparing to what. See also **44a**, **44b**, and **45i**.

FAULTY COMPARISON | **Like Wallace Stevens, her job strikes readers as unexpected for a poet.**   [It is not her job that is like the poet Wallace Stevens; her job is like his job.]

REVISED | **Like Wallace Stevens, she holds a job that strikes readers as unexpected for a poet.**

Revise sentences that ramble on to such an extent that they become tangled. Make sure your sentences have clear subjects and verbs, and use coordination or subordination effectively. Cut and check for action (**29**, **30**).

TANGLED | **The way I feel about getting what you want is that when there is a particular position or item that you want to try to get to do your best and not give up because if you give up you have probably missed your chance of succeeding.**

POSSIBLE REVISION | **To get what you want, keep trying.**

**40b** Position modifiers appropriately.

A modifier is a word or phrase that describes or limits another word or phrase. Avoid misplaced modifiers. Keep single words, phrases, and clauses that provide adjectival or adverbial information next to the sentence element that they modify.

*Take care with words such as* **only.** Place *only, even, just, nearly, merely,* or *simply* immediately before the word it modifies.

▶ She ~~only~~ likes ᴼⁿˡʸ Tom.   [Tom is the only one she likes.]

The meaning of a sentence changes significantly as the position of *only* changes, so careful placement is important.

▶ *Only* the journalist began to investigate the forgery.
[and nobody else]

▶ The journalist *only* began to investigate the forgery.
[but did not finish]

▶ The journalist began to investigate *only* the forgery.
[and nothing else]

*Place a phrase or clause close to the word it modifies.*

MISPLACED   **Sidel argues that young women's dreams will not always come true in her essay.**

[Will the dreams come true in Sidel's essay or does Sidel argue in her essay?]

REVISED   **In her essay, Sidel argues that young women's dreams will not always come true.**

*Consider the case for splitting an infinitive.* You split an infinitive when you place a word or phrase between *to* and the verb. *The New Oxford Dictionary of English* finds the use of split infinitives "both normal and useful," as in "To boldly go where no man has gone before…" (*Star Trek*). However, such splitting may irritate readers, especially when a clumsy sentence is the result, as in the following:

⎯⎯⎯ clumsy split infinitive *(to inform)* ⎯⎯⎯

▶ **We want to sincerely, honestly, and in confidence inform you of our plans for expansion.**

**40c** Avoid dangling modifiers.

A modifier that is not grammatically linked to the noun or phrase it is intended to describe is said to be dangling. An *-ing* or *-ed* modifier at the beginning of a sentence must provide information about the subject of the sentence.

DANGLING    **Walking into the house, the telephone rang.**

        [The sentence says the telephone was walking.]

DANGLING    **Delighted with the team's victory, the parade route was decorated by the fans.**

        [The sentence says the parade route was delighted.]

You can fix a dangling modifier in the following ways:

*Method 1*   Retain the modifier, but make the subject of the independent clause the person or thing modified.

REVISED    **Walking into the house, we heard the telephone ring.**

REVISED    **Delighted with the team's victory, the fans decorated the parade route.**

*Method 2*   Change the modifier phrase into a clause with its own subject and verb.

REVISED    **While we were walking into the house, the telephone rang.**

REVISED    **Because the fans were delighted with the team's victory, they decorated the parade route.**

**40d** Avoid shifts: from statements to commands, from indirect to direct quotation, and in point of view.

Sudden shifts in your sentences can disconcert readers. (See also **41h** on avoiding unnecessary shifts in verb tense.)

*Do not shift abruptly from statements to commands.*

> The students in this university should do more to keep the
>
>     They should pick
> place clean. ~~Pick~~ up the litter and treat the dorms like home.

*Do not shift a verb phrase from indirect to direct quotation, with or without quotation marks.* (See **41i** and **62d** ESL for more on quotations.)

SHIFT     The client told us that he wanted to sign the lease and would we prepare the papers.

REVISED     The client told us that he wanted to sign the lease and asked us to prepare the papers.

SHIFT     She wanted to find out whether any interest had accumulated on her account and was she receiving any money.

REVISED     She wanted to find out whether any interest had accumulated on her account and whether she was receiving any money.

*Do not shift point of view.*    Be consistent in using first, second, or third person pronouns. For example, if you begin by referring to *one*, do not switch to *you* or *we*. Also avoid shifting unnecessarily between third person singular and plural forms.

SHIFT     *One* needs a high salary to live in a city because *you* have to spend so much on rent and transportation.

POSSIBLE REVISIONS     *One* needs a high salary to live in a city because *one* has to spend so much on rent and transportation.

         *People* need a high salary to live in a city because *they* have to spend so much on rent and transportation.

         A high salary is necessary in a city because rent and transportation cost so much.

**40e**   Use a logical sequence after the subject: avoid faulty predication.

To avoid confusing readers, never use a subject and predicate that do not make logical sense together (see **37c**).

Building
▶ ~~The decision to build~~ an elaborate extension onto the train
station made all the trains arrive late.
[It was not the decision that delayed the trains, but the building
of the extension.]

Finding the
▶ ~~The~~ solution to the problem is a hard task.
[A solution is not a task.]

**40f**  Avoid faulty predication with definitions
and reasons.

When you write a definition of a term, use parallel structures on either
side of the verb *be*. In formal writing, avoid defining a term by using *is
when* or *is where* (or *was when, was where*).

FAULTY  **A tiebreaker in tennis *is where* they play one final game
to decide the set.**

REVISED  **A tiebreaker in tennis is the final deciding game of a
tied set.**

Writing about reasons, like writing definitions, has pitfalls. Avoid
*the reason is because* in Standard English. Grammatically, an adverb
clause beginning with *because* cannot follow the verb *be*. Instead, use
*the reason is that*, or recast the sentence.

FAULTY  ***The reason* Kournikova lost *is because* her opponent
was serving so well.**

POSSIBLE
REVISIONS  ***The reason* Kournikova lost *is that* her opponent was
serving so well.**

**Kournikova lost *because* her opponent was serving
so well.**

Note that Standard English requires *the reason that* and not *the reason
why*.

that
▶ The TV commentator explained the reason ~~why~~ Kournikova
lost.

[Another possibility here is to omit *that*.]

**40g** Avoid using an adverb clause as the subject of a sentence.

An adverb clause cannot function as the subject of a sentence. (See **37e** on adverb clauses.)

▶ ~~Because she swims~~ *Swimming* every day does not guarantee she is healthy.

[The subject is now a noun phrase, *Swimming every day,* instead of a clause, *Because she swims every day.*]

▶ When beavers eat trees⌃*, they* destroys the woods.

[The dependent clause *When beavers eat trees* is now attached to an independent clause with its own subject, *they.*]

**40h** Include all necessary words and apostrophes.

*Include necessary words in compound structures.* If you omit a verb form from a compound verb, the main verb form must fit into each part of the compound; otherwise, you must use the complete verb form (see **40j** on parallelism).

▶ He has always⌃*tried* and will always try to preserve his father's good name in the community. [*Try* fits only with *will,* not with *has.*]

*Include necessary words in comparisons.* (See also **45i**.)

▶ The volleyball captain is as competitive⌃*as* or even more competitive than her teammates.

[The comparative structures are *as competitive as* and *more competitive than.* Do not merge them.]

Sometimes you create ambiguity if you omit the verb in the second part of a comparison.

▶ He liked baseball more than his son⌃*did*. [Omitting *did* implies that he liked baseball more than he liked his son.]

*Include apostrophes with words that need them.*

> ▶ My mother's expectations differed from Jing-Mei's mother. [ 's ]

See also **45i** and **48c**.

## **40i** State the grammatical subject only once.

Even when a phrase or clause separates the subject and main verb of a sentence, do not restate the subject in pronoun form. (See also **62f** ESL.)

> [ restated subject ]
> ▶ The nurse who took care of my father for many years ~~she~~ gave him comfort and advice.

When the subject is a whole clause, do not add an *it* subject.

> ▶ What may seem moral to some ~~it~~ is immoral to others.

## **40j** Aim for parallelism.

The use of parallel structures helps produce cohesion in a text. Aim for parallelism in sentences and in longer passages. The following sentence contains parallel *-ing* phrases:

> ▶ They really enjoy   *playing* volleyball,
>                    *bicycling* on country roads,
>       and   *snorkeling* in the Gulf waters.

Sentences become confusing when you string together phrases or clauses that lack parallelism.

NOT PARALLEL    **He wants a new girlfriend, to get a house, and find a good job.**

PARALLEL    **He wants a new girlfriend, a house, and a good job.**

*Parallel structures with paired (correlative) conjunctions*   When your sentence contains correlative conjunctions, pairs such as *either . . . or, neither . . . nor, not only . . . but also, both . . . and, whether . . . or,* and *as . . . as,* the structure after the second part of the pair should be exactly parallel in form to the structure after the first part.

> [ to ]
> ▶ He made up his mind *either* to paint the van *or* sell it to another buyer. [*To paint* follows *either*; therefore, *to sell* should follow *or*.]

> playing
> ▶ **She loves** *both* **swimming competitively** *and* ~~to play~~ **golf.**

[An *-ing* form follows *both*; therefore, an *-ing* form should also follow *and*.]

> ▶ **The drive to Cuernavaca was** *not only* **too expensive** *but also*
> ~~was~~ **too tiring to do alone.** [*Too expensive* follows *not only*;
> therefore, *too tiring* should follow *but also*.]

***Parallel structures in comparisons*** When making comparisons
with *as* or *than*, use parallel structures.

> To drive
> ▶ ~~Driving~~ **to Cuernavaca is** *as* **expensive** *as* **to take the bus.**
> Taking
> ▶ ~~To take~~ **the bus is less comfortable** *than* **driving.**

# **41** Verbs

A verb will fit into one or more of the following sentences:

a. They want to _____ . It is going to _____ .
b. They will _____ .      It will _____ .

Identify a verb by checking that the *base form* (that is, the form listed as
a dictionary entry) fits these sentences.

## **41a** Verb forms in Standard English

Although you might use a variety of verb forms when you speak,
readers generally expect formal writing to conform to Standard English
usage. All verbs except *be* have five forms.

The five forms of *regular verbs* follow a predictable pattern. Once
you know the base form, you can construct all the others:

1. base form: the form listed in a dictionary;

2. *-s* form: the third person singular form of the present tense;

3. *-ing* form (the *present participle*): needs auxiliary verbs to function as
   a complete verb; can appear in a verbal phrase (see **37d**) and as a
   noun (gerund);

4. past tense form: functions as a complete verb, without auxiliary
   verbs;

5. past participle: often called the *–ed/en* form; needs auxiliary verbs to function as a complete verb (*has chosen, was chosen*); can appear in a phrase (*the chosen few; chosen for efficiency*).

REGULAR VERBS

| BASE | –s | *–ing* PRESENT PARTICIPLE | PAST TENSE | PAST PARTICIPLE |
|------|------|------|------|------|
| paint | paints | painting | painted | painted |
| smile | smiles | smiling | smiled | smiled |

In contrast, *irregular verbs* do not use *-ed* to form the past tense and the past participle. (See **41c** for the forms of the irregular verb *be*.)

IRREGULAR VERBS

| BASE | –s | *–ing* PRESENT PARTICIPLE | PAST TENSE | PAST PARTICIPLE |
|------|------|------|------|------|
| take | takes | taking | took | taken |
| go | goes | going | went | gone |

The following list shows some common irregular verbs. Notice the past tense form and past participle of each one.

| BASE FORM | PAST TENSE | PAST PARTICIPLE |
|------|------|------|
| arise | arose | arisen |
| bear | bore | born |
| beat | beat | beaten |
| become | became | become |
| begin | began | begun |
| bend | bent | bent |
| bet | bet | bet, betted |
| bind | bound | bound |
| bite | bit | bitten |
| bleed | bled | bled |
| blow | blew | blown |
| break | broke | broken |
| bring | brought | brought |
| build | built | built |
| burst | burst | burst |
| buy | bought | bought |
| catch | caught | caught |
| choose | chose | chosen |

| BASE FORM | PAST TENSE | PAST PARTICIPLE |
|---|---|---|
| cling | clung | clung |
| come | came | come |
| cost | cost | cost |
| creep | crept | crept |
| cut | cut | cut |
| deal | dealt | dealt |
| dig | dug | dug |
| do | did | done |
| draw | drew | drawn |
| drink | drank | drunk |
| drive | drove | driven |
| eat | ate | eaten |
| fall | fell | fallen |
| feed | fed | fed |
| feel | felt | felt |
| fight | fought | fought |
| find | found | found |
| flee | fled | fled |
| fly | flew | flown |
| forbid | forbad(e) | forbidden |
| forget | forgot | forgotten |
| forgive | forgave | forgiven |
| freeze | froze | frozen |
| get | got | gotten, got |
| give | gave | given |
| go | went | gone |
| grind | ground | ground |
| grow | grew | grown |
| hang* | hung | hung |
| have | had | had |
| hear | heard | heard |
| hide | hid | hidden |
| hit | hit | hit |
| hold | held | held |
| hurt | hurt | hurt |
| keep | kept | kept |
| know | knew | known |
| lay | laid | laid (see also **41b**) |
| lead | led | led |
| leave | left | left |

*Hang* meaning "put to death" is regular: *hang, hanged, hanged.*

| BASE FORM | PAST TENSE | PAST PARTICIPLE |
|---|---|---|
| lend | lent | lent |
| let | let | let |
| lie | lay | lain (see also **41b**) |
| light | lit, lighted | lit, lighted |
| lose | lost | lost |
| make | made | made |
| mean | meant | meant |
| meet | met | met |
| put | put | put |
| quit | quit | quit |
| read | read | read |
| ride | rode | ridden |
| ring | rang | rung |
| rise | rose | risen (see also **41b**) |
| run | ran | run |
| say | said | said |
| see | saw | seen |
| seek | sought | sought |
| sell | sold | sold |
| send | sent | sent |
| set | set | set (see also **41b**) |
| shake | shook | shaken |
| shine | shone | shone |
| shoot | shot | shot |
| shrink | shrank | shrunk |
| shut | shut | shut |
| sing | sang | sung |
| sink | sank | sunk |
| sit | sat | sat (see also **41b**) |
| sleep | slept | slept |
| slide | slid | slid |
| slit | slit | slit |
| speak | spoke | spoken |
| spend | spent | spent |
| spin | spun | spun |
| spit | spit, spat | spit |
| split | split | split |
| spread | spread | spread |
| spring | sprang | sprung |
| stand | stood | stood |
| steal | stole | stolen |
| stick | stuck | stuck |

| BASE FORM | PAST TENSE | PAST PARTICIPLE |
|---|---|---|
| sting | stung | stung |
| stink | stank, stunk | stunk |
| strike | struck | struck, stricken |
| swear | swore | sworn |
| sweep | swept | swept |
| swim | swam | swum |
| swing | swung | swung |
| take | took | taken |
| teach | taught | taught |
| tear | tore | torn |
| tell | told | told |
| think | thought | thought |
| throw | threw | thrown |
| tread | trod | trodden, trod |
| understand | understood | understood |
| upset | upset | upset |
| wake | woke | waked, woken |
| wear | wore | worn |
| weave | wove | woven |
| weep | wept | wept |
| win | won | won |
| wind | wound | wound |
| wring | wrung | wrung |
| write | wrote | written |

## **41b** Verbs commonly confused

You may need to give special attention to certain verbs that are similar in form but differ in meaning. Some of them can take a direct object; these are called *transitive verbs*. Others never take a direct object; these are called *intransitive verbs*. (See also **37c** and **62c** ESL.)

1. *rise:* to get up, to ascend (intransitive)

   *raise:* to lift, to cause to rise (transitive)

| BASE | –s | –ing | PAST TENSE | PAST PARTICIPLE |
|---|---|---|---|---|
| rise | rises | rising | rose | risen |
| raise | raises | raising | raised | raised |

▶ The sun *rose* at 5:55 a.m. today.

▶ She *raised* the blind and peeked out.

2. *sit:* to occupy a seat (intransitive)

   *set:* to put or place (transitive)

| BASE | –*s* | –*ing* | PAST TENSE | PAST PARTICIPLE |
|------|------|--------|------------|-----------------|
| sit  | sits | sitting | sat | sat |
| set  | sets | setting | set | set |

▶ He *sat* on the wooden chair.

▶ She *set* the vase on the middle shelf.

3. *lie:* to recline (intransitive)

   *lay:* to put or place (transitive)

| | | | | |
|------|------|--------|------|------|
| lie  | lies | lying | lay | lain |
| lay  | lays | laying | laid | laid |

    lay
▶ I ~~laid~~ down for half an hour.

    lying
▶ I was ~~laying~~ down when you called.

    Lay
▶ ~~Lie~~ the map on the floor.

In addition, note the verb *lie* ("to say something untrue"), which is intransitive.

| | | | | |
|------|------|--------|------|------|
| lie  | lies | lying | lied | lied |

▶ He *lied* when he said he had won three trophies.

## **41c** The forms of *be*, auxiliaries, and modal auxiliaries

The verb *be* has eight forms, including three present tense forms (*am, is, are*) and two past tense forms (*was, were*).

| BASE | PRESENT TENSE FORMS | –*ing* | PAST | PAST PARTICIPLE |
|------|---------------------|--------|------|-----------------|
| be   | am, is, are | being | was, were | been |

For more on the distinction between *being* and *been*, see page 314.

### LANGUAGE AND CULTURE

#### Language and Dialect Variation with *Be*

In some languages (Chinese and Russian, for example), forms of *be* used as an auxiliary ("She is singing") or as a linking verb ("He

*(Continued)*

*(Continued)*

is happy") can be omitted. In some spoken dialects of English (African American Vernacular, for example), subtle linguistic distinctions not possible in Standard English can be achieved: the omission of a form of *be* and the use of the base form in place of an inflected form (a form that shows number, person, mood, or tense) signal entirely different meanings.

| VERNACULAR | | STANDARD |
|---|---|---|
| He busy. | (temporarily) | He is busy now. |
| She be busy. | (habitually) | She is busy all the time. |

Standard English always requires the inclusion of an inflected form of *be*.

▶ Latecomers always at a disadvantage.
　　　　　　　are

An independent clause needs a complete verb. The *-ing* form and the past participle are not complete verbs because they do not show tense. They need auxiliary or modal auxiliary verbs to complete their meaning in a clause. (See **61b** ESL for the meanings of modal auxiliary verbs.)

| AUXILIARY VERBS | MODAL AUXILIARY VERBS | |
|---|---|---|
| *do*: does, do, did | will, would | shall, should |
| *be*: be, am, is, are, was,<br>　　were, being, been | can, could | may, might, must |
| *have*: has, have, had | | |

Auxiliary verbs and modal auxiliary verbs can be used in combination. Whatever the combination, the form of the main verb is determined by the auxiliary that precedes it, as in the following examples.

**WHICH FORM SHOULD I USE?**

1. After *do, does, did,* and the nine modal auxiliaries—*will, would, can, could, shall, should, may, might,* and *must*—use the base form.

▶ He *should stay.*

▶ They *must have* dinner soon.

▶ *Did* she *leave?*

**ESL Note** A modal auxiliary never changes form or takes an *-s* ending. ■

2. After *has, have,* and *had,* use the past participle.

▶ It *has snowed.*

▶ They should *have gone*
   [*not* They should *have went.*]

▶ They *had eaten* when I arrived.

In informal speech, we run sounds together, and the pronunciation may be mistakenly carried over into writing.

　　　　　　　　have
▶ **She should ~~of~~ left that job last year.**

The pronunciation of the contraction *should've* is probably responsible for the nonstandard form *should of.* Edit carefully for the appearance of the word *of* in place of *have* in verb phrases.

3. After *be, am, is, are, was, were,* and *been,* use the *-ing* form for active voice verbs.

▶ **She *is taking* her driving test.**　　▶ **You *were watching.***

▶ **He might have *been driving.***　　▶ **They could *be jogging.***

**ESL Note** To form a complete verb, always use a *be* auxiliary before the *-ing* form. The *-ing* form alone can never be a complete verb in a clause. See **61a** ESL. ■

4. After *be, am, is, are, was, were, been,* and *being,* use the past participle for passive voice (see **42**).

▶ **They *were taken* to a tropical island for their anniversary.**

▶ **The faucet should *be fixed.***

▶ **The pie might have *been eaten.***

▶ **The suspects are *being watched.***

**ESL Note** *Be* requires a modal before it to form a complete verb (*could be jogging; will be closed*). *Been* requires *have, has,* or *had* (*have been driving; has been eaten*). *Being* must be preceded by *am, is, are, was,* or *were* to form a complete verb and must be followed by an adjective or a past participle: *You are being silly. He was being followed.* ■

## 41d Verb tenses

Tenses indicate time as perceived by the speaker or writer. Verbs change form to indicate present or past time. (To indicate future time, English uses the modal auxiliary *will* as well as expressions such as *be going to*.) Closely related to tense is *aspect*, which allows a speaker or writer to indicate that an action is completed or in progress. For each time (present, past, and future), auxiliary verbs are used with the main verb to convey completed actions (perfect forms), actions in progress (progressive forms), and actions that are completed by some specified time or event and also emphasize the length of time in progress (perfect progressive forms).

The following examples illustrate aspects of active voice verbs referring to past, present, and future time. For passive voice verbs, see **42**.

PAST TIME

| | |
|---|---|
| Simple past | They *arrived* yesterday./They *did* not *arrive* today. |
| Past progressive | They *were leaving* when the phone rang. |
| Past perfect | Everyone *had left* when I called. |
| Past perfect progressive | We *had been sleeping* for an hour before you arrived. |

PRESENT TIME

| | |
|---|---|
| Simple present | He *eats* Wheaties every morning./He *does* not *eat* eggs. |
| Present progressive | They *are working* today. |
| Present perfect | She *has* never *read* Melville. |
| Present perfect progressive | He *has been living* here for five years. |

FUTURE TIME (USING *WILL*)

| | |
|---|---|
| Simple future | She *will arrive* soon. |
| Future progressive | They *will be playing* baseball at noon tomorrow. |
| Future perfect | He *will have finished* the project by Friday. |
| Future perfect progressive | By the year 2004, they *will have been running* the company for twenty-five years. |

Other modal auxiliaries can substitute for *will* and thus change the meaning: *must arrive, might be playing, may have finished, should have been running.* (See **61b** ESL.)

**ESL Note** Use simple tenses but not progressive forms with verbs expressing mental activity referring to the senses, preference, or thought, as well as with verbs of possession, appearance, and inclusion (for example, *smell, prefer, understand, own, seem, contain*).

possess
▶ They ~~are possessing~~ different behavior patterns.

smell
▶ I ~~am smelling~~ a rat. ■

## **41e** Present tenses

*Simple present*  Use the simple present tense for the following purposes:

1. To make a generalization

   ▶ We *turn* the clocks ahead every April.

2. To indicate an activity that happens habitually or repeatedly

   ▶ He *works* for Sony.

   ▶ They *take* vacations in Puerto Rico.

3. To discuss literature and the arts even if the work was written in the past or the author is no longer alive

   ▶ In *Zami,* Audre Lorde *describes* how a librarian *introduces* her to the joys of reading.

   When used in this way, the present tense is called the *literary present.* However, when you write a narrative of your own, use past tenses to tell about past actions.

   walked                                    kissed
   ▶ Then the candidate ~~walks~~ up to the crowd and ~~kisses~~ all the babies.

**ESL Note** In a dependent clause beginning with a conjunction such as *if, when, before, after, until,* or *as soon as,* do not use *will* to express future time. Use *will* only in the independent clause. Use the simple present in the subordinate clause.

▶ When they ~~will~~ arrive, the meeting will begin. ■

*Present progressive*   Use the present progressive to indicate an action in progress at the moment of speaking or writing.

▶ He *is playing* pool with his nephew.

*Present perfect and present perfect progressive*   Use the present perfect in the following instances:

1. To indicate that an action occurring at some unstated time in the past is related to present time

▶ They *have worked* in New Mexico, so they know its laws.

2. To indicate that an action beginning in the past continues to the present

▶ They *have worked* in New Mexico for three years.

If you state the exact time when something occurred, use the simple past tense, not the present perfect.

worked
▶ They ~~have worked~~ in Arizona three years ago.

Use the present perfect progressive when you indicate the length of time an action has been in progress up to the present time.

▶ They *have been dancing* for three hours.
   [This implies that they are still dancing.]

**41f**   Past tenses

Use the past tenses consistently. Do not switch to present or future for no reason (see **41h**).

*Simple past*   Use the simple past tense when you specify exactly when an event occurred.

▶ She *married* him last month.

When the sequence of past events is indicated with words like *before* or *after*, use the simple past for both events.

▶ She *knew* how to write her name before she *went* to school.

*Past progressive*   Use the past progressive for an activity in progress over time or at a specified point in the past.

▶ They *were working* all day yesterday.

▶ He *was lifting* weights when I called.

*Past perfect* Use the past perfect or the past perfect progressive only when one past event was completed before another past event or stated past time.

▶ Ben *had cooked* the whole meal by the time Sam arrived.

[Two events occurred: Ben cooked the meal; then Sam arrived.]

▶ He *had been cooking* for three hours when his sister finally offered to help.

[An event in progress—cooking—was interrupted in the past.]

Make sure that the past tense form you choose expresses your exact meaning.

▶ When the student protesters marched into the building at noon, the administrators *were leaving*.  [The administrators were in the process of leaving. They began to leave at, say, 11:57 a.m.]

▶ When the student protesters marched into the building at noon, the administrators *had left*.

[There was no sign of the administrators. They had left at 11 a.m.]

▶ When the student protesters marched into the building at noon, the administrators *left*.

[The administrators saw the protesters and then left at 12:01 p.m.]

**41g** *-ed* endings: past tense and past participle forms

Both the past tense form and the past participle of regular verbs end in *-ed*. This ending causes writers trouble because in speech the ending is often dropped—particularly when it blends into the next sound.

▶ They wash *ed* two baskets of laundry last night.

Standard English requires the *-ed* ending in the following instances.

1. To form the past tense of a regular verb

   ▶ He ask *ed* to leave early.

2. To form the expression *used to,* indicating past habit

   ▶ They use *d* to smoke.

3. To form the past participle of a regular verb for use with the auxiliary *has, have,* or *had* in the active voice or with forms of *be (am, is, are, was, were, be, being, been)* in the passive voice (see **42**)

▶ She has work~~ed~~ there for a long time. [Active]

▶ The work will be finish~~ed~~ tomorrow. [Passive]

4. To form a past participle for use as an adjective

▶ Put in some chop~~ped~~ meat.    ▶ The frighten~~ed~~ boy ran away.

*Note:* The following *-ed* forms are used with *be* or *get: concerned, confused, depressed, divorced, embarrassed, married, prejudiced, satisfied, scared, supposed (to), surprised, used (to), worried.* Do not omit the *-d* ending.

▶ I was surprise~~d~~ to see how many awards he had won.

▶ The general was suppose~~d~~ to be in charge.

▶ Parents get worr~~ied~~ when their children are depress~~ed~~.

Do not confuse the past tense form and the past participle of an irregular verb. A past tense form stands alone as a complete verb, but a past participle does not.

▶ He ~~drunk~~ drank too much last night.  ▶ You could have ~~went~~ gone alone.

▶ She ~~done~~ did her best.    ▶ The bell was ~~rang~~ rung five times.

**41h**  Avoiding unnecessary tense shifts

If you use tenses consistently throughout a piece of writing, you help readers understand what is happening and when. Check that your verbs consistently express present or past time, both within a sentence and from one sentence to the next.

| Tense Shifts | Selecting a jury *was* very difficult. The lawyers *ask* many questions to discover bias and prejudice; sometimes the prospective jurors *had* the idea they *are acting* in a play. |
|---|---|
| Revised | Selecting a jury *was* very difficult. The lawyers *asked* many questions to discover bias and prejudice; sometimes the prospective jurors *had* the idea they *were acting* in a play. |

When you write about events or ideas presented by another writer, use the literary present (see **41e**).

▶ The author illustrate**s** the images of women in two ways, using advertisements and dramas on TV. One way shows women who advance**d** their careers by themselves, and the other shows those who use**d** beauty to gain recognition.

Tense shifts are appropriate in the following instances:

1. When you signal a time change with a time word or phrase

signal for switch from past to present

▶ Harold *was* my late grandfather's name, and *now* it *is* mine.

2. When you follow a generalization (present tense) with a specific example of a past incident

generalization

▶ Some bilingual schools *offer* intensive instruction in English.

specific example

My sister, for example, *went* to a bilingual school where she *studied* English for two hours every day.

## **41i**  Tenses in indirect quotations

An indirect quotation reports what someone said. It does not use quotation marks. When the verb introducing an indirect quotation is in a present tense, the indirect quotation should preserve the tense of the original direct quotation. See also **40d** and **62d** ESL.

DIRECT     "The client *has signed* the contract."

INDIRECT   present     indirect quotation

The lawyer *tells* us that the client *has signed* the contract.

When the introductory verb is in a past tense, use forms that express past time in the indirect quotation.

DIRECT     "The meetings *are* over and the buyer *has signed* the contract."

INDIRECT   past     direct quotation

Our lawyer *told* us that the meetings *were* over and the buyer *had signed* the contract.

In longer passages, preserve the sequence of tenses showing past time throughout the whole indirect quotation.

▶ **Our lawyer, Larraine, told us that the meetings *were* over and the buyer *had signed* the contract. Larraine's firm *had reassigned* her to another case, so she *was leaving* the next day.**

*Note:* Use a present tense after a past tense introductory verb only if the statement is a general statement that holds true in present time.

▶ **Our lawyer *told* us she *is* happy with the progress of the case.**

**41j**  Verbs in conditional sentences, wishes, requests, demands, and recommendations

*Conditions*  When *if* or *unless* is used to introduce a dependent clause, the sentence expresses a condition. Four types of conditional sentences are used in English; two refer to actual or possible situations, and two refer to speculative or hypothetical situations. The Key Points box gives examples of these four types.

---

**KEY POINTS**

**Verb Tenses in Conditional Sentences**

| MEANING EXPRESSED | *IF* CLAUSE | INDEPENDENT CLAUSE |
|---|---|---|
| 1. Fact | Simple present | Simple present |

▶ **If people *earn* more, they *spend* more.**

| | | |
|---|---|---|
| 2. Prediction/ possibility | Simple present | *will, can, should, might* + base form |

▶ **If you *turn* left here, you *will end up* in Mississippi.**

| | | |
|---|---|---|
| 3. Speculation about present or future | Simple past *or* subjunctive *were* | *would, could, should, might* + base form |

*(Continued)*

*(Continued)*

▶ If he *had* a cell phone, he *would use* it.
[But he does not have one.]

▶ If she *were* my lawyer, I *might win* the case.
[But she is not.]

| 4. Speculation about past | Past perfect (*had* + past participle) | *would have* *could have* *should have* *might have* } + past participle |
|---|---|---|

▶ If they *had saved* the diaries, they *could have sold* them.
[But they did not save them.]

**USE OF SUBJUNCTIVE *WERE* IN PLACE OF *WAS*** With speculative conditions about the present and future using the verb *be, were* is used in place of *was* in the dependent *if* clause. This use of *were* to indicate hypothetical situations involves what is called the *subjunctive mood.*

▶ If my aunt *were* sixty-five, she *could get* a discount air fare.
[My aunt is sixty.]

**BLENDING** Some blending of time and tenses can occur, as in the case of a condition that speculates about the past in relation to the effect on the present.

▶ If I *had bought* a new car instead of this old wreck, I *would feel* a lot safer today.

**USE OF *WOULD*** When writing Standard English, use *would* only in the independent clause, not in the conditional clause. However, *would* occurs frequently in the conditional clause in speech and in informal writing.

▶ If the fish fry committee ~~would show~~ showed more initiative, people might attend their events more regularly.

▶ If I ~~would have~~ had heard him say that, I would have been angry.

**WOULD, COULD, AND MIGHT WITH CONDITIONAL CLAUSE UNDERSTOOD** *Would, could,* and *might* are used in independent clauses when no conditional clause is present. These are situations that are contrary to fact, and the conditional clause is understood.

▶ I *would* never *advise* her to leave college without a degree. She *might come back* later and blame me for her lack of direction.

*Wishes*  Like some conditions, wishes deal with speculation. For a present wish—about something that has not happened and is therefore hypothetical and imaginary—use the past tense or subjunctive *were* in the dependent clause. For a wish about the past, use the past perfect: *had* + past participle.

A WISH ABOUT THE PRESENT

▶ I wish I *had* your attitude.

▶ I wish that Shakespeare *were* still alive.

A WISH ABOUT THE PAST

▶ Some union members wish that the strike *had* never *occurred*.

▶ He wishes that he *had bought* a lottery ticket.

*Requests, demands, and recommendations*  The subjunctive also appears after certain verbs, such as *request, command, insist, demand, move* (meaning "propose"), *propose,* and *urge*. In these cases, the verb in the dependent clause is the base form, regardless of the person and number of the subject.

▶ The dean suggested that students *be* allowed to vote.

▶ He insisted that she *submit* the report.

▶ I move that the treasurer *revise* the budget.

Some idiomatic expressions preserve the subjunctive in standard English—for example, *far* be *it from me, if need* be, *as it* were.

---

## 42  Passive Voice

In the active voice, the grammatical subject is the doer of the action, and the sentence tells "who's doing what." The passive voice tells what *is done to* the subject of the sentence. The person or thing doing the action may or may not be mentioned but is always implied: "My car was repaired" (by somebody at the garage).

ACTIVE

ACTIVE

                  ⌐— subject —⌐   active voice verb   ⌐— direct object —⌐
▶ **Alice Walker**      **wrote**      *The Color Purple.*

PASSIVE

                              passive voice
        ⌐————— subject —————⌐   ⌐— verb —⌐   ⌐— doer or agent —⌐
▶ *The Color Purple* **was written**  **by Alice Walker.**

**42a** Know when to use the passive voice.

Use the passive voice sparingly. A general rule is to use the passive voice only when the doer or agent in your sentence (the person or thing acting) is unknown or is unimportant (see **42c**) or when you want to connect the topics of two clauses (see **31a** and **42d**).

▶ **The pandas are rare. Two of them will be returned to the wild.**

**ESL Note** Use the passive voice only with verbs that are transitive in English. Intransitive verbs such as *happen, occur,* and *try (to)* are not used in the passive voice.

▶ **The ceremony ~~was~~ happened yesterday.**

                                    *have*
▶ **Morality is an issue that ~~was~~ tried to explain ~~by~~**
   **many philosophers.**                              ∎

**42b** Know how to form the passive voice.

The complete verb of a passive voice sentence consists of a form of the verb *be* followed by a past participle.

                         verb: *be* +
        receiver        past participle
        ⌐— as subject —⌐   ⌐——————⌐   doer omitted or named after *by*
▶ **The windows**   **are cleaned**   **(by someone) every month.**

▶ **The windows** *were being cleaned* **yesterday afternoon.**

▶ **The windows** *will have been cleaned* **by the end of the workday.**

Auxiliaries such as *would, can, could, should, may, might,* and *must* can also replace *will* when the meaning demands it.

▶ **The windows** *might be cleaned* **next month.**

**42c** Use passive voice when the doer or agent is unknown or unimportant.

▶ He had a lot of people working for him, maybe sixty, and most of them liked him most of the time. Three of them *will be* seriously *considered* for his job.   —Ellen Goodman, "The Company Man"

In scientific writing, the passive voice is often preferred to indicate objective procedures. Scientists and engineers are interested in analyzing data and in performing studies that other researchers can replicate. The individual doing the experiment is therefore relatively unimportant and usually is not the subject of the sentence.

▶ The experiment *was conducted* in a classroom. Participants *were instructed* to remove their watches prior to the experiment.

If you are writing in the humanities, however, question each use of the passive voice, and ask yourself whether you need it.

**42d** Use the passive voice to connect the subject of a sentence to what has gone before.

Notice how the passive voice preserves the topic chain of *I* subjects in the following passage (see also **31a**):

▶ I remember to start with that day in Sacramento [. . .] when I first entered a classroom, able to understand some fifty stray English words. The third of four children, I *had been preceded* to a Roman Catholic school by an older brother and sister.
—Richard Rodriguez, *Hunger of Memory*

**42e** Do not overuse the passive voice.

Generally your writing will be clearer and stronger if you name the subject and use verbs in the active voice to tell "who's doing what." If you overuse the passive voice, the effect will be heavy and impersonal (see **30a**).

| UNNECESSARY PASSIVE | He *was alerted* to the danger of drugs by his doctor and *was persuaded* by her to enroll in a treatment program. |
| REVISED | His doctor alerted him to the danger of drugs and persuaded him to enroll in a treatment program. |

## 43 Subject-Verb Agreement

In standard English, a third person singular subject takes a singular verb (with -*s*), and a plural subject takes a plural verb (with no -*s*).

| SINGULAR SUBJECT | PLURAL SUBJECT |
|---|---|
| A baby *cries*. | Babies *cry*. |
| He *loses*. | They *lose*. |
| His brother *plays* baseball. | His brothers *play* baseball. |

### 43a Basic principles of subject-verb agreement

When you use the present tense, subject and verb must agree in person (first, second, or third) and number (singular or plural). In English, the ending -*s* is added to both nouns and verbs, but for very different reasons.

1. An -*s* ending on a noun is a plural signal: *her brothers* (more than one).

2. An -*s* ending on a verb is a singular signal; -*s* is added to a third person singular verb in the present tense: *Her plumber wears gold jewelry.*

**KEY POINTS**

**Two Key Points about Agreement**

1. Follow the "one -*s* rule." Generally, you can put an -*s* on a noun to make it plural, or you can put an -*s* on a verb to make it singular. (But see the irregular forms *is* and *has*, on p. 327.) An -*s* on both subject and verb is not Standard English.

| FAULTY AGREEMENT | **My friends comes over every Saturday.** |
|---|---|
| | [Violates the "one -*s* rule"] |

| POSSIBLE REVISIONS | **My friend comes over every Saturday.** |
|---|---|
| | **My friends come over every Saturday.** |

*(Continued)*

*(Continued)*

2. Do not omit a necessary *-s*.

▶ His supervisor want <sup>ꜱ</sup> him to work the night shift.

▶ The book <sup>ꜱ</sup> on my desk describe life in Tahiti.

▶ She *uses* her experience, *speaks* to the crowds, and *win* <sup>ꜱ</sup> their confidence.

Most simple present verbs show agreement with an *-s* ending. The verb *be*, however, has three instead of two present tense forms. In addition, *be* is the only verb to show agreement in the past tense, where it has two forms: *were* and the third person singular *was*.

### SUBJECT-VERB AGREEMENT

| BASE FORM | like | have | be | do |
|---|---|---|---|---|
| **SIMPLE PRESENT: SINGULAR** | | | | |
| First person: I | like | have | am | do |
| Second person: you | like | have | are | do |
| Third person: he, she, it | likes | has | is | does |
| **SIMPLE PRESENT: PLURAL** | | | | |
| First person: we | like | have | are | do |
| Second person: you | like | have | are | do |
| Third person: they | like | have | are | do |

## LANGUAGE AND CULTURE

### Issues of Subject-Verb Agreement

Many languages make no change in the verb form to indicate number and person, and several spoken versions of English, such as London Cockney, Caribbean Creole, and African American Vernacular (AAV), do not observe the standard rules of agreement.

▶ **Cockney: He** *don't* **never wear that brown whistle.**

[The standard form is *doesn't*; other nonstandard forms in this sentence are *don't never* (a double negative) and *whistle*— short for *whistle and flute*, rhyming slang for *suit*.]

▶ **AAV: She** *have* **a lot of work experience.**

*(Continued)*

*(Continued)*

Use authentic forms like these when quoting direct speech; for your formal academic writing, though, follow the subject-verb agreement conventions of Standard English.

**ESL Note** Modal auxiliaries never add an -s ending and any verb form following immediately must be a base form: I *can sing*; she *should go*; he *might be* leaving; she *will have* been promoted (**41c** and **61b** ESL). ■

## 43b Words between the subject and verb

When words separate the subject and verb, find the verb and ask "Who?" or "What?" about it to determine the subject. Ignore the intervening words.

▶ **The child picking flowers looks tired.**

[Who looks tired? The subject, *child*, is singular.]

▶ **Her collection of baseball cards is valuable.**

[What is valuable? The subject, *collection*, is singular.]

▶ **The government's proposals about preserving the environment**

**cause controversy.**

[What things cause controversy? The subject, *proposals*, is plural.]

Do not be confused by intervening words ending in -s, such as *always* and *sometimes*. The -s ending still must appear on a present tense verb if the subject is singular.

▶ **His assistant always ~~make~~ ˢmistakes.**

Phrases introduced by *as well as, along with*, and *in addition to* that come between the subject and the verb do not change the number of the verb.

▶ **His daughter, as well as his two sons, ~~want~~ ˢhim to move nearby.**

## 43c Agreement with linking verbs and complement

Linking verbs such as *be, seem, look*, and *appear* are followed by a complement, and a subject complement should not be confused with a subject (see **37c**). Make the verb agree with the subject stated before the linking verb, not with the noun complement that follows the verb.

| plural | singular | singular | plural |
|---|---|---|---|
| ┌─ subject ─┐ | ┌ complement ┐ | ┌─ subject ─┐ | ┌complement┐ |

▶ **Rare books are her passion.**   ▶ **Her passion is rare books.**
          plural verb                        singular verb

▶ **My favorite part of city life *is* the parties.**

▶ **Parties *are* my favorite part of city life.**

## 43d  Subject after verb

When the subject follows the verb in the sentence, make the subject and verb agree.

**1. Questions**   In a question, the auxiliary verb agrees with the subject.

        singular
     ┌─ subject ─┐
▶ *Does* **the editor agree to the changes?**

        ┌─────── plural subject ───────┐
▶ *Do* **the editor and the production manager agree to them?**

**2. Initial here *or* there**   When a sentence begins with *here* or *there*, the verb agrees with the subject.

        singular
     ┌subject┐
▶ **There *is* a reason to rejoice.**

     ┌─ plural subject ─┐
▶ **There *are* many reasons to rejoice.**

However, avoid excessive use of initial *there* (see **30b**): *We have a reason to rejoice.*

**ESL Note**   It does not follow the same pattern as *here* and *there*. The verb in a sentence beginning with *it* is always singular.

▶ **It *is* hundreds of miles away.** ■

**3. Inverted word order**   When a sentence begins not with the subject but with a phrase preceding the verb, the verb still agrees with the subject (see also **34d** and **37c**).

```
                              plural
      ┌── prepositional phrase ──┐  verb ┌── plural subject ──┐
```
▶ **In front of the library sit two stone lions.**

[Who or what performs the action of the verb? Two stone lions do.]

## **43e** Tricky singular subjects

*1.* **Each *and* every** *Each* and *every* may seem to indicate more than one, but grammatically they are singular words, used with a singular verb.

▶ **Each of the cakes *has* a different frosting.**

▶ **Every change in procedures *causes* problems.**

*2.* **-ing *verb form as subject*** With a subject beginning with the *-ing* verb form (called a *gerund*), always use a singular verb form.

```
  singular
  ┌ subject ┐
```
▶ **Playing the piano in front of a crowd *causes* anxiety.**

*3.* **Singular nouns ending in -s** Some nouns that end in -s *(news, economics, physics, politics, mathematics, statistics)* are not plural. Use them with a singular verb.

▶ **The news *has* been bad lately.**   ▶ **Politics *is* dirty business.**

*4.* **Phrases of time, money, and weight** When the subject is regarded as one unit, use a singular verb.

▶ **Five hundred dollars *seems* too much to pay.**

▶ **Seven years *was* a long time to spend at college.**

*5.* **Uncountable nouns** An uncountable noun *(furniture, jewelry, equipment, advice, happiness, honesty, information, knowledge)* encompasses all the items in its class. An uncountable noun does not have a plural form and is always followed by a singular verb (**60b** ESL).

▶ **That advice *makes* me nervous.**

▶ **The information found in the press *is* not always accurate.**

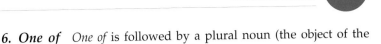

**6. *One of*** *One of* is followed by a plural noun (the object of the preposition *of* ) and a singular verb form.

▶ One of her friends *loves* to tango.

▶ One of the reasons for his difficulties *is* that he spends too much money.

For agreement with *one of* and *the only one of* followed by a relative clause, see **46c**.

**7. The number of/a number of** The phrase *the number of* is followed by a plural noun (the object of the preposition *of*) and a singular verb form.

▶ The number of reasons *is* growing.

With *a number of*, meaning "several," use a plural verb.

▶ A number of reasons *are* listed in the letter.

**8. *The title of a work or a word referred to as the word itself*** Use a singular verb with the title of a work or a word referred to as the word itself. Use a singular verb even if the title or word is plural in form. See also **52a** and **52c**.

▶ Cats *has* finally ended its long run on Broadway.

▶ In her story, the word <u>dudes</u> *appears* five times.

**43f** Collective nouns

Generally, use a singular verb with a collective noun (*class, government, family, jury, committee, group, couple, team*) if you are referring to the group as a whole.

▶ My family *goes* on vacation every year.

Use a plural verb if you wish to emphasize differences among individuals or if members of the group are thought of as individuals.

▶ His family *are* mostly artists and musicians.

▶ The jury *are* from every walk of life.

If that usage seems awkward, revise the sentence.

▶ **His close relatives *are* mostly artists and musicians.**

▶ **The members of the jury *are* from every walk of life.**

Some collective nouns, such as *police, poor, elderly,* and *young,* always take plural verbs.

▶ **The elderly *deserve* our respect.**

## **43g** Compound subjects

***With* and**   When a subject consists of two or more parts joined by *and,* treat the subject as plural and use a plural verb.

┌─────────── plural subject ───────✎ plural verb
▶ **His instructor and his advisor *want* him to change his major.**

However, if the parts of the compound subject refer to a single person or thing, use a singular verb.

┌────── singular subject (one person) ──✎ singular verb
▶ **The restaurant's chef and owner *makes* good fajitas.**

┌singular subject ✎singular verb
▶ **Fish and chips *is* a popular dish in England, but it is no longer served wrapped in newspaper.**

***With* each *or* every**   When *each* or *every* is part of a compound subject, the verb is singular.

▶ **Every toy and game *has* to be put away.**

▶ **Each plate and glass *looks* new.**

***With* or *or* nor**   When the parts of a compound subject are joined by *or* or *nor,* the verb agrees with the part nearer to it.

▶ **Her sister or her parents *plan* to visit her next week.**

▶ **Neither her parents nor her sister *drives* a station wagon.**

## **43h** Indefinite pronouns and quantity words

Words (indefinite pronouns) that refer to nonspecific people or things and words and phrases that refer to quantity can be tricky. Some take a singular verb; some take a plural verb; and some take a singular or a plural verb, depending on what they refer to. Some are used alone as a pronoun; others are used with a countable or uncountable noun in a noun phrase (for more on this, see **60a** and **60b** ESL). In addition, usage may differ in speech and writing.

## Indefinite pronouns used with a singular verb

| | | |
|---|---|---|
| anybody | everyone | nothing |
| anyone | everything | somebody |
| anything | nobody | someone |
| everybody | no one | something |

▶ **Nobody** *knows* **the answer.**

▶ **Someone** *has* **been sitting on my chair.**

▶ **Everyone** *agrees* **on the author's intention**

▶ **Everything about the results** *was* **questioned in the review.**

## Quantity words referring to a countable noun and used with a singular verb

| | |
|---|---|
| another | every |
| each | neither (see p. 335) |
| either | none (see p. 335) |

▶ **Another company** *has* **bought the land.**

▶ **Each of the chairs** *costs* **more than $300.**

▶ **Of the two options, neither** *was* **acceptable.**

▶ **Every poem** *contains* **a stark image.**

## Quantity words referring to an uncountable noun and used with a singular verb

| | |
|---|---|
| a(n) _____ amount (of) | (a) little |
| a great deal (of) | much (of) |
| less (see p. 335) | |

▶ **Less** *has* **been accomplished than we expected.**

▶ **A great deal of information** *is* **being released.**

▶ Much of the machinery *needs* to be repaired.

▶ An enormous amount of equipment *was* needed to clean up the spilled oil.

### Quantity words referring to a plural countable noun and used with a plural verb

| | |
|---|---|
| both | many |
| a couple/number of | other/others |
| (a) few (see **64c** ESL) | several |
| fewer (see p. 335) | |

▶ She has written two novels. Both *receive* praise.

▶ Many *have* gained from the recent stock market rise.

▶ Few of his fans *are* buying his recent book.

▶ A number of articles *refer* to the same statistics.

### Quantity words used with a plural verb to refer to a plural countable noun or with a singular verb to refer to an uncountable noun

| | | | |
|---|---|---|---|
| all | half | most | some |
| any | more | no | |

▶ All the students *look* healthy.
   [The plural countable noun *students* takes a plural verb.]

▶ All the furniture *looks* old.
   [The uncountable noun *furniture* takes a singular verb.]

▶ You gave me some information. More *is* necessary.
   [*More* refers to the uncountable noun *information*.]

▶ You gave me some facts. More *are* needed.
   [*More* refers to the countable noun *facts*.]

▶ Some of the jewelry *was* recovered.
   [The uncountable noun *jewelry* takes a singular verb.]

▶ Some of the windows *were* open.
   [The plural countable noun *windows* takes a plural verb.]

## *A note on* none, neither, less, *and* fewer

**NONE**  Some writers prefer to use a singular verb after *none (of)*, because *none* means "not one": *None of the contestants has smiled.* However, as *The American Heritage Dictionary* (4th ed.) points out about *none*, "The word has been used as both a singular and a plural noun from old English onward." In formal academic writing, a singular or a plural verb is therefore technically acceptable: *None of the authorities has* (or *have*) *greater tolerance on this point than H. W. Fowler.* As with many issues of usage, however, readers form preferences. Check to see if your instructor prefers the literal singular usage.

**NEITHER**  The pronoun *neither* is, like *none*, technically singular: *The partners have made a decision; neither wants to change the product.* In informal writing, however, you will see it used with a plural verb, especially when it is followed by an *of* phrase: *Neither of the novels reveal a polished style.* Ask your instructor about his or her preferences.

**LESS AND FEWER**  Technically, *less* refers to a singular uncountable noun (*less spinach*), *fewer* to a plural countable noun (*fewer beans*). In journalism and advertising, and especially on supermarket signs (*12 items or less*), *less* is often used in place of *fewer*. In formal writing, however, use *fewer* to refer to a plural word: *In the last decade, fewer Olympic medalists have been using steroids.*

For agreement with *one of*, see page 331. For agreement with *one of* and *the only one of* followed by a relative clause, see **46c**.

## **43i** Demonstrative pronouns and adjectives *(this, that, these, those)*

A demonstrative adjective must agree in number with the noun it modifies: *this solution, these solutions; that problem, those problems.*

| SINGULAR | PLURAL |
|----------|--------|
| this     | these  |
| that     | those  |

A demonstrative pronoun must agree in number with its antecedent (see **44d**).

▶ The mayor is planning changes. These will be controversial.

## **43j** Possessive pronoun as subject

The antecedent of a possessive pronoun standing alone determines whether the verb is singular or plural. Possessive pronouns such as *mine, his, hers, ours, yours,* and *theirs* can refer to both singular and plural antecedents (see **44d**).

singular
subject             singular verb
▶ **Her average is good, but** *mine is* **better.**

plural
subject             plural verb
▶ **His grades are good, but** *mine are* **better.**

## **43k** Subject clauses beginning with *what*

When a clause introduced by *what* functions as the subject of an independent clause, use a third person singular verb in the independent clause.

subject
▶ **What they are proposing** *concerns* **us all.**

When the verb is followed by the linking verb *be* and a plural complement, some writers use a plural verb. However, some readers may object.

▶ **What I need** *are* **black pants and an orange shirt.**

You can avoid the issue by revising the sentence to eliminate the *what* clause.

▶ **I need black pants and an orange shirt.**

## **44** Pronouns

A pronoun is a word that substitutes for a noun, a noun phrase, or another pronoun (see **37b**).

▶ **Jack's hair is so long that** *it* **hangs over** *his* **collar.**

## **44a** Use the correct forms of personal pronouns.

Personal pronouns change form to indicate person (first, second, or third), number (singular or plural), and function in a clause.

## KEY POINTS

### Forms of Personal Pronouns

|  | SUBJECT | OBJECT | POSSESSIVE + NOUN | POSSESSIVE (NO NOUN FOLLOWING) |
|---|---|---|---|---|
| First person singular | I | me | my | mine |
| First person plural | we | us | our | ours |
| Second person singular and plural | you | you | your | yours |
| Third person singular | he | him | his | his |
|  | she | her | her | hers |
|  | it | it | its | its (rare) |
| Third person plural | they | them | their | theirs |

*After a linking verb* In formal academic writing, use the subject form of a personal pronoun after a linking verb. (See **37c** on linking verbs.)

▶ **Was that Minnie Driver? It was *she*.**

[Informal: "It was her."]

▶ **It was *she* who sent the flowers.**

[Many writers would revise this sentence to sound less formal: "She was the one who sent the flowers."]

*After a verb and before an infinitive* Use the object form of a personal pronoun after a verb and before an infinitive. When a sentence has only one object, this principle is easy to apply.

▶ **The dean wanted *him* to lead the procession.**

Difficulties occur with compound objects.

           him and me
▶ **The dean wanted ~~he and I~~ to lead the procession.**

*In a compound subject or compound object with* **and: I** *or* **me; he** *or* **him?** To decide which pronoun form to use with a compound subject or compound object, mentally recast the sentence with only the pronoun in the subject or object position.

subject ─── object ───
▶ He and his sister invited my cousin and me to their party.
[He invited me.]

I
▶ Jenny and ~~me~~ went to the movies.

[If *Jenny* is dropped, you would say *I went to the movies*, not *me went to the movies*. Here you need the subject form, *I*.]

me
▶ They told my brother and ~~I~~ to wait in line.

[If *my brother* is dropped, you would say *They told me to wait in line*. Here you need the object form, *me*.]

*After a preposition*    After a preposition, you need an object form.

▶ I started off rapping for people just like myself, people who were in awe of wealth and flash. It was a conversation *between me* and *them*.              —Ice-T, *Observer,* 27 Oct. 1991

He                                                                    me
▶ ~~Him~~ and his brother waved to my colleague and ~~I~~.

[He waved to my colleague. They waved to me.]

me
▶ Between you and ~~I~~, the company is in serious trouble.

*In appositive phrases and with* we *or* us *before a noun*    When using a personal pronoun in an appositive phrase (a phrase that gives additional information about a preceding noun), determine whether the noun that the pronoun refers to functions as subject or as object in its own clause.

direct object ◄     appositive phrase
▶ The supervisor praised only two employees, Ramon and me.

subject ◄   appositive phrase
▶ Only two employees, Ramon and I, received a bonus.

Similarly, when you consider whether to use *we* or *us* before a noun, use *us* when the pronoun is the direct object of a verb or preposition, *we* when it is the subject.

object of preposition
▶ LL Cool J waved to us fans.

subject
▶ We fans have decided to form a club.

*In comparisons*   When writing comparisons with *than* and *as*, decide on the subject or object form of the personal pronoun by mentally completing the meaning of the comparison. (See also **45i**.)

▶ **She is certainly not more intelligent than I.**   [. . . than I am]

▶ **Jack and Sally work in the same office; Jack criticizes his boss more than she.**   [. . . more than Sally does.]

▶ **Jack and Sally work in the same office; Jack criticizes his boss more than her.**   [. . . more than he criticizes Sally.]

**44b**   Use appropriate possessive forms of pronouns.

*Distinguish between the adjective form of the possessive personal pronoun and the pronoun itself, standing alone.*

▶ **The large room with three windows is *her* office.**

[*Her* is an adjective.]

▶ **The office is *hers*.**

[*Hers*, the possessive pronoun, can stand alone.]

▶ **The little room on the left is *mine*.**

[*Mine*, the possessive pronoun, can stand alone.]

*Note:* The word *mine* does not follow the spelling pattern of *hers, theirs, yours,* and *ours.* The form *mines* is not Standard English.

When a possessive pronoun functions as a subject, its antecedent determines singular or plural agreement for the verb. (See **43j**.)

▶ **My shirt is cotton; hers *is* silk.**   [Singular antecedent and singular verb]

▶ **My gloves are black; hers *are* yellow.**   [Plural antecedent and plural verb]

*Possessive pronoun before an* **-ing** *form*   Generally, use a possessive personal pronoun before an *-ing* verb form used as a noun.

▶ **We would appreciate *your* participating in the auction.**

▶ **We were surprised at *their* winning the marathon.**

Sometimes the *-ing* form is a participle functioning as an adjective. In that case, the pronoun preceding the *-ing* form should be the object form.

▶ **We saw *them* giving the runners foil wraps.**

*No apostrophe with possessive personal pronouns*   Even though possessive in meaning, the pronouns *yours, ours, theirs, his,* and *hers* should never be spelled with an apostrophe. Use an apostrophe only with the possessive form of a noun.

▶ **That coat is *Maria's*.**          ▶ **These books are the *twins'*. (48c)**

▶ **That is *her* coat.**          ▶ **These are *their* books.**

▶ **That coat is *hers*.**          ▶ **These books are *theirs*.**

*No apostrophe with* **its** *as a possessive pronoun*   The word *it's* is not a pronoun; it is the contraction of *it is* or *it has*. An apostrophe is never used with *its*, the possessive form of the pronoun *it* (see also **48f**).

▶ **The paint has lost *its* gloss.**

▶ ***It's* not as glossy as it used to be.**   [It is not as glossy….]

*Comparisons using possessive forms*   Note how using *them* in place of *theirs* in the following sentence would change the meaning by comparing suitcases to roommates, not suitcases to suitcases.

▶ **It's really hard to be roommates with people if your suitcases are much better than *theirs*.**     —J. D. Salinger, *The Catcher in the Rye*

Forgetting to use the appropriate possessive form in the next example, too, could create a misunderstanding: are you comparing a house to a person, or his house to her house?

▶ **I like his house more than I like her.**
                                                                          s
                                                                          ^

**44c**   Make a pronoun refer to a clear antecedent.

A pronoun substitutes for a noun, a noun phrase, or a pronoun already mentioned. The word or phrase that a pronoun refers to is known as the pronoun's *antecedent*. Antecedents should always be clear and explicit.

▶ **Although the Canadian skater practiced daily with *her* trainers, *she* didn't win the championship.**

*State a specific antecedent.*   Be sure to give a pronoun such as *they* or *it* an explicit antecedent.

No SPECIFIC
ANTECEDENT
   **When Mr. Rivera applied for a loan, they outlined the procedures for him.**

   [The pronoun *they* lacks an explicit antecedent.]

REVISED
   **When Mr. Rivera applied to bank officials for a loan, *they* outlined the procedures for him.**

When you use a pronoun, make sure it does not refer to a posses-sive noun or to a noun within a prepositional phrase.

▶ In ~~George Orwell's~~ "Shooting an Elephant," ~~he~~ reports an inci-dent that shows the evil effects of imperialism.

   George Orwell

   [The pronoun *he* cannot refer to the possessive noun *Orwell's*.]

   Lance Morrow's essay
▶ ~~In the essay by Lance Morrow, it~~ points out the problems of choosing a name.

   [*It* refers to *essay*, which functions as the object of the preposition *in* and therefore cannot function as an antecedent.]

*Avoid ambiguous pronoun reference.*   Readers should never wonder what your pronouns refer to.

AMBIGUOUS
   **My husband told my father that he should choose the baby's name.**   [Does *he* refer to *husband* or *father*?]

REVISED
   **My husband told my father to choose the baby's name.**

REVISED
   **My husband wanted to choose the baby's name and told my father so.**

AMBIGUOUS
   **He had to decide whether to move to**

   **California. This was not what he wanted to do.**

   [Does *This* refer to making the decision or to moving to California?]

REVISED
   **He had to decide whether to move to California. The decision was not one he wanted to make.**

REVISED
   **He had to decide whether to move to California. Moving there was not something he wanted to do.**

**44d** Make a pronoun agree in number with its antecedent.

A plural antecedent needs a plural pronoun; a singular antecedent needs a singular pronoun.

*Make a demonstrative pronoun agree with its antecedent.* The demonstrative pronouns *this* and *that* refer to singular nouns; *these* and *those* refer to plural nouns: *this/that house, these/those houses* (**43i**).

singular antecedent

▶ He published his autobiography two years ago. This was his first book.

plural antecedent

▶ One reviewer praised his honesty and directness. Those were qualities he had worked hard to develop.

*Make a pronoun agree with a generalized (generic) antecedent.* Generic nouns name a class or type of person or object, such as *a student* meaning "all students" or *a company* meaning "any company" or "all companies." Do not use *they* to refer to a singular generic noun.

singular antecedent · plural pronoun

FAULTY AGREEMENT When a student is educated, they can go far in the world.

singular antecedent · singular pronoun

REVISED When a student is educated, he or she can go far in the world.

plural antecedent · plural pronoun

REVISED When students are educated, they can go far in the world.

Increasingly, you see in advertising, journalism, and informal writing a plural pronoun referring to a singular antecedent, as in the following:

faulty agreement

▶ One day *your child* turns sixteen and you let *them* borrow the keys to the wagon.

However, in formal academic writing, many readers may still expect a pronoun to agree with its antecedent. Often the best solution is to make the antecedent plural.

▶ We should judge a ~~person~~ *people* by who they are, not by the color of their skin.

*Make a pronoun agree with an indefinite pronoun or quantity word.* Indefinite pronouns, such as *everyone, somebody,* and *nothing* (p. 333), are singular in form and used with a singular verb. Some quantity words, such as *each, either, every,* and *neither,* are also singular in form (p. 333). A singular antecedent needs a singular pronoun to refer to it. But which singular pronoun should be used—*he, she,* or both? To avoid gender bias (**33f** and **44e**) and possible clumsiness, some writers use the plural *they* to refer to a singular indefinite pronoun. Some readers, however, may object to this usage, so revising the sentence is a good idea.

| | |
|---|---|
| SINGULAR PRONOUN WITH GENDER BIAS | **Everyone picked up his marbles and ran home to do his homework.** |
| REVISED BUT CLUMSY | **Everyone picked up his or her marbles and ran home to do his or her homework.** |
| REVISED BUT INFORMAL | **Everyone picked up their marbles and ran home to do their homework.** |
| | [The plural pronoun *their* refers to a singular antecedent.] |
| PROBABLY BEST | **The children all picked up their marbles and ran home to do their homework.** |

*Make a pronoun agree with the nearer antecedent when the parts of a compound antecedent are joined by* **or** *or* **nor.** When the elements of a compound antecedent are connected by *or* or *nor*, a pronoun agrees with the element that is nearer to it. If one part of the compound is singular and the other part is plural, put the plural antecedent closer to the pronoun and have the pronoun agree with it.

▶ Either my friend or my brother has left *his* bag in the hall.

▶ Neither Bill nor the campers could find *their* soap.

*Make a pronoun agree with a collective noun.* Use a singular pronoun to refer to a collective noun (*class, family, jury, committee, couple, team*) if you are referring to the group as a whole.

▶ The class revised *its* examination schedule.

▶ The committee has not yet completed *its* report.

Use a plural pronoun if members of the group named by the collective noun are considered to be acting individually.

▶ The committee began to cast *their* ballots in a formal vote.

**44e**  Avoid gender bias in pronouns.

***Personal pronouns***  For many years, the pronoun *he* was used routinely in generic references to unspecified individuals in certain roles or professions, such as student, teacher, doctor, lawyer, and banker; and *she* was used routinely in generic references to individuals in roles such as nurse, secretary, or typist. This usage is now considered biased language.

| NOT APPROPRIATE | When an accountant learns a foreign language, *he* gains access to an expanded job market. |
| --- | --- |

To revise such sentences that make general statements about people, roles, and professions, use one of the following methods:

1.  Use a plural antecedent plus *they* (see also **33f** and **44d**).

▶ When accountants learn a foreign language, *they* gain access to an expanded job market.

2.  Rewrite the sentence to eliminate the pronoun.

▶ An accountant who learns a foreign language gains access to an expanded job market.

3.  Use a singular antecedent plus *he or she*.

▶ When an accountant learns a foreign language, *he or she* gains access to an expanded job market.

The problem with option 3 is that awkward and repetitive structures can result when such a sentence is continued.

▶ When an accountant learns a foreign language, *he or she* gains access to an expanded job market once *he or she* has decided on *his or her* specialty.

Use the *he or she* option only when a sentence is relatively short and does not repeat the pronouns.

See also agreement with indefinite pronouns (**43h** and **44d**).

### 44f  Be consistent in your point of view.

Keep the point of view from which you are writing consistent through the careful use of pronouns.

INCONSISTENT  **We are all born with some of *our* personality already established in *us*. However, *I* believe that experiences also help shape who *you* are.**

REVISED  **We are all born with some of *our* personality already established in *us*. However, experiences also help shape who *we* are.**

### 44g  Use the pronoun *you* appropriately.

In formal writing, do not use the pronoun *you* when you mean "people generally." Use *you* only to address readers directly.

APPROPRIATE  **If *you* turn to the next page, *you* will find an excerpt from Edith Wharton's novel that will help *you* appreciate the accuracy of the details in this film.**

▶ **While growing up, ~~you~~ face arguments with ~~your~~ parents.**
         teenagers              their

Avoid shifting from third person pronouns to *you*.

▶ **It doesn't matter if young professionals are avid music admirers or comedy fans; ~~you~~ can find anything ~~you~~ want in the city.**
              they           they

### 44h  Use standard forms of intensive and reflexive pronouns.

Intensive pronouns emphasize a previously mentioned noun or pronoun. Reflexive pronouns identify a previously mentioned noun or pronoun as the person or thing receiving the action.

INTENSIVE  **The president *himself* appeared at the gates.**

REFLEXIVE  **He introduced *himself*.**

| INTENSIVE AND REFLEXIVE PRONOUNS | | |
|---|---|---|
| | SINGULAR | PLURAL |
| First person | myself | ourselves |
| Second person | yourself | yourselves |
| Third person | himself | themselves |
| | herself | |
| | itself | |

Forms such as *hisself, theirself,* and *theirselves* occur in spoken dialects but are not Standard English.

**44i** Use *who* and *whom* and *whoever* and *whomever* correctly.

In all formal writing situations, distinguish between the subject and object forms of the pronouns used to form questions (interrogative pronouns) or to introduce a noun clause (**37e**).

| SUBJECT | OBJECT |
|---|---|
| who | whom (or, informally, who) |
| whoever | whomever |

*In questions* In a question, ask yourself whether the pronoun is the subject of its clause or the object of the verb. Test the pronoun's function by rephrasing the question as a statement, substituting a personal pronoun for *who* or *whom*.

▶ **Who wrote that enthusiastic letter?**
[*He* wrote that enthusiastic letter. Subject: use *who*.]

▶ **Whoever could have written it?**
[*She* could have written it. Subject: use *whoever*.]

▶ **Who[m] were they describing?**
[*They* were describing *him*. Object: *whom* (formal), though *who* is common in such contexts both in speech and in writing.]

*In noun clauses* When introducing a dependent clause with a pronoun, determine whether to use the subject or object form by examining the pronoun's function in the clause. Ignore expressions such as *I think* or *I know* when they follow the pronoun; they have no effect on the form of the pronoun.

subject of clause
▶ **They want to know who runs the business.**

subject of clause (who runs the business)

▶ They want to know **who** I think runs the business.

object of *to* [the manager reports to him or her]

▶ They want to know **whom** the manager reports to.

subject of clause

▶ I will hire **whoever** is qualified.

object of *recommends*

▶ I will hire **whomever** my boss recommends.

For uses of *who* and *whom* in relative clauses, see **46a**.

## 45  Adjectives and Adverbs

*Adjectives* describe, or modify, nouns or pronouns. They do not add -s or change form to reflect number or gender.

▶ Analysts acknowledge the *beneficial* effects of TV.

▶ He tried a *different* approach.

▶ The depiction of rural life is *accurate*.

▶ She keeps her desk *tidy*.

**ESL Note**  Do not add -s to an adjective that modifies a plural noun.

▶ He tried three *differents* approaches.  ■

*Adverbs* modify verbs, adjectives, and other adverbs, as well as whole clauses.

▶ She settled down *comfortably*.

▶ The patient is demanding a *theoretically* impossible treatment.

▶ *Apparently*, the experiment was a success.

## 45a Use correct forms of adjectives and adverbs.

No single rule indicates the correct form of all adjectives and adverbs.

*Adverb: adjective + -ly*  Many adverbs are formed by adding *-ly* to an adjective: *soft/softly; intelligent/intelligently*. Sometimes when *-ly* is added, a spelling change occurs: *easy/easily; terrible/terribly*.

*Adjectives ending in -ic*  To form an adverb from an adjective ending in *-ic*, add *-ally* (*basic/basically; artistic/artistically*), except for *public*, whose adverb form is *publicly*.

*Adjectives ending in -ly*  Some adjectives, such as *friendly, lovely, timely*, and *masterly*, already end in *-ly* and have no distinctive adverb form.

adjective

▶ She is a friendly person.

┌— adverbial phrase —┐

▶ She spoke to me in a friendly way.

*Irregular adverb forms*  Certain adjectives do not add *-ly* to form an adverb:

| ADJECTIVE | ADVERB |
|-----------|--------|
| good | well |
| fast | fast |
| hard | hard |

adjective

▶ He is a good cook.

adverb

▶ He cooks well.

adjective

▶ She is a hard worker.

adverb

▶ She works hard.

[*Hardly* is not the adverb form of *hard*. Rather, it means "barely," "scarcely," or "almost not at all": *I could* hardly *breathe in that stuffy room.*]

**Note:** *Well* can also function as an adjective, meaning "healthy" or "satisfactory": *A well baby smiles often. She feels well.*

## 45b Know when to use adjectives and adverbs.

In speech, adjectives (particularly *good, bad*, and *real*) are often used to modify verbs, adjectives, or adverbs. This is nonstandard usage. Use an adverb to modify a verb or an adverb.

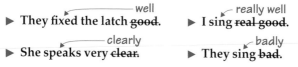

well

▶ They fixed the latch ~~good~~.

really well

▶ I sing ~~real good~~.

clearly

▶ She speaks very ~~clear~~.

badly

▶ They sing ~~bad~~.

**45c** Use adjectives after linking verbs.

After linking verbs (*be, seem, appear, become*), use an adjective to modify the subject. (See **37c** on subject complements.)

▶ That steak is good.

▶ Her new coat seems tight.

▶ She feels bad because she sings so badly.

Some verbs (*appear, look, feel, smell, taste*) are sometimes used as linking verbs, sometimes as action verbs. If the modifier tells about the subject, use an adjective. If the modifier tells about the action of the verb, use an adverb.

ADJECTIVE    She looks *confident* in her new job.

ADVERB    She looks *confidently* at all the assembled partners.

ADJECTIVE    The waiter feels *bad*.

The steak smells *bad*.

ADVERB    The chef smelled the lobster *appreciatively*.

**45d** Use correct forms for compound adjectives.

A compound adjective consists of two or more words used as a unit to describe a noun. Many compound adjectives contain the past participle *-ed* verb form: *flat-footed, barrel-chested, broad-shouldered, old-fashioned, well-dressed, left-handed*. Note the forms when a compound adjective is used before a noun: hyphens, past participle (*-ed*) forms where necessary, and no noun plural (*-s*) endings.

▶ They have a *five-year-old* daughter. [Their daughter is five years old.]

▶ She gave me a *five-dollar* bill. [She gave me five dollars.]

▶ He is a *left-handed* pitcher. [He pitches with his left hand.]

For more on hyphenation, see **56b**.

## 45e Know where to position adverbs.

An adverb can be placed in various positions in a sentence.

▶ *Enthusiastically,* **she ate the sushi.**

▶ **She** *enthusiastically* **ate the sushi.**

▶ **She ate the sushi** *enthusiastically.*

**ESL Note** Do not place an adverb between a verb and a short direct object (**62b** ESL).

▶ **She ate** |*enthusiastically*| **the sushi** ■

Put adverbs that show frequency (*always, usually, frequently, often, sometimes, seldom, rarely, never*) in one of four positions:

1. At the beginning of a sentence

▶ *Sometimes* **I just sit and daydream instead of writing.**

When *never, seldom,* or *rarely* occurs at the beginning of the sentence, word order is inverted (see also **34d** and **37c**).

▶ *Never will* **I let that happen.**

2. Between the subject and the main verb

▶ **They** *always* **arrive half an hour late.**

3. After a form of *be* or any auxiliary verb (such as *do, have, can, will, must*)

▶ **They are** *always* **unpunctual.**

▶ **She is** *seldom* **depressed.**

▶ **He has** *never* **lost a game.**

4. In the final position

▶ **He goes to the movies** *frequently.*

*Note:* Never place the adverb *never* in the final position.

## 45f Know the usual order of adjectives.

When two or more adjectives modify a noun, they usually occur in the order listed in the Key Points box. Commas separate coordinate adjectives of evaluation; their order can be reversed, and the word *and* can be inserted between them (**47g**). No commas separate adjectives in the other categories listed in the box.

---

**KEY POINTS**

**Order of Adjectives**

1. Determiner: articles (*a, an, the*), demonstrative adjectives (*this, that, these, those*), possessives (*its, our*), quantity words (*many, some*), numerals (*five, nineteen*)
2. Adjective of evaluation: *interesting, delicious, comfortable, inexpensive, heavy*
3. Adjective describing size: *little, big, huge*
4. Adjective describing shape: *round, square, long*
5. Adjective describing age: *new, young, old*
6. Adjective describing color: *white, red*
7. Adjective describing national origin: *Italian, European*
8. Adjective describing religious faith: *Catholic, Buddhist*
9. Adjective describing material: *oak, ivory, wooden*
10. Noun used as an adjective: *kitchen* cabinet, *writing* desk

---

▶ **the lovely old oak writing desk**

▶ **many little white ivory buttons**

▶ **that beautiful long kitchen table**

▶ **her efficient, hardworking assistant**

   [Commas between coordinate adjectives of evaluation]

As a general rule, avoid long strings of adjectives. Two or three adjectives of evaluation, size, shape, age, color, national origin, faith, or material should be the limit.

**45g** Avoid double negatives.

Adverbs like *hardly, scarcely,* and *barely* are considered negatives, and the contraction *-n't* stands for the adverb *not.* Some languages and dialects allow the use of more than one negative to emphasize an idea, but Standard English allows only one negative in a clause. Avoid double negatives.

| Double Negative | **We do*n't* have *no* excuses.** |
| Revised | **We do*n't* have *any* excuses. [or] We have *no* excuses.** |

| Double Negative | **She did*n't* say *nothing*.** |
| Revised | **She did*n't* say *anything*. [or] She said *nothing*.** |

| Double Negative | **They ca*n't* *hardly* pay the rent.** |
| Revised | **They can *hardly* pay the rent.** |

## **45h** Know the comparative and superlative forms of adjectives and adverbs.

The *comparative* and *superlative* forms of adjectives and adverbs are used for comparisons. Use the comparative form to compare two people, places, things, or ideas; use the superlative to compare more than two.

***Regular forms*** Add the ending *-er* to form the comparative and *-est* to form the superlative of both short adjectives (those that have one syllable or those that have two syllables and end in *-y* or *-le*) and one-syllable adverbs. (Change *-y* to *-i* if *-y* is preceded by a consonant: *icy, icier, iciest*.) Generally, a superlative form is preceded by *the* (*the shortest distance*).

|  | COMPARATIVE (COMPARING TWO) | SUPERLATIVE (COMPARING MORE THAN TWO) |
| --- | --- | --- |
| short | shorter | shortest |
| pretty | prettier | prettiest |
| simple | simpler | simplest |
| fast | faster | fastest |

With longer adjectives and with adverbs ending in *-ly*, use *more* (for the comparative) and *most* (for the superlative). Note that *less* (comparative) and *least* (superlative) are used with adjectives of any length (*less bright, least bright; less effective, least effective*).

|  | COMPARATIVE | SUPERLATIVE |
| --- | --- | --- |
| intelligent | more intelligent | most intelligent |
| carefully | more carefully | most carefully |
| dangerous | less dangerous | least dangerous |

If you cannot decide whether to use *-er/-est* or *more/most*, consult a dictionary. If there is an *-er/-est* form, the dictionary will say so.

*Note:* Do not use the *-er* form with *more* or the *-est* form with *most*.

▶ **The first poem was ~~more~~ better than the second.**

▶ **Boris is the ~~most~~ fittest person I know.**

***Irregular forms*** The following common adjectives and adverbs have irregular comparative and superlative forms:

|            | COMPARATIVE | SUPERLATIVE |
|------------|-------------|-------------|
| good       | better      | best        |
| bad        | worse       | worst       |
| much/many  | more        | most        |
| little     | less        | least       |
| well       | better      | best        |
| badly      | worse       | worst       |

***Using* than *with comparative forms*** To compare two people, places, things, or ideas, use the comparative form and the word *than*. If you use a comparative form in your sentence, you need *than* to let readers know what you are comparing with what.

*than the previous one*
▶ **This course of action is more efficient.**
                                           ^

Comparative forms are also used without *than* in an idiomatic way.

▶ **The *harder* he tries, the *more satisfied* he feels.**

▶ **The *more*, the *merrier*.**

## 45i  Avoid faulty or incomplete comparisons.

Make sure that you state clearly what items you are comparing. Some faulty comparisons can give readers the wrong idea. See **40h**, **44a**, **44b**.

INCOMPLETE  **He likes the parrot better than his wife.**

To avoid suggesting that he prefers the parrot to his wife, clarify the comparison by completing the second clause.

REVISED  **He likes the parrot better *than his wife does*.**

Edit sentences like the following:

▶ My essay got a higher grade than Maria.ᐟs

[Compare the two essays, not your essay and Maria.]

▶ Williams's poem gives a more objective depiction of the

painting than Auden.ᐟs

[To compare Williams's poem with Auden's poem, you need to include an apostrophe; otherwise, you compare a poem to the poet W. H. Auden.]

Comparisons must also be complete. If you say that something is "more efficient," your reader wonders, "More efficient than what?"

▶ Didion shows us a home that makes her feel more tied to her

roots. *than her home in Los Angeles does* [Include the other part of the comparison.]

## 46  Relative Clauses and Relative Pronouns

Relative clauses are introduced by relative pronouns: *who, whom, whose, which,* and *that.* Relative clauses are also called *adjective clauses* because they modify nouns and noun phrases as adjectives do. Relative clauses follow the nouns to which they refer. A dependent relative clause refers to a word or words (its *antecedent*) in an independent clause. (See **37e**.)

┌─ relative clause ─┐
▶ The girl *who* can't dance says the band can't play.

—Yiddish proverb

### 46a  Use an appropriate relative pronoun.

The forms of relative pronouns vary in speech and writing and in informal and formal usage. In academic writing, use the relative pronouns designated *formal* in the discussion that follows.

*Human antecedents*   In formal writing, use *who, whom,* and *whose* to refer to people.

RELATIVE PRONOUNS: HUMAN ANTECEDENTS

| SUBJECT | OBJECT | POSSESSIVE |
|---------|--------|------------|
| who | whom (sometimes omitted) that (informal) | whose |

For *who* and *whom* as question words, see **44i**.

The form of the relative pronoun depends on the pronoun's grammatical function in its own clause. To identify the correct form, restate the clause, using a personal pronoun.

subject of clause

▶ **The teachers who challenge us are the ones we remember.**

[*They* challenge us.]

object of clause

▶ **The teachers whom the students honored felt proud.**

[The students honored *them. Whom* may be omitted.]

possessive

▶ **The teachers whose student evaluations were high won an award.**   [*Their* student evaluations were high.]

Phrases such as *I know, he thinks,* and *they realize* inserted into a relative clause do not affect the form of the pronoun.

subject of clause

▶ **We should help children who we realize cannot defend**

**themselves.**   [*They* cannot defend themselves.]

*Nonhuman antecedents: animals, things, and concepts*   Standard English, unlike languages such as Spanish, Arabic, and Thai, uses different relative pronouns for human and for nonhuman antecedents. Use *that* or *which* to refer to nonhuman antecedents. Never use *which* to refer to a human antecedent.

who

▶ **The teacher ~~which~~ taught me math in high school was strict.**

RELATIVE PRONOUNS: NONHUMAN ANTECEDENTS

| SUBJECT | OBJECT | POSSESSIVE |
|---------|--------|------------|
| that | that (sometimes | of which (formal) |
| which | omitted) | whose (informal) |
| | which (sometimes | |
| | omitted) | |

Use the relative pronoun *that* to refer to an antecedent naming an animal, a thing, or a concept (such as *success* or *information*). When the relative pronoun *that* functions as the direct object in its clause, it can be omitted.

▶ **They stayed at a hotel *that* had two pools and a sauna.**

[*That* is the subject of the relative clause.]

▶ **They stayed at a hotel *that* their friends had recommended.**

[*That* is the direct object in the relative clause.]

▶ **They stayed at a hotel their friends had recommended.**

[*That* as direct object in the relative clause can be omitted.]

▶ **They stayed at a hotel the name *of which* I can't remember.**
[Formal]

▶ **They stayed at a hotel *whose* name I can't remember.**
[Informal]

See **46d** and **46g** for the use of *that* and *which* in restrictive and nonrestrictive clauses.

**46b** Make the verb agree with the antecedent of a subject relative pronoun.

Determine subject-verb agreement within a relative clause by asking whether the antecedent of a subject relative pronoun is singular or plural.

▶ The book that *is* at the top of the bestseller list gives advice about health.   [The singular noun *book* is the antecedent of *that*, the subject of the singular verb *is* in the relative clause.]

▶ The books that *are* at the top of the bestseller list give advice about health, success, and making money.

[The plural noun *books* is the antecedent of *that*, the subject of the plural verb *are* in the relative clause.]

**46c** Check agreement in relative clauses after *one of* and *the only one of.*

The phrase *one of* is followed by a plural noun phrase. However, the verb can be singular or plural, depending on the meaning.

▶ **Juan is one of the employees who *work* long hours.**

[Several employees work long hours. Juan is one of them. The plural word *employees* is the antecedent of *who*, the subject of the plural verb *work* in the relative clause.]

— antecedent —  singular verb
▶ **Juan is the only one of the employees who *works* long hours.**

[Only Juan works long hours.]

**46d** Distinguish between restrictive and nonrestrictive relative clauses.

The two types of relative clauses, restrictive and nonrestrictive, fulfill different functions and need different punctuation (**47d**).

RESTRICTIVE **The people *who live in the apartment above mine* make a lot of noise at night.**

NONRESTRICTIVE **The Sullivans, *who live in the apartment above mine,* make a lot of noise at night.**

*Restrictive relative clause* A restrictive relative clause provides information essential for identifying the antecedent and restricting its scope.

FEATURES

1. The clause is not set off with commas.
2. An object relative pronoun can be omitted.
3. *That* (not *which*) is preferred for reference to nonhuman antecedents.

▶ **The teachers *who challenge us* are the ones we remember.**

[The independent clause—"The teachers are the ones"—leads us to ask, "Which teachers?" The relative clause provides information that is essential to completing the meaning of the subject; it restricts the meaning from "all teachers" to "the teachers who challenge us."]

▶ **The book [*that*] *you gave me* was fascinating.**

[The relative pronoun *that* is the direct object in its clause ("You gave me the book") and can be omitted.]

*Nonrestrictive relative clause*  A nonrestrictive relative clause provides information that is not essential for understanding the antecedent. It refers to and describes a proper noun (which names a specific person, place, or thing and begins with a capital letter) or a noun that is identified and unique.

FEATURES

1. The antecedent is a unique, designated person or thing.

2. The clause is set off by commas.

3. *Which* (not *that*) is used to refer to a nonhuman antecedent.

4. An object relative pronoun cannot be omitted.

▶ **The book *War and Peace*, which you gave me, was fascinating.**

[The independent clause—"The book *War and Peace* was fascinating"—does not promote further questions, such as "Which book?" The information in the relative clause ("which you gave me") is almost an aside and not essential for understanding the independent clause.]

**46e**  Check relative clauses beginning with quantity words (*most of, some of, one of*).

Relative clauses beginning with a quantity word such as *some, none, many, much, most,* or *one* followed by *of which* or *of whom* are always nonrestrictive.

▶ **They selected five candidates, one of whom would get the job.**

▶ **The report mentioned five names, none of which I recognized.**

**ESL Note**  You need only the relative pronoun, not a personal pronoun in addition.

*most of whom*
▶ **I tutored some students, ~~which most of them~~ were my classmates.**  ■

**46f** Take care when a relative clause contains a preposition.

When a relative clause contains a relative pronoun within a prepositional phrase, do not omit the preposition. Keep in mind these three points:

1. Directly after the preposition, use *whom* or *which*, never *that*.

```
            ┌──── relative clause ────┐
```
▶ The man *for whom* we worked last year has just retired.

2. If you place the preposition after the verb, use *that* (or you can omit *that*), but do not use *whom* or *which*.

        [that]
▶ The man ~~whom~~ we worked for was efficient.

3. Do not add an extra personal pronoun object after the preposition at the end of the relative clause.

▶ The company [that] I worked for ~~it~~ last summer has gone bankrupt.

**46g** Know when to use *that* as a relative pronoun.

**When to use that**    In Standard English, for a nonhuman antecedent, use *that* rather than *which* in the subject position and use *that* (or omit *that*) as an object in a restrictive relative clause. Never use *what* as if it were a relative pronoun.

       that
▶ The book ~~which~~ won the prize is a love story.

       [that]
▶ The deal ~~what~~ she was trying to make fell through.

       [that]
▶ Everything ~~which~~ she does for United Way is appreciated.

Use *that* rather than *who* when referring to groups of people.

       that
▶ The class ~~who~~ meets here is late.

**When not to use that**    In the following instances, use *which* or *whom* instead of *that*.

1. In nonrestrictive clauses supplying extra information (see **46d**)

▶ Ellsvere Shopping Center, *which* was sold last month, has changed the whole area.

2. Directly following a preposition

▶ **The woman to *whom* I was talking is a famous physicist.**

In informal contexts, however, the preposition is likely to occur at the end of the clause; in this case, *that* can be used or omitted.

▶ **The woman [that] I was talking to is a famous physicist.**

**46h** Position a relative clause close to its antecedent.

To avoid ambiguity, place a relative clause as close as possible to its antecedent. (See also **40b** on misplaced modifiers.)

AMBIGUOUS **He searched for the notebook all over the house that his friend had forgotten.** [Had his friend forgotten the house?]

REVISED **He searched all over the house for the notebook that his friend had forgotten.**

**46i** Avoid using a pronoun after a relative clause to rename the antecedent.

Although this kind of usage occurs in informal speech and in many other languages, avoid it in formal writing. (See also **62f** ESL.)

▶ **My colleague who moved to Italy three years ago and has his own apartment in Milan ~~he~~ has a good life.**

**46j** Use *where* and *when* as relative pronouns when appropriate.

When you refer to actual or metaphoric places and times, you can use *where* to replace *in which, at which,* or *to which,* and you can use *when* to replace *at which, in which,* or *on which.* Do not use a preposition with *where* or *when.*

▶ **The morning on which she graduated was warm and sunny.**

▶ **The morning *when* she graduated was warm and sunny.**

▶ **The village in which he was born honored him last year.**

▶ **The village *where* he was born honored him last year.**

Use *where* or *when* only if actual time or physical location is involved.

according to which
▶ **The influence of the Sapir-Whorf hypothesis, ~~where~~ behavior is regarded as influenced by language, has declined.**

# PART 8

## Punctuation, Mechanics, and Spelling

# PART 8　Punctuation, Mechanics, and Spelling

When you think about how many ways you can say "That's great" to convey different meanings, you will realize the importance of intonation to speech. In writing, punctuation replaces intonation. It is much more than a set of obscure rules, much more than a few marks to split up sentences. Punctuation serves to regulate the flow of information through a sentence, showing readers how to read your ideas: how to separate, anticipate, and emphasize individual words, phrases, clauses, and sentences. The following headline from the *New York Times*, "Stock Fraud Is Easier, and Easier to Spot," says that stock fraud is not only easy to engage in but also easy to detect. Without the comma, however, the sentence would send a different message: it would say that detecting stock fraud is becoming increasingly easy.

Keep in mind that there is no ideal model of punctuation, no prescribed length for a sentence. Where a sentence ends and divides depends on its meaning and your style. The writer Ernest Hemingway advised writers to keep punctuation conventional: "The game of golf would lose a good deal if croquet mallets and billiard cues were allowed on the putting green. You ought to be able to show that you can do it a good deal better than anyone else with the regular tools before you have a license to bring in your own improvements" (Letter of 15 May 1925, *Selected Letters*, ed. Carlos Baker, 1981).

# 47 Commas

A comma separates parts of a sentence; a comma alone does not separate one sentence from another. When readers see a comma, they think, "These parts of the sentence are being separated for a reason." When you can't decide whether to use commas, follow this general guideline: "When in doubt, leave them out." Readers find excessive use of commas more distracting than a few missing ones.

## 47a Two checklists—Commas: Yes, Commas: No

The two checklists provide general rules of thumb. Details and more examples of each rule follow in the rest of section **47**.

---

 **KEY POINTS**

**Commas: Yes**

1. Before a coordinating conjunction (*and, but, or, nor, so, for, yet*) to connect independent clauses, but optional if the clauses are short (**47b**)

   ▶ He frowned, but she did not understand why he was worried.

2. After most introductory words, phrases, or clauses (**47c**)

   ▶ After the noisy party, the neighbors complained.

3. Before and after extra (nonrestrictive) information included in a sentence ("extra commas with extra information") (**47d**)

   ▶ My father, a computer programmer, works late at night.

   *(Continued)*

---

*(Continued)*

4. Around transitional expressions (**47e**)

   ▶ **The ending, however, is disappointing.**

5. To separate three or more items in a series (**47f**)

   ▶ **They ordered eggs, bacon, and potatoes.**

6. Between coordinate evaluative adjectives (**45f** and **47g**)

   ▶ **We ate a delicious, well-prepared, and inexpensive meal.**

7. After a verb that introduces a quotation (**47h**)

   ▶ **She gasped, "We haven't a moment to lose!"**

### KEY POINTS

**Commas: No (see 47i)**

1. Not between subject and verb

   ▶ **The man in the baggy blue jeans is her English teacher.**

   However, use two commas to set off any extra information inserted between subject and verb (see **47d**).

2. Not before part of a compound structure that is not an independent clause

   ▶ **She won the trophy and accepted it graciously.**

3. Not *after* a coordinating conjunction connecting two independent clauses, but *before* it

   ▶ **The movie tried to be engaging, but it failed miserably.**

4. Not between two independent clauses without a coordinating conjunction (use either a period and a capital letter or a semicolon instead)

   ▶ **He won; she was delighted.**

5. Not between an independent clause and a following dependent clause introduced by *after, before, because, if, since, unless, until,* or *when,* and neither before nor after the subordinating conjunction

   *(Continued)*

*(Continued)*

▶ **She will continue working for the city until she has saved enough for graduate school.**

6. Not before a clause beginning with *that*

▶ **They warned us that the meeting would be difficult.**

7. Not before and after essential, restrictive information

▶ **The player who scored the goal became a hero.**

8. Not between a verb and its object or complement

▶ **The best gifts are food and clothes.**

9. Not after *such as*

▶ **Popular fast food items, such as hamburgers and hot dogs, tend to be high in fat.**

---

**47b**   Use a comma before a coordinating conjunction to connect independent clauses.

When you connect independent clauses with a coordinating conjunction (*and, but, or, nor, so, for, yet*), place a comma before the conjunction.

▶ **The managers are efficient, but personnel turnover is high.**

▶ **The juggler juggled seven plates, and we all cheered.**

If the independent clauses are short, you may omit the comma before the conjunction.

▶ **He offered to help and he meant it.**

---

**47c**   Use a comma after most introductory words, phrases, and clauses.

The comma signals to readers that the word, phrase, or clause has conveyed an idea, and that the introductory part has ended. It says, in effect, "Now wait for the independent clause."

▶ **If you blow out all the candles, your wishes will come true.**

Often a comma is essential to prevent misreading.

MISREADING
POSSIBLE
**When active viruses can spread easily.**

REVISED
**When active, viruses can spread easily.**

The comma after the introductory material tells readers to expect the subject and verb of the independent clause.

**47d** Use commas to set off extra (nonrestrictive) phrases and clauses.

When a phrase or clause provides extra information that could be omitted without changing the meaning of the independent clause, the phrase or clause is said to be *nonrestrictive*. Use commas to set off a nonrestrictive element, to signal that the extra information it presents does not limit the meaning of the independent clause (**37e**). A phrase or clause that limits or restricts the meaning of the independent clause is said to be *restrictive*. Do not use commas with restrictive information.

NONRESTRICTIVE **We'll attend, even though we'd rather not.**

RESTRICTIVE **We'll attend if we can.**

*Commas around appositive phrases* Use commas to set off an appositive phrase (a phrase that renames or gives additional information about a prior noun or pronoun). If the phrase were omitted, readers might lose some interesting details but would still be able to understand the message.

appositive
phrase
▶ **She loves her car, a red Toyota.**

appositive phrase
▶ **His dog, a big Labrador retriever, is afraid of mice.**

▶ **Salinger's first novel, *The Catcher in the Rye,* captures the language and thoughts of teenagers.**

[The commas are used because the title provides supplementary information about the first novel, not information that identifies which novel the writer means. See also **47i**, item 7.]

*Commas around nonrestrictive participle and prepositional phrases* Nonrestrictive participle and prepositional phrases add extra descriptive, but not essential, information.

▶ My boss, wearing a red tie and a green shirt, radiated the holiday spirit.

▶ The poet's study, in which she spent her final months, is now a shrine.

*Commas around extra information in nonrestrictive relative clauses* When you give nonessential information in a relative clause introduced by *who, whom,* or *which* (never *that*), set the clause off by commas.

▶ My boss, who wears bright colors, is a cheerful person.

[The independent clause "My boss is a cheerful person" does not lead readers to ask "Which boss?" The relative clause does not restrict the meaning of *boss.*]

▶ His recent paintings, which are hanging in our local restaurant, show dogs in various disguises.    [The relative clause, introduced by *which*, merely provides the additional fact that his recent paintings are on display in the restaurant.]

Do not use commas to set off essential, restrictive information (**46d** and **47i**).

        ⌐ restricts *people* to a subgroup ⌐
▶ People who wear bright colors send an optimistic message.

[The relative clause, beginning with *who*, restricts "people" to a subgroup: not all people send an optimistic message; those who wear bright colors do.]

**47e** Use commas to set off transitional expressions.

Transitional expressions and conjunctive adverbs connect or weave together the ideas in your writing and act as signposts for readers. See **2d** for a list of these expressions. Use commas to set off a transitional expression from the rest of the sentence.

▶ Most Labrador retrievers, however, are courageous.

*Note:* When you use a transitional expression such as *however, therefore, nevertheless, above all, of course,* or *in fact* at the beginning of an independent clause, end the previous clause with a period or a semi-colon. Then place a comma after the transitional expression.

▶ **The party was a success. In fact, it was still going on at 2 a.m.**

**47f** Use commas to separate three or more items in a series.

Readers see the commas between items in a series and think, "This is a list." If you said the sentence aloud, you would pause between items; in writing, you use commas to separate them.

▶ **Searching through the drawer, the detective found a key, a stamp, three coins, and a photograph.**

**47g** Use commas to separate coordinate evaluative adjectives.

Adjectives are *coordinate* when their order can be reversed and the word *and* can be inserted between them without any change in meaning. Coordinate adjectives (*beautiful, delicious, exciting, noisy*) make subjective and evaluative judgments rather than providing objectively verifiable information about, for instance, size, shape, color, or nationality (**45f**). Separate coordinate adjectives with commas.

▶ **He hires people who are energetic, efficient, and polite.**

Do not, however, put a comma between the final adjective of a series and the noun it modifies.

▶ **Energetic, efficient, and polite salespeople are in demand.**

No comma is necessary to separate adjectives that provide information about size, shape, age, color, national origin, religion, or material.

▶ **Entering the little old stone house brought back memories of her childhood.**

**47h** Use a comma to separate a direct quotation from the verb that introduces it.

The verb may come either before or after the quotation.

▶ **When asked what she wanted to be later in life, she replied, "An Olympic swimmer."**

▶ "I want to be an Olympic swimmer," she announced confidently.
[The comma is inside the quotation marks.]

**47i**   When not to use commas: nine rules of thumb

*1. Do not use a comma to separate a verb from its subject.*

▶ The gifts she received from her colleagues made her realize her value to the company.

▶ Interviewing so many women in the United States helped the researcher understand the "American dream."

Between a subject and verb, you might put two commas around inserted material, but never use just one comma.

```
     ┌──── subject ────┐
```
▶ The engraved plaque, given to her by her colleagues on her

    *verb*
last day of work, made her feel respected.

*2. Do not use a comma within a compound structure when the second part of the compound is not an independent clause.*

▶ Amy Tan has written novels and adapted them for the screen.

▶ Tan has written about her mother and the rest of her family.

*3. Do not use a comma after a coordinating conjunction that connects two sentences.*   The comma goes *before* the conjunction, not *after* it.

▶ *The Joy Luck Club* is supposed to be good, but I missed it when it came to my local movie theater.

*4. Do not use a comma to connect two independent clauses when no coordinating conjunction is present.*   Instead, end the first clause with a period and make the second clause a new sentence, or insert a semicolon between the clauses. Use a comma only if you connect the clauses with a coordinating conjunction. See **39** for ways to correct a comma splice, the error that results when two independent clauses are incorrectly connected with a comma.

▶ Amy Tan has written novels; they have been adapted for the screen.

**5. *Do not use a comma to separate an independent clause from a following dependent clause introduced by* after, before, because, if, since, unless, until, *or* when.**

▶ The test results were good because all the students had studied in groups.

**6. *Do not use a comma to separate a clause beginning with* that *from the rest of the sentence.***

▶ The girl in Tan's story tried to convey to her mother that she did not have to be a child prodigy.

*Note:* A comma can appear before a *that* clause when it is the second comma of a pair before and after extra information inserted as a nonrestrictive phrase.

▶ He skates so fast, despite his size, that he will probably break the world record.

**7. *Do not use commas around a phrase or clause that provides essential, restrictive information.***

▶ Alice Walker's essay "Beauty: When the Other Dancer Is the Self" discusses coping with a physical disfigurement.

[Walker has written more than one essay. The title restricts the noun *essay* to one specific essay.]

Similarly, a restrictive relative clause introduced by *who, whom, whose, which,* or *that* is never set off by commas. The clause provides essential, identifying information (see **46d** and **47d**).

▶ The teachers praised the children who finished on time.

[The teachers didn't praise all the children; they praised only the ones who finished on time.]

**8. *Do not use a comma to separate a verb from its object or complement.***

▶ The qualities required for the job are punctuality, efficiency, and the ability to work long hours.

**9. *Do not use a comma after* such as.**

▶ They bought kitchen supplies such as detergent, paper towels, and garbage bags.

**47j** Special uses of commas

*With an absolute phrase*  Use a comma to set off a phrase that modifies the whole sentence (an absolute phrase).

▸ The audience looking on in amusement, the valedictorian blew kisses to all her favorite instructors.

*With a date*  Use a comma to separate the day from the year in a date.

▸ On May 14, 1998, the legendary singer Frank Sinatra died.
[Do not use a comma before the year when the day precedes the month: 14 May 1998.]

*With numbers*  Use a comma (never a period) to divide numbers into thousands.

▸ 1,200      ▸ 515,000      ▸ 34,000,000

No commas are necessary in years (*2002*), numbers in addresses (*3501 East 10th Street*), or page numbers (*page 1008*).

*With titles*  Use commas around a person's title or degree.

▸ Stephen L. Carter, Ph.D., gave the commencement speech.

*With the parts of an address*

▸ Alice Walker was born in Eatonton, Georgia, in 1944.

However, do not use a comma before a ZIP code: Newton, MA 02159.

*With a conversational tag or tag question*

▸ Yes, Salinger's daughter, like others before her, has produced a memoir.

▸ She has not won a Pulitzer prize, has she?

*With a direct address or salutation*

▸ Whatever you build here, Mr. Trump, will cause controversy.

# 48 Apostrophes

Apostrophes indicate ownership or possession (*Fred's books, the government's plans*). They can also signal omitted letters (*who's, can't*).

**48a** Two checklists—Apostrophe: Yes, Apostrophe: No

### KEY POINTS

**Apostrophe: Yes**

1. Use -'s for the possessive form of all nouns except plural nouns that end with -s: *the hero's misfortune, the actress's Academy Award*.

2. Use an apostrophe alone for the possessive form of plural nouns that end with -s: *actresses' lives, the heroes' misfortunes*.

3. Use an apostrophe to indicate the omission of letters in contracted forms such as *didn't* and *they're*.

4. Use *it's* only for "it is" or "it has": *It's a good idea; it's been a long time.* (The possessive form of the pronoun *it* is spelled with no apostrophe: *The house lost its roof.*)

### KEY POINTS

**Apostrophe: No**

1. Generally, do not use an apostrophe to form the plurals of nouns. (See **48e** for rare exceptions.)

2. Never use an apostrophe before an -s ending on a verb.

3. Do not write possessive pronouns *(hers, its, ours, yours, theirs)* with an apostrophe.

4. Do not use an apostrophe to form the plural of names: *the Browns*.

5. Do not use an apostrophe to indicate possession by inanimate objects such as buildings and items of furniture; instead, use *of*: *the roof of the hotel, the back of the desk*.

## 48b Use -'s to signal possession.

As a general rule, to signal possession, use -'s with singular nouns, with indefinite pronouns, and with plural nouns that do not form the plural with -s.

| | |
|---|---|
| the child's books | anybody's opinion |
| the children's toys | today's world |
| this month's budget | Mr. Jackson's voice |
| someone else's idea | their money's worth |

**Individual and joint ownership**   To indicate individual ownership, make each owner possessive.

▶ **Updike's and Roth's recent works received glowing reviews.**

To show joint ownership, make only the last owner possessive: *Sam, Sue, and Pat's house.*

**Compound nouns**   Add -'s to the last word in a compound noun.

▶ **my brother-in-law's car**

**Singular nouns ending in -s**   When a singular noun ends in -s, add -'s as usual for the possessive.

▶ **Thomas's toys**        ▶ **my boss's instructions**

However, when a singular noun ending in -s is a long word or ends with a *z* or *eez* sound, an apostrophe alone is sometimes used: *Charles' theories, Erasmus' rhetoric, Euripides' dramas.*

## 48c Use only an apostrophe to signal possession in plural nouns already ending in -s.

Add only an apostrophe when a plural noun already ends in -s.

▶ **the students' suggestions**        ▶ **my friends' ambitions**
    [more than one student]                  [more than one friend]

Remember to include an apostrophe in comparisons with a noun understood (**40h** and **45i**):

▶ **His views are different from other professors'.**
    [... from other professors' views]

## **48d** Use an apostrophe in contractions.

In a contraction (*shouldn't, don't, haven't*), the apostrophe appears where letters have been omitted. To test whether an apostrophe is in the correct place, mentally replace the missing letters. The replacement test, however, will not help with the following:

won't     will not

*Note:* Some readers object to contractions in formal academic writing because they view them as colloquial and informal. It is safer not to use contractions unless you know your readers' preferences.

| | | | |
|---|---|---|---|
| can't | cannot | they'd | they had *or* they would |
| didn't | did not | they're | they are |
| he's | he is *or* he has | it's | it is *or* it has |
| 's | is, has, *or* does (How's it taste?) | let's | let us (Let's go.) |

Never place an apostrophe before the -s ending of a verb:

▶ **The author let's his characters take over.**

An apostrophe can also take the place of the first part of a year or decade.

▶ **the greed of the '80s**     ▶ **the Spirit of '76**

   [the 1980s]           [the year 1776]

*Note:* Fixed forms spelled with an apostrophe, such as *o'clock* and the poetic *o'er*, are contractions ("of the clock," "over").

## **48e** Use -'s for plurals in two special instances.

*1. Use -'s for the plural form of letters of the alphabet.* Italicize or underline only the letter, not the plural ending (**52c**).

▶ **Maria picked all the *M*'s out of her alphabet soup.**

▶ **Georges Perec's novel called *A Void* has no *e*'s in it at all.**

*2. Use -'s for the plural form of a word referred to as the word itself.* Italicize or underline the word named as a word, but do not italicize or underline the -'s ending (**52c**).

▶ **You have too many *but*'s in that sentence.**

MLA and APA prefer no apostrophe in the plural form of numbers, acronyms, and abbreviations (**54f**).

the 1900s    CDs    FAQs    BAs

However, you will frequently see such plurals spelled with -'s. Just be consistent in your usage.

Never use an apostrophe to signal the plural of common nouns or personal names: *big bargains, the Jacksons*.

## **48f** Distinguish between *it's* and *its*.

When deciding whether to use *its* or *it's*, think about meaning. *It's* is a contraction meaning "it is" or "it has." *Its* is the possessive form of the pronoun *it* and means "belonging to it." See also **44b**.

▶ **It's a good idea.**    ▶ **The committee took its time.**

## **49** Quotation Marks

Quotation marks indicate where a quotation begins and ends. The text between the quotation marks repeats the exact words that someone said, thought, or wrote. For omitting words, see **51g**.

## **49a** Guidelines for using quotation marks

### KEY POINTS

**Quotation Marks: Basic Guidelines**

1. Quote exactly the words used by the original speaker or writer.
2. Pair opening quotation marks with closing quotation marks to indicate where the quotation ends and your ideas begin.
3. Use correct punctuation to introduce and end a quotation, and place other marks of punctuation carefully in relation to the quotation marks.
4. Enclose the titles of short works in quotation marks.

## **49b** Punctuation introducing and ending a quotation

*After an introductory verb, use a comma followed by a capital letter to introduce a direct quotation.*

▶ Calvin Trillin makes a good point when he says, "As far as I'm concerned, *whom* is a word that was invented to make everyone sound like a butler."  — "Whom Says So?"

*Use a colon after a complete sentence introducing a quotation, and begin the quotation with a capital letter.*

▶ Woody Allen always tries to make us laugh even about serious issues like wealth and poverty: "Money is better than poverty, if only for financial reasons." —*Without Feathers*

*When a quotation is integrated into the structure of your own sentence, use no special introductory punctuation other than the quotation marks.*

▶ Phyllis Grosskurth comments that "anxiety over money was driving him over the brink." —*Byron*

*Put periods and commas inside quotation marks, even if these punctuation marks do not appear in the original quotation.*

▶ When Henry Rosovsky characterizes Bloom's ideas as "mind-boggling," he is not offering praise. —*The University*

In a documented paper, when you use parenthetical citations after a short quotation at the end of a sentence, put the period at the end of the citation, not within the quotation. See **49f** for long quotations.

▶ Geoffrey Wolff observes that when his father died, there was nothing to indicate "that he had ever known another human being" (11). —*The Duke of Deception*

*Put question marks and exclamation points inside the quotation marks if they are part of the original source, with no additional period.* When your sentence is a statement, do not use a comma or period in addition to a question mark or exclamation point.

▶ She asked, "Where's my mama?"

*Put a question mark, exclamation point, semicolon, or colon outside the closing quotation marks.*    If your sentence contains punctuation that is your own, not part of the original quotation, do not include it within the quotation marks.

▶ **The chapter focuses on this question: Who are "the new American dreamers"?**

## 49c  Quotation marks in dialogue

Do not add closing quotation marks until the speaker changes or you interrupt the quotation. Begin each new speaker's words with a new paragraph.

interruption
⌐ of quotation ¬
▶      **"I'm not going to work today," he announced. "Why should I? I worked all weekend. My boss is away on vacation. And I have a headache."**

⌐———— change of speaker ————¬
**"Honey, your boss is on the phone," his wife called from the bedroom.**

If a quotation from one speaker continues for more than one paragraph, place *closing* quotation marks at the end of only the *final* paragraph of the quotation. However, place *opening* quotation marks at the beginning of every paragraph, so readers realize that the quotation is continuing.

## 49d  Double and single quotation marks

Enclose quotations in double quotation marks. Enclose a quotation within a quotation in single quotation marks. (British usage is different.)

▶ **Margaret announced, "I have read 'The Lottery' already."**

## 49e  Quotation marks around titles of short works

In your writing, enclose in quotation marks the title of any short works you mention, such as a short story, poem, article, song, or chapter.

▶ **Ishmael Reed's essay "America: The Multinational Society" begins with an illuminating quotation.**

▶ **"Everything That Rises Must Converge"** [short story]

▶ **"Kubla Khan"** [poem]

**49f** When not to use quotation marks

*Do not put quotation marks around indirect quotations.*

▶ One woman I interviewed said that her husband argued like a lawyer.

*Do not put quotation marks around clichés, slang, or trite expressions.* Instead, revise to eliminate the cliché, slang, or trite expression. See also **33d** and **33g**.

involvement.
▶ All they want is ~~"a piece of the action."~~

*Do not put quotation marks at the beginning and end of long indented quotations.* When you use MLA style to quote more than three lines of poetry or four typed lines of prose, indent the whole passage one inch (or ten spaces) from the left margin. Do not enclose the quoted passage in quotation marks, but retain any internal quotation marks. See **10c** for an illustration.

*On the title page of your own paper, do not put quotation marks around your essay title.* Use quotation marks in your title only when your title contains a quotation or the title of a short work.

▶ The Advantages of Bilingual Education

▶ Charles Baxter's "Gryphon" as an Educational Warning

## 50 Semicolons

A period separates independent clauses with finality; a semicolon provides a less distinct separation, indicating more to come. As Lewis Thomas comments in his essay "Notes on Punctuation": "The period tells you that that is that; if you didn't get all the meaning you wanted or expected, anyway you got all the writer intended to parcel out and now you have to move along. But with a semicolon there you get a pleasant little feeling of expectancy; there is more to come [. . .]." Use a semicolon instead of a period when the ideas in two independent clauses are very closely connected and you want readers to expect more.

**50a** Connect two independent clauses with a semicolon to avoid a run-on sentence or a comma splice.

The use of a semicolon between closely related independent clauses creates a compound sentence (**34c**).

▶ **Biography tells us about the subject; biographers also tell us about themselves.**

A comma between the two independent clauses would produce a comma splice, and no punctuation at all would produce a run-on sentence (see **39**). Do not use a capital letter to begin a clause after a semicolon. Semicolons are often used when the second independent clause contains a transitional expression like *however, moreover, in fact, nevertheless, above all,* or *therefore.* (See **2d** and **31c** for more on transitional expressions.)

▶ **The results of the study support the hypothesis; however, further research with a variety of tasks is necessary.**

**50b** Use semicolons to separate items in a list containing internal commas.

Items in a list are usually separated by commas. However, to avoid ambiguity, use semicolons to separate listed items when internal commas are present.

▶ **When I cleaned out the refrigerator, I found a chocolate cake, half-eaten; some canned tomato paste, which had a blue fungus growing on the top; and some possibly edible meat loaf.**

**50c** When not to use a semicolon

*Do not use semicolons interchangeably with colons.* A colon (**51b**), not a semicolon, is used to introduce a list or explanation.

▶ **They contributed a great deal of food : salad, chili, and dessert.**

*Do not use a semicolon after an introductory phrase or dependent clause, even if the phrase or clause is long.* Using a semicolon would produce a fragment. Use a comma instead.

▶ **Because the training period was so long and arduous for all the players , the manager allowed one visit by family and friends.**

*Do not overuse semicolons.* Use a semicolon in place of a period only when the link between two independent clauses is strong.

# 51 Other Punctuation Marks

## 51a Periods, question marks, and exclamation points

These three punctuation marks are grouped together because they mark the end of a sentence. The MLA, in its list of Frequently Asked Questions at <http://www.mla.org>, recommends leaving one space after a punctuation mark at the end of a sentence but sees "nothing wrong with using two spaces after concluding punctuation marks." Ask your instructor for her or his preference. In a list of works cited, however, whether in MLA or APA style, leave only one space after each period in an entry.

*Periods* **(.)**   Use a period to end a sentence or signal an abbreviation.

**Mr.**     **Ms.**     **Dr.**     **Rev.**     **etc.**     **Tues.**     **i.e.**

**a.m./p.m.** (or **A.M./P.M.** See also **54c.**)

*Note:* In MLA style, do not use periods in uppercase initials of names of government agencies or other organizations, acronyms (abbreviations pronounced as words), Internet abbreviations, degrees, or common time indicators. See **54b**.

| ACLU | BA | HUD | NAACP | NPR |
| AD | FAQ | IBM | NASA | PhD |
| AIDS | HTML | IRS | NOW | URL |

*Question marks* **(?)**   A question mark at the end of a sentence signals a direct question.

▶ **What is he writing?**

Questions are useful devices to engage readers' attention. You ask a question and then provide an answer.

▶ **Many cooks nowadays are making healthier dishes. How do they do this? For the most part, they use unsaturated oil.**

A question mark can be used to express uncertainty in a sentence that is a statement.

▶ "She jumped in?" he wondered.

▶ Plato (427?–347 BC) founded the Academy at Athens.

Do not use a question mark with an indirect question (**40d** and **62d** ESL).

▶ Nobody asked him what he was writing.

*Exclamation points* (**!**)    An exclamation point at the end of a sentence indicates that the writer considers the statement amazing, surprising, or extraordinary. Avoid overuse. Let your words and ideas carry the force of any emphasis you want to communicate. When you do use an exclamation point, use it only at the end of a sentence, and do not accompany it with a period, comma, or question mark.

## 51b  Colons

A colon (:) follows an independent clause and introduces information that balances or explains that clause. A colon tells readers, "What comes next will tell you more about what you just read." When you use a colon, make sure that the sentence parts on each side of it balance or exemplify each other.

*Use a colon after an independent clause to introduce a list.*

▶ The students included three pieces of writing in their portfolios: a narrative, an argument, and a documented paper.

*Use a colon after an independent clause to introduce an explanation or elaboration.*

▶ The author has performed a remarkable feat: she has maintained suspense to the last page.

Some writers prefer to use a capital letter after a colon introducing an independent clause. Be consistent in your usage.

*Use a colon followed by a capital letter to introduce a rule or principle.*

▶ The main principle of public speaking is simple: Look at the audience.

*Use a colon in salutations, precise time notations, titles, and biblical citations.*

| | |
|---|---|
| Letters and memos | Dear Chancellor Witkin:<br>To: The Chancellor |
| Hours and minutes | 7:20 p.m. |
| Titles and subtitles | *Backlash: The Undeclared War against<br>American Women* |
| Biblical citations | Genesis 37:31–35. [Here, a period could<br>be used in place of the colon.] |

*Do not use a colon directly after a verb (such as a form of* **be** *or* **include***), a preposition, or* **such as.**

▶ The two main effects were the improvement of registration and an increase in the numbers of advisers.

▶ The book includes a preface, an introduction, an appendix, and an index.

▶ They packed many different items for the picnic, such as taco chips, salsa, bean salad, pita bread, and egg rolls.

In addition, do not use a colon after *for example, especially,* or *including.*

▶ His taste is so varied that his living room includes, for example, antiques, modern art, and art deco lighting fixtures.

## **51c** Dashes

Dashes (—) suggest a change of pace. They alert readers to something unexpected or to an interruption. Form a dash by typing two hyphens, putting no extra space before, between, or after them. Recent software will transform the two hyphens into one continuous dash.

▶ Armed with one weapon—his wit—he faced the crowd.

▶ The accused gasped, "But I never—" and fainted.

▶ In America there are two classes of travel—first class and with children.       —Robert Benchley, in Robert E. Drennan, *The Algonquin Wits*

Commas can be used to set off appositive phrases, but dashes are preferable when the phrase itself contains commas.

▶ The contents of his closet—torn jeans, frayed jackets, and suits shiny on the seat and elbows—made him reassess his priorities.

## **51d** Parentheses

Use parentheses to mark an aside or provide additional information.

▶ **Chuck Yeager's feat (breaking the sound barrier) led to increased competition in the space industry.**

Also use parentheses to enclose citations in a documented paper and to enclose numbers or letters preceding items in a list.

▶ **(3) A journalist reports that in the course of many interviews, he met very few people who were cynical about the future of the country (Lamb 5).**

## **51e** Brackets

*Square brackets* **([ ])**   When you insert words or make changes to words within a quotation, enclose the inserted or changed material in square brackets. Be careful to insert only words that help the quotation fit into your sentence grammatically or that offer necessary explanation. Do not insert words that substantially change the meaning.

▶ **Maxine Hong Kingston agrees with reviewer Diane Johnson that the memoir form "can neither [be] dismiss[ed] as fiction nor quarrel[ed] with as fact."**

On occasion, you may need to use brackets to insert the Latin word *sic* (meaning "thus") into a quoted passage in which an error occurs. Using *sic* tells readers that the word or words that it follows were present in the original source and are not your own.

▶ **Richard Lederer tells of a man who did "exercises to strengthen his abominable [sic] muscles."**

Square brackets are also used in MLA style around ellipsis dots that you add to signal an omission (**51g**).

*Angle brackets* **(< >)**   Angle brackets are used to enclose e-mail addresses and URLs (Web addresses), particularly in an MLA-style works-cited list. See **12e** and **57a**.

## **51f** Slashes

Use slashes (/) to separate two or three lines of poetry quoted within your own text. For quoting more than three lines of poetry, see **10c**.

▶ **Philip Larkin asks a question that many of us relate to: "Why should I let the toad** *work* **/ Squat on my life?"**

Slashes are also used in expressions such as *and/or* and *he/she* to indicate options. Be careful not to overuse these expressions. See also **33f**.

## **51g** Ellipsis dots

When you omit material from a quotation, indicate the omission—the ellipsis—by using spaced dots (. . .). The following passage by Ruth Sidel, on page 27 of *On Her Own*, is used in the examples that follow.

> These women have a commitment to career, to material well-being, to success, and to independence. To many of them, an affluent life-style is central to their dreams; they often describe their goals in terms of cars, homes, travel to Europe. In short, they want their piece of the American Dream.

*Words omitted from the middle of a quotation*   Use three ellipsis dots when you omit material from the middle of a quotation. MLA style calls for square brackets around the dots so that readers will know that the dots are not part of the original text (**10c**).

MLA   **Ruth Sidel reports that the women in her interviews "have a commitment to career [. . .] and to independence" (27).**

APA   **Ruth Sidel reports that the women in her interviews "have a commitment to career . . . and to independence" (1990, p. 27).**

*Words omitted at the end of your sentence*   When you omit part of a quotation and the omission occurs at the end of your own sentence, insert a period after the closing bracket (MLA style), followed by the closing quotation marks, making four dots in all.

▶ **Ruth Sidel presents interesting findings about jobs and money: "These women have a commitment to career, to material well-being [. . .]."**

When a parenthetical reference follows the quoted passage, put the final sentence period after the parenthetical reference:

▶ **Ruth Sidel presents interesting findings about jobs and money: "These women have a commitment to career, to material well-being [. . .]" (27).**

*Complete sentence omitted* When you omit a complete sentence or more, insert three ellipsis dots (in brackets for MLA style).

► Sidel tells us how "an affluent life-style is central to their dreams; [. . .] they want their piece of the American dream" (27).

*Line of poetry omitted* When you omit one or more lines of poetry from a long, indented quotation, indicate the omission with a line of dots—enclosed in square brackets if you are using MLA style.

► This poem is for the hunger of my mother
[ . . . . . . . . . . . . . . . . . . ]
who read the Blackwell's catalogue
like a menu of delights
and when we moved from Puerto Rico to the States
we packed 100 boxes of books and 40 of everything else.
                              —Aurora Levins Morales, *Class Poem*

*When not to use ellipsis dots* Do not use ellipsis dots when you quote only a word or a phrase because it will be obvious that material has been omitted:

► The women Sidel interviewed see an "affluent life-style" in their future.

*Note:* Use three dots to indicate uncertainty, a pause, or an interruption.

► After watching the mystery for two hours, I braced myself for those annoying words, "To be continued . . .".

## 52 Italics and Underlining

Use italic type or underlining to highlight a word, phrase, or title in your own writing. Most word processing programs offer italic type. Usually, though, in manuscript form, underlining is more distinctive and therefore preferred, particularly in bibliographical lists and in material to be graded or typeset. Ask your instructor which to use. For underlining when writing online, see **57b**.

► Woolf's novel *Orlando* was written for Vita Sackville-West.

► In The Psychology of Time , we learn about perceptions of filled and empty time.

**52a** Italicize or underline titles of long, whole works.

In the body of an essay, italicize or underline the titles of books, magazines, newspapers, plays, films, TV series, long poems, musical compositions, Web sites, online databases, and works of art.

- ▶ **The Sun Also Rises**
- ▶ *Survivor*
- ▶ **Newsweek**
- ▶ *The English Patient*
- ▶ **Mona Lisa**
- ▶ *InfoTrac*

Do not italicize or underline the names of sacred works such as the Bible, books of the Bible (Genesis, Psalms), and the Koran (Qur'an). Also do not italicize or underline the titles of documents and laws, such as the Declaration of Independence, the Constitution, and the Americans with Disabilities Act.

Do not italicize or underline the titles of short works, such as poems, short stories, essays, and articles; use quotation marks (**49e**). Do not italicize or underline the title of your own essays on your title page (**49f**).

**52b** Italicize or underline names of specific ships, trains, airplanes, and spacecraft.

- ▶ **Mayflower**
- ▶ *Silver Meteor*
- ▶ *Mir*

Do not underline or italicize the abbreviations sometimes preceding them: USS *Constitution.*

**52c** Italicize or underline letters, numerals, and words referring to the items themselves, not to what they represent.

- ▶ The sign had a large **P** in black marker and a **3** in red.
- ▶ *Zarf* is a useful word for some board games.

**52d** Italicize or underline words from other languages.

Expressions not commonly used in English should be italicized or underlined. Do not overuse such expressions because they tend to sound pretentious.

- ▶ The chef decided to put *moules paysanne* on the menu.

Do not italicize common expressions: et al., croissant, film noir, etc.

**52e** Avoid italicizing or underlining for emphasis.

hair-raising.
▶ **The climb was ~~so scary~~.**

Select a word that conveys the emphasis you want to express.

## 53 Capitalization

Always consult a dictionary if you are not sure whether to capitalize a word.

**53a** Capitalize proper nouns and proper adjectives.

Begin the names of specific people, places, and things with a capital letter.

| TYPES OF PROPER NOUNS AND ADJECTIVES | EXAMPLES |
|---|---|
| Names of people | Albert Einstein, Madonna, T. S. Eliot, Bill Gates |
| Names of nations, continents, planets, stars, and galaxies | Hungary, Asia, Mercury, the North Star, the Milky Way |
| Names of mountains, rivers, and oceans | Mount Everest, the Thames, the Pacific Ocean |
| Names of public places and regions | Golden Gate Park, the Great Plains, the Midwest |
| Names of streets, buildings, and monuments | Rodeo Drive, the Empire State Building, the Roosevelt Memorial |
| Names of cities, states, and provinces | Toledo, Kansas, Nova Scotia |
| Days of the week and months | Wednesday, March |
| Holidays | Labor Day, the Fourth of July |
| Organizations and companies | the Red Cross, Microsoft Corporation |
| Institutions (including colleges, departments, schools, government offices, and courts of law) | University of Texas, Department of English, School of Business, Defense Department, Florida Supreme Court |

| TYPES OF PROPER NOUNS AND ADJECTIVES | EXAMPLES |
|---|---|
| Historical events, named periods, and documents | the Civil War, the Renaissance, the Roaring Twenties, the Declaration of Independence |
| Religions, deities, revered persons, and sacred texts | Buddhism, Islam, Muslim, Baptist, Jehovah, Mohammed, the Torah, the Koran (Qur'an) |
| Races, tribes, nations, nationalities, and languages | the Navajo, Greece, Greek, Spain, Spanish |
| Registered trademarks | Kleenex, Apple, Bic, Nike, Xerox |
| Names of ships, planes, and spacecraft | the USS *Kearsage,* the *Spirit of St. Louis,* the *Challenger* |

*Note:* Do not capitalize nouns naming general classes or types of people, places, things, or ideas: *government, jury, mall, prairie, utopia, traffic court, the twentieth century, goodness, reason.* For the use of capital letters in online writing, see **57c**.

**53b** Capitalize a title before a person's name.

▶ The reporter interviewed Senator Thompson.

▶ The residents cheered Grandma Jones.

Do not use a capital letter when a title is not attached to a person's name.

▶ Each state elects two senators.

▶ My grandmother is ninety years old.

When a title substitutes for the name of a known person, a capital letter is often used.

▶ Have you spoken with the Senator [senator] yet?

**53c** Capitalize major words in titles.

In titles of published books, journals, magazines, essays, articles, films, poems, and songs, use a capital letter at the beginning of all words except articles *(the, a, an),* coordinating conjunctions *(and, but, or, nor, so, for, yet), to* in an infinitive *(to stay),* and prepositions unless they begin or end a title or subtitle.

▶ "A Matter of Identity"

▶ "Wrestling with the Angel: A Memoir"

**53d** Guidelines for using a capital or lowercase letter after a colon or at the beginning of a quotation

*Should a capital letter be used at the beginning of a clause after a colon?* Usage varies. Usually a capital letter is used if the clause states a rule or principle (**51b**). Make your usage consistent.

*Should a capital letter be used at the beginning of a quotation?* Capitalize the first word of a quoted sentence if it is capitalized in the original passage.

▶ **Quindlen says, "This is a story about a name," and thus tells us the topic of her article.**

Do not capitalize when you quote part of a sentence.

▶ **When Quindlen says that she is writing "a story about a name," she is telling us the topic of her article.**

## 54 Abbreviations

For abbreviations commonly used in online writing, see **57e**.

**54a** Abbreviate titles used with people's names.

Use an abbreviation, followed by a period, for titles before or after names. The following abbreviated titles precede names: *Mr., Mrs., Prof., Dr., Gen.,* and *Sen.* (Note that *Ms.* is not an abbreviation, yet it is followed by a period.) The following abbreviated titles follow names: *Sr., Jr., PhD, MD, BA,* and *DDS.* Do not use a title both before and after a name: *Dr. Benjamin Spock* or *Benjamin Spock, MD.* Do not abbreviate a title if it is not attached to a specific name.

doctor
▶ He went to the ~~dr.~~ twice last week.

**54b** Abbreviate the names of familiar institutions, countries, tests, diplomas, individuals, and objects.

Use abbreviations of the names of well-known institutions (*UCLA, YWCA, FBI, IBM*), countries (*USA* or *U.S.A.*), tests and diplomas (*SAT, GED*), individuals (*FDR*), and objects (*DVD*). If you use a specialized abbreviation, first use the term in full followed by the abbreviation in parentheses; then use the abbreviation.

▶ **The Graduate Record Examination (GRE) is required by many graduate schools. GRE preparation is therefore big business.**

**54c** Abbreviate terms used with numbers.

Use the abbreviations such as *BC, AD, a.m., p.m., $, mph, wpm, mg, kg,* and other units of measure only when they occur with specific numbers.

▶ **35 BC** [meaning "before Christ," now often replaced with BCE, "before the Common Era"]

▶ **AD 1776** [*anno domini,* "in the year of the Lord," now often replaced with *CE,* "Common Era," used after the date: 1776 CE]

▶ **2:00 a.m./p.m.** [*ante* or *post meridiem,* Latin for "before or after midday"] Alternatives are A.M./P.M. or AM/PM. Be consistent.

But do not use these abbreviations and other units of measure when no number is attached to them.

▶ **His family gave him a wallet full of $̲ to spend on vacation.**
               *money*

▶ **They arrived late in the ~~p.m.~~**
          *afternoon.*

**54d** Abbreviate common Latin terms.

In notes, parentheses, and source citations, use abbreviations for common Latin terms. In the body of your text, use the English meaning.

| ABBREVIATION | LATIN | ENGLISH MEANING |
| --- | --- | --- |
| etc. | et cetera | and so on |
| i.e. | id est | that is |
| e.g. | exempli gratia | for example |
| cf. | confer | compare |

| ABBREVIATION | LATIN | ENGLISH MEANING |
|---|---|---|
| N.B. | nota bene | note well |
| et al. | et alii | and others |

## 54e Do not abbreviate words to save time and space.

In formal writing, write in full expressions such as the following:

| | |
|---|---|
| & | and |
| bros. | brothers [Use "Bros." only if it is part of the official name of a business.] |
| chap. | chapter |
| Mon. | Monday |
| nite | night |
| NJ | New Jersey [Abbreviate the name of a state only in an address, a note, or a reference.] |
| no. | number [Use the abbreviation only with a specific number: "No. 17 on the list was deleted."] |
| Oct. | October [Write names of days and months in full, except in some works-cited lists.] |
| soc. | sociology [Write names of academic subjects in full.] |
| thru | through |
| w/ | with |

## 54f Use -s (not -'s) for the plural form of an abbreviation.

Do not use an apostrophe to make an abbreviation plural (48e).

▶ **She has over a thousand CDs.**  ▶ **Both his VCRs are broken.**

## 55 Numbers

Conventions for using numerals (actual figures) or words vary across the disciplines.

## 55a Use the conventions of the discipline.

### In the humanities and in business letters

Use words for numbers expressible in one or two words and for fractions (*nineteen, fifty-six, two hundred, one-half*).

Use numerals for longer numbers *(326; 5,625; 7,642,000).*

Use a combination of words and numerals for whole millions, billions, and so on *(45 million, 1 billion).*

### In scientific and technical writing

Use numerals for all numbers above nine.

Use numerals for numbers below ten only when they show precise measurement, as when they are grouped and compared with other larger numbers *(5 of the 39 participants),* or when they precede a unit of measurement *(6 cm),* indicate a mathematical function *(8%; 0.4),* or represent a specific time, date, age, score, or number in a series.

Use words for fractions: *two-thirds.*

**55b** In both the humanities and the sciences, spell out numbers that begin a sentence.

▶ **One hundred twenty-five members voted for the new bylaws.**

▶ **Six thousand fans have already bought tickets.**

**ESL Note** Even after plural numbers, use the singular form of *hundred, thousand,* and *million.* Add *-s* only when there is no preceding number.

▶ **Five *hundred* books were damaged in the flood.**

▶ ***Hundreds* of books were damaged in the flood.** ■

**55c** Use numerals in special instances.

In nonscientific writing, use numerals for the following:

| | |
|---|---|
| Time and dates | 6 p.m. on 31 May 1995 |
| Decimals | 20.89 |
| Statistics | median score 35 |
| Addresses | 16 East 93rd Street |
| Chapter, page, scene, and line numbers | chapter 5, page 97 |
| Quantities appearing with abbreviations or symbols | 6°C (for temperature Celsius), $21, 6′7″ |
| Scores | The Knicks won 89–85. |

For percentages and money, numerals and the symbol (*75%*, *$24.67*) are usually acceptable, or you can spell out the expression if it is fewer than four words (*seventy-five percent, twenty-four dollars*).

**55d** Use *-s* (not *-'s*) for the plural form of numerals.

▶ in the 1980s    ▶ They scored in the 700s in the SATs.

## 56 Hyphenation

Use hyphens to divide a word or to form a compound. For the use of hyphens online, see **57d**.

**56a** Hyphens with prefixes

Many words with prefixes are spelled without hyphens: *cooperate, nonrestrictive, unnatural.* Others are hyphenated: *all-inclusive, anti-intellectual.* Always use a hyphen when the main word is a number or a proper noun: *all-American, post-1990.* If you are unsure about whether to insert a hyphen before a prefix, check a dictionary.

**56b** Hyphens in compound nouns and adjectives

Some compound nouns are written as one word (*toothbrush*), others as two words (*coffee shop*), and still others with one or more hyphens (*role-playing, father-in-law*). Always check an up-to-date dictionary.

Hyphenate compound adjectives preceding a noun: *a well-organized party, a law-abiding citizen, a ten-page essay.* When the modifier follows the noun, no hyphen is necessary: *The party was well organized. Most citizens try to be law abiding. The essay was ten pages long.*

Do not insert a hyphen between an *-ly* adverb and an adjective or after an adjective in its comparative (*-er*) or superlative (*-est*) form: *a tightly fitting suit, a sweeter sounding melody.*

**56c** Hyphens in spelled-out numbers

Use hyphens when spelling out two-word numbers from twenty-one to ninety-nine. (See **55** for more on spelling out numbers.)

▶ **Twenty-two applicants arrived early in the morning.**

Also use a hyphen in spelled-out fractions: *two-thirds of a cup.*

### 56d End-of-line hyphens

Most word processors either automatically hyphenate words or automatically wrap words around to the next line. Choose the latter option to avoid the strange and unacceptable word division that sometimes appears with automatic hyphenation.

## 57 Online Guidelines

### 57a Punctuation in URLs

Punctuation marks communicate essential information in Web site addresses—Uniform Resource Locators (URLs)—and in e-mail addresses. Be sure to include all marks when you write an address, and if you need to spread a URL over more than one line, split it after a slash (MLA style) or before a punctuation mark. Do not split the protocol (<http://>). Use angle brackets to enclose e-mail and Web addresses. Do not include any additional punctuation within the angle brackets.

▶ **The Modern Language Association, whose Web site is at <http://www.mla.org>, provides examples of documenting Web sources.**

### 57b Underscoring, underlining, and italics online

In World Wide Web pages and in HTML (hypertext markup language), underlining indicates a link to another site, so underlining is not available for other uses. When you write for publication on the Web, use italics to indicate titles and other usually underlined expressions. In e-mail, use underscore marks instead of italics and underlining, as in this sentence:

▶ **Just read Joyce's _Ulysses_ to get a flavor of Dublin.**

[The underscore marks precede and follow the word that would have been italicized or underlined.]

## **57c** Capital letters online

Lowercase and capital (uppercase) letters are significant (the technical term is *case-sensitive*) in e-mail addresses and URLs, so keep careful records of which are used. If you make a mistake, you will be unable to make a connection. Similarly, the names of many systems and search engines have specialized capitalization (WebCrawler, AltaVista).

Avoid using capitalized text (the whole text, not just initial letters) in e-mail communications and electronic discussion groups. In both places, the prolonged use of capital letters is regarded as "shouting" and may offend readers. See also **20c**.

## **57d** Hyphens online

Some e-mail addresses include hyphens, so never add a hyphen to indicate that you have split an address between lines. When an e-mail address includes a hyphen, do not break the line at a hyphen because readers will not know whether the hyphen is part of the address.

Technological vocabulary changes quickly. We already have new combined words such as *online* and *download.* You will find both *e-mail* and *email.* The MLA prefers the hyphenated spelling, *e-mail,* but the tendency is for common words like this to move toward closing up. Whichever form you use, use it consistently.

## **57e** Asterisks and abbreviations online

*Asterisks* **(\*)**   Some older e-mail providers do not support text features such as italics or underlining. In such cases, use asterisks before and after a word or phrase for emphasis.

▶ They were \*decidedly\* antagonistic.

*Abbreviations*   Many abbreviations in the electronic world have become standard fare: *CD-ROM, RAM, PIN,* and more. In addition, the informal world of online communication leads to informal abbreviations, at least in personal e-mail messages. Abbreviations such as *BTW* ("by the way") and *TTYTT* ("to tell you the truth") are used in e-mail but never appear in more formal written communication.

## 58 Spelling

Get into the habit of using a dictionary and a word processor with a spelling check program. Even if you check your spelling with computer software, you still need to proofread. A program will not alert you to a correctly spelled word used in the wrong place (such as *cite* used in place of *sight* or *site*).

### 58a Plurals of nouns

*Regular plural forms*   The regular plural of nouns is formed by adding *-s* or *-es* to the singular word.

essay, essays                match, matches

To form the plural of a compound noun, attach the *-s* to the main noun in the phrase.

mothers-in-law                passersby

Proofread carefully for plural forms that form the plural with *-s* but make other changes, too, such as the following:

*-f* OR *-fe* ⟶ *-ves*                (*Exceptions:* beliefs, roofs, chiefs)

thief, thieves
wife, wives

| *-o* ⟶ *-oes* | *-o* ⟶ *-os* |
|---|---|
| potato, potatoes | hero (sandwich), heros |
| tomato, tomatoes | photo, photos |
| hero (man), heroes | piano, pianos |

| CONSONANT + *-y* ⟶ *-ies* | VOWEL + *-y* ⟶ *-ys* |
|---|---|
| family, families | toy, toys |
| party, parties | monkey, monkeys |

### *Irregular plural forms* (no *-s* ending)

| | |
|---|---|
| man, men | foot, feet |
| woman, women | tooth, teeth |
| child, children | mouse, mice |

*Plural forms borrowed from other languages*   Words borrowed from other languages, particularly Greek and Latin words, frequently borrow the plural form of the language, too.

| | |
|---|---|
| basis, bases | nucleus, nuclei |
| thesis, theses | vertebra, vertebrae |
| hypothesis, hypotheses | alumnus (m.), alumni |
| criterion, criteria | alumna (f.), alumnae |

*Plural forms with no change*   Some words have the same form in singular and plural: *moose, deer, sheep, fish.*

## **58b** Doubling consonants

Doubled consonants form a link between spelling and pronunciation because the doubling of a consonant signals a short vowel sound.

*Double the consonant when the verb stem contains one vowel plus one consonant in one syllable.*

slip, slipping, slipped     hop, hopping, hopped

The doubled consonant preserves the short vowel sound. Compare the pronunciation of *hop, hopping, hopped* with *hope, hoping, hoped.* Compare the vowel sounds in *write, writing,* and *written.*

*Double the consonant when the verb stem contains two or more syllables with one vowel plus one consonant in the final stressed syllable.*

refer, referring, referred     control, controlling, controlled

Compare *travel, traveling,* which has the stress on the first syllable. (See the Language and Culture box on p. 401 for variants in British English.)

*Double the consonant when the suffix -er or -est is added to one-syllable adjectives ending in one vowel plus one consonant.*

big, bigger, biggest     hot, hotter, hottest

*Double the l when adding -ly to an adjective that ends in one -l.*

careful, carefully     successful, successfully

## **58c** Spelling with -*y* or -*i*

| VERB ENDS IN CONSONANT + -*y* | -*ies* | -*ying* | -*ied* |
|---|---|---|---|
| cry | cries | crying | cried |
| study | studies | studying | studied |

| VERB ENDS IN VOWEL + -*y* | -*ys* | -*ying* | -*yed* |
|---|---|---|---|
| play | plays | playing | played |

*Exceptions:* pay/paid, say/said, lay/laid

| VERB ENDS IN VOWEL + -*e* | -*ies* | -*ying* | -*ied* |
|---|---|---|---|
| die | dies | dying | died |

| TWO-SYLLABLE ADJECTIVE ENDS IN -*y* | -*i* WITH A SUFFIX |
|---|---|
| happy | happier, happily, happiness |

| TWO-SYLLABLE ADJECTIVE ENDS IN -*ly* | -*lier* | -*liest* |
|---|---|---|
| friendly | friendlier | friendliest |

## **58d** Internal *ie* or *ei*

This traditional rhyme helps with the decision about whether to use *ie* or *ei*: "*I* before *e*/ Except after *c*/Or when sounded like *ay*/ As in *neighbor* and *weigh*."

The following examples illustrate those guidelines:

| *i* BEFORE *e* | *e* BEFORE *i* AFTER *c* | *e* BEFORE *i* WHEN SOUNDED LIKE *ay* |
|---|---|---|
| believe | receive | vein |
| relief | ceiling | reign |
| niece | deceive | sleigh |

*Exceptions:*

| *i* BEFORE *e* EVEN AFTER *c* | *e* BEFORE *i*, NOT AFTER *c* | |
|---|---|---|
| conscience | height | seize |
| science | either/neither | foreign |
| species | leisure | weird |

## **58e**   Adding a suffix

### *Keep a silent -e before an -ly suffix.*

immediate, immediately     sure, surely

*Exceptions:* true, truly; whole, wholly; due, duly

### *Keep a silent -e before a suffix beginning with a consonant.*

state, statement     force, forceful     rude, rudeness

*Exceptions:* acknowledge, acknowledgment; judge, judgment; argue, argument

### *Drop a silent -e before a suffix beginning with a vowel.*

hope, hoping          observe, observant
write, writing         remove, removable

*Exceptions:* enforce, enforceable; change, changeable. Retaining the *-e* preserves the soft sound of the preceding consonant.

### *With adjectives ending in -le, drop the -le when adding -ly.*

sensible, sensibly

### *With adjectives ending in -ic, add -ally to form the adverb.*

basic, basically     characteristic, characteristically

*Exception:* public, publicly

### *Pay attention to the suffixes -able, -ible, -ant, -ent, -ify, and -efy.*   More words end in *-able* than in *-ible*. Here are some of the most common *-ible* words:

| | | | |
|---|---|---|---|
| eligible | incredible | irresistible | legible |
| permissible | responsible | terrible | visible |

Unfortunately there are no rules of thumb to help you decide whether to use the suffix *-ant* or *-ent*. Learn common words with these suffixes, and have your dictionary handy for others.

| -ANT | -ENT |
|---|---|
| defiant | confident |
| observant | convenient |
| relevant | existent |
| reluctant | imminent |
| resistant | independent |

The suffix *-ify* is more common than *-efy*. Learn the four *-efy* words:

    liquefy     putrefy     rarefy     stupefy

## **58f** Accents, umlauts, tildes, and cedillas

Words and names in languages other than English may be spelled with special marks over or under a letter, such as an accent (é or è), an umlaut or dieresis (ö), a tilde (ñ), or a cedilla (ç). Your word processing program probably provides these characters (in Microsoft Word, go to Insert/Symbol/Font). If it does not, insert them by hand.

### LANGUAGE AND CULTURE

**Different Englishes**

Differences exist in the meaning and spelling of words in varieties of the English language, such as Caribbean, Indian, and African American Vernacular. Here are some common spelling differences in British and American English:

| BRITISH | AMERICAN | BRITISH | AMERICAN |
|---------|----------|---------|----------|
| colour | color | theatre | theater |
| humour | humor | centre | center |
| learnt | learned | criticise | criticize |
| travelled | traveled | judgement | judgment |
| cheque | check | defence | defense |

Here are some common differences in meaning. Note the potential for confusion.

| BRITISH | AMERICAN |
|---------|----------|
| bonnet (of car) | hood |
| windscreen | windshield |
| boot | trunk |
| car park | parking lot |
| dual carriageway | divided highway |
| roundabout | traffic circle, rotary |
| nappy | diaper |

*(Continued)*

*(Continued)*

| BRITISH | AMERICAN |
| --- | --- |
| dummy | pacifier |
| pudding | dessert |
| eiderdown | comforter |
| braces | suspenders |
| vest | undershirt |
| waistcoat | vest |
| trousers | pants |
| pants | underwear |
| over the road | across the street |
| chips | french fries |
| crisps | potato chips |

# PART 9

*For Multilingual/ESL Writers*

# 59 Culture, Language, and Writing

The abbreviation *ESL* ("English as a second language") is commonly used in college curricula, professional literature, and the press. However, the term is not really broad enough to include many individuals who grew up speaking languages other than English. Many so-called second-language students speak three or four languages besides English, depending on their life and educational circumstances and the languages spoken at home. Along with being bilingual or multilingual, ESL students are also multicultural, equipped with all the knowledge and experience that those terms imply.

## 59a Cultural, rhetorical, and linguistic differences—not deficits

If your first language is not English, you may not be totally fluent yet in English, but as you learn, it is a good idea to see your knowledge of language and culture as an advantage rather than a problem. Unlike many monolingual writers (individuals who know only one language), you are able to know different cultures in an in-depth way and to switch at will among varied linguistic and rhetorical codes. Rather than having only one language, one culture, and one culturally bound type of writing, you have a broader perspective—more to think about, more to write about, more resources to draw on as you write, and far more comparisons to make among languages, writers, writing, and culture. You bring your culture with you into your writing, and as you do so, you help shape and reshape the culture of North America. The questions in the Key Points box will help you examine your unique situation.

**KEY POINTS**

**Cultural, Rhetorical, and Linguistic Differences**

Consider the following questions. Discuss them with members of your family or with friends who share your cultural background.

1. What three features of your native culture stand out for you as significantly different from features of North American culture?

*(Continued)*

*(Continued)*

(These features might relate to customs, holidays, religion, relationships, the structure of family life and responsibility, growing up and adolescence, work and entertainment, or educational practices.) List them.

2. How have these three cultural issues affected you as a student and as a writer?

3. When you read articles, essays, and letters in your first language and in English, do you notice any differences in approach to the topic and in style? How would you characterize those differences?

4. How does your culture view references to classic texts and to the work of others? Does every reference to another writer's ideas have to be documented? Why or why not? (See **9b** for more on Western views of plagiarism.)

5. Write a paragraph in your native language about your experiences as a writer. What considerations occupied you as you wrote (for example, content, organization, grammar, punctuation)? How different are they from the considerations you have when you write in English?

6. List five linguistic features of English that cause you trouble when you write—problem areas where you may make mistakes in sentence structure or grammar. Decide why you make mistakes in these areas: Are mistakes caused by the influence of your native language? Or do mistakes occur when you construct a hypothesis about English that turns out to be false?

7. For each of the five problem areas you have isolated, write down the corresponding usage in your native language. What light does the comparison throw on why these particular features of English cause you problems?

## **59b** Language learning and errors

Even for language learners who are learning well, errors are inevitable. They are not a sign of laziness or stupidity. Welcome and embrace your errors; study them; learn from them. Errors show language learning in progress. If you make no errors while you are learning to speak or write a new language, perhaps you are being too careful and using only what you know to be correct. Be willing to take risks and try new words, new expressions, new combinations. That is the way to expand your repertoire.

When you make an error, make a note of it. Consider why you made the error. Analyzing the causes of errors will help you understand how to edit them and avoid them in the future.

Readers are most likely to be disturbed by errors when the content and flow of ideas are not clear. A thoughtful, well-written essay that contains a few errors will usually win out over a sloppy, flimsy piece of work that is grammatically flawless. Errors, however, do distract attentive readers, and you need to learn how to edit for accuracy. Sections **60–64** address some problems faced by many language learners. Consult those sections as you need to, along with the ESL Notes and Language and Culture boxes appearing throughout this book, which address not just errors but cultural differences. Part 7 addresses problems that many writers face, whether they speak one or more than one language.

## 59c Language guide to transfer errors

Errors in writing in a new language can occur when you are grappling with new subject matter and difficult topics. You concentrate on ideas and clarity, but because no writer can do everything at once, you fail to concentrate on editing.

The language guide on pages 408–411 identifies several problem areas for multilingual/ESL writers. It shows grammatical features (column 1) of specific languages (column 2) that lead to an error when transferred to English (column 3). Of course, the guide covers neither all linguistic problem areas nor all languages. Rather, it lists a selection, with the aim of being useful and practical. Included in the guide are references to Caribbean Creole (listed simply as "Creole"), a variety of English with features differing from Standard English. Use the guide to raise your awareness about your own and other languages.

If you think of a feature or a language that should be included in the guide, please write to the author at the publisher's address or send a message at the publisher's Web site at <college.hmco.com/keys.html>. This Web site also provides links to sites specifically designed for multilingual students.

| LANGUAGE FEATURES | LANGUAGES | SAMPLE TRANSFER ERRORS IN ENGLISH |
|---|---|---|
| **ARTICLES (60c–60f)** | | |
| No articles | Chinese, Japanese, Russian, Swahili, Thai, Urdu | *Sun is hot.* *I bought book.* *Computer has changed our lives.* |
| No indefinite article with profession | Arabic, Creole, French, Japanese, Korean, Vietnamese | *He is student.* *She lawyer.* |
| Definite article with days, months, places, idioms | Arabic | *She is in the bed.* *He lives in the Peru.* |
| Definite article used for generalization | Farsi, French, German, Greek, Portuguese, Spanish | *The photography is an art.* *The books are more expensive than the disks.* |
| No article for generalization with singular noun | Creole | *Bird can fly.* |
| Definite article used with proper noun | French, German, Greek, Portuguese, Spanish | *The Professor Brackert teaches in Frankfurt.* |
| No definite article | Hindi, Turkish | *Store on corner is closed.* |
| No indefinite article | Korean (uses *one* for *a;* depends on context) | *He ran into one tree.* |
| **VERBS AND VERBALS (61)** | | |
| *Be* can be omitted. | Arabic, Chinese, Creole, Russian | *India more religious than Britain.* *She working now.* *He cheerful.* |
| No progressive forms | French, German, Greek, Russian | *They still discuss the problem.* *When I walked in, she slept.* |
| No tense inflections | Chinese, Creole, Thai, Vietnamese | *He arrive yesterday.* *When I was little, I always walk to school.* |

| LANGUAGE FEATURES | LANGUAGES | SAMPLE TRANSFER ERRORS IN ENGLISH |
|---|---|---|
| No inflections for person and number | Creole, Chinese, Japanese, Korean, Russian, Thai | *The singer have a big band.* *She work hard.* |
| Past perfect formed with *be* | Arabic | *They were arrived.* |
| Different tense boundaries from English | Arabic, Chinese, Creole, Farsi, French | *I study here for a year.* *He has left yesterday.* |
| Different limits for passive voice | Creole, Japanese, Korean, Russian, Thai, Vietnamese | *They were stolen their luggage.* *My name base on Chinese characters.* *The mess clean up quick.* *A miracle was happened.* |
| No *-ing* (gerund)/ infinitive distinction | Arabic, Chinese, Farsi, French, Greek, Portuguese, Spanish, Vietnamese | *She avoids to go.* *I enjoy to play tennis.* |
| Infinitive not used to express purpose | Korean | *I go out for having my dinner.* |
| Overuse of progressive forms | Hindi, Urdu | *I am wanting to leave now.* |

## WORD ORDER AND SENTENCE STRUCTURE (62)

| | | |
|---|---|---|
| Verb precedes subject | Arabic, Hebrew, Russian, Spanish (optional), Tagalog | *Good grades received every student in the class.* |
| Verb-subject order in dependent clause | French | *I knew what would propose the committee.* |
| Verb after subject and object | Bengali, German (in dependent clause), Hindi, Japanese, Korean, Turkish | *. . . (when) the teacher the money collected.* |

| LANGUAGE FEATURES | LANGUAGES | SAMPLE TRANSFER ERRORS IN ENGLISH |
|---|---|---|
| Coordination favored over subordination | Arabic | Frequent use of *and* and *so*. |
| Relative clause or restrictive phrase precedes noun it modifies | Chinese, Japanese, Korean, Russian | *The enrolled in community college student . . .*<br>*A nine-meter-high impressive monument to Lenin . . .*<br>*He gave me a too difficult for me book.* |
| Adverb can occur between verb and object or before verb | French, Urdu (before verb) | *I like very much clam chowder.*<br>*They efficiently organized the work.* |
| *That* clause rather than an infinitive | Arabic, French, Hindi, Russian, Spanish | *I want that you stay.*<br>*I want that they try harder.* |
| Inversion of subject and verb rare | Chinese | *She is leaving and so I am.* |
| Conjunctions occur in pairs | Chinese, Farsi, Vietnamese | *Although she is rich, but she wears simple clothes.*<br>*Even if I had money, I would also not buy that car.* |
| Subject (especially pronoun) can be omitted | Chinese, Italian, Japanese, Spanish, Thai | *Is raining.* |
| Commas set off a dependent clause | German, Russian | *He knows, that we are right.* |
| No equivalent of *there is/there are* | Japanese, Korean, Portuguese, Russian, Spanish, Thai (adverb of place and *have*) | *This article says four reasons to eat beans.*<br>*In the garden has many trees.* |

| LANGUAGE FEATURES | LANGUAGES | SAMPLE TRANSFER ERRORS IN ENGLISH |
|---|---|---|

## NOUNS, PRONOUNS, ADJECTIVES, ADVERBS (**60a**, **60b**, **44**, **45**)

| LANGUAGE FEATURES | LANGUAGES | SAMPLE TRANSFER ERRORS IN ENGLISH |
|---|---|---|
| Personal pronouns restate subject | Arabic, Gujarati, Spanish | *My father he lives in California.* |
| No human/nonhuman distinction for relative pronoun (*who/which*) | Arabic, Farsi, French, Russian, Spanish, Thai | *Here is the student which you met her last week.* *The people which arrived . . .* |
| Pronoun object included in relative clause | Arabic, Chinese, Farsi, Hebrew | *The house that I used to live in it is big.* |
| No distinction between subject and object forms of pronouns | Chinese, Gujarati, Korean, Spanish, Thai | *I gave the forms to she.* |
| Nouns and adjectives have same form. | Chinese, Japanese | *She is very beauty woman.* *They felt very safety on the train.* |
| No distinction between *he* and *she*, *his* and *her* | Bengali, Farsi, Gujarati, Thai | *My sister dropped his purse.* |
| No plural form after a number | Creole, Farsi | *He has two dog.* |
| No plural (or optional) forms of nouns | Chinese, Japanese, Korean, Thai | *Several good book . . .* |
| No relative pronouns | Korean | *The book is on the table is mine.* |
| Different perception of countable/uncountable | Japanese, Spanish | *I bought three furnitures.* *He has five chalk.* |
| Adjectives show number. | Spanish | *I have helpfuls friends.* |
| Negative before verb | Spanish | *Jack no like meat.* |
| Double negatives used routinely | Spanish | *They don't know nothing.* |

## 60 Nouns and Articles

### 60a Categories of nouns

Nouns in English fall into various categories. A *proper noun* names a unique person, place, or thing and begins with a capital letter: *Walt Whitman, Lake Superior, Grand Canyon, Vietnam Veterans Memorial, Tuesday.* A *common noun* names a general class of persons, places, or things and begins with a lowercase letter: *bicycle, furniture, plan, daughter, home, happiness.* Common nouns can be further categorized as countable and uncountable.

A *countable noun* can have a number before it (*one, two,* and so on) and has a plural form. Countable nouns frequently add *-s* to indicate the plural: *picture, pictures; plan, plans.* Use singular countable nouns after *a, an, the, this, that,* and singular quantity words (**43h**). Use plural countable nouns after *the, these, those,* and plural quantity words (**43h**).

An *uncountable noun* cannot be directly counted. It has no plural form: *furniture, advice, information.* Use uncountable nouns after *the, this, that,* and certain quantity words (**43h** and **60b**).

| COMMON NOUNS | |
|---|---|
| COUNTABLE | UNCOUNTABLE |
| machine, engine (machines, engines) | machinery |
| tool, hammer (tools, hammers) | equipment |
| bicycle, ship (bicycles, ships) | transportation |
| chair, desk (chairs, desks) | furniture |
| description, fact (descriptions, facts) | information |
| necklace, earring (necklaces, earrings) | jewelry |
| view, scene (views, scenes) | scenery |
| tip, suggestion (tips, suggestions) | advice |

### 60b Uncountable nouns

Follow these guidelines:

1. Do not use a number, a plural word like *these* and *those,* or a plural quantity word (such as *many* or *several*) before an uncountable noun. An uncountable noun has no plural form.

▶ She gave me several informations.
      ^some

2. Never use an uncountable noun with *a* or *an,* except in the phrase *a little*.

▶ **Puerto Rico has a̸ lovely scenery.**

3. Make an uncountable noun agree with a singular verb: *That information* is *useful.*

4. Use the following before an uncountable noun:

- no article (called the *zero article*) for a generalization: *Information is free.*
- a singular word such as *this* or *that*: *This equipment is jammed.*
- a possessive (see **44b**): *His advice was useless.*
- a quantity word or phrase for nonspecific reference (see pp. 333 and 334 in **43h**): *They gave us some advice. They gave us a little advice.*
- *the* for specific reference: *The information we found was all wrong.*

5. Some nouns are invariably uncountable and are listed as such in a language learners' dictionary such as *The American Heritage ESL Dictionary.* Learn the most common uncountable nouns, and note the ones that end in *-s* but are nevertheless singular:

*A mass made up of parts:* clothing, equipment, furniture, garbage, homework, information, jewelry, luggage, machinery, money, scenery, traffic, transportation

*Abstract concepts:* advice, courage, education, fun, happiness, health, honesty, information, knowledge, success

*Natural substances:* air, blood, cotton, hair, heat, ice, rice, sunshine, water, wood, wool

*Diseases:* diabetes, influenza, measles

*Games:* chess, checkers, soccer, tennis

*Subjects of study:* biology, economics, history, physics

6. Use an uncountable noun in a countable sense—that is, indicate a quantity of it—by adding a word or phrase that indicates quantity. The noun itself will always remain singular: three pieces of *furniture,* two bits of *information,* many pieces of *advice.*

7. Be aware that some nouns can be countable in one context and uncountable in another.

### GENERAL CLASS (UNCOUNTABLE)

He loves *chocolate*. [all chocolate, in whatever form]

*Time* flies.

We all hang on to *life*.

### A COUNTABLE ITEM OR ITEMS

She gave him *a chocolate*. [one piece of candy from a box]

She then gave him *three chocolates*.

They are having *a good time*.

Try it *several times*.

He is leading *a hedonistic life*.

A cat is said to have *nine lives*.

### SPECIFIC REFERENCE

*The chocolate* you gave me is delicious. [specific chocolate]

*The time* is ripe for action.

*The life* he is leading is hedonistic.

*Note:* The concept of countability varies across languages. Japanese makes no distinction between countable and uncountable nouns. In French, Spanish, and Chinese, the word for *furniture* is a countable noun; in English, it is not. In Russian, the word for *hair* is countable and is used in the plural.

## **60c** Basic rules for articles

1. Use *the* whenever a reference to a common noun is specific and unique for writer and reader (see **60d**).

   ▶ He loves $\overset{\text{the}}{\wedge}$ house that she bought.

2. Do not use *a* or *an* with a plural countable noun.

   ▶ They cited ~~a~~ reliable surveys.

3. Do not use *a* or *an* with an uncountable noun.

   ▶ He gave ~~a~~ helpful advice.

4. Use *a* before a consonant sound: *a bird, a house, a unicorn.* Use *an* before a vowel sound: *an egg, an ostrich, an hour, an ugly vase.* Take spe-

cial care with the sounds associated with the letters *h* and *u*, which can have either a consonant or a vowel sound.

5. To make a generalization about a countable noun, do one of the following:

   - Use the plural form: *Lions are majestic.*
   - Use the singular with *a* or *an*: *A lion is a majestic animal.*
   - Use the singular with *the* to denote a classification: *The lion is a majestic animal.*

6. A countable singular noun can never stand alone, so make sure that a countable singular noun is preceded by an article or by a demonstrative pronoun (*this, that*), a number, a singular word expressing quantity, or a possessive.

   A (Every, That, One, Her) nurse
   ▶ ~~Nurse~~ has a difficult job.
   ⌃

7. In general, though there are many exceptions, use no article with a singular proper noun (*Mount Everest*), and use *the* with a plural proper noun (*the Himalayas*). See **60f**.

## 60d *The* for a specific reference

When you write a common noun that both you and your readers know refers to one or more specific persons, places, things, or concepts, use the article *the*. The reference can be specific in two ways: outside the text or inside it.

### Specific reference outside the text

   ▶ **I study *the* earth, the sun, and the moon.** [the ones in our solar system]

   ▶ **She closed *the* door.** [of the room she was in]

   ▶ **Her husband took *the* dog out for a walk.** [the dog belonging to the couple]

### Specific reference inside the text

   ▶ ***The* kitten that her daughter brought home had a distinctive black patch above one eye.** [a specific kitten—one that was brought home]

▶ Her daughter found *a* kitten. When they were writing a lost-and-found ad that night, they realized that *the* kitten had a distinctive black patch above one eye. [The second mention is to a specific kitten identified earlier—the one her daughter found.]

▶ He bought *the most expensive* bicycle in the store. [A superlative makes a reference to one specific item.]

## 60e Which article? Four basic questions

Multilingual writers often have difficulty choosing among the articles *a, an,* and *the* and the *zero article* (no article at all). Languages vary greatly in their representation of the concepts conveyed by English articles (see the Language Guide to Transfer Errors in **59c**).

The Key Points box lists four questions to ask about a noun to decide whether to use an article and, if so, which article to use.

---

**KEY POINTS**

**Articles at a Glance: Four Basic Questions about a Noun**

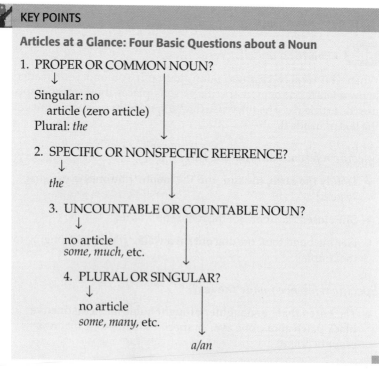

1. PROPER OR COMMON NOUN?
   ↓
   Singular: no
     article (zero article)
   Plural: *the*

2. SPECIFIC OR NONSPECIFIC REFERENCE?
   ↓
   *the*

3. UNCOUNTABLE OR COUNTABLE NOUN?
   ↓
   no article
   *some, much,* etc.

4. PLURAL OR SINGULAR?
   ↓
   no article
   *some, many,* etc.

   *a/an*

You can use the questions to decide which article, if any, to use with the noun *poem* as you consider the following sentence:

▶ **Milton wrote __?__ moving poem about the blindness that afflicted him before he wrote some of his greatest works.**

1. Is the noun a proper noun or a common noun?

   COMMON  **Go to question 2.**

2. Does the common noun refer to a specific person, place, thing, or idea known to both writer and reader as unique or is the reference nonspecific?

   NON-      [*Poem* is not identified to the reader in the same way that
   SPECIFIC  *blindness* is. We know the reference is to the blindness that afflicted Milton before he wrote some of his greatest works. However, there is more than one "moving poem" in literature.] **Go to question 3.**

3. Is the noun uncountable or countable?

   COUNTABLE  [We can say *one poem, two poems.*] **Go to question 4.**

4. Is the noun plural or singular?

   SINGULAR  [The first letter in the noun phrase *moving poem* is *m*, a consonant sound.] **Use *a* as the article.**

   ▶ **Milton wrote *a* moving poem about the blindness that afflicted him before he wrote some of his greatest works.**

## 60f  Proper nouns and articles

***Singular proper nouns: Use with no article***  Examples are *Stephen King, General Powell, Central America, Italy, Golden Gate Park, Hollywood Boulevard, Cornell University, Lake Temagami, Mount St. Helens, Thursday, July.* There are, however, many exceptions.

EXCEPTIONS: SINGULAR PROPER NOUNS WITH *THE*

Proper nouns with a common noun and *of* as part of the title: *the University of Texas, the Fourth of July, the Museum of Modern Art, the Statue of Liberty*

Highways: *the New Jersey Turnpike, the Long Island Expressway*

Buildings: *the Eiffel Tower, the Prudential Building*

Hotels and museums: *the Hilton Hotel, the Guggenheim Museum*

Countries named with a phrase: *the United Kingdom, the Dominican Republic*

Parts of the globe: *the North Pole, the West, the East*

Seas, oceans, gulfs, rivers, and deserts: *the Mediterranean Sea, the Atlantic Ocean, the Persian Gulf, the Yangtze River, the Mojave Desert*

Historical periods and events: *the Enlightenment, the October Revolution*

**Plural proper nouns: Use with the**  Examples are *the United States, the Great Lakes, the Himalayas, the Philippines, the Chinese* (people).

## 61  Verbs and Verbals

A clause needs a complete verb consisting of one of the five verb forms (**41a**) and any necessary auxiliaries. A verbal cannot serve as the verb of a clause. It is a form derived from a verb: an *-ing* form, a past participle (ending in *-ed* for a regular verb), or an infinitive (*to* + base form). Because readers get so much information from verbs and verbals, they have a relatively low level of tolerance for error, so make sure you edit with care.

### 61a  The *be* auxiliary

*Inclusion*  (See also **41c**.) The *be* auxiliary must be included in a verb phrase in English, though in languages such as Chinese, Russian, and Arabic it can be omitted.

> are
> ▶ They studying this evening.
> ^

> been
> ▶ They have studying since dinner.
> ^

*Sequence*  (See also **41c**.) What comes after a *be* auxiliary? You have two options:

- The *-ing* form follows a verb in the active voice: He *is sweeping* the floor.

- The past participle follows a verb in the passive voice: The floor *was swept* yesterday.

### 61b  Modal auxiliary verbs: form and meaning

The modal auxiliary verbs (*will, would, can, could, shall, should, may, might,* and *must*) do not change form, never add an *-s* ending, and are always followed by a base form without *to*: *could* go, *should* ask, *must* arrive, *might have* seen, *would be* sleeping. (See also **41c**.)

The following list summarizes the common meanings of modal auxiliary verbs.

MEANINGS OF MODAL VERBS

| MEANING | PRESENT AND FUTURE | PAST |
| --- | --- | --- |
| 1. Intention | *will, shall* | *would* |

▶ She *will* explain.      ▶ **She said that she *would* explain.**

*Shall* is used mostly in questions: *Shall I buy that big green ceramic horse?*

| | | |
| --- | --- | --- |
| 2. Ability | *can (am/is/are able to)* | *could (was/were able to)* |

▶ **He *can* cook well.** [He is able to cook well.]

▶ **He *could* not read until he was eight.** [He was not able to read until he was eight.]

Do not use both *can* and *able to* together:

am
▶ **I ~~can~~ not able to give you that information.**

| | | |
| --- | --- | --- |
| 3. Permission | *may, might, can, could* | *could, might* |

▶ ***May* I open the window?** [*Might* or *could* is more tentative.]

▶ **She said I *could* leave early.**

| | |
| --- | --- |
| 4. Polite question | *would, could* |

▶ ***Would* you please pass the carrots?**

▶ ***Could* you possibly help me?**

| | | |
| --- | --- | --- |
| 5. Speculation | *would (could, might)* | *would (could, might) + have + past participle* |

▶ **If I had time, I *would* bake a cake.**

▶ **If I had studied, I *would have* passed the test.**

(See also **41j**.)

| | | |
| --- | --- | --- |
| 6. Advisability | *should* | *should + have + past participle* |

▶ **You *should* go home and rest.**

▶ **You *should have* taken your medication.**
[Implied here is "But you did not."]

### MEANINGS OF MODAL VERBS

| MEANING | PRESENT AND FUTURE | PAST |
|---|---|---|
| 7. Necessity (stronger than *should*) | *must* (or *have to*) | *had to* + base form |

▶ He *must* apply for a new driver's license.

▶ She *had to* apply last month.

| | | |
|---|---|---|
| 8. Prohibition | *must* + *not* | |

▶ You *must not* leave until we tell you to.

| | | |
|---|---|---|
| 9. Expectation | *should* | *should* + *have* + past participle |

▶ You *should* receive the check soon.

▶ You *should have* received the check a week ago.

| | | |
|---|---|---|
| 10. Possibility | *may, might* | *might* + *have* + past participle |

▶ They *might* be at home now.

▶ She *might have* gone to the movies.

| | | |
|---|---|---|
| 11. Logical assumption | *must* | *must* + *have* + past participle |

▶ She's late; she *must* be stuck in traffic.

▶ She *must have* taken the wrong route.

| | | |
|---|---|---|
| 12. Repeated past action | | *would* (or *used to*) + base form |

▶ When I was a child, I *would* spend hours drawing.

## **61c** Verbs followed by an infinitive

Some verbs are followed by an infinitive (*to* + base form), others by an *-ing* form of the verb. Such combinations are called *verb chains*, and they are often highly idiomatic. Note the following features.

### *Verb + infinitive*

▶ His father *wanted to rule* the family.

These verbs are commonly followed by an infinitive (*to* + base form):

| | | | | |
|---|---|---|---|---|
| agree | choose | fail | offer | refuse |
| ask | claim | hope | plan | venture |
| beg | decide | manage | pretend | want |
| bother | expect | need | promise | wish |

Note any differences between English and your own language. For example, the Spanish word for *refuse* is followed by the equivalent of an *-ing* form.

▶ He refused ~~criticizing~~ the system.
*to criticize*

*Position of a negative*   In a verb + infinitive pattern, the position of the negative affects meaning. Note the difference in meaning that the position of a negative (*not, never*) can create.

▶ He did *not* decide to buy a new car. His wife did.

▶ He decided *not* to buy a new car. His wife was disappointed.

*Verb + noun or pronoun + infinitive*   Some verbs are followed by a noun or pronoun and then an infinitive. See also **44a** for pronouns before an infinitive.

▶ The librarian *advised them to use* a better database.

Verbs that follow this pattern are *advise, allow, ask, cause, command, convince, encourage, expect, force, help, need, order, persuade, remind, require, tell, urge, want, warn.*

Spanish and Russian use a *that* clause after verbs like *want*. In English, however, *want* is followed by an infinitive.

▶ Rose wanted ~~that~~ her son ~~would~~ become a doctor.
*to*

**Make, let,** *and* **have**   After these verbs, use a noun or pronoun and a base form of the verb (without *to*).

▶ He *made his son practice* for an hour.

▶ They *let us leave* early.

▶ She *had her daughter wash* the car.

Note the corresponding passive voice structure with *have:*

▶ We *have the car washed* once a month.

**61d**　Verbs followed by an *-ing* verb form used as a noun

▶ I can't help *laughing* at Dennis Miller.

The *-ing* form of a verb used as a noun is known as a *gerund*. The verbs that are systematically followed by an *-ing* form make up a relatively short and learnable list.

| | | | | |
|---|---|---|---|---|
| admit | consider | enjoy | miss | resist |
| appreciate | delay | finish | postpone | risk |
| avoid | deny | imagine | practice | suggest |
| be worth | discuss | keep | recall | tolerate |
| can't help | dislike | | | |

　　　　　　　　　inviting
▶ We considered ~~to invite~~ his parents.

　　　　　　　　　hearing
▶ Most people dislike ~~to hear~~ cell phones at concerts.

Note that a negation comes between the verb and the *-ing* form:

▶ During their vacation, they enjoy *not* getting up early every day.

**61e**　Verbs followed by an infinitive or an *-ing* verb form

Some verbs can be followed by either an infinitive or an *-ing* verb form (a gerund) with almost no discernible difference in meaning: *begin, continue, hate, like, love, start.*

▶ She loves *cooking.*　　　　▶ She loves *to cook.*

The infinitive and the *-ing* form of a few verbs, however (*forget, remember, try, stop*), signal different meanings:

▶ He remembered *to mail* the letter.　[an intention]

▶ He remembered *mailing* the letter.　[a past act]

**61f**　*-ing* and *-ed* verb forms used as adjectives

Both the present participle (*-ing* verb form) and the past participle (ending in *-ed* in regular verbs) can function as adjectives (see **41a** and **41g**). Each form has a different meaning: the *-ing* adjective indicates that the word modified produces an effect; the past participle adjective indicates that the word modified has an effect produced on it.

▶ The *boring* cook served baked beans yet again.

[The cook produces boredom. Everyone is tired of baked beans.]

▶ The *bored* cook yawned as she scrambled eggs.

[The cook felt the emotion of boredom as she did the cooking, but the eggs could still be appreciated.]

| PRODUCES AN EFFECT | HAS AN EFFECT PRODUCED ON IT |
|---|---|
| amazing | amazed |
| amusing | amused |
| annoying | annoyed |
| confusing | confused |
| depressing | depressed |
| disappointing | disappointed |
| embarrassing | embarrassed |
| exciting | excited |
| interesting | interested |
| satisfying | satisfied |
| shocking | shocked |
| worrying | worried |

*Note:* Do not drop the *-ed* ending from a past participle. Sometimes in speech it blends with a following *t* or *d* sound, but in writing the *-ed* ending must be included.

▶ I was surprise to see her wild outfit.

▶ The researchers were concern that the results were contaminated.

## 62 Sentence Structure

Languages structure the information in sentences in many ways. For more on sentence structure, see **37c** and **40**.

### 62a Inclusion of a subject

In some languages, a subject can be omitted. In English, you must include a subject in every clause, even just a filler subject such as *there* or *it*.

▶ The director's business partners lost money, and *there* were
immediate effects on the share prices.

▶ He went bankrupt because *it* was too easy to borrow money.

Do not use *it* to point to a long subject that follows.

▶ We can say that ~~it~~ |does not matter| the historical period of
the society|.

## 62b  Order of elements

*Expressions of time and place*    Put adverbs and adverb phrases of
time and place at the beginning or end of a clause, not between the
verb and its direct object.

▶ The quiz show host congratulated |many times| the winner|.

*Descriptive adjective phrases*    Put a descriptive adjective phrase
after, not before, the noun it modifies.

▶ I would go to |known only to me| places|.

*Order of subject, verb, object*    Languages vary in their basic word
order for the sentence elements of subject (S), verb (V), and direct object (DO). In English, the most commonly occurring sentence pattern
is S + V + DO ("Children like candy"). See also **37c**.

▶ ~~Good grades received every~~ *Every* student in the class *received good grades*.

## 62c  Direct and indirect objects

Some verbs—such as *give, send, show, tell, teach, find, sell, ask, offer, pay,
pass,* and *hand*—can be followed by both a direct object and an indirect
object. The indirect object is the person or thing to whom or to which,
or for whom or for which, something is done. It follows the verb and
precedes the direct object (**37c**).

                    ┌─ IO ─┐ ┌── DO ──┐
▶ He gave his mother some flowers.

        IO  ┌── DO ──┐
▶ He gave her some flowers.

An indirect object can be replaced with a prepositional phrase that *follows* the direct object:

prepositional phrase

▸ He gave some flowers to his mother.

Some verbs—such as *explain, describe, say, mention*, and *open*—are never followed by an indirect object. However, they can be followed by a direct object and a prepositional phrase with *to* or *for*:

to me

▸ She explained ~~me~~ the election process.

to us

▸ He described ~~us~~ the menu.

Note that *tell*, but not *say*, can take an indirect object.

told

▸ She ~~said~~ him the secret.

## **62d** Direct and indirect quotations and questions

In a direct quotation or direct question, the exact words used by the speaker are enclosed in quotation marks. In an indirect quotation or indirect question, the writer reports what the speaker said, and quotation marks are not used. Changes also occur in pronouns, time expressions, and verb tenses (**41i**).

direct quotation

▸ He said, "I have lost my notebook."

indirect quotation

▸ He said that he had lost his notebook.

direct question

▸ He asked, "Have you seen it?"

indirect question

▸ He asked if we had seen it.

***Direct and indirect quotations***   Usually you must make several changes when you rewrite a direct quotation as an indirect quotation. You will do this often when you write college papers and report the views of others. Avoid shifts from direct to indirect quotations (**40d**).

| TYPE OF QUOTATION | EXAMPLE |
|---|---|
| 1. *Direct quotation* with quotation marks and present tense | The young couple said, "The price *is* too high." |
| *Indirect quotation:* no quotation marks; tense change (**41i**) | The young couple said that the price *was* too high. |

| TYPE OF QUOTATION | EXAMPLE |
|---|---|
| 2. *Direct quotation* with first person pronoun and present tense | He insisted, "*I understand* the figures." |
| *Indirect quotation:* change to third person pronoun; tense change (**41i**) | He insisted that *he understood* the figures. |
| 3. *Direct quotation* of a command | "Cancel the payment," her husband said. |
| *Indirect quotation:* verb + *to* | Her husband *said* [told her] *to* cancel the payment. |
| 4. *Direct quotation* with expressions of time and place | The bankers said, "*We will* work on this deal *tomorrow*." |
| *Indirect quotation:* expressions of time and place not related to speaker's perspective; tense change (**41i**); change to third person pronoun | The bankers said *they would* work on *that* deal *the next day*. |
| 5. *Direct quotation* of spoken words and phrases | The clients said, "Well, no thanks; *we won't* wait." |
| *Indirect quotation:* spoken words and phrases omitted or rephrased; tense change (**41i**) | The clients thanked the bankers but said *they would not* wait. |

**Direct and indirect questions**   When a direct question is reported indirectly, it loses the word order of a question and also loses the question mark. Sometimes changes in tense are necessary (see **41i**).

|  | V     S |
|---|---|
| DIRECT QUESTION | The buyer asked, "*Are* the goods ready to be shipped?" |

|  | S     V |
|---|---|
| INDIRECT QUESTION | The buyer asked if the goods *were* ready to be shipped. |

|  | V   S |
|---|---|
| DIRECT QUESTION | The boss asked, "What *are* they doing?" |

|  | S     V |
|---|---|
| INDIRECT QUESTION | The boss asked what they *were* doing. |

| | |
|---|---|
| DIRECT QUESTION | V S "Why *did* they *send* a letter instead of a fax?" her secretary asked. |

| | |
|---|---|
| INDIRECT QUESTION | S V Her secretary asked why they [had] *sent* a letter instead of a fax. |

Use only a question word or *if* or *whether* to introduce an indirect question. Do not use *that* as well.

▶ Her secretary asked ~~that~~ why they sent a letter instead of a fax.

**62e** Dependent clauses

In some languages, a subordinating conjunction (such as *although* or *because*) can be used along with a coordinating conjunction (*but, so*) or a transitional expression (*however, therefore*) in the same sentence. In English, only one is used.

| | |
|---|---|
| FAULTY | *Although* he loved his father, *but* he did not have much opportunity to spend time with him. |
| POSSIBLE REVISIONS | *Although* he loved his father, he did not have much opportunity to spend time with him. |
| | He loved his father, *but* he did not have much opportunity to spend time with him. |
| FAULTY | *Because* she had been trained in the church, *therefore* she was sensitive to the idea of audience. |
| POSSIBLE REVISIONS | *Because* she had been trained in the church, she was sensitive to the idea of audience. |
| | She had been trained in the church, *so* she was sensitive to the idea of audience. |
| | She had been trained in the church; *therefore,* she was sensitive to the idea of audience. |

See **47e** for the punctuation of transitional expressions.

**62f** Unnecessary pronouns

Do not restate the simple subject of a sentence as a pronoun. See also **40i**.

▶ Visitors to the Statue of Liberty ~~they~~ have worn the steps down.

▶ **The advisor who told me about dyslexia ~~he~~ is a man I will never forget.**

In a relative clause introduced by *whom, which,* or *that,* do not include a pronoun that the relative pronoun has replaced. See also **46f.**

▶ **The house that I lived in ~~it~~ for ten years has been sold.**

## 63 Prepositions in Idiomatic Expressions

Prepositions appear in phrases with nouns and pronouns, and they also combine with adjectives and verbs in various ways. Learn the idioms one by one, as you come across them.

### 63a Idioms with three common prepositions

Learn the idiomatic uses of prepositions by writing them down in lists when you come across them in your reading. Here is a start:

IN

in July, in 1999, in the morning, in the drawer, in the closet, in Ohio, in Milwaukee, in the cookie jar, in the library stacks, singing in the rain, in the United States, in his pocket, in bed, in school, in class, in Spanish, in time (to participate in an activity), in love, the letter in the envelope

ON

on the menu, on the library shelf, on Saturday, on 9 September 1999, on Union Street, on the weekend, on the roof, a ring on her finger, an article on education, on the moon, on earth, on occasion, on time (punctual), on foot, on the couch, knock on the door, the address on the envelope

AT

at 8 o'clock, at home, at a party, at night, at work

### 63b Adjective + preposition

When you are writing, use a dictionary to check the specific prepositions used with an adjective.

▶ He is *afraid of* spiders.     ▶ She was *interested in* bees.

Some idiomatic adjective + preposition combinations are *afraid of, ashamed of, aware of, fond of, full of, jealous of, proud of, suspicious of, tired of, interested in, grateful to* (someone), *grateful for* (something), *responsible to* (someone), *responsible for* (something), *anxious about, content with,* and *satisfied with.*

## 63c  Verb + preposition

Some idiomatic verb + preposition combinations are *concentrate on, congratulate* (someone) *on* (success or good fortune), *depend on, insist on, rely on, consist of, take care of, apologize to* (someone) *for* (an offense or error), *blame* (someone) *for* (an offense or error), *thank* (someone) *for* (a gift or favor), *complain about, worry about, laugh at, smile at, explain* (facts) *to* (someone), *throw* (an object) *to* (someone waiting to catch it), *throw* (an object) *at* (someone not expecting it), *arrive in* (a country or city), and *arrive at* (a building or an event). Keep a list of others you notice.

## 63d  Phrasal verbs

Prepositions and a few adverbs (such as *away* and *forward*) can combine with verbs in such a way that they no longer function as prepositions or ordinary adverbs. They are then known as *particles.* Only a few languages other than English—Dutch, German, and Swedish, for example—have this verb-plus-particle (preposition or adverb) combination, which is called a *phrasal verb.* Examples of English phrasal verbs are *put off* and *put up with.*

The meaning of a phrasal verb is entirely different from the meaning of the verb alone. Note the idiomatic meanings of some common phrasal verbs.

| | |
|---|---|
| break down [stop functioning] | run across [meet unexpectedly] |
| get over [recover from] | run out [become used up] |
| look into [examine] | take after [resemble] |

Always check the meanings of such verbs in a specialized dictionary such as *The American Heritage English as a Second Language Dictionary.*

A particle can be followed by a preposition to make a three-word combination:

▶ She *gets along with* everybody.  [She is friendly toward everybody.]

Other three-word verb combinations are

| | |
|---|---|
| catch up with [draw level with] | look forward to [anticipate] |
| look down on [despise] | put up with [endure] |
| look up to [admire] | stand up for [defend] |

***Position of direct objects with two-word phrasal verbs*** Some two-word transitive phrasal verbs are separable. The direct object of these verbs can come between the verb and the accompanying particle.

▶ She *put off* her dinner party.   [She postponed her dinner party.]

▶ She *put* her dinner party *off*.

When the direct object is a pronoun, however, always place the pronoun between the verb and the particle.

▶ She *put* it *off*.

Some commonly used phrasal verbs that follow that principle are listed here. They can be separated by a noun as a direct object; they must be separated when the direct object is a pronoun.

| | | |
|---|---|---|
| call off [cancel] | give up [surrender] | make up [invent] |
| fill out [complete] | leave out [omit] | turn down [reject] |
| find out [discover] | look up [locate] | turn off [stop] |

Most dictionaries list phrasal verbs that are associated with a particular verb, along with their meanings and examples. Develop your own list of such verbs from your reading.

**63e** Preposition + -*ing* verb form used as a noun

The -*ing* verb form that functions as a noun (the *gerund*) frequently occurs after a preposition.

▶ They congratulated him *on winning* the prize.

▶ Sue expressed interest *in participating* in the fundraiser.

▶ He ran three miles *without stopping*.

▶ The cheese is the right consistency *for spreading*.

*Note:* Take care not to confuse *to* as a preposition with *to* used in an infinitive. When *to* is a preposition, it is followed by a noun, a pronoun, a noun phrase, or an -*ing* form, not by the base form of a verb.

> ⌐infinitive ⌐
> ► They want *to adopt* a child.

> preposition + *-ing* form (noun)
> ► They are looking forward *to adopting* a child.

Check which to use by testing a noun replacement:

> ► They are looking forward to parenthood.

Note also *be devoted to, be/get used to* (see **63f**).

---

**63f** The difference between *get used to* and *used to*

For multilingual writers of English, the distinction between *used to* + base form and *be/get used to* + *-ing* (gerund) is difficult.

> ► He *used to work* long hours.
>
> [He did in the past but doesn't anymore. The infinitive form follows *used* in this sense.]

> ► Air traffic controllers *are used to dealing* with emergencies.
>
> [They are accustomed to it. The *-ing* form follows *be/get used to*.]

---

**64 Frequently Asked ESL Editing Questions**

**64a** When do I use *no* and *not*?

*Not* is an adverb that negates a verb, an adjective, or another adverb. *No* is an adjective and therefore modifies a noun.

> ► She is *not* wealthy.   ► She is *not* really poor

> ► The author does *not* intend to deceive the reader.

> ► The author has *no* intention of deceiving the reader.

---

**64b** What is the difference between *too* and *very*?

Both *too* and *very* intensify an adjective or adverb, but they are not interchangeable. *Too* indicates excess. *Very* indicates degree, meaning "extremely."

> ► It was *very* hot.

▶ **It was *too* hot to sit outside.** [*Too* occurs frequently in the pattern *too* + adjective or adverb + *to* + base form of verb.]

▶ **The Volvo was *very* expensive, but he bought it anyway.**

▶ **The Volvo was *too* expensive, so he bought a Ford instead.**

### 64c   Does *few* mean the same as *a few*?

*A few* is the equivalent of *some*. *Few* is the equivalent of *hardly any*; it has more negative connotations than *a few*. Both expressions are used with countable plural nouns. Although *a* is not generally used with plural nouns, the expression *a few* is an exception.

some
▶ **She feels fortunate because she has *a few* helpful colleagues.**

hardly any
▶ **She feels depressed because she has *few* helpful colleagues.**

You might prefer to use only the more common *a few* and use *hardly any* in sentences where the context demands *few*. Similar expressions used with uncountable nouns are *little* and *a little*.

some
▶ **She has *a little* time to spend on work-related projects.**

hardly any
▶ **She has *little* time to spend on recreation.**

### 64d   How do I distinguish *most, most of*, and *the most*?

*Most* expresses a generalization, meaning "nearly all."

▶ ***Most* Americans like ice cream.**

When a word like *the, this, these, that,* or *those* or a possessive pronoun (such as *my, their*) precedes the noun to make it specific, *most of* is used. The meaning is "nearly all of."

▶ **I did *most of* this needlework.**

▶ ***Most of* his colleagues work long hours.**

*The most* is used to compare more than two people or items.

▶ **Bill is *the most* efficient of all the technicians.**

**64e** What structures are used with *easy, hard,* and *difficult*?

The adjectives *easy, hard,* and *difficult* cause problems for speakers of Japanese and Chinese. All of the following patterns are acceptable in English.

▶ It is *easy* for me to change a fuse.

▶ It is *easy* to change a fuse.

▶ To change a fuse is *easy* for me.

▶ To change a fuse is *easy*.

▶ Changing a fuse is *easy* for me.

▶ Changing a fuse is *easy*.

▶ I find it *easy* to change a fuse.

However, a sentence like the following needs to be edited in English into one of the patterns listed above or as follows:

think it is
▶ I am *easy* to change a fuse.

**64f** How do I use *it* and *there* to begin a sentence?

Use *there* to indicate that something exists (or existed) or happens (or happened). See also **30b**.

There
▶ It was a royal wedding in my country two years ago.

There
▶ It is a tree on the corner of my block.

Use *it* for weather, distance, time, and surroundings.

▶ It is a long way to Tipperary.  ▶ It is hot.

Use *it* also in expressions such as *it is important, it is necessary,* and *it is obvious,* emphasizing the details that come next. See also **30b**.

▶ It is essential for all of you to sign your application forms.

*It* or *there* cannot be omitted as a filler subject.

it
▶ As you can see, is dark out already.

**64g** Which possessive pronoun do I use: *his* or *her*?

In some languages, the form of the pronoun used to indicate possession changes according to the gender of the noun that follows it, not according to the pronoun's antecedent. In French, for instance, *son* or *sa* means "his" or "her," the form being determined by the noun the pronoun modifies.

▶ **Marie et sa mère**    [Marie and her mother]

▶ **Pierre et sa mère**    [Pierre and his mother]

▶ **Pierre et son père**    [Pierre and his father]

In English, however, the gender of a possessive *(his, her,* or *its)* is always determined by the antecedent.

▶ **I met Marie and her mother.**    ▶ **I met Pierre and his mother.**

# PART 10

## Glossaries and Index

# PART 10    Glossaries and Index

# 65 Glossary of Usage

Listed in this glossary are words that are often confused (*affect/effect*, *elicit/illicit*), misspelled (*alright*, *it's/its*), or misused (*hopefully*). Also listed are nonstandard words (*irregardless*, *theirself*) and colloquial expressions (*a lot*, *OK*) that should be avoided in formal writing.

**a, an**   Use *an* before words that begin with a vowel sound (the vowels are *a*, *e*, *i*, *o*, and *u*): *an apple, an hour* (silent *h*). Use *a* before words that begin with a consonant sound: *a planet, a yam, a ukelele, a house* (pronounced *h*).

**accept, except, expect**   *Accept* is a verb: *She accepted the salary offer. Except* is usually a preposition: *Everyone has gone home except my boss. Expect* is a verb: *They expect to visit New Mexico on vacation.*

**adapt, adopt**   *Adapt* means "to adjust" and is used with the preposition *to: It takes people some time to adapt to the work routine after college. Adopt* means "to take into a family" or "to take up and follow": *The couple adopted a three-year-old child. The company adopted a more aggressive policy.*

**advice, advise**   *Advice* is a noun: *Take my advice and don't start smoking. Advise* is a verb: *He advised his brother to stop smoking.*

**affect, effect**   In their most common uses, *affect* is a verb, and *effect* is a noun. To *affect* is to have an *effect* on something: *Pesticides can affect health. Pesticides have a bad effect on health. Effect*, however, can be used as a verb meaning "to bring about": *The administration hopes to effect new health care legislation. Affect* can also be used as a noun in psychology, meaning "a feeling or emotion."

**all ready, already**   *All ready* means "totally prepared": *The students were all ready for their final examination. Already* is an adverb meaning "by this time": *He has already written the report.*

**all right, alright**   *All right* is standard. *Alright* is nonstandard.

**all together, altogether**   *All together* is used to describe acting simultaneously: *As soon as the boss had presented the plan, the managers spoke up all together. Altogether* is an adverb meaning "totally," often used before an adjective: *His presentation was altogether impressive.*

**allude, elude**   *Allude* means "to refer to": *She alluded to his height. Elude* means "to avoid": *He eluded her criticism by leaving the room.*

**allusion, illusion**   The noun *allusion* means "reference to": *Her allusion to his height made him uncomfortable.* The noun *illusion* means "false idea": *He had no illusions about being Mr. Universe.*

**almost, most**   Do not use *most* to mean *almost*: *Almost* [not *Most*] *all my friends are computer literate.*

**alot, a lot of, lots of**    *Alot* is nonstandard. *A lot of* and *lots of* are regarded by some as informal for *many* or *a great deal of: They have performed many research studies.*

**ambiguous, ambivalent**    *Ambiguous* is used to describe a phrase or act with more than one meaning: *The ending of the movie is ambiguous; we don't know if the butler really committed the murder. Ambivalent* describes lack of certainty and the coexistence of opposing attitudes and feelings: *The committee is ambivalent about the proposal for restructuring the company.*

**among, between**    Use *between* for two items, *among* for three or more: *I couldn't decide between red or blue. I couldn't decide among red, blue, or green.*

**amount, number**    *Amount* is used with uncountable expressions: *a large amount of money, work, or effort. Number* is used with countable plural expressions: *a large number of people, a number of attempts.* See **60b** ESL.

**an**    See *a*.

**and**    Avoid using *and* to mean "to": <u>not</u> *Try and find me* <u>but</u> *Try to find me.*

**anyone, any one**    *Anyone* is a singular indefinite pronoun meaning "anybody": *Can anyone help me? Any one* refers to one from a group and is usually followed by *of* + plural noun: *Any one* [as opposed to any two] *of the suggestions will be considered acceptable.*

**anyplace**    The standard *anywhere* is preferable.

**anyway, anywhere, nowhere; anyways, anywheres, nowheres**    *Anyway, anywhere,* and *nowhere* are standard forms. The others, ending in *-s,* are not.

**apart, a part**    *Apart* is an adverb: *The old book fell apart.* "A part" is a noun phrase: *I'd like to be a part of that project.*

**as, as if, like**    See *like*.

**as regards, in regard to**    See *in regard to*.

**at**    Avoid ending a question with *at*: <u>not</u> *Where's the library at?* <u>but</u> *Where's the library?*

**awful**    Avoid using *awful* to mean "bad" or "extremely": <u>not</u> *He's awful late.* <u>but</u> *He's extremely late.*

**a while, awhile**    "A while" is a noun phrase: *a while ago; for a while. Awhile* is an adverb meaning "for some time": *They lived awhile in the wilderness.*

**bad, badly**    *Bad* is an adjective, *badly* an adverb. Use *bad* after linking verbs (such as *am, is, become, seem*): *They felt bad after losing the match.* Use *badly* to modify a verb: *They played badly.*

**because, because of**    *Because* is a subordinating conjunction used to introduce a dependent clause: *Because it was raining, we left early. Because of* is a two-word preposition: *We left early because of the rain.*

**being as, being that**   Avoid. Use *because* instead: *Because* [not *Being as*] *I was tired, I didn't go to class.*

**belief, believe**   *Belief* is a noun: *She has radical beliefs. Believe* is a verb: *He believes in an afterlife.*

**beside, besides**   *Beside* is a preposition meaning "next to": *Sit beside me. Besides* is a preposition meaning "except for": *He has no assistants besides us. Besides* is also an adverb meaning "in addition": *I hate horror movies. Besides, there's a long line.*

**better**   See *had better.*

**between**   See *among.*

**breath, breathe**   The first word is a noun, the second a verb: *Take three deep breaths. Breathe in deeply.*

**can't hardly**   This expression is nonstandard. See *hardly.*

**cite, site, sight**   *Cite* means "to quote or mention"; *site* is a noun meaning "location"; *sight* is a noun meaning "view": *She cited the page number in her paper. They visited the original site of the abbey. The sight of the skyline from the plane produced applause from the passengers.*

**complement, compliment**   As verbs, *complement* means "to complete or add to something," and *compliment* means "to make a flattering comment about someone or something": *The wine complemented the meal. The guests complimented the hostess on the fine dinner.* As nouns, the words have meanings associated with the verbs: *The wine was a fine complement to the meal. The guests paid the hostess a compliment.*

**compose, comprise**   *Compose* means "to make up"; *comprise* means "to include." *The conference center is composed of twenty-five rooms. The conference center comprises twenty-five rooms.*

**conscience, conscious**   *Conscience* is a noun meaning "awareness of right and wrong." *Conscious* is an adjective meaning "awake" or "aware." *Her conscience troubled her after the accident. The victim was still not conscious.*

**continual, continuous**   *Continual* implies repetition; *continuous* implies lack of a pause. *The continual interruptions made the lecturer angry. Continuous rain for two hours stopped play.*

**could care less**   This expression is often used but is regarded by some as nonstandard. In formal English, use it only with a negative: *They could not care less about their work.*

**custom, customs, costume**   All three words are nouns. *Custom* means "habitual practice or tradition": *a family custom. Customs* refers to taxes on imports or to the procedures for inspecting items entering a country: *go through customs at the airport.* A *costume* is "a style of dress": *a Halloween costume.*

**dairy, diary** The first word is associated with cows and milk, the second with daily journal writing.

**desert, dessert** *Desert* can be pronounced two ways and can be a noun with the stress on the first syllable *(the Mojave Desert)* or a verb with the stress on the second syllable: *When did he desert his family?* The noun *desert* means "a dry, often sandy, environment." The verb *desert* means "to abandon." *Dessert* (with stress on the second syllable) is the sweet course at the end of a meal.

**different from, different than** Standard usage is *different from: She looks different from her sister.* However, *different than* appears frequently in speech and informal writing, particularly when *different from* would require more words: *My writing is different than* [in place of *different from what*] *it was last semester.*

**discreet, discrete** *Discreet* means "tactful": *Be discreet when you talk about your boss. Discrete* means "separate": *They are researching five discrete topics.*

**disinterested, uninterested** *Disinterested* means "impartial or unbiased": *The mediator was hired to make a disinterested settlement. Uninterested* means "lacking in interest": *He seemed uninterested in his job.*

**due to the fact that, owing to the fact that** Wordy. Use *because* instead: *They stopped the game because* [not *due to the fact that*] *it was raining.*

**each, every** These are singular pronouns; use them with a singular verb. See also **43h** and **44d.**

**each other, one another** Use *each other* with two; use *one another* with more than two: *The twins love each other. The triplets all love one another.*

**effect** See *affect.*

**e.g.** Use *for example* or *for instance* in place of this Latin abbreviation.

**elicit, illicit** *Elicit* means "to get or draw out": *The police tried in vain to elicit information from the suspect's accomplice. Illicit* is an adjective meaning "illegal": *Their illicit deals landed them in prison.*

**elude** See *allude.*

**emigrate, immigrate** *Emigrate from* means "to leave a country"; *immigrate to* means "to move to another country": *They emigrated from Ukraine and immigrated to the United States.* The noun forms *emigrant* and *immigrant* are derived from the verbs.

**eminent, imminent** *Eminent* means "well known and noteworthy": *an eminent lawyer. Imminent* means "about to happen": *an imminent disaster.*

**etc.** This abbreviation for the Latin *et cetera* means "and so on." Do not let a list trail off with *etc.* Rather than *They took a tent, a sleeping bag, etc.,* write *They took a tent, a sleeping bag, cooking utensils, and a stove.*

**every, each**  See *each*.

**everyday, every day**  *Everyday* (one word) is an adjective meaning "usual": *Their everyday routine is to break for lunch at 12:30.* *Every day* (two words) is an adverbial expression of frequency: *I get up early every day.*

**except, expect**  See *accept*.

**explicit, implicit**  *Explicit* means "direct": *She gave explicit instructions.* *Implicit* means "implied": *A tax increase is implicit in the proposal.*

**farther, further**  Both words can refer to distance: *She lives farther (further) from the campus than I do.* *Further* also means "additional" or "additionally": *The management offered further incentives. Further, the union proposed new work rules.*

**female, male**  Use these words as adjectives, not as nouns in place of *man* and *woman*: *There are only three women* [not *females*] *in my class. We are discussing female conversational traits.*

**few, a few**  For the distinction, see **64c** ESL.

**fewer, less**  Formal usage demands *fewer* with plural countable nouns *(fewer holidays), less* with uncountable nouns *(less sunshine).* However, in informal usage, *less* with plural nouns commonly occurs, especially with *than: less than six items, less than ten miles, fifty words or less.* In formal usage, *fewer* is preferred.

**first, firstly**  Avoid *firstly, secondly,* and so on when listing reasons or examples. Instead, use *first, second.*

**flaunt, flout**  *Flaunt* means "to show [something] off," or "to display in a proud or boastful manner." *Flout* means "to defy or to show scorn for." *When she flaunted her jewels, she flouted good taste.*

**get married to, marry**  These expressions can be used interchangeably: *He will get married to his fiancée next week. She will marry her childhood friend next month.* The noun form is *marriage: Their marriage has lasted thirty years.*

**had better**  Include *had* in Standard English, although it is often omitted in advertising and in speech: *You had better* [not *You better*] *try harder.*

**hardly**  This is a negative word. Do not use it with another negative: <u>not</u> *He couldn't hardly walk.* <u>but</u> *He could hardly walk.*

**height**  Note the spelling and pronunciation: not *heighth.*

**heroin, heroine**  Do not confuse these words. *Heroin* is a drug; *heroine* is a brave woman. *Hero* may be used for an admirable person of either sex.

**hisself**  Nonstandard; instead use *himself.*

**hopefully**  This word is an adverb meaning "in a hopeful manner" or "with a hopeful attitude": *Hopefully, she e-mailed her résumé.* Avoid using *hopefully* in place of *I hope that:* <u>not</u> *Hopefully, she will get the job.* <u>but</u> *I hope that she will get the job.*

**illicit, elicit** See *elicit.*

**illusion, allusion** See *allusion.*

**immigrate, emigrate** See *emigrate.*

**imminent, eminent** See *eminent.*

**implicit, explicit** See *explicit.*

**imply, infer** *Imply* means "to suggest in an indirect way": *He implied that further layoffs were unlikely. Infer* means "to guess" or "to draw a conclusion": *I inferred that the company was doing well.*

**incredible, incredulous** *Incredible* means "difficult to believe": *The violence of the storm was incredible. Incredulous* means "skeptical, unable to believe": *They were incredulous when he told them about his daring exploits in the whitewater rapids.*

**in regard to, as regards** Use one or the other. Do not use the nonstandard *in regards to.*

**irregardless** Nonstandard; instead use *regardless: He selected a major regardless of the preparation it would give him for a career.*

**it's, its** The apostrophe in *it's* signals not a possessive but a contraction of *it is* or *it has. Its* is the possessive form of the pronoun *it: The city government agency has produced its final report. It's available upon request.* See also **48f.**

**kind, sort, type** In the singular, use each of these with *this* and a singular noun: *this type of book.* Use in the plural with *these* and a plural noun: *these kinds of books.*

**kind of, sort of** Do not use these to mean "somewhat" or "a little." *The pace of the baseball game was somewhat* [not *kind of* ] *slow.*

**knew, new** *Knew* is the past tense of the verb *know. New* is an adjective meaning "not old."

**lend, loan** *Lend* is a verb, and *loan* is ordinarily used as a noun: *Our cousins offered to lend us some money, but we refused the loan.*

**less, fewer** See *fewer.*

**lie, lay** Be sure not to confuse these verbs. *Lie* does not take a direct object; *lay* does. See **41b.**

**like, as, as if** In formal usage, *as* and *as if* are subordinating conjunctions and introduce dependent clauses: *She walks as her father does. She looks as if she could eat a big meal. Like* is a preposition and is followed by a noun or pronoun, not by a clause: *She looks like her father.* In speech, however, and increasingly in writing, *like* is often used where formal usage dictates *as* or *as if: She walks like her father does. He looks like he needs a new suit.*

**loan** See *lend, loan.*

**loose, lose** *Loose* is an adjective meaning "not tight": *This jacket is comfortable because it is so loose. Lose* is a verb (the past tense form and past participle are *lost*): *Many people lose their jobs in a recession.*

**lots of, alot, a lot of** See *alot.*

**marital, martial** *Marital* is associated with marriage, *martial* with war.

**may be, maybe** *May be* consists of a modal verb followed by the base form of the verb *be; maybe* is an adverb meaning "perhaps." If you can replace the expression with *perhaps,* make it one word: *They may be there already, or maybe they got caught in traffic.*

**most, almost** See *almost.*

**myself** Use only as a reflexive pronoun *(I told them myself)* or as an intensive pronoun *(I myself told them).* Do not use *myself* as a subject pronoun: not *My sister and myself won.* but *My sister and I won.*

**nowadays** All one word. Be sure to include the final *-s.*

**nowhere, nowheres** See *anyway.*

**number, amount** See *amount.*

**of a** Do not use *of a* after an adjective: not *She's not that good of a player.* but *She's not that good a player.*

**off, off of** Use only *off,* not *off of: She drove the car off* [not *off of*] *the road.*

**oftentimes** Do not use. Prefer *often.*

**OK, O.K., okay** Reserve these forms for informal speech and writing. Choose another word in a formal context: not *Her performance was OK.* but *Her performance was satisfactory.*

**one another** See *each other.*

**owing to the fact that** See *due to the fact that.*

**passed, past** *Passed* is a past tense verb form: *They passed the deli on the way to work. He passed his exam. Past* can be a noun *(in the past),* an adjective *(in past times),* or a preposition *(She walked past the bakery).*

**plus** Do not use *plus* as a coordinating conjunction or a transitional expression. Use *and* or *moreover* instead: *He was promoted, and* [not *plus*] *he received a bonus.* Use *plus* as a preposition meaning "in addition to": *His salary plus his dividends placed him in a high tax bracket.*

**precede, proceed** *Precede* means "to go or occur before": *The Roaring Twenties preceded the Great Depression. Proceed* means "to go ahead": *After you pay the fee, proceed to the examination room.*

**pretty** Avoid using *pretty* as an intensifying adverb. Instead use *really, very, rather,* or *quite: The stew tastes very* [not *pretty*] *good.* Often, however, the best solution is to avoid using any adverb: *The stew tastes good.*

**principal, principle** *Principal* is a noun *(the principal of a school)* or an adjective meaning "main" or "most important": *His principal motive was monetary gain. Principle* is a noun meaning "standard or rule": *He always acts on his principles.*

**quite, quiet** Do not confuse the adverb *quite,* meaning "very," with the adjective *quiet* ("still" or "silent"): *We were all quite relieved when the audience became quiet.*

**quote, quotation** *Quote* is a verb. Do not use it as a noun; use *quotation: The quotation* [not *quote*] *from Walker tells the reader a great deal.*

**real, really** *Real* is an adjective; *really* is an adverb. Do not use *real* as an intensifying adverb: *She acted really* [not *real*] *well.*

**reason is because** Avoid *the reason is because.* Instead, use *the reason is that* or rewrite the sentence. See **40f.**

**regardless** See *irregardless.*

**respectable, respectful, respective** *Respectable* means "presentable, worthy of respect": *Wear some respectable shoes to your interview. Respectful* means "polite or deferential": *Parents want their children to be respectful to adults. Respective* means "particular" or "individual": *The friends of the bride and the groom sat in their respective seats in the church.*

**rise, raise** *Rise* is an intransitive verb: *She rises early every day. Raise* is a transitive verb: *We raised alfalfa last summer.* See **41b**.

**sale, sell** *Sale* is a noun: *The sale of the house has been postponed. Sell* is a verb: *They are still trying to sell their house.*

**should (could, might) of** Nonstandard; instead use *should have: You should have paid.* See **41c,** p. 314.

**since** Use this subordinating conjunction only when time or reason is clear: *Since you insist on helping, I'll let you paint this bookcase.* Unclear: *Since he got a new job, he has been happy.*

**site, sight, cite** See *cite.*

**sometimes, sometime, some time** The adverb *sometimes* means "occasionally": *He sometimes prefers to eat lunch at his desk.* The adverb *sometime* means "at an indefinite time": *I read that book sometime last year.* The noun phrase *some time* consists of the noun *time* modified by the quantity word *some: After working for Honda, I spent some time in Brazil.*

**sort, type, kind** See *kind.*

**sort of, kind of** See *kind of.*

**stationary, stationery** *Stationary* is an adjective meaning "not moving" (*a stationary vehicle*); *stationery* is a noun referring to the paper on which you write letters.

**supposedly** Use this, not *supposably: She is supposedly a great athlete.*

**than, then** *Then* is a time word; *than* must be preceded by a comparative form: *bigger than, more interesting than.*

**their, there, they're** *Their* is a pronoun indicating possession; *there* indicates place or is used as a filler in the subject position in a sentence; *they're* is the contracted form of *they are: They're over there, guarding their luggage.*

**theirself, theirselves, themself** Nonstandard; instead use *themselves.*

**to, too, two** Do not confuse these words. *To* is a sign of the infinitive and a common preposition; *too* is an adverb meaning *also; two* is the number: *She is too smart to agree to report to two bosses.*

**undoubtedly** This is the correct word, not *undoubtably.*

**uninterested, disinterested** See *disinterested.*

**used to, get (become) used to** These expressions share the common form *used to.* But the first, expressing a past habit that no longer exists, is followed by the base form of a verb: *He used to wear his hair long.* (Note that after *not,* the form is *use to: He did not use to have a beard.*) In the expression *get (become) used to, used to* means "accustomed to" and is followed by a noun or an *-ing* form: *She couldn't get used to driving on the left when she was in England.* See also **63f ESL.**

**way, ways** Use *way* to mean "distance": *He has a way to go. Ways* in this context is nonstandard.

**wear, were, we're** *Wear* is a verb; *were* is a past tense form of *be; we're* is a contraction for *we are.*

**weather, whether** *Weather* is a noun; *whether* is a conjunction: *The weather will determine whether we go on the picnic.*

**who, whom, which, that** See **46a** and **46g.**

**whose, who's** *Whose* is a possessive pronoun: *Whose goal was that? Who's* is a contraction of *who is* or *who has: Who's the player whose pass was caught? Who's got the ball?*

**your, you're** *Your* is a pronoun used to show possession. *You're* is a contraction for *you are: You're wearing your new shoes today, aren't you?*

**66** Glossary of Grammatical Terms

**absolute phrase** A phrase consisting of a noun followed by a participle (*-ing* or past participle) and modifying an entire sentence: *Flags flapping in the wind,* the stadium looked bleak. **37d.**

**acronym** A pronounceable word formed from the initials of an abbreviation: *NATO, MADD, NOW.* **51a.**

**active voice** Attribute of a verb when its grammatical subject performs the action: The dog *ate* the cake. **42.** See also *passive voice.*

**adjective** The part of speech that modifies a noun or pronoun: A *happy* child. She is *happy.* **37b, 45.** See also *comparative; coordinate adjective; superlative.*

**adjective clause** A dependent clause beginning with a relative pronoun (*who, whom, whose, which,* or *that*) and modifying a noun or pronoun: The writer *who won the prize* was elated. Also called a *relative clause.* **46.**

**adverb** The part of speech that modifies a verb, an adjective, or another adverb. Many adverbs end in *-ly:* She ran *quickly.* He is *really* successful. The children were *well* liked. **37b, 45.** See also *comparative; conjunctive adverb; frequency adverb; superlative.*

**adverb clause** A dependent clause that modifies a verb, an adjective, or an adverb and begins with a subordinating conjunction: He left early *because he was tired.* **37e.**

**agent** The person or thing doing the action described by a verb in the active voice: *His sister* won the marathon. **42a.**

**agreement** The grammatical match in person, number, and gender between a verb and its subject or between a pronoun and its antecedent (the word the pronoun refers to): The *benefits continue; they are* pleasing. The *benefit continues; it is* pleasing. **43, 44d.**

**antecedent** The noun that a pronoun refers to: My *son* who lives nearby found a *kitten. It* was black and white. **44c, 44d, 46a.**

**appositive phrase** A phrase occurring next to a noun and used to describe it: His father, *a factory worker,* is running for office. **37d, 44a, 47d.**

**article** *A, an* (indefinite articles), or *the* (definite article). Also called a *determiner.* **60c ESL, 60d ESL, 60e ESL.**

**aspect** Nature of the relationship between the action of a verb and time. Aspects are perfect, progressive, and perfect progressive. **41d.**

**auxiliary verb** A verb that joins with another verb to form a complete verb. Auxiliary verbs are forms of *do, be,* and *have,* as well as the modal auxiliary verbs. **41c.** See also *modal auxiliary verb.*

**base form** The dictionary form of a verb, used in an infinitive after *to: see, eat, go, be.* **41a.**

**clause** A group of words that includes a subject and a verb. ; **37c, 37e.** See also *dependent clause; independent clause.*

**cliché** An overused, predictable expression: *as cool as a cucumber.* **33g.**

**collective noun** A noun naming a collection of people or things that are regarded as a unit: *team, jury, family.* For agreement with collective nouns, see **43f, 44d.**

**comma splice** The error that results when two independent clauses are incorrectly joined with only a comma. **39.**

**common noun** A noun that does not name a unique person, place, or thing. **60** ESL. See also *proper noun.*

**comparative** The form of an adjective or adverb used to compare two people or things: *bigger, more interesting.* **45h.** See also *superlative.*

**complement** A *subject complement* is a word or group of words used after a linking verb to refer to and describe the subject: Harry looks *happy.* An *object complement* is a word or group of words used after a direct object to complete its meaning: They call him a *liar.* **37c, 43c.**

**complete verb** A verb that shows tense. Some verb forms, such as *-ing* (present) participles and past participles, require auxiliary verbs to make them complete verbs. *Going* and *seen* are not complete verbs; *are going* and *has been seen* are complete. **38c, 41c.**

**complex sentence** A sentence that has one independent clause and one or more dependent clauses: *He wept when he won the marathon.* **34c.**

**compound adjective** An adjective formed of two or more words often connected with hyphens: a *well-constructed* house. **45d, 56b.**

**compound-complex sentence** A sentence that has at least two independent clauses and one or more dependent clauses: *She works in Los Angeles, but her husband works in San Diego, where they both live.* **34c.**

**compound noun** A noun formed of two or more words: *toothbrush, merry-go-round.* **56b.**

**compound predicate** A predicate consisting of two or more verbs and their objects, complements, and modifiers: He *whistles and sings in the morning.* **38e, 40h.**

**compound sentence** A sentence that has two or more independent clauses: *She works in Los Angeles, but her husband works in San Diego.* **34c.**

**compound subject** A subject consisting of two or more nouns or pronouns and their modifiers: *My uncle and my aunt* are leaving soon. **43g, 44a.**

**conditional clause** A clause introduced by *if* or *unless,* expressing conditions of fact, prediction, or speculation: *If we earned more,* we would spend more. **41j.**

**conjunction** The part of speech used to link words, phrases, or clauses. **37b, 37e, 43g.** See also *coordinating conjunction; correlative conjunctions; subordinating conjunction.*

**conjunctive adverb** A transitional expression used to link two independent clauses. Some common conjunctive adverbs are *moreover, however,* and *furthermore.* **2d, 37e.**

**connotation** The meanings and associations suggested by a word, as distinct from the word's denotation, or dictionary meaning. **33c.**

**contraction** The shortened form that results when an apostrophe replaces one or more letters: *can't* (for *cannot*), *he's* (for *he is* or *he has*), *they're* (for *they are*). **48d.**

**coordinate adjective** One of two or more evaluative adjectives modifying the same noun or pronoun. When coordinate adjectives appear in a series, their order can be reversed, and they can be separated by *and*. Commas are used between coordinate adjectives: the *comfortable, expensive car.* **45f, 47g.**

**coordinating conjunction** The seven coordinating conjunctions are *and, but, or, nor, so, for,* and *yet.* They connect sentence elements that are parallel in structure: He couldn't call, *but* he wrote a letter. **31c, 47b.**

**coordination** The connection of two or more ideas to give each one equal emphasis: *Sue worked after school,* so *she didn't have time to jog.* **31c.**

**correlative conjunctions** A pair of conjunctions joining equivalent elements. The most common correlative conjunctions are *either… or, neither… nor, both…and,* and *not only… but also: Neither* my sister *nor* I could find the concert hall. **40j.**

**countable noun** A common noun that has a plural form and can be used after a plural quantity word (such as *many* or *three*): one *book,* three *stores,* many *children.* **60a** ESL, **60e** ESL.

**dangling modifier** A modifier that fails to modify the noun or pronoun it is intended to modify: <u>not</u> *Turning the corner,* the lights went out. <u>but</u> *Turning the corner, we* saw the lights go out. **40c.**

**demonstrative pronoun** The four demonstrative pronouns are *this, that, these,* and *those: That* is my glass. **43i.**

**denotation** A word's dictionary meaning. See also *connotation.* **33b, 33c.**

**dependent clause** A clause that cannot stand alone as a complete sentence and needs to be attached to an independent clause. A dependent clause begins with a subordinating word such as *because, if, when, although, who, which,* or *that: When it rains, we* can't take the children outside. **37e.**

**diction** Choice of appropriate words and tone. **33.**

**direct object**   The person or thing that receives the action of a verb: They ate *cake* and *ice cream.* **37c, 62c** ESL.

**direct quotation**   A person's words reproduced exactly and placed in quotation marks: *"I won't be home until noon,"* she said. **9d, 10c, 40d, 62d** ESL.

**double negative**   The use of two negative words in the same sentence: He does *not* know *nothing.* This usage is nonstandard and needs to be avoided: *He does not know anything. He knows nothing.* **45g.**

**ellipsis**   Omission of words from a quotation, indicated by three dots (in MLA style enclosed in brackets): "I pledge allegiance to the flag [. . .] and to the republic for which it stands [. . .]." **51g.**

**etymology**   The origin of a word. **33b.**

**euphemism**   A word or phrase used to disguise literal meaning: She is *in the family way* [meaning "pregnant"]. **33g.**

**faulty predication**   The error that results when subject and verb do not go together logically: <u>not</u> The *decrease* in stolen cars *has diminished* in the past year. <u>but</u> The *number* of stolen cars *has decreased* in the past year. **40e.**

**figurative language**   The use of unusual comparisons or other devices to draw attention to a specific meaning. See *metaphor; simile.* **5b, 33e.**

**filler subject**   *It* or *there* used in the subject position of a clause, followed by a form of *be*: *There are* two elm trees on the corner. **30b, 43d, 64f** ESL.

**first person**   The person speaking or writing: *I* or *we.* **44a.**

**fragment**   A group of words that is punctuated as if it were a sentence but is grammatically incomplete because it lacks a subject or a predicate or begins with a subordinating word: *Because it was a sunny day.* **38.**

**frequency adverb**   An adverb that expresses time (such as *often, always,* or *sometimes*). It can be the first word in a sentence or be used between the subject and the main verb, after an auxiliary verb, or as the last word in a sentence. **45e.**

**fused sentence**   See *run-on sentence.*

**gender**   Classification of a noun or pronoun as masculine *(Uncle John, he),* feminine *(Ms. Torez, she),* or neuter *(book, it).* **44e, 64g** ESL.

**generic noun**   A noun referring to a general class or type of person or object: A *student* has to write many papers. **44d.**

**gerund**   The *-ing* verb form used as a noun: *Walking* is good for the health. **43e, 61** ESL, **63e** ESL. See also *verbal.*

**helping verb**   See *auxiliary verb.*

**imperative mood**   Verb mood used to give a command: *Follow* me. **34b.**

**indefinite pronoun**   A pronoun that refers to a nonspecific person or thing: *anybody, something.* **43h, 44d.**

**independent clause**   A clause that has a subject and predicate and is not introduced by a subordinating word. An independent clause can function as a complete sentence. *Birds sing. The old man was singing a song.* Hailing a cab, *the woman used a silver whistle.* **31c, 37e.**

**indicative mood**   Verb mood used to ask questions or make statements. It is the most common mood. **34b.**

**indirect object**   The person or thing to whom or to which, or for whom or for which, an action is performed. It comes between the verb and the direct object: He gave his *sister* some flowers. **37c, 62c** ESL.

**indirect question**   A question reported by a speaker or writer, not enclosed in quotation marks: They asked *if we would help them.* **62d** ESL.

**indirect quotation**   A description or paraphrase of the words of another speaker or writer, integrated into a writer's own sentence and not enclosed in quotation marks: He said *that they were making money.* **10c, 40d, 62d** ESL.

**infinitive**   The base form, or dictionary form, of a verb, preceded by *to: to see, to smile.* **41a, 61c** ESL, **61e** ESL.

**infinitive phrase**   An infinitive with its objects, complements, or modifiers: *To wait for hours* is unpleasant. He tries hard *to be punctual.* **37d.**

**intensive pronoun**   A pronoun ending in *-self* or *-selves* and used to emphasize its antecedent: They *themselves* will not attend. **44h.**

**interjection**   The part of speech that expresses emotion and is able to stand alone: *Aha! Wow!* Interjections are seldom appropriate in academic writing. **37b.**

**interrogative pronoun**   A pronoun that introduces a direct or indirect question: *Who* is that? I don't know *what* you want. **43k, 44i.**

**intransitive verb**   A verb that does not take a direct object: Exciting events *have occurred.* He *fell.* **37c, 42a.** See also *transitive verb.*

**inverted word order**   The presence of the verb before the subject in a sentence; used in questions or for emphasis: *Do you expect* an award? Not only *does she do* gymnastics, but she also wins awards. **30b, 37c, 43d.**

**irregular verb**   A verb that does not form its past tense and past participle with *-ed: sing, sang, sung; grow, grew, grown.* **41a.**

**linking verb**   A verb connecting a subject to its complement. Typical linking verbs are *be, become, seem,* and *appear:* He *seems* angry. A linking verb is intransitive; it does not take a direct object. **37c, 41c, 44a, 45c.**

**mental activity verb**   A verb not used in a tense showing progressive aspect: *prefer, want, understand:* <u>not</u> He *is wanting to leave.* <u>but</u> He *wants* to leave. **41d.**

**metaphor** A figure of speech implying a comparison but not stating it directly: a *gale* of laughter. **5b, 33e.**

**misplaced modifier** An adverb (particularly *only* and *even*) or a descriptive phrase or clause positioned in such a way that it modifies the wrong word or words: She showed the ring to her sister *that her aunt gave her.* **40b.**

**mixed structure** A sentence with two or more types of structures that clash grammatically: *By doing* her homework at the last minute *caused* Meg to make many mistakes. **40a, 40e, 40f.**

**modal auxiliary verb** The nine modal auxiliaries are *will, would, can, could, shall, should, may, might,* and *must.* They are followed by the base form of a verb: *will go, would believe.* Modal auxiliaries do not change form. **41c, 61b** ESL.

**modifier** A word or words that describe another noun, adverb, verb, phrase, or clause: He is a *happy* man. He is smiling *happily.* **45.**

**mood** The mood of a verb tells whether the verb states a fact (*indicative:* She *goes* to school); gives a command (*imperative: Come* back soon); or expresses a condition, wish, or request (*subjunctive:* I wish you *were* not leaving). **41j.** See also *imperative mood; indicative mood; subjunctive mood.*

**nonrestrictive phrase or clause** A phrase or clause that adds extra or nonessential information to a sentence and is set off with commas: His report, *which he gave to his boss yesterday,* received enthusiastic praise. **46d, 47d.**

**noun** The part of speech that names a person, place, thing, or idea. Nouns are proper or common and, if common, countable or uncountable. **37b, 60** ESL. See also *collective noun; common noun; compound noun; countable noun; generic noun; noun clause; proper noun; uncountable noun.*

**noun clause** A dependent clause that functions as a noun: I like *what you do.* **37e.**

**number** The indication of a noun or pronoun as singular (one person, place, thing, or idea) or plural (more than one). **43a, 44d.**

**object of preposition** The noun or pronoun (along with its modifiers) that follows a preposition: on *the beach.* **37d.**

**paragraph** A group of sentences set off in a text, usually on one topic. **2a, 2c.**

**parallelism** The use of coordinate structures that have the same grammatical form: She likes *swimming* and *playing* tennis. **40j.**

**participle phrase** A phrase beginning with an *-ing* verb form or a past participle: The woman *wearing a green skirt* is my sister. *Baffled by the puzzle,* he gave up. **34e, 37d.** See also *verbal.*

**particle**    A word (frequently a preposition or adverb) that combines with a verb to form a phrasal verb, a verb with an idiomatic meaning: get *over,* take *after.* **63d** ESL.

**passive voice**    Attribute of a verb when its grammatical subject is the receiver of the action that the verb describes: The book *was written* by my professor. **30c, 42.** See also *active voice.*

**past participle**    A verb form that in regular verbs ends with *-ed.* The past participle needs an auxiliary verb to function as the complete verb of a clause: *has chosen, was cleaned, might have been told.* The past participle can function alone as an adjective. **41a, 41c, 41d, 41g, 61f** ESL.

**perfect progressive tense forms**    Verb tenses that show actions in progress up to a specific point in present, past, or future time. For active voice verbs, use forms of the auxiliary *have been* followed by the *-ing* form of the verb: *has/have been living, had been living, will have been living.* **41d.**

**perfect tense forms**    Verb tenses that show actions completed by present, past, or future time. For active voice verbs, use forms of the auxiliary *have* followed by the past participle of the verb: *has/have arrived, had arrived, will have arrived.* **41d.**

**person**    The form of a pronoun or verb that indicates whether the subject is doing the speaking (first person, *I* or *we*); is spoken to (second person, *you*); or is spoken about (third person, *he, she, it,* or *they*). **43a, 44a.**

**phrasal verb**    An idiomatic verb phrase consisting of a verb and a preposition or adverb called a particle: *put off, put up with.* **63d** ESL.

**phrase**    A group of words that lacks a subject or predicate and functions as a noun, verb, adjective, or adverb: *under the tree, has been singing, amazingly simple.* **37d.** See also *absolute phrase; appositive phrase; infinitive phrase; participle phrase; prepositional phrase.*

**possessive**    The form of a noun or pronoun that indicates ownership. Possessive pronouns include *my, his, her, their, theirs,* and *whose: my* boat, *your* socks. The possessive form of a noun is indicated by an apostrophe or an apostrophe and *-s: Mario's* car, the *children's* nanny, the *birds'* nests. **43j, 44b, 48a, 48b.**

**predicate**    The part of a sentence that contains the verb and its modifiers and that comments on or makes an assertion about the subject. To be complete, a sentence needs a subject and a predicate. **37c.**

**prefix**    Letters attached to the beginning of a word that change the word's meaning: *un*necessary, *re*organize, *non*stop. **56a.**

**preposition**    The part of speech used with a noun or pronoun in a phrase to indicate time, space, or some other relationship. **37b, 46f, 63** ESL. The noun or pronoun is the object of the preposition: *on the table, after dinner, to her.* Examples of prepositions:

| about | among | between | for | near | past | under |
|-------|--------|---------|-----|------|------|-------|
| above | around | by | from | of | since | until |
| across | at | despite | in | off | through | up |
| after | before | down | inside | on | till | with |
| against | behind | during | into | out | to | within |
| along | below | except | like | over | toward | without |

**prepositional phrase**   A phrase beginning with a preposition and including the object of the preposition and its modifiers: The head *of the electronics company* was waiting *for an hour*. **37d, 38a, 46f.**

**present participle**   The *-ing* form of a verb, showing an action as being in progress or continuous: They are *sleeping*. Without an auxiliary, the *-ing* form cannot function as a complete verb but can be used as an adjective: *searing* heat. When the *-ing* form is used as a noun, it is called a gerund: *Skiing* can be dangerous. **41a, 43e, 61d** ESL, **61f** ESL. See also *verbal*.

**progressive tense forms**   Verb tenses that show actions in progress at a point or over a period of time in past, present, or future time. They use a form of *be* + the *-ing* form of the verb: They *are working*; he *will be writing*. **41d, 41e, 41f.**

**pronoun**   The part of speech that takes the place of a noun, a noun phrase, or another pronoun. Pronouns are of various types: personal *(I, they)*; possessive *(my, mine, their, theirs)*; demonstrative *(this, that, these, those)*; intensive and reflexive *(myself, herself)*; relative *(who, whom, whose, which, that)*; interrogative *(who, which, what)*; and indefinite *(anyone, something)*. **37b, 43i, 43j, 44.**

**pronoun reference**   The connection between a pronoun and its antecedent. Reference should be clear and unambiguous: The *lawyer* picked up *his* hat and left. **44c.**

**proper noun**   The capitalized name of a specific person, place, or thing: *Golden Gate Park, University of Kansas*. **37b, 53a, 60f** ESL. See also *common noun*.

**quantity word**   A word expressing the idea of quantity, such as *each, every, several, many,* and *much*. Subject-verb agreement is tricky with quantity words: *Each* of the students *has* a different assignment. **43h.** See also *agreement*.

**reflexive pronoun**   A pronoun ending in *-self* or *-selves* and referring to the subject of a clause: They incriminated *themselves*. **44h.**

**regular verb**   Verb that ends with *-ed* in its past tense and past participle forms. **41a.**

**relative clause**   See *adjective clause*.

**relative pronoun**   Pronoun that introduces a relative clause: *who, whom, whose, which, that*. **46.**

**restrictive phrase or clause**   A phrase or clause that provides information essential for identifying the word or phrase it modifies. A restrictive phrase or clause is not set off with commas: The book *that is first on the best-seller list* is a memoir. **46d, 47i.**

**run-on sentence**   The error that results when two independent clauses are not separated by a conjunction or by any punctuation: not *The dog ate the meat the cat ate the fish.* but *The dog ate the meat; the cat ate the fish.* Also called a *fused sentence.* **39.**

**second person**   The person addressed: *you.* **44a, 44g.**

**shifts**   Inappropriate switches in grammatical structure, such as from one tense to another or from statement to command or from indirect to direct quotation: not Joan asked *whether I was warm enough* and *did I sleep well.* but Joan asked *whether I was warm enough and slept well.* **40d, 41h.**

**simile**   A figure of speech that makes a direct comparison: She has a laugh *like a fire siren.* **5b, 33e.**

**simple tense forms**   Verb tenses that show present, past, or future time with no perfect or progressive aspects: they *work,* we *worked,* she *will work.* **41d, 41e, 41f.**

**split infinitive**   An infinitive with a word or words separating *to* from the base verb form: *to successfully complete.* This structure has become acceptable. **40b.**

**Standard English**   "The variety of English that is generally acknowledged as the model for the speech and writing of educated speakers." This *American Heritage Dictionary,* 4th edition, definition warns that the use of the term is "highly elastic and variable" and confers no "absolute positive evaluation." **33d, 37.**

**subject**   The noun or pronoun that performs the action of the verb in an active voice sentence or receives the action of the verb in a passive voice sentence. To be complete, a sentence needs a subject and a verb. **37c, 38d, 40i, 62a** ESL.

**subjunctive mood**   Verb mood used in conditions and in wishes, requests, and demands: I wish he *were* here. She demanded that he *be* present. **41j.**

**subordinate clause**   See *dependent clause.*

**subordinating conjunction**   A conjunction used to introduce a dependent adverb clause: *because, if, when, although, since, while.* **37e, 38b.**

**suffix**   Letters attached to the end of a word that change the word's function or meaning: gentle*ness*, humor*ist*, slow*er*, sing*ing*. **58e.**

**superlative**   The form of an adjective or adverb used to compare three or more people or things: *biggest; most unusual; least effectively.* **45h, 60d** ESL. See also *comparative.*

**synonym**   A word that has the same or nearly the same meaning as another word: *quick, rapid; stanza, verse; walk, stroll; shiny, sparkling.* **33b.**

**tense** The form of a verb that indicates time. Verbs change form to distinguish present and past time: he *goes;* he *went.* Various structures are used to express future time, mainly *will* + the base form, or *going to* + the base form. Closely associated with time is *aspect* (perfect and progressive), which expresses the relation between the action of the verb and past, present, and future time. **41d.** See *aspect;* see also *perfect progressive tense forms; perfect tense forms; progressive tense forms; simple tense forms.*

**third person** The person or thing spoken about: *he, she, it, they,* or nouns. **43a, 44a.**

**topic chain** Repetition of key words or related words throughout a passage to aid cohesion. **31a, 42d.**

**transitional expression** A word or phrase used to connect two independent clauses. Typical transitional expressions are *for example, however,* and *similarly:* We were able to swim today; *in addition,* we took the canoe out on the river. A semicolon frequently connects the two independent clauses. **2d, 47e, 50a.**

**transitive verb** A verb that takes an object—the person or thing that receives the action (in the active voice): Dogs *chase* cats. When transitive verbs are used in the passive voice, the subject receives the action of the verb: Cats *are chased* by dogs. **41b, 42a, 42b.** See also *intransitive verb.*

**uncountable noun** A common noun that cannot follow a plural quantity word (such as *several* or *many*) is never used with *a* or *an,* is used with a singular third person verb, and has no plural form: *furniture, happiness, information.* **37b, 43e, 60b** ESL.

**verb** The part of speech that expresses action or being and tells what the subject of the clause is or does. The complete verb in a clause might require auxiliary or modal auxiliary verbs to complete its meaning. **37b, 41, 61** ESL. See also the following entries for more specific information:

| | | |
|---|---|---|
| *active voice* | *linking verb* | *predicate* |
| *agreement* | *mental activity verb* | *present participle* |
| *aspect* | *modal auxiliary verb* | *progressive tense forms* |
| *auxiliary verb* | *mood* | *regular verb* |
| *base form* | *passive voice* | *simple tense forms* |
| *complete verb* | *past participle* | *subjunctive mood* |
| *compound predicate* | *perfect progressive* | *tense* |
| *indicative mood* | *tense forms* | *transitive verb* |
| *infinitive* | *perfect tense forms* | *verb chain* |
| *intransitive verb* | *phrasal verb* | *voice* |
| *irregular verb* | | |

**verbal** A form, derived from a verb, that cannot function as the main verb of a clause. The three types of verbals are the infinitive, the *-ing* participle, and the past participle. A verbal can function as a noun, adjective, or adverb. **61** ESL, **63e** ESL.

**verb chain** Combination of an auxiliary verb, a main verb, and verbals: She *might have promised to leave;* they *should deny having helped* him. **61** ESL.

**voice**   Transitive verbs (verbs that take an object) can be used in the active voice *(He is painting the door)* or the passive voice *(The door is being painted).* **42.**

**zero article**   The lack of an article *(a, an,* or *the)* before a noun. Uncountable nouns are used with the zero article when they make no specific reference. **60b** ESL, **60e** ESL.

**Credits** *(continued from copyright page iv)*

Collins, Chuck, and Felice Yeskel. *Economic Apartheid in America: A Primer on Economic Inqeuality and Insecurity.* New York: New Press. Graph ("Where Do You Sit?"). Reprinted by permission of United for a Fair Economy. Illustration copyright © United for a Fair Economy (http://www.ufenet.org).

Kuechler, Manfred. Dept. of Sociology, Hunter College <http://maxweber.hunter>.cuny.edu/eres/docs/eres/SOC241.00_KUECHLER/hw4-fb.htm> (7 August 2000). Graphs ("Start of Regular Computer Use" (pie chart; bar graph). Used by permission.

Marsh, Allison. Web pages. <http:/www.student.richmond.edu/~amarsh/index.html>. Reprinted by permission of Allison Marsh.

Microsoft Word 2000. Four screen shots, reprinted by permission from Microsoft Corporation.

National Telecommunications and Information Administration. *Falling through the Net: Toward Digital Inclusion. A Report on Americans' Access to Technology Tools.* Oct. 2000. Table 1–2 <http://www.ntia.doc.gov/ntiahome/fttn00/charts00.html#t31>. Figure 1–8 <http://www.ntia.doc.gov/ntiahome/fttn00/charts00.html F11> (November 2000).

Rahman, Yousuf. "Working in the Public/Private Sector" (PowerPoint slide). Office of Management and Budget, 75 Park Place, New York, New York, 10007.

Raimes, Emily. "New York City" (PowerPoint slide).

Sax, L. J., et al. *An Overview of the 1999 Freshman Norms.* Los Angeles Higher Education Research Institute, UCLA, 1999 <http://www.gseis.ucla.edu/heri/executive.htm> (28 November 2000). Graphs ("Growing Freshman Stress"; "High School Grade Inflation"). Reprinted by permission.

**Part 6**   *American Heritage Dictionary of the English Language,* 4th ed. Definition of "graduate." Copyright © 2000 by Houghton Mifflin. Reproduced by permission.

Baker, Nicholson. "Deadline." *New Yorker* 24 June 2000, 49.

*Chicago Manual of Style FAQ.* <http://www.press.uchicago.edu/Misc/Chicago/cmosfaq.html>. 28 August 2000. Reprinted by permission of the University of Chicago Press.

Kipfer, Barbara Ann. Entry on "privacy." *Roget's Twenty-first Century Thesaurus.* New York: Phillip Lieff/Dell, 1992. 653.

Marshall, Paule. *Brown Girl, Brownstones.* New York: Feminist Press, 1981. 12.

Pinsky, Robert. "Letting Go." *New York Times Book Review* 6 Jan. 1991, sec. 7: 1+. Reprinted by permission of the author.

Roth, Philip. *Patrimony.* New York: Simon and Schuster, 1991.

Sidel, Ruth. *On Her Own: Growing Up in the Shadow of the American Dream.* New York: Penguin, 1990. 27, 33.

**Part 7**   Allen, Woody. *Death* (a play). New York: Random House, 1975.

*American Heritage Dictionary of the English Language,* 4th ed. Definition of "Standard English." Copyright © 2000 by Houghton Mifflin.

Rodriguez, Richard. *Hunger of Memory.* Boston: David Godine, 1981. 11.

**Part 8**   Larkin, Philip. "Toads." *The Less Deceived, Philip Larkin: Collected Poems.* Ed. Anthony Thwaite. London: Marvell, 1989. By permission of the Marvell Press, England and Australia.

Morales, Aurora Levins. "Class Poem." *Getting Home Alive.* Ed. Aurora Morales and Rosario Morales. Ithaca, NY: Firebrand. 45–47. Copyright © 1986 by Aurora Levins Morales. Used with permission from Firebrand Books, Ithaca, NY.

Sidel, Ruth. *On Her Own: Growing Up in the Shadow of the American Dream.* New York: Penguin, 1990. 27, 33. Copyright © 1990 by Penguin.

**Part 10**   *American Heritage Dictionary of the English Language,* 4th ed. Definition of "Standard English." Copyright © 2000 by Houghton Mifflin.

**Page 494**   Houghton Mifflin, *A Guide for Authors.* Copyright © 1998 by Houghton Mifflin Company. Used by permission.

# Index

*Note: An asterisk (\*) refers to a page number in the Glossary of Grammatical Terms.*